D1083288

THE FIRST 125 YEARS

The two presidents of The Co-op League: Dr. J. P. Warbasse (left), 1916-41; Murray D. Lincoln, 1941—present.

The two most recent League executive directors: E. R. Bowen (left), 1934-46; Jerry Voorhis, 1946—present.

The First 125 Years

by

FLORENCE E. PARKER

A History of Distributive and Service Cooperation in the United States, 1829-1954

Printed by
COOPERATIVE PUBLISHING ASSOCIATION
Superior, Wisconsin, U. S. A.

8

DEDICATION

This book has grown out of some 35 years' observation and study of the American cooperative scene.

I was very fortunate in that my job and my personal interest and sympathy coincided. In my work as specialist on cooperatives in a Government office, as observer at all of the Cooperative Congresses except that of 1918, and as a member of many cooperative organizations, I was able to view and ponder cooperative developments while at the same time being far enough removed to maintain some detachment and impartiality.

Still fairly young when I first began to read cooperative literature, attend meetings, and absorb the cooperative philosophy, I then envisioned cooperatives as instruments entirely of brotherhood and sweetness and light. This illusion was rudely shattered at the very first Cooperative Congress I attended—that of 1920. For that meeting was marked by a knock-down and drag-out oral battle between the Cooperative League's representatives (notably its president) and those of regional organizations of the Midwest and Far West whose practices deviated from accepted Rochdale methods. At that Congress I learned that even cooperators were not exempt from the American passion for bigness and speed and that some of them would resort to questionable tactics to obtain "results."

This was the first of a long series of revelations showing that the cooperative movement is above all one of *people*—people of all sorts and descriptions: Some who joined only because of what they could get out of it in dollars and cents. Some who did not by any means disdain the possible economic advantages, but also caught a gleam of something shining beyond. And some who envisioned the store or other enterprise merely as a valuable means to the larger end of a broader, fuller life open to an ever-growing circle of people, with services provided for use and not profit. For this ultimate aim, thousands have worked and sacrificed with single-minded devotion and a few have even laid down their lives.

This is not to say that anywhere near all the effort has been on a selfless, lofty plane. The cooperative movement has by no means been free of personal ambition, of bitter antipathies, of petty bickering and politicking, or of many honest differences of opinion as to ways and means. All of these have been present, and many a cooperative has been torn and even wrecked, primarily because two men or two factions could not get along with each other and neither would yield.

Since the cooperative movement is one of personalities, it is peculiarly subject to all of the human characteristics. Its successes are the result of the higher qualities of leadership, high ideals, perseverance, and courage. Its failures have been the result of human frailties, of inexperience and short vision.

By and large, I venture to say, few if any economic movements have elicited more devoted, disinterested service than the cooperative movement. Over the years certain cooperators stand out like beacon lights. The names of hundreds of these workers are as well known to other cooperators as those in their own families. Some of them are mentioned in this history. But, in addition, are the many thousands who have rendered almost anonymous service, recognized by few outside their immediate circle, but who in the aggregate have formed that hard core of the faithful without whom the movement would have died out long ago.

It is to that vast nameless group that this book is dedicated.

In my thoroughly satisfying task as historian and compiler of facts, I have had the assistance throughout the years from hundreds of persons within and without the movement. In the actual writing, also, a number of persons have given both time and encouragement.

Foremost among them is Dr. James P. Warbasse, a founder and long-time president of the Cooperative League of the USA, without which it is probable that, even now, there might be no *organized* consumers' cooperative movement in this country. To Dr. Warbasse I am indebted for the unrestricted freedom of his personal files and vast accumulation of data, which provided a multitude of facts as well as an invaluable background for the understanding of events. Dr. Arthur E. Albrecht, of the College of the City of New York, turned over to me a mass of source material as well as the partially completed manuscript of a history which he had begun but had never had time to finish. Many facts and "leads" were obtained from that contribution.

To a number of others I am grateful for information and for the reading of portions of this history and for many suggestions and criticisms. Among them are Mrs. Frank Albertson, Hayes Beall, Philip Brown, Joseph Gilbert, A. J. Hayes, I. H. Hull, Erick Kendall, Waldemar Niemela, Udo Rall, Jerry Voorhis, A. W. Warinner, Colston E. Warne, and Leslie E. Woodcock.

I submit this admittedly imperfect report as a badly needed beginning toward filling the historical vacuum in the cooperative movement of the United States. It should have been undertaken many years ago. In the years that have gone by, much valuable material (especially that contained in cooperative periodicals) has been allowed to be destroyed and thus lost to history.

The lack of an adequate history of the American cooperative movement has had an unfortunate result: Knowing little of what has gone by, new groups of cooperators can never profit by the mistakes of the past. Successive generations waste time and effort trying out ideas that had long ago been tested and discarded.

My own book does, I hope, bring together in conveniently usable form some of the facts of yesteryear that will enable present-day cooperators not only to see where we have been but to visualize where we are going.

Not all of this history makes pleasant reading. But it is my belief that mistakes teach perhaps as much as successes and that the movement as a whole can profit by facing up to them.

In this work effort has been made to check carefully the facts presented. Some I know through personal participation or observation; for most I have had to depend on printed sources or the personal recollection of others. In the occasional instances in which authorities disagreed, I have chosen the more authoritative. Undoubtedly, some of my opinions and some of my interpretations of events will be questioned. For such and for any inadvertent inaccuracies I accept full responsibility. I do not expect complete agreement. What I ask is that my story be read thoughtfully for what it may teach.

Washington, D. C. Florence E. Parker

July 25, 1955

LIST OF ILLUSTRATIONS

Errata

Page 5. The third paragraph which reads: "By mid-1948," should read: "By mid-1848"; and the following paragraph should read: "The 1849 convention . . ." Page 434 is erroneously numbered 334.

CONTENTS

INTRODUCTION.—COOPERATION AND HOW IT WORKS

"Cooperation" means working together. A cooperative association is therefore a group of people who join together to provide themselves with goods or services, by joint effort, on a nonprofit basis. The essence of cooperation is participation in a common enterprise for the common good.

Kinds of Cooperatives

Cooperative associations fall, roughly, into two classes—producers' and consumers'—according as they serve the needs of the members in those capacities. A cooperative creamery, for example, may be either a producers' or a consumers' cooperative. If its function is to market the milk turned over to it by the members who produced it on their farms, it is a producers' cooperative. If, however, it processes and distributes milk for consumption by the members' families, it is a consumers' cooperative.

Producers' cooperatives.—There are various types of producers' cooperatives, of which by far the most important in the United States are the farmers' processing and marketing associations.

Two other types of producer associations are those of industrial workers: the workers' productive associations, and the self-help cooperatives. The former are cooperative workshops—small factories of various kinds, owned and operated by the workers in them. This kind of cooperative has never reached any considerable development in this country. Self-help associations were ephemeral organizations started among the unemployed, in times of depression, to exchange their labor for goods and services and to barter commodities and services among themselves.

Consumers' cooperatives.—"Consumers' cooperation" embraces a wide variety of activities in the distributive and service industries, and even in production for consumer needs. These include such distributive enterprises as stores, gasoline stations, etc., and organizations to provide such services as housing and medical care.

In this country some of the branches of consumers' cooperation have developed independently of the others and even have their own national organizations. Among them are the electricity associations and the credit unions.

Scope of Present Study

This history is confined to the consumers' cooperatives. Inevitably it overlaps into farmers' cooperation, because not only were agriculturists and their organizations among the first to start consumers' cooperatives in this country, but farmers' cooperatives still form the majority of the consumer distributive associations here.

How It All Started

The consumers' cooperative movement, as we know it today, was started in 1844 by 28 poverty-stricken workers of Rochdale, England, in protest against the evils resulting from unemployment, underemployment, extortionate prices, and adulteration of goods. They decided to pool their small funds and supply themselves. Each subscribed to one pound sterling, to be paid in at the rate of twopence a week. Such small sums were at first sufficient only for the purchase of small quantities of flour, sugar, butter, and oatmeal, and with these commodities as their stock in trade, they opened a small store. As they had to earn their living during the day and could not afford to hire labor for the business, the store was open only a few hours on Monday and Saturday evenings.

Their program, however, was as ambitious as their store business was modest. They aimed to do no less than "arrange the powers of production, distribution, education, and government" so as to establish "a self-supporting home colony of united interests." Although they never were able to attain these exalted ends, their association, the Rochdale Society of Equitable Pioneers, made progress from the first and, indeed, is still in successful operation after more than a century. Its example, copied first in England, eventually spread around the world.

The Rochdale Principles

For the operation of their association, the Rochdale Pioneers evolved what have come to be known as the Rochdale principles and practices, now recognized as standards wherever consumers' cooperation is found.

The Rochdale principles are—

1. Open membership, without restriction as to sex, or political, religious, or other affiliation.
2. Democratic control by the members.

   Each member has only one vote, regardless of how much he has invested in the cooperative's share capital. In the cooperative it is the man, not his wealth, that is important.

   There is no voting by proxy. A member may vote by mail (if informed beforehand on the matter to be considered), but must cast his own vote; he cannot surrender it to another who acts as his "proxy."
3. Limited return on share capital.
4. Net savings returned to members in proportion to their patronage of the association.

   This is the main feature that distinguishes cooperatives from profit business.

Cooperative Practices

Three methods were also used by the Pioneers. These, although important, are not regarded as absolutely essential to the preservation of the cooperative character of an association. They are as follows:

1. Political and religious neutrality.
2. Continuous promotion of educational work, and regular appropriations therefor.
3. Business done for cash only.

Certain other practices, evolved over the years largely on the basis of practical experience, are widely observed by cooperatives:

1. Goods are distributed at current market prices.

   This serves two purposes: (a) It insures a margin to cover operating expenses. (b) It avoids the appearance of price cutting, which immediately arouses the antagonism of competing profit dealers.

2. Efficient bookkeeping and accounting, outside audits, and regular, understandable, and complete financial reports to members.

3. Bonding of all persons handling money.

4. Honest and full information to members about the merchandise handled; maintenance of high standards of quality; and, as far as possible, purchase of supplies made under good working conditions.

5. Affiliation as soon as possible with the nearest cooperative wholesale and educational organization.

The immediate object of the consumers' cooperative is economic—to make the pennies go farther, to eliminate the extra cost entailed by extravagant advertising and high-pressure salesmanship, to fill an increasing number of human wants on a nonprofit basis, and to return the savings to the members.

Like the original Pioneers' society, the present-day movement also has a far-reaching social philosophy. It stands as the champion of the consumer, in fighting against adulteration and for the maintenance of quality and for truth in advertising, in watching out for measures that are inimical to his interests as a consumer and as a citizen, in providing a measuring rod for comparison with profit business, in combatting the tendency to monopolistic concentration of economic power, and above all, in providing a channel for the exercise of the spirit of mutual helpfulness and brotherhood that is latent in all of us.

Part 1.

INFANCY OF AMERICAN DISTRIBUTIVE COOPERATION

Chapter 1. — EARLY COOPERATIVES

The Faint Beginnings

Cooperative workshops owned by the workers in them and colonies in which all property was owned in common were known in the United States as early as the last quarter of the eighteenth century. But not until the early 1800's did distributive cooperation begin.

In England and the Continent Rochdale cooperation was preceded by various experiments (such as those of Robert Owen, Charles Fourier, and others), all groping toward a solution of social problems by collective action. Although the same occurred in the United States, some time elapsed after the Rochdale Pioneers had formulated their "principles" before they became known in this country and even then their fundamental value for cooperation was not widely recognized.

The general belief is that distributive cooperation in this country dates from 1845. Actually, there were at least two such cooperatives as early as 1829. In that year a group of workers opened a store on North Fifth Street in Philadelphia, which charged dues of 20 cents per month for the privilege of trading there, and sold at cost. Another was organized in New York City in the same year, one of the organizers being the former secretary of an association in Brighton, England. Its membership never exceeded 40 and it gradually "faded out."

Two years after these associations were formed, "cooperative trading" was discussed at the first annual convention of the New England Association of Farmers, Mechanics and other Workingmen in February 1831. Some 40 cooperatives were reported to have been started as a result of the interest thus stimulated.

There appears to have been no further record of "cooperative agitation" until 1845, although the subject was discussed in numerous labor organizations, and goods were bought in bulk and sold at a margin sufficient to pay expenses.

The Protective Union Movement, 1845-67

At the suggestion of John G. Kaulback, Jr., a journeyman tailor and a member of the New England Association above mentioned, the organization undertook joint buying in order to increase the attendance at meetings. The first purchase consisted of a box of soap and half a chest of tea, at a saving of "at least 25 percent." A small "dividing" store was opened in a room over Boylston Market in Boston, on October 6, 1845, and the buying club was named First Workingmen's Protective Union. In a short time it had a hundred members. By the time the parent club was a year old, there were 12 divisions in operation in New England, one of which was formed by "a few working women in Lowell."

A central body, the Supreme Division of the Workingmen's Protective Union, was created on January 7, 1847.

The announced program of the Protective Union was "one of broad social amelioration," to be attained through "cooperation, mercantile and fraternal." Strict temperance and good moral character (attested by two "good, respectable references") were insisted upon; no person could join who used or sold intoxicating liquor. Indeed, the atmosphere in some instances appears to have been almost overpoweringly proper. Thus, the character of the store at Worcester was said to be such that "even the devotee of [tobacco] would instinctively lay aside his cigar or pipe on entering."[1]

Each division had its own purchasing agent. At first, business was conducted on the cost-plus plan, and only members were dealt with. Later, when these restrictions were lifted, nonmembers paid current market prices, whereas members either paid at reduced rates or received the difference in the form of dividends on shares.

Under the inducement supplied by the depression of 1846-49, great progress was made. Twenty-five divisions were represented at a convention held in October 1847.

Although this New England movement knew little about the Rochdale cooperatives, there was at least at first general adherence to such principles as cash sales and equality in voting. There is no record that refunds were paid on patronage in New England, but it appears that the Farmers & Mechanics Protective Co., at Weedsport, N. Y., did so. The secretary of the New England Protective Union stated that not until 1864 were cooperatives on the Rochdale plan established in or near Boston.

The wholesale buying was under the supervision of the central Board of Trade, composed of elected local buyers. Actual purchasing was done on commission by John Kaulback, board chairman. This was the first known instance of federation for wholesale purchasing in the United States.

By mid-1948, four-fifths of the 50-odd divisions were buying through the Board of Trade such things as drygoods, hardware, crockery, lamp oil, shoes, cheese, and flour.

The 1949 convention adopted a new constitution and changed the name of the organization to New England Protective Union (because the members now included persons from outlying rural areas) and that of the Supreme Division to Central Division. It also directed that a special effort be made to organize "associations of ladies."

In 1850, 106 new divisions were established, bringing the total to 207—mostly in New England, but including one each in Illinois and New York City and three in Canada—with 10,673 members. A "lady" was reported to have been engaged by the Central Division to purchase "fancy articles." By 1852 there were 403 divisions.

The business had also steadily increased. From 1848 to 1852 the purchases through the Central Division increased every year, rising from $112,500 to over a million. That of the local divisions also rose, from $638,600 in 1849 to $1,700,000 in 1852. As the latter figure covered only 165 of the existing 403 divisions, it is probable that the total local volume for that year exceeded $4,000,000.

The Protective Union network had thus become a forceful factor in both the retail and the wholesale market. The organization had the sympathetic interest of the various nonprofit and reform groups, the periodicals of which provided a friendly press for the cooperators.

Schism

Almost from the beginning, differences had arisen regarding cost-plus operation and the powers of the Central Division and the Board of Trade. Also, the resolution of the 1848 convention, forbidding extension of credit, was never fully accepted by the divisions.

The central Board of Trade had begun to be concerned by a distrust of John Kaulback on the part of the locals, by their complaints about prices, quality, delays, etc., and by their growing disposition to buy through other sources. Dissatisfaction culminated in 1853. After hearings by the Board of Trade, and a long-drawn-out controversy, he was forced to resign.

Growing difficulties soon began to be mirrored in the Union's paper, *The Journal*, and in the reports of the association. Discord and agitation continued, there was a gradual gravitation of shares into the hands of a dwindling number of stockholders, and trade through the Central Division for the year 1853 fell by 45 percent. By 1855, however, the central volume had risen somewhat and the 63 local divisions reporting had sales of $1,005,882, and a membership of 3,584. The geographic scope of the Union was indicated by the fact that its 1857 convention was attended by delegates from seven States—Connecticut, Maine, Massachusetts, New Hampshire, New York, Rhode Island, and Vermont.

The leaders were, however, becoming increasingly worried about the soundness of the Union structure. *The Journal* excoriated the incompetent, unfaithful, and scheming managers of some stores and clerks who resorted to craft and trickery. It reminded the members of the high social aims with which they had started, and warned that they should not be abandoned.

In the meantime, Kaulback's supporters had withdrawn in 1853 and formed the American Protective Union, for which he became buyer. Figures supplied by him to the Massachusetts Bureau of Statistics of Labor indicate that his agency's volume ran about half a million dollars annually above that of the New England Protective Union during the years 1853 through 1857. However, at a meeting in 1859, only 36 divisions were represented; two years before, Kaulback had claimed 350 units in at least ten States.

The American Union appears to have had no social aims, and the original Union's program also came to an end, for all practical purposes, at the time of schism in 1853.

During the four years after the split, the original Union organized about 250 new divisions, bringing the total to 756. Most of these were in New England, but the movement had also expanded into New York, Ohio, Illinois, and other midwest States. Oregon had a division and there were several in Canada.

Decline

The internal problems of both agencies became more and more difficult. In addition, there were opposition and blacklisting by merchants and employers, who spared no effort to create division and dissension. Competing merchants cut prices. From the cooperatives' own membership came complaints regarding quality of goods, prices, management of stores, and the temperance question. Divisions in the same town were competing with each other. Some withdrew from the central organizations and others failed. To all these were added the financial panic of 1857, with its resultant dislocations, and the economic uncertainties incident to the Civil War which was impending.

Both agencies began to decline about 1858 and gradually the whole system fell to pieces. The Central Divisions of both organizations were gone by 1860. Kaulback's purchasing agency survived until 1863 and that of the NEPU until 1867.

By this time the local union stores had mostly disappeared. The majority had disbanded without loss to the members, and some even returned large amounts of earnings accumulated while in operation. Many sold out to private storekeepers or to a group of the members. Some survived, however, and prospered for many years.

By 1886 there were only four survivors—in Worcester, New Bedford, and Natick, Mass., and Salmon Falls, N. H.[2]

Appraisal

The men who pioneered the New England Protective Union had high social ideals and the most advanced ideas. They agitated for such measures as the 10-hour day, factory legislation, universal education, extension of the right of suffrage, a mechanic's lien law, and the abolition of capital punishment, slavery, war, and imprisonment for debt. As the movement spread, however, new members joined who knew nothing and cared less about such causes and were concerned only with getting low prices and large dividends. As the idealistic pioneers fell into the background, the stores "became the arena for a competition that never scrupled at a trade that would bring dividends."[3] Even at its peak, however, the organization was never able to command the greater part of its members' patronage.

It was an early demonstration of internal dissension and weakness and of unsound business practices by the divisions which, combined with deteriorating economic conditions and finally the Civil War, were more than the organization could withstand. The Protective Union movement did, however, furnish an example to later movements not only of mistakes to be avoided, but of high-minded aims the value of which was not destroyed by its economic failure.

Cooperation Among the Mormons, 1864-1893

A few years after the decline of the Protective Union in the East, a semicooperative movement developed, quite independently, in Utah, under the sponsorship of the Church of Latter Day Saints of Jesus Christ. Its system of stores was preceded by several scattered associations—in Brigham City (1864), Spanish Fork (1867), and Lehi (1868). The Lehi store was opened as a result of a journey to England by Israel Evans of Lehi, on a church mission. It was probably the only one in Utah established under Rochdale influence; it had no effect on the cooperative program of the Mormon Church, however, and indeed soon merged into the latter's State-wide system.

The general church program for distributive cooperation was initiated by Brigham Young, as a move to keep distributive facilities in the hands of Mormons. Zion's Cooperative Mercantile Institution (ZCMI) started business in Salt Lake City in March 1869, with Mr. Young as president. In the next few years cooperative retail stores were opened in nearly every Mormon community in Utah.

Any member of the LDS Church who was of good moral character and had paid his tithes was eligible to join a cooperative store. Shares were $100 each, and each share carried a vote (a requirement of the State law); directors, however, had only one vote each.

During the period 1868-80, 146 local branches were opened in 126 towns in 24 counties, and nearly every church ward in Salt Lake City had a cooperative store. They were usually very successful and paid dividends (on shares) running as high as 300 percent.

ZCMI supplied the local stores on a cost-plus basis. During its first 4½ years' operation, the wholesale returned dividends amounting to 78 percent on shares. It went into the manufacture of shoes and clothing. The depression of 1873, however, compelled it to close several branches as well as its grocery, dry-goods, and clothing departments. By April 1875 it was again out of debt and had also erected a new building.

During its first 18 years' operation, 1869-87, ZCMI paid $1,544,344 in dividends on shares.

For a while its network held nearly a monopoly of the mercantile business in Utah. By 1882, however, the church "felt itself able to open the field to all merchants, and with that date began the decline of the local cooperatives."[4] Many were forced into bankruptcy by the depression of 1893, and most of those surviving were joint-stock rather than cooperative enterprises; all earnings were paid on shares, voting was on a share basis, and the stock had tended to drift into the hands of a few. By 1917, although about 150 stores were still active, they no longer had any close connection with ZCMI. Only 8 were left by 1935.[5]

The local store associations had certain cooperative features in the beginning, but ZCMI itself (still in successful retail operation) was never democratically controlled.

Appraisal

From the moment of the Mormon colonists' descent into the then treeless, arid Salt Lake valley, close community action in every direction was necessary for mere survival. The Mormon cooperative movement was therefore a natural development of that long-established habit. The fundamental flaw in their organizations was the requirement of voting by shares, which allowed the gradual shift of control into the hands of a few stockholders, who received all the earnings, thus transforming the associations into joint-stock companies.

Chapter 2.—COOPERATIVES OF FARM MOVEMENTS

Farmers were quick to see the value of cooperation and to promote it in an organized way. The Patrons of Husbandry (Grangers), although not the first to use the Rochdale principles in this country, supported them with the full power of a coordinated movement. For more than 15 years, beginning in 1867, Grange cooperation was outstanding. The Farmers' Alliance, which followed in 1874, patterned its cooperative activities upon those of the Grange.

Patrons of Husbandry (The Grange Movement), 1867-85[1]

The Grange movement began in Washington, D. C., on December 4, 1867, when the Order of the Patrons of Husbandry was formed on the initiative of Oliver H. Kelly, previously a farmer but then a clerk in the U. S. Bureau of Agriculture.

From the beginning, the Grange was a sponsor of "cooperation in all things." Its "Declaration of Principles" set forth its desire to bring "producers and consumers, farmers and manufacturers, into the most direct and friendly relations possible. Hence we must dispense with the surplus middlemen, not that we are unfriendly to them, but we do not need them."

At first the Granges had appointed local and State purchasing agents and at one time there were business agencies in more than 25 States. The system had worked so poorly, however, that the members lost faith in them.

In 1873 the executive committee of the National Grange made a field study of distributive cooperation and recommended to the next year's meeting that a national business agency be established. In 1875 the national convention approved the printing of a set of rules embodying the Rochdale principles, which the executive committee had drawn up. As a result, genuinely cooperative stores began to appear here and there, and spread rapidly. Hundreds of stores were thus established. A representative was sent to England to study the movement there, and the National Grange thereafter devoted its main efforts to disseminating cooperative literature and encouraging the formation of Rochdale cooperatives.

From 1873 to 1874 the Grange business operations more than tripled. The annual savings were estimated at $100 per capita for 400,000 active Grangers. The average saving on tea, sugar, coffee, kerosene, etc., was reported to be 5 to 15 percent; on clothing, 10 to 20 percent; and on implements and machinery, 34 to 40 percent.

At the peak of the order and of its cooperative development, there were Grange stores throughout New England, the Midwest and South, and even on the Pacific Coast. The greatest development was in the Middle West. Nearly all the counties in Ohio and nearly half in Illinois had Patrons' stores. At least five States had wholesales.

The Patrons, however, did not confine themselves to cooperative stores. Encouraged by their early successes, "they rushed pell mell into all sorts of business schemes" without considering how to obtain the capital and business ability to carry them out.[2] State and local Granges branched out into grain elevators, warehouses, grist mills, pork-packing plants, bag factories, brick yards, blacksmith shops, machinery and implement works, broom factories, cotton gins, cotton-yarn mills, and transport by rail and ship. At least four banks were started—three in California and one in Olathe, Kans. Many township or county fire insurance companies were formed, as well as Statewide companies in California, Kansas, New Hampshire, and Maine. Life insurance was also undertaken, but it never was as successful as the fire insurance.

Appraisal

The Grange movement as a whole had about spent its force by 1885. By the middle 90's, not a single Grange manufacturing or commercial enterprise aside from the stores was left. Numerous individual store associations continued to operate, however, and some of these were conspicuously successful for many years.[3]

The business enterprises had to contend with lack of experience in working together; difficulty in getting the farmers to meetings; falling away of member support and patronage;

almost total lack of business experience or ability; poor and sometimes dishonest management; and the hard times during and following the Civil War. Where the cash system was adhered to, farmer members withdrew because the store denied them credit. Where credit was given, losses were sustained on bad accounts. Either way, the store lost out.

The Patrons were also weakened by the appearance on the scene of a rival order, the Farmers' Alliance, which largely superseded it eventually in both the South and West.

The Patrons did not achieve their declared objective of revolutionizing distributive and manufacturing business or of eliminating the middleman. But, great sums were saved to the members each year. There seems to be no doubt, either, that the Grange stores helped to bring down the general price level in their locality, so that nonmembers also benefited. The advantages therefore far outweighed the occasional losses. The order also deserves credit for its efforts to promote genuine Rochdale cooperation.

The Farmers' Alliance, 1874-93

The Farmers' Alliance was a secret order that consisted of two separate movements having little or no connection with each other. One was the National Farmers' Alliance, the main strength of which was in the upper Mississippi Valley; the other, mainly in the South, was the National Farmers' Alliance and Industrial Union, commonly called the Southern Alliance.

National Alliance

A group of members of the New York State Grange started the northern Alliance in March 1877, with the idea of its becoming a spokesman for the Grange on political matters.

The first really effective step was the formation of the Farmers' Alliance for Cook County, Ill., on April 15, 1880, by Milton George, a Chicago newspaper editor. This was a nonsectarian association that also admitted Negroes to membership.

The order thereafter had an immediate success, attributed largely to the prevailing hard times and the drought in the farm areas. The Alliance began to decline after 1882, when the early enthusiasm had been exhausted. It revived during the winter of 1884-85, because of poor prices for wheat, and spread into the Dakota Territory and even into Colorado and California. By November 1890 it had 10 State organizations, and five others in process. There were numerous locals in other States in which no step had been taken toward State federation.

At first the Alliance merely arranged for members' discounts from private merchants, in return for a pledge that all the members' patronage would go to them. Such a pledge was hard to enforce, however, and usually the arrangement did not last long.

A fire, hail, and life insurance association was started in Dakota and later one was organized in Washington, D. C. The Alliance was also instrumental in starting a cooperative movement akin to that of the Grangers. Where an Alliance unit was formed, there was likely to be, also, an insurance association, cooperative store, grain elevator, cheese factory, or cotton gin. Some of these were reported to have underbid their competitors by 25 to 50 percent.

Some well-managed associations operated for a considerable period. Their main obstacle was the fact that their capital was sufficient only for a strictly cash business, whereas the average farmer demanded credit periodically.

Purchasing agencies operated on the commission plan were more successful, especially in Iowa, Minnesota, and Nebraska. In North Carolina and Dakota Territory, agencies were started as joint-stock companies.

The Farmers' Alliance became active in California in 1890. It organized a group of local enterprises and a State buying agency. Contrary to the methods of the national organization, the California stores operated on Rochdale principles. Alliance members also had cooperative flour mills in San Miguel and Gilroy and a tannery at Paso Robles. In 1895 the Alliance was instrumental in obtaining the passage of an improved State cooperative law which introduced the one-vote principle, irrespective of number of shares held. This law proved to be a great incentive to the spread of cooperation and was adopted by several other States.

Southern Alliance

The Southern Alliance came into being in Texas to promote cooperative effort in catching horse thieves and in purchasing supplies.

The main channel of business was the Farmers' Alliance Exchange which began business in September 1887, at Dallas, Tex. At first only a marketing organization, it began purchasing farm implements, then drygoods, groceries, and farm supplies. Similar exchanges were organized in Mississippi and Georgia in 1888 and in South Carolina in 1889. By mid-1889 a majority of the southern States had business agencies.

Appraisal

The Farmers' Alliance rendered the South, especially, a great service in helping to put farm crops on a cash basis; formerly only cotton was a cash crop, all others being bartered at the local merchants' stores for food, clothing and other necessaries. Its cooperative stores also acted as price regulators, as sources of savings for members, and as a means of raising standards of retail service. At a meeting of State agents in 1890 it was claimed that Alliance agencies were doing a business of about $10 million.

No information is available as to the total number of stores and agencies at the high point of Alliance development. Eventually all disappeared except a reorganized association at Green, Kans.[4]

Perhaps the greatest mistake made by this movement was the close involvement of the stores with the fortunes of the order. The Alliance became active in politics, promoting such issues as free coinage of silver and warehouses operated by the U. S. Treasury for the benefit of farmers. Alliance members ran for many public offices and the whole energies of the movement became directed on these activities rather than the cooperatives. The latter were already weak when the order declined, and did not survive.

Patrons of Industry, 1889-1900

During the period 1886-92, other farmers' organizations known as The Wheel and The Alliance tried unsuccessfully to establish cooperative stores in the South.

They were followed by the Patrons of Industry, which was a movement to combine farmers and laborers into a single organization. Its purpose was "to promote their rights and interests by protecting them by means of independent cooperative political action from the rapacity and avaricious greed of organized monopoly." It began about 1889 to organize in Michigan; by 1890 it had close to 80,000 members in that State.

Thence the order spread over about 13 States of the Midwest and Northwest. By the middle nineties many of the locals had started cooperative stores or were doing collective buying. Of these, only one is known to have survived.[5]

Chapter 3.—COOPERATIVES OF LABOR MOVEMENTS

Knights of St. Crispin, 1867-74

Beginning in 1869, the cooperative idea began to take hold in the labor movement. Thus, the platform of the Labor Reform Party in 1871 contained a plank that demanded laws extending to cooperation the same facilities, aid, and encouragement that had "heretofore been given to railroads and other enterprises." The principal leadership, however, was supplied by the International Grand Lodge of the Knights of St. Crispin of North America. This was an association of shoemakers (St. Crispin was their patron saint), organized in Milwaukee in March 1867. Incorporators were Newell Daniels, formerly of Milford, Mass., and six associates.

During the first half of 1869, 30 to 40 cooperative stores were opened by local lodges in Massachusetts, and the State lodge was urging the passage of a State law permitting it to incorporate and handle local funds for collective buying of coal, groceries, etc., in wholesale quantities. Such a law was obtained in 1870.

Three types of cooperative plans were favored: Informal buying clubs, cooperative stores, and cooperative factories. Cooperation was endorsed and all the lodges were urged to invest their surplus funds in workers' productive enterprises, to form buying clubs and stores, and to set aside all or part of the earnings for the assistance of cooperative factories. Many new cooperative stores and shoe factories resulted.

The Knights as a whole had a rapid growth until the end of 1870, reaching a strength variously estimated at 30,000 to 60,000, associated in some 250 lodges. The Knights' decline, beginning in 1870, was hastened by "rash strikes" and particularly by the crushing defeat of one in Lynn, Mass. By 1872, although most of the cooperative stores and workshops were reported still doing well, the membership of the order itself had fallen to 13,000. An attempt to revive the organization in 1874-78 was without success, except temporarily in Massachusetts.

The cooperative stores disappeared along with the labor organization.

Knights of Labor, 1869-90

The Noble Order of Knights of Labor was formed in Philadelphia on Thanksgiving Day, 1869, by seven garment cutters under the leadership of Uriah S. Stephens. It was begun as a secret society, and for a long time even its name was never used publicly, the organization being referred to as the "Five Stars."

The Knights of Labor had grown out of an organization called the Industrial Brotherhood, which had declared for "the establishment of cooperative institutions, productive and distributive." This pronouncement was carried over into the constitution of the Knights in 1878, but a change in wording 6 years later favored only "a cooperative industrial system."

Several attempts to commit the order itself to operating cooperatives were without success. A plea for a cooperative system, both distributive and productive, to be started and controlled by the order, was rejected by the convention of 1880. Two years later the officers organized a Cooperative Fund and levied a monthly assessment. A revolt over the compulsory feature of this levy resulted in its being made voluntary.

Neither the Cooperative Association nor the Cooperative Board created by the convention of 1882 was ever very active. The Board did recommend that the local assemblies "use every effort to establish cooperatives," but, as it was never given any funds (though some were authorized by a later convention), the Board could never take any action itself.

Probably of greater influence was the continuous campaign for cooperatives, especially consumers' cooperatives, carried on for nearly a year in the Knights' *Journal of United Labor.*

By 1883 there were some 50 or 60 cooperative stores, nearly all of which followed the Rochdale plan. They were all closed organizations, admitting only Knights to membership and dealing only with members. Many of the store associations were very secretive and carried on their deliberations behind closed doors. There was one small cooperative store in Michigan of which it was even said that its "very existence was kept secret" from all but the members.

In the South, after 1880, the Knights of Labor had become a predominantly farm group, allied with the Populist movement. There as in other places where the Knights were strong, cooperatives of various kinds were started—among them stores, marketing associations, and cooperative workshops. The stores were organized particularly in towns where there was only a company store that exploited the workers. These do not appear to have been very long-lived. Figures for 1887 did not show any in the South, but there were 18 Knights of Labor stores in Maine, 10 or more in Illinois and Ohio, 3 each in Minnesota and Wyoming, 2 each in Iowa and Kansas, and 1 each in Colorado and Massachusetts. All had disappeared by 1913.

Strike failures contributed to the decline of the order. Thereafter it began to lose its hold on the semiskilled and unskilled urban industrial workers who had been its mainstay. Organization on a trade rather than industrial basis came in with the formation of the American Federation of Labor in 1886. The Knights of Labor thereupon began working among country people—small merchants, mechanics, and farmers. It was on the decline, however, and came to an end a few years later.

The Knights were champions of all sorts of causes, political, social and economic, that promised to improve the condition of the workers.[1] Possibly this very diversity of interest weakened their influence in any one direction. In cooperation, they divided their attention between distributive and productive enterprises, but with greater emphasis on the latter. They scattered their fire, lacked practical business experience, and financed their businesses inadequately.

The order's contribution to the consumers' cooperative movement was inconsiderable. A substantial proportion of its comparatively few stores were only semicooperative. In the productive field its enterprises served mainly to point up vividly the weaknesses of industrial cooperation.

Sovereigns of Industry, 1874-79

The Sovereigns of Industry had a greater and more lasting cooperative impact, in spite of the short life of the order.

The idea underlying the Sovereigns' program was conceived by William H. Earle, a fruit grower in Worcester, Mass. He had studied the Grangers' experience (had in fact been a Grange organizer) and thought that there should be a corresponding secret organization for industrial workers. A group of 15 laboring men, called into meeting by him in Springfield, in January 1874, drew up a constitution and formed the National Council of the Order of Sovereigns of Industry—a secret society with passwords and a ritual.

The first subordinate council was organized, appropriately, at Worcester. Other councils began to be formed almost immediately in Massachusetts and the neighboring States.

The Sovereigns aimed at "wise and kindly measures" for "organized resistance to the organized encroachment of the monopolies and other evils of the existing industrial and commercial system," and the promotion of "mutual fellowship and cooperative action among the producers and consumers of wealth throughout the earth." It declared: "We wage no wars with persons or classes, but only with wrongs, discords and hardships, which have existed too long."

The first State council was that organized for Massachusetts in April 1874. At a year-end meeting 100 councils, with some 10,000 members, were represented.

By 1875, although the order was less than 2 years old, it had taken root in a majority of the States. State councils had been organized in 11 States and were in process in 3 others. Membership was largest in Connecticut, Massachusetts, and Rhode Island. Local councils were formed as far west as the Pacific Coast.

In mid-year 101 councils (of 175) had some kind of purchasing arrangements. Massachusetts alone had 48 such councils.

The main emphasis, however, was on obtaining reduced prices from retailers, in consideration for the large potential patronage represented by the membership, and about half of the councils never progressed beyond this stage. Discounts ranged from 5 to 50 percent.

In the next few years emphasis shifted and Sovereign stores sprang up all over the eastern and central parts of the United States. The order never got a real foothold in the South, though there were a few individual members as far south as Maryland in the early years, and some enterprises were started as a result of Sovereign influence. Several independent associations already in existence also affiliated. A wholesale was started in New Haven, Conn.

Although other labor groups and their leaders had declared for cooperative action, the Sovereigns were the first labor organization to put the main emphasis on consumers' cooperation. President Earle was an ardent advocate of Rochdale cooperation and it was probably due to his influence that for 2 years the Sovereigns kept in the field two paid lecturers, one of whose duties was to "instruct the people in cooperation."

Nearly half of the Sovereign stores operated on the Rochdale plan from the beginning. In 1876 the National Council issued its *Plan for Organization and Management of Cooperative Stores*, which set forth all the Rochdale principles and gave model bylaws and bookkeeping forms.

The Sovereigns' stores thus marked the period of transition from workers' joint-stock cooperative companies to workers' Rochdale cooperatives.

Savings to members through cooperation were estimated at 15 percent on purchases.

The order reached its peak in the winter of 1875-76, but its very success carried the seeds of disaster. It grew too fast to be sound, for it included "too many ignorant, discordant elements." The panic of 1873 and the hard times of 1874-79 caused loss of members, who transferred their patronage to private dealers giving credit, and stopped paying dues, with the result that many Sovereign activities had to be dropped. President Earle resigned his office for reasons of health, and his successor appeared to be more interested in politics than in cooperation. The Sovereigns went out of existence in 1879.

The dissolution of the order did not involve the genuinely cooperative stores, a majority of which went on operating for some years, and some were unusually long lived.[2] Even in those that suspended operation, there was in many cases no financial failure. Indeed, some were so prosperous that a few members found it profitable to buy up the stock gradually and thus transform them into ordinary stock companies.

Students of the cooperative movement agree that the Sovereigns of Industry, its leaders, and its cooperative program were all animated by the highest ideals. The stores that failed did so because of the disregard of the Rochdale principles, poor management, and lack of member support—the same causes that operate today.

Chapter 4.—OTHER FEDERATED MOVEMENTS

The Labor Exchanges, 1889-1906

The "labor exchange" movement began in 1889 with the incorporation of the first (and parent) unit in Sedalia, Mo., by G. B. de Bernardi of Independence.

The primary object was to provide employment by facilitating the exchange of commodities and services, thus enabling the workers to buy food, clothing and home comforts. Membership was open to any person of good character, not addicted to intemperance or of immoral habits, who was willing to work in a useful occupation.

Members were invited to bring in for sale "any product of labor," receiving therefor a check representing its estimated wholesale price, which could be used to buy any articles on display. They were also urged to pay cash or deposit money with the Exchange.[1] (Private merchants were sometimes induced to accept labor-exchange checks, but usually only at a discount.)

At first the movement took hold primarily among the industrial workers; later it had even more success in the small towns and rural districts. By mid-1896 the membership represented "almost every trade, profession, and calling," and 135 local exchanges with 6,000 members had been started in 32 States.

It was reported that in southern California alone there were 22 exchanges. In that State (and in Washington), though the national leadership opposed orthodox cooperation, the exchanges tended to become Rochdale consumers' cooperatives. In fact, the first cooperative in California to bear the name of Rochdale was organized in Dos Palos in 1896 as Branch No. 135 of the Labor Exchange at Independence, Mo. It was started in order to break a one-store monopoly in the town and at the same time find an outlet for the members' produce. In 1899 the store incorporated, taking the name Dos Palos Rochdale Co. It had a long and successful history. Until 1912 it never failed to pay a patronage fund. It declined during the next few years, however, and was out of business by 1920.

The Exchange movement as a whole attained a moderate degree of success and was still in operation in 1906, but did not prosper on the scale its founder had expected.

Cooperative Union of America, 1895-99

The Cooperative Union of America was formed in Cambridge, Mass., on September 5, 1895, to act as educational organization and coordinating body for local cooperatives. During its first year letters were sent to all the known cooperatives, bylaws were formulated for their guidance, and a study of the cooperative laws was made.

The Union had also joined the International Cooperative Alliance. The next year it sent delegates to a national convention in St. Louis at which the American Cooperative Union (never more than a paper organization) was formed.[2]

The high point of the Union's activity and influence appears to have been reached in 1897 and it was in that year also that it drafted a bill for a cooperative law for Massachusetts, presumably to amend or supplant a law passed in 1866. There is no evidence of any success in this move.

Its members then numbered 14 associations—12 in New England and one each in New Jersey and New York. (Total membership never exceeded this number.) They included a few of the old Protective Union cooperatives as well as new, independent associations.

The Union, which depended on voluntary contributions for the greater part of its income, was having trouble making ends meet as early as mid-1897. Part of the difficulty doubtless lay in the general economic situation, which was serious; thousands were walking the streets, unemployed.

The last issue of its *News* was that for February 1899. The Union went out of existence shortly afterward—a victim of nonsupport by the local associations and of the dissolution of the Cambridge Cooperative Association which had been its mainstay.

This organization was one composed primarily of intellectuals. Among its organizers were Prof. F. G. Peabody of Harvard University and Rev. Robert E. Ely of Cambridge. Prof. John Graham Brooks of Harvard was on its board, as well as N. O.

Nelson of St. Louis; and Rev. Edward Everett Hale served a term as vice president. During its 3-year publication, the *American Cooperative News* received many contributions from people famous in literature and philanthropy.

The Union was never very successful, however, in rallying the local cooperatives to its banner, though they did send increasing numbers of representatives to its meetings. Its chief contribution, in my opinion, was that it served as a unifying force in disseminating news of cooperatives throughout the United States. Its paper continually carried items on cooperatives in other areas, and was practically the only source for such information.

After the disappearance of the Union, the local associations "withdrew into their restricted local interests, and made no further attempt to keep in touch with distant societies."[8]

Chapter 5.—EARLY INDEPENDENT COOPERATIVES, 1860-1900

There were, in this early period, numerous, sometimes rather isolated cooperatives not sponsored by any organization but formed by people interested in cooperation for the sake of its philosophy or for the possible pecuniary benefits or both. These associations rarely had access to the services of a central federation which could act as clearing house of information or as wholesale supplier. Most of them "lived and died in obscurity, known only to a small circle of interested persons."[1] Some, however, displayed an astounding vitality and functioned vigorously over long periods of time.

By 1866, "practically every important industrial town between Boston and San Francisco" had some form of distributive cooperative.[2] Because of the lack of any central sources of information, however, the data on these associations are very scattered and fragmentary, and only a few highlights can be given here.

Eastern States

Pennsylvania has the honor of being the first State to produce a cooperative on the accepted Rochdale plan—Union Cooperative Association No. 1, organized December 16, 1862, in Philadelphia. Its orthodoxy was attributable to one of the organizers' having obtained a copy of the constitution and bylaws of the Rochdale Society of Equitable Pioneers. By 1886 it had three branches. Excessive overhead caused it to go into the red, and it failed in that same year.

Its influence, the rapidly rising prices, and a series of articles in *Fincher's Trades' Review* (a trade-union publication) caused the formation of many other cooperatives independent of any sponsoring organization. Most of these, though not all, had failed by 1868.

The Philadelphia Industrial Cooperative Society, organized in 1874, at its zenith (1883) had over 2,500 members and eight stores, and did an annual business of nearly a quarter of a million dollars. Thereafter it declined, going out of business in 1890 as a result of ineffective boards of directors, ill-advised expansion, and a penny-pinching labor policy.

In the same State during the nineties, coal miners started a number of independent stores, mainly in and around Pittsburgh. One, Banksville Cooperative Association (1890), was still operating in 1917 and was then the oldest cooperative in Pennsylvania. The Juniata Cooperative Association lasted from 1895 till the late 1920's.

Maine, which had participated in both the Grange and Sovereigns programs, also had a few cooperatives without organizational sponsorship. Among these were several owned by English textile workers at Skowhegan, Sabattus, and Lisbon Falls, that survived long after the sponsored movements had disappeared.

Although Maryland appears to have had relatively little cooperative activity, it had one association that was successful during its entire long existence—the Lonaconing Cooperative Association in the coal-mining region of western Maryland, organized in March 1874. During the depression of 1920-21 it went on a cash basis. Many of the members, unemployed, had no ready money and sales fell off. The members then voted to sell out. When the books were closed, in May 1921, each member received the full value of his shares plus a bonus of 20 percent. A report to the U. S. Bureau of Labor Statistics on the reasons for dissolution concluded: "Anyway, they got tired of running the store"—an ironic epitaph for an association that during its 47-year operation had returned more than $100,000 on patronage to the workers of this little town!

Immediately after the Civil War, numerous Negro organizations sprang up throughout the city of Baltimore. These included grocery stores, coal yards, and other businesses, which failed eventually for want of capital or trained management.

In Massachusetts, between 1860 and 1865, several cooperative stores were started in the Boston area, none of which lasted for more than a few years. Another revival occurred just after the end of the Civil War, stimulated at least in part by the passage of a State cooperative law in 1866. Between that year and 1885, at least 30 to 40 stores (and probably others of which there is no present record) were opened. Massachusetts was probably the leading cooperative State, and one historian observed that the future of cooperation "seemed never so bright as today."[3]

Among the more successful stores was the Arlington Cooperative Society, organized in 1884 among the employees of the Arlington textile mill at Lawrence. By the end of 1889 it had two branch stores and a fuel yard, besides discount arrangements with local dealers for the purchase of shoes, clothing, drygoods, stoves, and hardware. At its peak this cooperative had 3,440 members—an almost unprecedented number for those days and a very respectable one even now. From 1885 to 1890 it paid refunds ranging from 7 to 9 percent. It made the mistake of allowing control to drift into the hands of the manager (who proved dishonest) and woke up to the danger only when it was too late. It went out of business in 1908.

The same State had other, even longer-lived, cooperatives—at Worcester (two associations), Lawrence, and Gardner. These four cooperatives had life spans ranging from 37 to 57 years. On the dissolution of the German Cooperative Association in Worcester, a $50 premium was paid on all shares. When the Gardner cooperative closed its doors, each member received $23 for every $5 share held by him.

In New Jersey the earliest independent of record was the Fruit Growers Union & Cooperative Store at Hammonton, doing marketing and operating a general store, started in 1867. Between 1881 (when a State cooperative law was enacted) and 1895, 33 distributive associations were organized under its terms, of which 25 actually went into operation. Fifteen were already out of business by 1895. Among the survivors was the Trenton Cooperative Society (1885) that in the first 12 years of operation returned $104,864 on patronage. Another small wave of interest brought forth eight independent cooperatives between 1896 and 1902.

Mention has already been made of the year 1829 association in New York—believed to be the very first cooperative in the United States. The next of record in this State were the Farmers & Mechanics Trading Co. at Seneca Falls, started in 1872, and a store in New York City in 1875. At least five others opened in the years 1877-96. Among them was the Port Jervis Cooperative Society (1877) which operated until 1922, when its charter expired. The charter had already been renewed once; no explanation was given for the failure to do so again, after 45 years of service.

The independent cooperative movement in Rhode Island, never extensive, included one veteran cooperative. It was the Pascoag United Cooperative Association at Burrillville, composed of textile workers and farmers, which was in operation for 46 years—from 1888 to 1934.

In Vermont, the Orange County Farmers Exchange at Bradford operated nearly as long—from 1891 to 1936.

Midwest

Illinois had seven independent cooperatives, of which one outlived all the rest. It was the Leclaire Cooperative Association at Edwardsville, owned by the N. O. Nelson employees and organized in 1892. It had a great success and was one of the bright spots in the cooperative movement until about 1920, when it lost its cooperative features.

As early as 1878, Wisconsin had at least 20 independent stores, the majority of which were affiliated to a State federation. These gradually disappeared one by one.[4] In Ohio the store at Washingtonville (1891) operated until late in the 1930's. Iowa had 15 known independent cooperatives in 1898, and some 13 others were opened during the next year, mainly by farmers.[5]

Minnesota also had a considerable number, among them the Minneapolis Mercantile Co. (a grocery started by coopers in 1885), the Brainerd Cooperative Co. (1886), and the Duluth Cooperative Mercantile Co. (1887) which admitted only trade-unionists to membership. Some of the independents started during the decade beginning with 1890 lasted for notably long periods. They included the Lake Shore Cooperative Mercantile Co. at Butternut (1894) which operated for 51 years. The Bear Park Cooperative Mercantile Co. at Gary and the Nelson and Albin Cooperative Mercantile Association at St. James, both organized in 1894, are still in operation.[6]

Records of early independent cooperatives in Michigan are sparse. One, however, deserves mention—the Tamarack Cooperative Association. Started by copper miners in 1890, it prospered for many years and at one time was reported to be doing the largest business of any store, cooperative or profit, north of Milwaukee. Its sales in 1920 exceeded $856,000. Up to 1919 it never failed to pay a patronage refund, usually returning from 8 to 13 percent. After the end of World War I, however, the mines closed down for the first time in 50 years, and many members moved away in search of work. The association found itself with $98,000 in accounts receivable, but miraculously was able to collect nearly all of it; losses from these debts proved to be less than one-half of 1 percent.

The slump in copper mining continued for many years, during which Tamarack by 1930 had become virtually a ghost town. A survey by the U. S. Bureau of Labor Statistics in that year disclosed that, although the association was still in operation, it had deteriorated in many ways. Members had to show $200 annual purchases at the store in order to receive patronage refunds. They had ceased to take much interest, and the manager was for all practical purposes in complete control. Employees were treated with exceptional generosity for those days, each receiving 10 days' paid vacation each year, sick leave with pay, and a $1,500 life insurance policy paid for by the association.

Business dwindled during the depression and the Tamarack cooperative had operating losses each year from 1932 through 1936. It still had 1,530 "paper" members, but most of them had moved away. The business was closed in 1939, after half a century of operation.

Western States

The first independent consumers' cooperative of record in California was the Cooperative Union Store, started in San Francisco in the latter part of 1867. By 1875 six consumers' cooperatives were in operation on essentially Rochdale principles. Ironically, they fell victim to the prosperity that followed the panic of 1873 and to the reaction following too rapid a growth. By 1885 most of the cooperatives had become either joint-stock companies or the property of individuals. Two years later there was still little cooperative activity; the people were said to be so prosperous that cooperation made little headway, but semicooperative schemes were "abundant." A few cooperatives were started in the decade of the nineties.

Southern States

Though there were few cooperatives in the South, Louisiana was the scene of a one-man movement for cooperation in the person of N. O. Nelson, who had become a convert to Rochdale cooperation, kept in touch with cooperatives throughout the United States, and took part in many of their gatherings.[7] He built up a chain, Nelson Cooperative Stores, in and around New Orleans (and a single store in St. Louis). Although he intended that these should become real cooperatives eventually, he said in 1911 that they were not cooperative yet and he did not call them such (in spite of their name).

By 1917, Nelson Cooperative Stores included 61 retail stores, four meat markets, a bakery, a milk-pasteurization plant, a coffee-roasting plant, a condiment mill, and a 1,500-acre farm. He was still trying to attract members, offering them the expectation of savings of "at least 20 percent on the retail price."

No evidence could be found that the consumers, as members, ever did take hold and make the stores really cooperative.

Students' Cooperative Bookstores

One distinctive type of independent cooperative in the early period consisted of the students' stores selling books and other supplies, which began to be formed as early as the 1880's.

With a complete student turnover every four years, it was difficult to retain member ownership and control. In most cases, the organization usually became, eventually, a trusteeship affair, with actual control vested in trustees who were commonly members of the faculty. "Dividends" on purchases continued to be paid, but the student purchaser had no vote and therefore no voice in determination of policies. At present, few of the college bookstores are even semi-cooperative.

Among the earliest of which there is a present record were stores at the universities of Tennessee (1862), Harvard (1882), California (1884), and Yale (1885). All except that in Tennessee are still in operation, but only the Harvard association has any semblance of student ownership and control.

In the decade 1890-99, bookstores were opened at Wisconsin, Texas, Cornell, and Stanford. The stores at Texas and Stanford still have some cooperative features, but those at Cornell and Wisconsin have not been cooperative since about 1905. From 1900 to 1909 university bookstores were started in Illinois, Kansas, Missouri, New Jersey (Princeton), Ohio (Cincinnati), and Washington. Only the Princeton organization is still operating, as a (semi) cooperative.

Summary and Conclusion

Scattered though the independent cooperatives were, geographically, in the aggregate they formed quite a respectable number. Also, in spite of few cooperative laws—and almost no good ones—a substantial proportion of the associations followed Rochdale principles. They appear to have had no general program but pursued one aim: operation of a business enterprise usually a store.

Ordinarily they were not sufficiently concentrated geographically for wholesaling, although the subject was discussed here and there. In Iowa and Wisconsin (and possibly other States) there were informal federations for education and exchange of experience.

As has been seen, some of the independent cooperatives had long histories of success that profit business might envy. The truth of the matter was, however, that with these exceptions, the independent associations usually went their own way—and eventually out of existence at such a rate as to make wholesale federation impracticable. No firm business could be built on such ephemeral organizations as most of them were.

Some met bitter opposition and stiff competition from profit merchants. Depression, unemployment among the members, money panics, etc., added to their hardships. Much if not most of the trouble lay within, however. Insufficient capital for efficient operation, mismanagement, poor management, extension of credit, overexpansion—these were recurring reasons for dissolution. But the underlying cause was member failure, apathy ("they got tired"), lack of patronage, and lack of participation in the affairs of the association. Even a cursory examination of the records discloses an appalling number of cases in which a prosperous cooperative, doing its job well, was allowed to become the creature of one man (generally the manager), or finally to drift into the hands of a few persons who knew a good thing when they saw it. In their way, the independents thus provided object lessons in both success and failure.

Chapter 6.—SITUATION AT THE END OF THE CENTURY

The waves of cooperative activity prior to 1900 had been strong but fairly brief. They appeared to be alternately or concurrently proletarian or agrarian in origin. The first cooperatives were those of industrial workers, in the Protective Union movement. Then followed the Granger movement (agrarian), accompanied almost identically in time by the Crispins, Knights of Labor, and Sovereigns of Industry (all industrial). The Farmers' Alliance (agrarian), next in sequence, was followed by the Cooperative Union of America (mainly urban in character).

Most of the early historians were inclined to regard the whole history of consumers' cooperation in the United States up to that time as one of failure, and Randall even doubted that cooperative distribution could ever become a success in the United States, for "only a slow-thinking, penny-counting, frugal and painstaking people" can succeed in cooperation.[1]

Bemis told the First International Cooperative Congress, in 1895, that there were then no National or State cooperative federations, no central sources of information (governmental or cooperative), and no cooperative papers. There were ten failures to one success, and the existing associations were not growing much.

Reporting to the U. S. Bureau of Labor Statistics, the next year, he noted that in many States cooperative effort consisted only of collective buying. Apart from Utah which had a semi-cooperative movement of its own, there were then but five centers of cooperative activity in the United States—in California, Kansas, Massachusetts, New Jersey, and Texas. Even in Texas, cooperation had "greatly declined." An attempt was being made to federate the associations in Kansas.

Fifteen associations formed since 1886 were still in operation. Of these, five were in Kansas, three each in California, and New Jersey, and one each in Michigan, Minnesota, New York, and Pennsylvania.

Bemis estimated the total cooperative business in New England (now almost entirely on the Rochdale basis) as about twice as great as ten years previously, or about $2,372,000 and the business elsewhere as about $900,000 (as compared with about $1 million in 1886). The average rate of patronage refund on the 1895 business was 6.8 percent in New England and 3.5 percent elsewhere. In some associations, also, the members were receiving, either directly from merchants or through the cooperative, trade discounts on goods not handled by the latter.

The membership of the New England cooperatives early in 1896 totaled 10,692. Adding to this the 6,115 members in known associations elsewhere, the 6,000 members of the 135 labor exchanges in the West and South, and the estimated membership for possibly 20 or more undiscovered associations, Bemis reached a total figure of at least 25,000.

Cummings expressed the opinion (though not in connection with the above figures) that cooperative statistics gave the movement "an appearance of coherence and stability which it does not possess. Indeed, these diverse, widely scattered, and disconnected remnants can scarcely be said to constitute a movement in any proper sense of the term."[2]

Records of the U. S. Bureau of Labor Statistics indicate the existence in 1900 of at least 96 consumers' cooperatives in 23 States. Massachusetts was in the lead with 20, followed by Kansas and Minnesota (10 each), California and Texas (6 each), and Iowa, New York and Wisconsin (5 each). Of the active associations, 17 were Grange cooperatives, 12 had been started by the Farmers' Alliance, seven by the Sovereigns, and three by the Protective Union. Five were students' cooperatives and 52 were independently organized. These figures did not include the 100 or more semi-cooperative organizations of the Mormons.

The collective-buying agencies of the Protective Union, the Grange State agencies, and the two wholesales of the Grangers and the Sovereigns had all disappeared. A new wholesale was just getting under way in California which offered great promise and was the only federated cooperative business in the United

States. Elsewhere such cooperative activity as remained was carried on by individual groups operating their own little retail businesses, with little or no communication with other cooperatives.

A central federation, independent of outside movements but responsive to and controlled by the local cooperatives could have provided a coordinating and stabilizing influence, as well as wise guidance. The experience of the Cooperative Union of America, however, indicated that the local associations were not yet sufficiently convinced of the value of such a federation to give it the necessary financial and moral support.

Part II.

COOPERATION
IN THE NEW CENTURY

Chapter 7.—PRE-WAR PERIOD, 1900-16

Interest in cooperation began to quicken again, just before the end of the nineteenth century, but for reasons different from those in the early years: Rapid economic development had produced an increased social solidarity and a greater feeling of economic dependence; also the people were beginning to rebel against the high prices set by monopolies. As cooperatives appeared to be a possible counter-measure, several organizations were formed to promote them, and the Socialist Party began to preach cooperation as the only solution for the "tremendous waste of the present system of distribution." Two farm organizations—the Farmers Union and the American Society of Equity—both formed in 1902, also began to promote cooperatives. As a result of all these factors, there was a gradual expansion of the cooperative movement, particularly in California, the North Central States, and parts of New England, until about 1910. Thereafter occurred a slow decline until about the time of the United States' entrance into World War I, in 1917.

A year-long study by Ira Cross, for 1905, revealed widespread but still mostly uncoordinated activities throughout the country. The Midwest had by now definitely taken the lead. Of 343 cooperatives discovered, 138 were there; 98 were in the far West, and 42 were in New England. The total membership was estimated at 76,146 and the annual business at $265,500,000. The greatest volume of business was now coming from the farmers, not the urban industrial workers.

This period also saw the formation of many cooperatives among immigrant groups—a development that continued for the next 10 or 15 years.

Some movement toward coordination of cooperative activity was likewise evident. Federations for education and exchange of experience were being organized: Pacific Coast Cooperative Union (California), formed in 1899; Kansas State Cooperative Association (1901), having 35 affiliated stores by 1904; and the Washington State Cooperative Union (1903), having 24 members (stores, creameries and shingle mills) by 1905. Nearly 10 years later (1914), the Iowa Cooperative Store Federation was organized and by the next year had 35 member associations.[1]

Cooperation in the East

In the East, the revival of cooperation in the early 1900's occurred among both the rural and urban people. In part this was due to renewed activity by the Grangers. It also included a number of cooperative coal yards formed in New England during the coal strike of 1902. (Ten years later, all but a few coal associations had become joint-stock companies).

Labor unions (especially those of coal miners) were organizing cooperative stores, as a weapon of defense against the Citizens' Alliance, an organization of retail merchants and professional men which was trying to destroy the trade-unions. The coal miners, it was said, had been inspired by speeches and articles by John Mitchell, president of the United Mine Workers, after a trip to Europe.

Cooperative Association of America

Among the more interesting and unusual of the organizations in this period was one that was neither farmer nor unionist —the Cooperative Association of America. It was formed in January 1899, by Bradford Peck (owner of a large department store in Lewiston, Maine), with himself as president.

The declared purposes were threefold: To provide employment to workers, to run stores and buying clubs, and to provide old-age security through pensions and other means. Although cooperative distribution was one facet, the program resembled the old Owenite philosophy rather than that of Rochdale. The participants in the plan were to be of two classes—the "co-workers" (people employed in the enterprise) who paid a fee of $300; and associate members who paid $2 per year and subscribed for shares at $25 each, with the privilege of using the facilities of the buying clubs and stores.

The first enterprises undertaken were a cooperative cafe, opened in 1900 (and closed at the year's end) and a store to serve Lewiston and Auburn, opened late in 1901. In August a book and job printing plant in Boston was bought, among the duties of which was the printing of the association's monthly, *The American Cooperator.*

The humanitarian aspects of Mr. Peck's plan had attracted a group of clergymen, editors, educators, reformers, and others.[2] However, notwithstanding Mr. Peck's subsidies, it did not seem equally appealing to the workers whom it was intended to benefit. Perhaps the investment required from "co-workers" was too much; perhaps the scheme was too patriarchal; perhaps going in too many directions at once—consumers' cooperation, industrial cooperation, profit sharing, and outright philanthropy. At any rate, three years after CAA was launched, only 28 persons had become co-workers; they constituted less than a fourth of the number employed in the business. About 30 others had applied for membership.

By 1907 CAA had discontinued the payment of patronage refunds. Mr. Peck had withdrawn from the CAA, and the business was being run by the workers.

By 1913 all of the affiliates were out of business, as a result of mismanagement or of nonsupport by the members. The department store was still operating, but on a profit-sharing rather than cooperative plan, and the Boston Cooperative Exchange (started in 1904) was also active, "trying to induce private retailers to adopt cooperative methods." The rest is silence.[3]

The (Jewish) Cooperative League

In New York City, in 1907, a group of persons (some of whom later were among the founders of the present Cooperative League of the USA) formed a small retail cooperative in the Bronx, with only a few dozen members.

This undercapitalized store failed in the 1907 money panic, but one of its members, Hyman I. Cohn, a salesman, had become so imbued with the cooperative idea that he began preaching it in season and out. One of the results of his incessant advocacy was The Cooperative League, organized in March 1909, of which he was elected vice president.[4]

An ambitious welfare program was also planned. Members who had been "continuous" patrons of the league stores and who became incapacitated by accident or illness, "not caused by vicious habits," would be entitled to draw free goods from the store for not to exceed 12 weeks. Amounts so drawn were to be limited in amount to the value of the member's average weekly purchases during the 12 weeks preceding incapacity.

Although the league announced that it would start a bakery, actually its first enterprise was a hat store at 159 Delancey Street. With a capital of only $238, collected over a period of two years, the store opened with a fairly large stock "procured on the credit of one of the members." It had an instant and rather astonishing success. Then, flushed with triumph, and acting on the urging of Mr. Cohn, the directors took over "on terms" the factory that had been supplying the hats. Two more stores were opened—one uptown and one in the Brownsville section of Brooklyn.

The novelty of the enterprise seemed to appeal to the imagination of the East Siders and business boomed. By the time of the first general assembly of the league, in June 1912, the membership consisted of 72 branches of the Workmen's Circle, eight labor unions, and 446 individuals. The cooperative association in Troy, N. Y., had also applied for membership—the only one outside New York City to do so.

Problems began to appear in the hat business, however. The league had only several hundred members and these would need at most only one or two hats a year. Nevertheless, it had to dispose of many thousands of hats annually in order to operate the factory at capacity and meet the overhead expense. Therefore three additional stores were opened, and each added a men's furnishing department. Unfortunately, "what active sympathy there was in the Jewish quarter for the league had concentrated on the Delancey Street store."[5] None of the other stores could be made to pay.

For a while the original store met the losses of the others, but finally the factory and losing stores had to be sold. The association reorganized in 1914 as the Industrial and Agricultural Cooperative Association, branched out into other lines, and was very successful for a considerable time. At its peak it operated two restaurants, two boarding houses, and a meat market, and had an annual payroll of $20,000. The association went out of business in the middle 1920's.

The original association (the league), though short-lived, had an influence far beyond its size and business territory. In 1913 it even sent a delegate to the Glasgow congress of the International Cooperative Alliance, which it had joined in 1912. The league's efforts were responsible also for the establishment of a cooperative information bureau by the Socialist Party, the literature and activities of which led to the organization of many cooperatives, all over the country.

Cooperation in the Midwest

Between 1900 and 1905, the Illinois coal miners began to be interested in cooperation. By 1905 there were ten cooperative stores in the State, of which about half were miners' organizations. During the next five years, however, the cooperative movement failed to hold its own, as the workers were more concerned with union and political activity, and the farmers were enjoying a period of relative prosperity in which there was no particular need for the benefits of cooperation. There were, however, several rather unusual associations. One was a mail-order organization, First National Cooperative Society, started in Chicago in 1903 by Julius Kahn. It appears to have been financially successful from the first, paying dividends on capital of never less than 10 percent, in addition to a 5-percent discount on orders.

After a series of difficulties during which Mr. Kahn was indicted for fraud and then acquitted, the business was sold in April 1906. Mr. Kahn then organized a new association, the Cash Buyers Cooperative Union, which later sold out to the Consumers-Alliance National.

The Consumers-Alliance National was formed on March 4, 1911, under the leadership of James H. Brower. It was planned as a national organization for discount arrangements with private merchants and mail-order purchasing, and to run cooperative stores which would be branches of the parent association.

Thirteen local councils had been formed by September 1911. Mr. Brower died the next month, however, and G. P. Bethel took over the work. Inadequately capitalized stores were opened at Galesburg and Staunton. Thereafter the organization declined. Membership dissension had wrecked the Staunton group by

1915. The store at Galesburg took the name, Consumers-Alliance National, when the headquarters organization dissolved (about 1915), and struggled along. In 1921 it merged with the Knox County Cooperative (which operated a coal yard), under the name Galesburg Cooperative Society. The latter went out of business in 1925.

Kansas was among the leaders in cooperation in this period. A State-wide survey in 1913 revealed 175 genuinely cooperative associations, but only 17 of them were stores. Among the others was the Farmers Union Cooperative Association of Mitchell County (with five grain elevators, three cream stations, four stores, and a service station reported to be handling "coal oil and gasoline"). Thus, the Mitchell County cooperative was the first to be recorded as handling gasoline in this country. It is still in successful operation.[8]

Many of the Kansas stores had been sponsored by the Farmers Union and Farmers Equity Union. The current policy of the Grange in that State was to encourage the pooling of purchases rather than the operation of stores.

In 1914, Minnesota had 126 cooperative stores. Some of them were old-established organizations dating from the early waves of cooperation. The greater part, however, were those promoted by the Right Relationship League, which also was responsible for a notable increase in the number of cooperative stores in Wisconsin between 1910 and 1912, mainly in the rural areas. By 1916 the latter State had 57 farmers' cooperative stores, two-thirds of which had been started since 1910.

Cooperation in the West

Toward the end of the century, following the example of the Dos Palos Rochdale Co. and assisted by the Farmers' Alliance, Rochdale stores were promoted in California and other parts of the West. Thus, by the beginning of 1904, Washington had 12 Rochdale stores, as well as several creameries and three cooperative communities.

Colorado in this period had two short-lived developments promoted by the Western Federation of Miners and the Farmers Union of Colorado.

Ground Swell in California

In California, the Pacific Coast Cooperative Union was formed in November 1899, for the "study and propagation of cooperative ideas." By the end of the year a going wholesale business had been purchased and renamed Rochdale Wholesale Co. In recognition of the need for a larger base for the wholesale (there were then only six local cooperatives in operation), an organization bureau was started, and a paper, *The Cooperative Journal,* began publication in January 1900.

The next decade was one of rapid growth. By 1902 there were about 60 stores; and three years later, 68, of which 51 were operating on Rochdale principles. The end of 1906 showed about 100 stores.

California was now the leading cooperative State, with what was termed "easily the most successful and strongest cooperative system in the United States."

Economic conditions had favored the expansion of the movement. All that had to be done during this time was to "open your store and business rolled in." "Almost any kind of business could succeed in California."

Although the Rochdale Wholesale Co. suffered from the earthquake and fire of 1906, necessitating its temporary removal to Oakland, it had recovered by the end of the year.

A turning point was reached in the panic of 1907. By the end of the year the nearly 100 stores were "all in a state of rapid decline." The wholesale "had to get 85 percent of its business from ordinary small merchants in order to survive."[7] Member associations owed it long-overdue accounts, and it was frequently embarrassed for funds to meet its own obligations. Nevertheless it had been able to build up its business to $335,000 per year by 1910.

Agitation for a central company through which to channel the local business to the wholesale crystallized into the California Rochdale Co. in 1911, but the results of this move did not come up to expectations.

Loss of stores by dissolution (in 1911, ten stores went out of business in a few months) was overcome by organizing new branches. By early 1912, 12 branches were in operation. The wholesale at mid-year had 36 regular customers (all but the Berkeley association in country districts). Some stores, however, had already sold out to their managers and others were in process of doing so.

The wholesale netted nearly $9,000 on its 1912 volume of some $350,000, and the business was reported to be "in a flourishing condition," with prospects brighter than in a long time. This optimism was belied by events, however. Although a strictly cash policy was put into effect in June 1913, it was too late. The California Rochdale Co. failed before the end of the year, and the 10 branches still remaining were closed.

By this time the Rochdale Wholesale Co., also, was in a precarious state. Fewer than 30 of the 100-odd independent Rochdale associations remained.

The movement "seemed to have received a fatal blow." To nearly everyone future prospects for cooperation seemed hopeless.[8] A few persons realized that if cooperation was to be revived, it must be through education and adherence to "true and tried principles of cooperation."[8] In this emergency, the Pacific Cooperative League was organized under the California cooperative law in 1913. Its history is given in a later section.

Retrospect

Cooperative activity was chiefly among the farmers in this period. Working-class cooperation remained disorganized and for the most part ineffective. With a few exceptions, the labor movement had not yet become convinced of the value of distributive cooperation. The recurring crop of spurious cooperatives (which usually failed, wiping out all the capital invested) helped to discourage the general public with the idea of cooperation.

The years 1914 and 1915 saw the disappearance or near-eclipse of a number of apparently promising developments, notably in New Jersey, Minnesota (Right Relationship League), and Pennsylvania.

Many of the proponents of cooperation in this time were liberals who evidently were not clear in their own minds just what it was they were after. Consequently, their programs were often a melange of consumers' cooperation, productive cooperation, and pure philanthropy, with a little profit sharing thrown in for good measure. They seem to have been thoroughly imbued with the idea that they must "make no *little* plans," however. Probably there have never been more grandiose (even though well-intentioned) schemes than were dreamed up in this decade and that of the twenties. All proved to be will-of-the-wisps that eluded the grasp and ended in failure.

Impracticality and failure to appreciate the value of education were the main disabilities of the promoters. The father of the present cooperative movement, looking back over the early days in the East, commented:

> "I realize that I was associated with as impractical an aggregation of zealots, and yet earnest and self-sacrificing devotees to an ideal, as are recorded in the annals of cooperation. Most of the societies that they started failed within two years; but the few leaders went to their little stores, carried home bags of groceries which they made themselves believe were heavenly essences, and looked upon their dwindling businesses as sputtering fuses about to blow up the citadel of capitalism."[9]

Impractical leaders, reliance upon a single person whose death or withdrawal destroyed the enterprise, poor judgment, unsound business practices, and adverse economic conditions—all these played their part. Possibly the greatest drawback in the failures was the inability to gain and hold that member support without which no cooperative can succeed. As will be seen, to a great extent this was due to the fact that so many associations were started on whipped-up enthusiasm, but without a sound basis of felt need. Patronage waned as enthusiasm cooled, leaving another enterprise stranded.

The most successful in this period, as is commonly the case, were not the ones that made a "splash." They were usually the quiet groups, often with a common bond of nationality or church affiliation, whose members knew the meaning and value of cooperation. Among them were the 60-odd Finnish stores in the Lake Superior region of Minnesota and Wisconsin.

Nevertheless, it was true that, as one participant said:

". . . all those early failures, those sometimes apparently futile efforts, were necessary to any solid foundation for a successful movement. It was the period of tilling and sowing. Much of the seed fell on barren ground. Most of the sowers are now forgotten. I feel, however, that their deeds should not pass on entirely unrecorded. They gave the most that any man can give; they gave themselves at a time when there was no reward for effort—not even glory."[10]

Chapter 8.—"PROMOTED" COOPERATION

The Right Relationship League, 1905-15

The Right Relationship League was responsible for the organization of a large part of the consumers' cooperatives that got under way in the North Central States during the decade, 1905-15. The League's offshoots were similarly active in the same region.

The Right Relationship League was incorporated in Minneapolis, on January 6, 1905. The RRL was not itself a cooperative, but was run by three of the incorporators—E. J. Van Horn (president), W. F. Vedder (treasurer), and E. Marion Tousley (secretary).[1]

The League's practice was to go into a territory, hold meetings, and arouse enthusiasm for a locally owned cooperative store. When enough members and capital ($5,000 to $10,000) had been pledged, negotiations were begun for the purchase of the store, inventory, and good will of an existing business. The theory was that it was undesirable to start additional stores, as there were already too many.

Most of the earliest associations were intended to serve a whole county and their names so indicated. (Beginning about 1909, the new associations were organized to serve a single town only.) By 1907 there were 14 county associations (in Minnesota, Wisconsin, North Dakota, and even Missouri) which together had nearly 50 stores and over 3,000 members and an estimated annual business of nearly a million dollars.

(The local group was usually organized with three departments—store, creamery, and grain elevator—or three associations were started, each performing one of these functions. League publicity and reports, however, always emphasized the store business and the cooperatives were always referred to as stores.)

Notwithstanding a previous unfruitful experience, the 1908 convention voted to establish a wholesale, to do collective buying.

The Cooperative Wholesale Co. was accordingly incorporated in October 1909. By January 18 stores had paid in $50 each; 6 others had subscribed for shares but not paid. It soon developed that the locals not only could not pay cash as required, but still less could they buy shares. The wholesale was never mentioned in print again, though it lingered on for several years.

The League had been very active during these first years. It had started its own paper, *Cooperation,* and an auditing department, and had issued model bylaws and set up a badly needed uniform accounting system for the stores, besides sponsoring drafts of new or amending legislation in Minnesota and Wisconsin.

Only seven of the oldest (county) associations were represented at the 1910 convention, but delegates were present from 24 organized on a town basis. Secretary Tousley reported that the league membership included 54 cooperatives with 86 stores and 7,700 members. The total business in 1909 was estimated at $3 million.

Although some restiveness had been evident as early as 1909, even under the League's loose supervision, one feature of the 1910 meeting was "an almost unanimous" vote in favor of three resolutions looking toward more complete central control over the League members.

By the end of the next year there were claimed to be "fully 140 stores" on the RRL plan. On "urgent demand," an office had even been opened in Seattle.[2]

Toward the end of 1910 *Cooperation* reported that only a few failures had occurred, but what proportion of the stores were successful from the cooperative point of view "is another question." Possibly three-fourths of the members failed to grasp the essentials of cooperation. As a whole they were failing to assume responsibility and were also failing in loyalty. They lacked the missionary spirit as well. The editor warned that, instead of paying out all the earnings in patronage refunds, they should leave them in the business. "Promissory notes won't capitalize cooperation."

In 1911 three stores were sold back to the original owners, two were sold at auction because of insufficient volume of business, and four became regular corporations. Excessive inventory and credit were general, and the rural members (a majority of the total) were experiencing hard times.

Then the League's chief auditor left in midsummer with a blast at its methods that put the organization on the defensive. To quiet reports reflecting on its integrity, the League requested the University of Minnesota to examine all of its transactions, covering about 4 years.

The latter's report, issued after 8 months' investigation, exonerated the League officers, calling the mistakes that had been made "errors of judgment rather than motive." The League's plan and methods were approved "for the present stage of the movement," but "no work of this sort should be carried on without adequate supervision." The officers had made up a deficit of nearly $6,500 in the auditing department and one of $5,600 on the magazine, from their own pockets. Their average remuneration during the 4 years was "a little more than $1,800" each per year. "This certainly seems a small remuneration," considering the risks.[3]

Possibly as a result of the charges, changes were taking place in the League and its methods. W. F. Vedder resigned in May 1913[4] and E. J. Van Horn in June 1914. Up to this time enthusiastic accounts, with names, had been published regarding new associations in process of formation. In October 1914 it was noted that the organization work was "not advancing as rapidly as might be desired." Thereafter, new groups if mentioned at all were referred to only in general terms that prevented identification.

The requirement that new cooperatives must subscribe to *Cooperation* for each of their members was abandoned in August 1914. This resulted in a rapid decline in circulation. By the end of the year the total edition (which at its peak had hit 5,000) numbered less than 3,000 and only 200 were individual subscriptions. The paper suspended publication a month or two later.

The League itself appears to have discontinued operation not long afterwards.

Successors of the League

E. M. Tousley next appeared as manager of the American Rochdale League, Minneapolis, which seems to have been established about 1915. This body also operated on the principle of buying up existing stores.[5]

A companion organization, American Rochdale Stores Co., was started for commercial purposes in March 1918. By 1920 it reported 9 stores in South Dakota and 4 in Wyoming, with a total membership of 815. Its financial statement for the year showed a business of $1,060,000. By 1926 both the League and the store company were out of existence.

In the meantime, E. J. Van Horn had started another promotion body, Northwestern Cooperative League (also in Minneapolis), of which he was president. It followed the same practice as the other leagues in buying up going businesses. It was his boast that the League never put anyone out of business; the owner was taken over along with the business.[6] New cooperatives were organized on the triple system—stores, creameries, and elevators. There was a central accounting system which new units were encouraged to accept.

The Northwestern Cooperative League reported in August 1920 that 73 stores organized by it had total sales in 1919 amounting to nearly $3½ million. These stores included 24 in Minnesota, 10 in South Dakota, 4 in Iowa, 15 in Wisconsin, 15 in North Dakota, and 5 in Montana.

The League was still in existence in 1926 but evidently not very active. H. N. Hanchett (its secretary-treasurer) reported—from Florida—that there had been a great falling off of work since 1920, but this of course was "only temporary." No later evidence of the existence or activity of the League could be found.

Record of the Local Associations

Records now available indicate that the Right Relationship League organized at least 200 store associations, of which 91 were in Minnesota, 54 in Wisconsin, 20 in North Dakota, with a few each in 10 other States (Illinois, Indiana, Iowa, Kansas, Michigan, Missouri, Montana, Ohio, South Dakota, and Washington).

Some reached substantial proportions. Thus, the Goodhue County Cooperative Co. at Red Wing, Minn., in 1920 had 7 branches, 800 members, and an annual business of nearly

$750,000. Another, Polk County Cooperative Co. at Amery, Wis., expanded into a 10-store chain with 600 members.

A considerable number operated for long periods. A few were still alive at last reports—eight in Minnesota, two in Wisconsin, three in Michigan, and one in Iowa. There are no known survivors in the other States.

The Northwestern Cooperative League was responsible for some 120 cooperatives in the North Central States and Montana. As a group, its stores appear to have been of shorter average duration than those of the RRL, possibly because most of them were still very young and inexperienced when the 1921-22 depression struck. Some pulled through and lived until the late 1920's and a few even lasted through several years of the Great Depression. Those still operating include four in Minnesota, two in North Dakota, and one each in South Dakota and Wisconsin.

Only about twoscore associations were promoted—in Michigan and Ohio—by the American Organization Bureau in Chicago, operated by W. F. Vedder. Three of the Michigan cooperatives were alive at last reports.

The activities of Tousley's American Rochdale League seem to have been confined mainly to South Dakota, with occasional forays into other Midwest and Western States. Altogether, this organization was accountable for the formation of some 30 associations. There is only one known League store still in existence.

The Leagues in Retrospect

Opinions of historians and cooperative leaders vary as to the bona fides of the directors of these leagues. Some thought they looked upon the cooperative movement mainly as a means of livelihood—and undoubtedly this *was* a consideration. Others believed that they (especially Mr. Tousley) were motivated by a genuine belief in cooperation on the Rochdale plan. Certainly the Right Relationship League always preached and, as far as the printed record goes, practised simon-pure Rochdale cooperation: Each member one vote only, continuous educational work, interest on capital limited, patronage refunds to members, and, (unusual for those days) also to nonmembers, though at half rates.

The faults of all the leagues, as this writer sees them, lay in (1) the practice of purchasing privately owned stores, often with shopworn goods and sometimes at too high a valuation, (2) starting cooperatives with far too little advance educational work in the cooperative method and on the basis of insufficient local desire or demand, and (3) often hiring as manager the former owner, who knew nothing and cared less about cooperation and probably had no real desire to see the cooperative succeed.

The RRL, at least, made a real contribution in its journal's continual exposition of genuinely cooperative methods, in its insistence upon the necessity of good accounting, and in its realization of the importance of federation for educational work and for wholesaling.

As has been seen, the four organization bodies were responsible for the formation of at least 356 associations which the present writer has traced, and probably for others undiscovered. On these known associations the survival rate may seem low; only 25 or about 7 percent, overcame the obstacles faced over periods ranging from 25 to 50 years.[7]

In my opinion, however, these rates are actually remarkably high, considering all the factors: (1) The unsound basis on which they were formed, (2) the generally inadequate membership base and low capitalization (and in addition, the fact that many members never paid up their capital pledges), (3) the difficulties met (at least one and, for many, two world wars, two depressions, and the drought and other bad agricultural conditions in the rural areas), and (4) the necessity for continual membership renewal in the 30 to 50 years that have elapsed since the associations were organized. Whatever the motives that underlay the formation of these cooperatives, the survival record as a whole is not one of which to be ashamed.

Chapter 9.—BEGINNINGS OF COORDINATION

When the war broke out in Europe in 1914, cooperative enthusiasm was generally rather low in this country, except in the Midwest (where the Right Relationship League was busy) and in California (where a new organization was trying to salvage the remains of an earlier movement). Elsewhere, there were still scattered remnants of earlier waves, and a few new associations were being formed here and there. There were even a few moves (usually unsuccessful) toward area coordination. Most of the cooperatives, however, were going their own way, with little or no knowledge of what others were doing, even in their own region. The Rochdale principles were generally not well observed. The lessons of experience were either unknown or disregarded. Trial and error were killing, within a few months or years, a majority of such new cooperatives as were being formed.

It was truly a situation that called for some strong unifying force that would weld these disparate parts into something resembling a movement. That no central organization of this kind existed was not for want of intention. A number of conferences looking toward the formation of a national federation had been held, and two federations were actually organized—American Cooperative Union, in 1906, and American Cooperative Federation, in 1913. But in no case was there a follow-through, either because of lack of funds or because of inertia on the part of the local cooperatives.

Consumers' Cooperative Union

The first move that was to bear fruit began in a small way, with the contributed services of a few men gripped by a big idea and willing to make sacrifices to bring it into realization. The group included Hyman Cohn, Albert Sonnichsen, and William A. Kraus.[1]

They began by organizing the Cooperative Propaganda Publishing Association—later changed, first to Consumers' Cooperative Publishing Association, and then to Consumers' Cooperative Union. In May 1914 appeared the first issue of *The Cooperative Consumer.* The paper operated on an infinitesimal income and was kept going for a year and a half only through the good management of Mr. Kraus, its business manager.[2] Albert Sonnichsen was its editor.

That the time was ripe was evidenced by the calls for speakers, for assistance in organizing, and for literature, that began to pour in from all parts of the country.

As a member of the finance committee, to solicit contributions from private persons, Mr. Sonnichsen called upon Dr. James Peter Warbasse. "As a particular job, it was the most successful I ever undertook for cooperation"[3]—for Dr. Warbasse became a founder of the organization that developed into the present national League of consumers' cooperatives. To the devotion, persistence, and solid financial support of Dr. Warbasse can be attributed the lion's share of the credit for molding the scattered cooperatives into a genuinely Rochdale movement.[4]

The Present Cooperative League

A meeting at the Brooklyn home of Dr. and Mrs. Warbasse, on December 18, 1915, drew only a few persons. About 50 people came to another called for January 8, 1916, however, and they voted unanimously to establish an organization to promote consumers' cooperation in the United States. A committee was elected to draw up a constitution.

On March 18, 1916 the Cooperative League of America was formally organized and the constitution adopted.[5]

The new League absorbed the Consumers' Cooperative Union and took over the issuance of *The Cooperative Consumer.* That paper, resuming publication after a hiatus of 3 months, for want of funds, explained that the new League was not a federation of local associations, though such federation was desirable. Retail cooperatives were still too few in number for that. It would at first attempt to utilize the strength and contributions of individuals all over the United States. The League was therefore at present "a society of individual cooperators who propose to push a general campaign of propaganda until the societies shall be strong enough to undertake it for themselves."

Local cooperatives already in existence were urged to affiliate and eventually take over control of the League.

Minutes of the early board and committee meetings record the opening of an office at 2 W. Thirteenth Street, the installation of a telephone, and the hiring of an assistant secretary and two full-time office workers.[6] Mrs. Agnes Dyer Warbasse, wife of the president, served as educational director, without pay, from 1916 to 1928.[7]

The League in its early years unabashedly made use of celebrities interested in cooperation, to attract attention to its meetings and to the movement. Also, prominent people in various fields were invited to become members of an "advisory council" and their names were carried on the League's letterhead.

The League office was by now humming with industry. During its first year, more than 100,000 pieces of literature were printed and distributed.[8] The League had also collected a small library, established a speakers' bureau, and prepared speeches, articles, bylaws, and materials for exhibits. Circular letters had been sent to about 900 consumers' cooperatives, but the returns had been "very poor."

The Jewish Industrial and Agricultural Society and its offshoot, the Tenants League, were among the first to affiliate, having joined before the beginning of 1917. The League had made no special effort to obtain the affiliation of the retail cooperatives, feeling that it had little thus far to offer them.

There were also by now several small organizations doing collective buying,[9] and another similar association, Federation of Eastern States Cooperative Societies, was organized by delegates to the League's November 1917 meeting.

First National Congress of the League

A national convention was called by the Cooperative League, to be held at Springfield, Ill., September 25-27, 1918. The congress was primarily for distributive associations (only their delegates could vote, although other representatives could speak); and it rallied 185 delegates from 386 cooperatives. The meeting was hailed as demonstrating "closeness and sympathy" between cooperatives and trade-unions, and several speakers were present from the labor movement. In response to a direct question, President Warbasse said the League intended to maintain harmonious relations with both labor organizations and farmers' cooperatives. However, its field would be that of consumers' cooperation, "at the same time desiring to coordinate and harmonize the interests of the consumers with the interests of the producers."

On recommendation of a "committee on national unity," the meeting recognized the League as a national federation of consumers' cooperatives. A committee was appointed to draw up a constitution and bylaws for consideration at the next congress.

The other major topic for consideration was the advisability of organizing a national wholesale. After discussion such a wholesale was authorized, with membership open to all associations operating on the Rochdale plan. A temporary board of directors, composed of a representative of each of the seven districts having delegates at the congress,[10] was empowered "to enter into immediate negotiations with the cooperative wholesale organizations now in existence in order to merge them into the national wholesale as branches thereof."

Dr. Warbasse was elected president of the Cooperative League, Mabel Watson Cheel, treasurer, and Scott Perky, secretary.[11]

Aftermath of the Congress

Following the congress, cooperative conventions financed by the League were held in seven regions throughout the United States. All except that in the Tri-State (Pittsburgh) area passed resolutions on national unity and endorsing the Cooperative League as the central federation of consumers' cooperatives. This was the only time in the history of the League when so many areas had annual meetings under the sponsorship of the League. In the Southeast and the South Central States the conventions represented the result of promotional work by the League rather than actual cooperative development.

The League as a recognized national body was therefore under way. Though by no means as yet a representative federation of cooperatives, it had made some progress in that direction. It was becoming known throughout the country and was attaining some influence in the movement.

Chapter 10.—NEW INTEREST WITH ONSET OF WAR

Labor's Cooperatives

As prices began to rise, with wages lagging, industrial workers began to look for ways to stretch their earnings. To them and their labor unions consumers' cooperation appeared to be at least one way out. Among the first to recognize this was the American Federation of Labor.[1] Its 1917 annual meeting passed a resolution urging the establishment and strengthening of cooperatives, since they constituted the protection of the workers "in their relations with the merchants and businessmen." During the next few years the conventions of many national labor unions and State federations of labor endorsed the cooperative movement and recommended the opening of cooperative stores by their members.

The years 1917 through 1922 marked a high level of organization of cooperative stores by unionists. The railroad brotherhoods were among the most enthusiastic. In the West, some of the Pacific Cooperative League stores were organized among union railroad men. Other stores were started in railroad centers of the Carolinas and Dakotas.

In Illinois, Pennsylvania, and elsewhere, the coal miners were giving support either to cooperatives or to nonprofit, union-financed stores. At Virginia City, Nev., a meat market was opened, owned by the gold and silver miners' unions of Gold Hill and Virginia City—one of the few known consumers' cooperative ventures in Nevada.

The Seattle Situation

In Seattle the last years of the First World War and those immediately following were a period of social ferment and labor unrest. Strikes and lockouts were frequent, and in the financial stringency thus engendered the labor unionists became increasingly interested in cooperation. Their first enterprise, however, was a union-owned, not a cooperative business, the Cooperative Food Products Association, organized in December 1917, to assist the butchers and meatcutters against a lockout.

However, a really cooperative movement was also developing. Early in 1918 the Seattle Consumers' Cooperative Association was started and a grocery store was opened in midyear, with 133 members and $900 in capital.

The association began to boom after the 1918 Congress of the Cooperative League, at which the Seattle delegate was Carl E. Lunn, "a young Swede with a dynamic personality."[2] On his return to Seattle, Mr. Lunn threw himself with characteristic enthusiasm into the organization of new cooperative stores. The board of the cooperative association and the labor people caught fire from him and soon cooperative organizers were in action not only in Seattle but all over the Puget Sound area. The rallying cry was "Cooperation—The Big Idea."

This was the signal for one of the greatest mushroom cooperative growths this country has ever seen. Not only did new cooperatives spring up thick and fast; labor organizations also went into additional businesses, some of them purely trade-union in character and open only to unionists, others semi-cooperative in method and control.

The Cooperative Food Products Association was also expanding, taking on in the process more of the aspects of a consumers' cooperative. Its business for the 4½-month period ending July 31 totaled $1,198,446—a truly remarkable figure for those days. Early in 1920 the association bought the big South End Public Market, where it could have its own ice and cold-storage plant.

As the local stores grew in number, they began to agitate for a wholesale to serve them, and a committee was formed to raise funds for a branch of the National Cooperative Wholesale Association (Chicago).

During this period Dr. Warbasse, president of the Cooperative League, visited Seattle, but expressed his fears that the growth there was superficial and that something might crack. At a series of meetings he urged less-rapid expansion and more education. But this advice fell on deaf ears.

The branch warehouse was opened in October and Ernest Ames (San Francisco) was named as its manager. By this time

$30,000 in capital had been raised and a drive was on for $50,000 more.

The Seattle Consumers' Cooperative Association was designated to head the retail chain for the area. It then dropped the word, "Seattle," from its name and began to take over as branches such cooperatives outside the city as were willing to give up their independence. By October 1919 it claimed 1,460 members. The cooperative then had eight grocery stores, a coal yard, and two tailor shops, and was in process of organizing 12 other grocery stores.

The association was skating on thin ice, however. Salesmen were recruiting members so fast that the records did not keep up with them. An auditor called in by Mr. Ames found the association to be deeply in debt. There had been no separate accounting in the central office for the individual stores, and it was therefore impossible to determine which were "in the black" and which were losing money. Thousands of dollars received on shares had never been entered on the books. So chaotic were the records that even the creditors had to be written to, to find out how much was owed them. The result of the audit showed that member financing, in terms of capital actually paid in, averaged only 95 cents per person. On total capital sufficient for but a single store, the association had opened eight. It was, in fact, insolvent, and owed large amounts to the cooperative wholesale which had been supplying it with goods.

At the Northwest Cooperative Convention, in November 1919, Mr. Ames appealed to the delegates to face boldly the "real serious problems" that everyone knew existed. But apparently the delegates failed to realize the true situation, even then, for at this meeting the suggestion was made that a department store be started.

The cooperative situation was also beginning to be complicated by economic conditions. The *Seattle Union Record* pointed out that "idle thousands [were] vainly seeking work in Seattle," and that ex-servicemen were either unemployed or trying to sell apples.

In mid-1920 the Consumers' Cooperative Association had a recorded 1,700 members and was trying to operate six stores on $20,000 of paid-in capital. It owed the wholesale over

$18,000. On Mr. Ames' return from a business trip he asked for a receivership.[3] By that time, the local cooperatives were trying to withdraw and operate independently, "'without provision for the corporate debts and obligations.'"[4] Finally, Dalton Clarke, president of National, guaranteed that Chicago would bear the Seattle deficit.

Things went from bad to worse, and the Consumers was closed in midsummer, 1920, and the branch wholesale in August.

Then followed recriminations on a scale never known in the cooperative movement before or since. National Cooperative Wholesale Association blamed the Seattle situation on interference by Dr. Warbasse; the Cooperative League blamed the officers of the wholesale; and the local people blamed Ernest Ames.[5]

The present writer, who spent several weeks in Seattle in the winter of 1920-21, after tempers and emotions had begun to subside, talked to many persons involved in one capacity or another, as well as to interested observers who had remained outside the fray.

Inefficient and slipshod methods, overexpansion on inadequate capital, poor accounting, lack of cooperative understanding, and unfulfilled and unfulfillable promises all played their part in this situation. The interference of cooperators from outside, even though well-intentioned, had the result only of creating further dissension and division. The impetus for the Seattle wholesale warehouse appears to have come from the local people, but National's officers (in their efforts to extend National's base) were quick to take advantage of the opportunity offered. Actually, the collapse of the whole national wholesale movement and its retail branches was imminent and the Seattle situation, although uglier than most, was only one of many similar ones throughout the country.

With the closing of Consumers' Cooperative Association and the wholesale warehouse, practically all the affiliated stores also went down. The reaction from the fiasco almost put the Cooperative Food Products Association out of business as well. However, since it had stood aloof during the whole affair and operated strictly within its means, it pulled through, at least for a while.

When the shipyards closed down in 1921, however, its volume of business fell from $120,000 to $12,000 per month. As Frank Rust (secretary of the Trade-Union Savings and Loan Association) phrased it, the cooperative was in the position of delivering a yeast cake in a 4-ton truck.

Several steps were taken in an attempt to save the situation. The slaughterhouse was sold as well as the milk condensary and some land (all at a loss). The cooperative moved to smaller quarters, but this proved to have been a mistake. It was still liable for the lease on its old location, which had a year to run. The new store was alongside "three of the worst price cutters in town." The transient trade, substantial in the former location, was lost in the new place and the total volume proved to be insufficient to pay the overhead. The remaining assets were finally taken over about the middle of 1922 by the Associated Grange Warehouse of Seattle.

It was many years before the cooperative movement could live down the memory of the debacle in Seattle.

Plant Cooperatives

An interesting but transitory development of the war and postwar period was the industrial employees' buying enterprises. Some of these were started as early as 1917. The Cooperative League reported in mid-1920 that it was receiving letters from companies in all parts of the country, asking for advice in starting cooperative stores for their employees. Connecticut was reported as having 18 employees' associations in 1920 and New York 20 in 1922.

The employee enterprises that resulted from this interest were of varying degree of cooperativeness. In one type, the company itself ran a store which sold at cost plus overhead. In another the store was managed and controlled by the employees, but subsidized by the firm as regards space, heat and light, and sometimes also the salary of the store clerk. In some cases the company pooled orders from the employees and bought commodities at wholesale; in others the employees themselves took the orders and did the buying. Some employers gave their workers a discount on all goods handled in the company's business, or made arrangements for discounts on employee purchases from local firms.

Most of the employee enterprises went out of business during the depression of the early twenties. However, the Lukens' Employees' Cooperative Store at Coatsville, Pa. (1920) was still in operation in 1952.

Farmers' Cooperatives

During this period the farmers were again taking an interest in consumers' cooperation. Grangers were organizing stores, notably in the States of Washington, Maine, and New Hampshire. In North Dakota the Nonpartisan League (a farm organization) had opened four cooperative stores by the end of 1917 and expected to have a hundred in the course of the next year. The Farmers' Union, one of whose principal aims was the encouragement of cooperatives, was fostering the organization of stores all through the Middle West (particularly in the Dakotas, Nebraska, and Kansas) and as far south as Kentucky, Tennessee, and North Carolina.

In 1919 Nebraska had 85 cooperative stores handling general merchandise and 4 lumber yards dealing in coal and building materials. The following year, the number of cooperative stores had risen to 114. Most of them were those of farmers, but 30-40 percent admitted nonfarm people to membership.

Cooperative stores were reported to be more popular among Missouri farmers in the early 1920's than were marketing associations. This was because of the immediate savings to the members in the stores and the "meager capital" needed for them. Some 6.8 percent of all the farms in the State were said to be purchasing through cooperatives in 1918.

A study made in Minnesota showed 189 farmers' stores in operation in 1921 as compared with 120 in 1913, 126 in 1914, and 102 in 1917 (this last figure was considered probably too low). The greatest development was in northeastern Minnesota, where the stores were the result of "racial homogeneity and a common language" (i.e., Finnish). The report also showed 6 oil associations, 10 lumber yards, 1 laundry, 167 mutual insurance companies, and 1,648 farmers' telephone companies.

Patrons Cooperative Mercantile Association, Cadmus, Kans. Oldest consumers' cooperative in U. S., dating from 1876

The first cooperative store in California
Founded in 1899 at Dos Palos

CO-OP LEAGUE BOARD, 1929.

Reading from left, front row: Mary E. Arnold, Harold I. Nordby, Dr. J. P. Warbasse, Cedric Long. Back row: Eskel Ronn, Matti Tenhunen, Waldemar Niemela, V. S. Alanne, A. W. Warinner, L. S. Herron, Jacob Liukku, Joseph Blaha.

Farmer-Labor Activities

One of the results of labor's interest was the calling of a joint Farmer-Labor Conference in Chicago in November 1919, attended by representatives of farm organizations, labor unions, and cooperatives. The meeting adopted a National Cooperative Manifesto declaring that the prevailing high prices were due to the "wasteful methods, speculation, and profiteering of the middlemen," and that the remedy was the elimination of the middlemen through cooperative organization. A committee of 12 was appointed to act as a joint board for developing cooperatives.

A second conference was called for February 1920, to "give effective aid to strengthening and developing the cooperative movement" (by establishing a Nationwide commission) and to work to bring together cooperative consumers and producers and thus eliminate speculation. The conference was attended by 400 delegates, representing an estimated 4 million persons.

Resolutions were passed endorsing the Rochdale system and favoring the establishment of a cooperative newspaper and news service. A committee was named to encourage direct trading between farmers and consumers, and one to establish banks for cooperatives, labor, and farm organizations.

All-American Cooperative Commission

As a result of these two conferences, the All-American Cooperative Commission was formed, with headquarters in Cleveland, Ohio.[6] It held a congress in February 1921, at which both farm organizations and labor unions were represented. (If the Cooperative League of the USA sent a delegate, the fact was not mentioned.)

The announced purpose of the meeting was the development of cooperative credit and banking[7] and the furtherance of direct trading between farmers and consumers.

The meeting went on record as favoring a system of Federal and State cooperative laws permitting cooperatives to carry on any type of business open to corporations, and endorsing the principle of collective bargaining for farmers and labor alike.

The Commission had a rather mixed reception in the consumers' cooperative movement, being favored as a national organization (in preference to the Cooperative League) by

National Cooperative Wholesale Association and Ernest Ames of the Pacific Cooperative League, but damned with faint praise by John Walker, president of Central States Cooperative Society and of Illinois Federation of Labor. The Commission's endeavor to obtain the endorsement of the American Federation of Labor was unsuccessful. The Cooperative League's attitude of mere tolerance was well expressed by Dr. Warbasse's comment on being told of the Commission's demise in 1925: "Well, that's over."

Farmer-Labor Exchange

An indirect result of the farmer-labor conferences and work of the All-American Cooperative Commission was the formation of the Farmer-Labor Exchange in November 1922, with offices in Chicago. Moving spirit in this organization was Charles F. Lowrie, secretary and manager.[8]

The first activity was to market directly to the consumers of the Chicago area (through cooperatives, trade-unions, etc.) honey produced by members of the Progressive Farmers of Idaho (connected with the Nonpartisan League of that State). Later, other commodities, such as potatoes and poultry, were added. The Exchange was selected as the means of distributing "union-mined coal from a union-owned mine" in Herrin, Ill., to unionists and organized farmers. The association also received the endorsement of the 1926 Chicago Federation of Labor convention.

The small size of the Exchange operations, notwithstanding all this, is indicated by the fact that in the 27 months ending March 1, 1925, business totaled only $19,560. It operated until 1933.

Extent of Consumers' Cooperation in 1920

The high point of interest and organization during this period was reached in the latter part of 1919 and the first half of 1920. A national study, covering wartime development and the situation in 1920, revealed about 2,600 consumers' cooperatives in active operation at the end of 1920. Reporting associations included 3 housing cooperatives, 8 providing meals and/or rooms, 2 irrigation associations, 4 printing and publishing plants, 10 bakery associations, and 2 laundries; all the rest were stores (mostly general stores).

The membership of the reporting associations averaged 282 and business $99,900. The greatest development was in the North Central States, which accounted for 60 percent of the associations, 53 percent of the membership, and 65.7 percent of the business done. The reports indicated little cooperative development in the South, either actually or in relation to population.

Fifty-six percent of the consumers' cooperatives reporting were in places of less than 2,500 population and 83 percent in places of less than 25,000. Reflecting the recent wide flurry of cooperative organization, more than two-fifths of the associations had been in business less than 2 years. Only 3.2 percent had been operating 25 years or more (but in New England, over 10 percent were in this group). The average age was 4 years and 11 months.

Many of the associations had been started in the immediate postwar years, which were a period of much idealism and high enthusiasm. Prospective members signed up, subscribed for shares, made a small down payment on them, and were told they could thereafter "eat their way in," letting patronage refunds pay for the rest of their shares.

As a result of this, most of the associations had only the minimum cash capital required for store operation—sufficient "only if the members are absolutely loyal to the store." And the degree of membership loyalty was problematical; in the cooperatives for which data on this point were obtained, members' patronage accounted for only 47 percent of total sales. Extension of credit was a problem, and accounting methods left much to be desired. On the other hand, operating expenses compared favorably with those of private stores, and three-fifths of the cooperatives were able to return patronage refunds for 1920—bad as operating conditions were—and these averaged 5.9 percent of sales.

Actually, this was not a bad showing, considering the fact that 1920 was one of unusual and uncertain business conditions, requiring experience and a high degree of business ability. Many of these young associations lacked both. Difficulties were compounded when unemployment began to be serious toward the end of 1920. Extension of credit (practiced by too many cooperatives) then became a prime cause of failure.

Chapter 11.—NEW ATTEMPTS AT WHOLESALING, 1910-20

Even in the early years of the cooperative movement, the subject of a cooperative source of wholesale supply for the retail stores kept cropping up, and a number of collective-buying agencies or wholesales were formed. But none had been able to command the full support of the local associations—even those that had helped to form it.

This fact and the first events in the new century made the prospects for cooperative wholesaling appear dubious.

In the Midwest, the "wholesale" of the Right Relationship League actually carried on only a little joint buying.

In New York, two abortive attempts were made at wholesaling, one just after the other. The American Wholesale Cooperative Society, promoted by Socialists under the leadership of William Church Osborne and Piet Vlag, began business in March 1910. The wholesale was a building with no foundation, however, and this lack Mr. Vlag undertook to remedy by organizing new stores; among its patrons were also some Italian and "cosmopolitan societies." Even so, its sales were only about $12,000 a year, and it went out of business by the end of 1911. It did, however, leave behind "a good sprinkling" of retail cooperatives in New Jersey and New York that it had organized.[1]

Shortly after this failure, the Cooperative Wholesale Corporation, also with headquarters in New York City, was incorporated in December 1913.[2] This organization also was unsuccessful, for lack of sufficient membership and patronage. "It began and ended as a dream,"[3] and dissolved in 1915.

In California (as already noted) the Rochdale Wholesale Co. flourished moderately for a while during the first few years of the century, then languished so badly that it was pulled out of bankruptcy only by the most strenuous measures on the part of a small band of devoted cooperators. It then became the subsidiary of the Pacific Cooperative League, an organization that had an extraordinary success for some years.

In the second half of the decade it appeared that cooperative wholesaling was really in the ascendant. In the 5-year period 1915-19 five regional wholesales were formed, serving nonfarm groups mainly: Central States Cooperative Society, Illinois (1915); Cooperative Central Exchange, Wisconsin (1917); Cooperative Wholesale Society of America, Minnesota (1917); Tri-State Cooperative Association, Pennsylvania (1918); and New England Cooperative Wholesale Society, Massachusetts (1919). In 1919, also, the National Cooperative Wholesale Association was organized.

Pacific Cooperative League

The Pacific Cooperative League was formed in 1913,[4] and by the end of the year had organized buying clubs and purchases on a mail-order basis, as well as direct-from-manufacturer sales of women's coats and suits.

By 1917, associate members of PCL numbered 1,100; their orders were pooled by the League, filled through the wholesale, and shipped directly to them. These buyers were scattered through northern and central California and even into Nevada. Wherever five or more families were close enough to pool their orders, a buying club was organized.

Not until after 4 years of preliminary work did the PCL attempt to organize any new stores. It then opened, as a branch of the League, a store in the little oil town of Rodeo.

In all of this work, Ernest Ames was the leader. He soon became president and general manager of the League and remained in those capacities throughout the rest of its existence.[5]

The operations of the League and its stores were centralized. All inventory was bought by the central office and it also did all the accounting. Several observers, including Dr. Warbasse, expressed the opinion that the success of the stores in the early years was due to this close supervision.

The movement accelerated very rapidly, partly because of popular dissatisfaction with the high prices and profiteering during the war years, and partly because of the interest of organized labor. PCL was endorsed by many labor organizations, including the State Federations of Labor in Arizona, California, and New Mexico.

By June 1919, the cooperative movement in California was almost entirely that of PCL.[6] "Insistent" requests for assistance in organizing were coming from Arizona, Nevada, New Mexico, and even Washington, Oregon, and Texas.

Over 20 new stores and established associations came into the League as branches in 1920, and "nearly 20" more were reported as in process of organizing.[7] Seven stores in Washington were stated to have affiliated with the League, which had opened an organization office in Portland, Oreg.

Farmers' Union Exchanges

Just before World War I the National Farmers' Union began to advocate the formation of State Exchanges to supply the local stores. Such exchanges were opened in at least nine States (California, Colorado, Iowa, Kansas, Kentucky, Nebraska, Oklahoma, South Dakota, and Washington—this last serving stores in Washington, Oregon and Idaho).

One of the first was the wholesale purchasing department of the Farmers' Union of Nebraska, opened in 1914. In 1917 it became a separate organization, all the shares of which were owned by its parent; in 1919 (taking advantage of a new amendment to the State law) it was reorganized and transformed into a federation of local cooperatives. This wholesale is still in successful operation.

The Colorado Farmers Union Exchange, at Denver, was in operation from 1918 to 1926; in South Dakota, the Farmers Union Exchange (also known as South Dakota Cooperative Service Co.), at Mitchell, ran for a few years beginning in 1917. The Kansas Farmers Union Jobbing Association started in June 1914 and operated at first (unsuccessfully) as a mail-order house. It became a jobber in 1920 for such things as groceries, general merchandise, farm supplies, and farm machinery, besides marketing farm produce. It is still in business, but has not been handling consumer goods for many years. The Farmers Union Central Exchange, St. Paul, formed in 1927, is still flourishing.

Central States Cooperative Society

By the end of 1914 the coal miners in Illinois had 14 cooperative stores and many more were in process. Although the mining areas were depressed (for the past 4 years the mines had been shut down from 1 day per week to as much as 7 months of the year in some places), the majority of the stores were reported to be "in pretty good shape"; a high proportion of total business, however, came from nonmembers.

John Walker (president of the Illinois Federation of Labor) and Duncan McDonald (secretary of District 12, United Mine Workers) called a meeting for late March 1915, which formed the Cooperative Society of Illinois,[8] designed to encourage the formation of cooperatives and provide a channel for education and exchange of experience.

By 1916 the number of miners' cooperatives had risen to 32, of which 16 had joined the Society. This progress was attributed to the personal efforts of Messrs. Walker and McDonald, as was also the passage of a State cooperative law. A few cooperatives had closed during the year, but more than three times as many had been formed.

The 1916 convention changed the name of the federation to Central States Cooperative Society, and authorized the hiring of an agent to make buying arrangements with wholesalers.

When the third convention met in September 1917, President Walker reported that there were about 50 stores in the mining areas and "quite a number" in industrial centers. Nearly all were "making rapid and substantial progress." There had been a tremendous spread of knowledge of cooperation and a great awakening of interest in it. However, only 10 stores had paid their dues. The Central States Cooperative Society had been kept going thus far by money from the miners' District 12 and the Illinois Federation of Labor. The national Cooperative League had provided funds for field work, and promised further financial assistance until the local associations could assume the burden.

The new secretary-treasurer (paid by the Cooperative League) took up his duties aggressively, arranging for a uniform system of accounting, and organizing new associations in seven towns. He complained that although the locals were willing to send delegates to meetings, they failed to become members of the federation.

The 1917 meeting had authorized the organization of a wholesale to which only affiliates of Central States would be admitted as members. It was to do only collective buying at first. Robert McKechan was named as buying agent.

Much of the discussion at the 1918 meeting centered on the question of the national wholesale. During President Walker's absence from the meeting, the delegates, under the urging of Messrs. McKechan, McDonald and Warbasse, passed a resolution pledging Central States to amalgamate with other wholesales in a new national wholesale. Mr. Walker, however, was adamant against such a move, and succeeded in keeping the Illinois federation independent. His judgment proved to be sound.

Secretary-treasurer Duncan McDonald reported that, for the first time, the federation was debt free and had a small balance, but the year had been a "trying one" for the local associations and three had gone out of business.

After the meeting, notwithstanding the lagging patronage from the local associations, wholesale manager McKechan bought a warehouse building in East St. Louis. The wholesale had almost no capital, and only the promise by the managers of 55 Rochdale associations to give it their patronage. Although everything possible was done to get them to make good on this promise, by the end of 1918 only seven cooperatives had joined the wholesale.

American Rochdale Plan

Failing to get sufficient support, the management in February 1919 began a new experiment. The association at Herrin had failed, but the miners there still wanted to do collective buying, though without forming a cooperative. The wholesale, therefore, began to sell in bulk to the local union, with a committee distributing the goods. Rapid expansion of the business followed, and soon a full-time distributing station was operated. This succeeded so well that miners in other towns began to demand similar service.

Thus began a new system of union-financed stores, operated as branches of the wholesale—a system later to be known as the American Rochdale Plan, which was heralded as an American adaptation of the English Rochdale system.

In 1919, 13 local associations joined. In the following year, 14 cooperatives affiliated, of which 5 surrendered their independence and became branches later in the year. Three of the associations that had joined in 1919 become branches in 1921.

By July 1919, when the next convention was held, it appeared that a profit of $2,620 had been made in the first half year's operations.[9] Sales increased steadily during the summer, and the September financial statement showed earnings of $1,496.[10] Before the year's end 15 stores had been opened, the wholesale reported a surplus of $20,783,[11] and enthusiasm for the new plan was high.

The American Plan was supported not only by the miners' unions but also by those of the railway workers, steel workers, and molders, among others. Outside observers (including the Cooperative League) were impressed by its apparent success.

Sales increased steadily throughout the first half of 1920. However, difficulties were beginning to appear. Expansion was being narrowed by the organization drives of National Cooperative Wholesale Association in northern Illinois, Indiana, and Iowa, and of the fraudulent Cooperative Society of America. Profit dealers were retaliating against the cost-plus operation of the Central States stores by price-cutting tactics of their own. Patrons were expressing dissatisfaction with the varying price mark-ups in the different stores. But the chief trouble lay in the failure of the wholesale to build up an efficient system of business controls over the local stores. The result was local mismanagement, poor auditing, and costly mistakes.

Nevertheless, the manager's report to the 1920 convention was optimistic. He disparaged orthodox Rochdale cooperation, saying that 14 of the 15 independent associations that had been taken over by the wholesale had been bankrupt.

By this time the organization had nearly $330,000 in capital, of which all but $25,511 had been supplied by labor organizations. The financial statement showed apparent 6-month earnings of nearly $14,500 on a business of slightly over a million dollars. On the strength of this showing, the wholesale paid 4 percent interest on capital and a 5-percent patronage refund to each of the Rochdale associations trading with it.[12]

The manager did point out a few unfavorable circumstances: The wholesale had been unable to take maximum advantage of cash discounts, because of lack of ready funds. The original

Rochdale associations were behind in their accounts by over $20,000 most of the time, and few of the American Plan stores had been able to raise adequate capital (sometimes not even enough to cover the amount of their inventory). The wholesale had not only to finance its own operations but to give them credit as well.

Dr. Warbasse, who was present at the meeting, predicted that the Illinois stores would revert eventually to "the old-fashioned Rochdale movement." In his opinion it was "rather stretching a point" to call the association's stores cooperatives. He could see many advantages in the American Plan, but also some disadvantages. Cooperation had to be independent of politics, religion, and labor organizations.

Later, an unsigned article in *Cooperation* (League periodical) characterized the American Plan stores as "cheap chain stores rather than cooperative stores." However, the "central control and administration guaranteed a degree of efficiency which is higher than hitherto found in most true Rochdale stores in Illinois." The American Plan stores were "succeeding where the true Rochdale stores have failed." The article went on to say that "It is quite possible that this method of approach to cooperation may be America's contribution to the movement," making it possible to compete with the big chains. Furthermore, "a strong central wholesale is being created."[13]

Cooperative Central Exchange

The Cooperative Central Exchange (now Central Cooperative Wholesale) was organized July 30, 1917.[14] A collection, to which delegates from 15 of the 19 local cooperatives represented contributed, netted $15.50, and this constituted the wholesale's entire original capital.[15] Collective buying for the local groups was begun in September, with John D. Nummivuori[16] as manager. By the end of the year, $480 had been accumulated in capital.

In 1918 the wholesale joined the Cooperative League—the first cooperative wholesale in the United States to do so. The Exchange was probably, also, the first regional wholesale[17] to undertake technical training: in 1918 it gave a 1-week course in bookkeeping with H. V. Nurmi[18] as instructor. Since that time educational courses have been given every year, even during wars and depressions. V. S. Alanne[19] was engaged in 1920 as full-time educational director, and the length of the term was increased to 6 weeks.

In 1918 a 3-story headquarters building was purchased, and a bakery was opened the next year. In this period the original 15 member associations increased to 40 (all of Finnish membership), the business increased and earnings were made each year. Back of these facts lay the extreme hardships of the early years, the struggle to pay the bills, and the long hours of devoted work contributed by the Finns who were the wholesale's officers. Among the problems was that of obtaining supplies; frequently manufacturers refused to sell goods to the Exchange, because of protests from their other customers. Nevertheless persistence and hard work won out and the wholesale grew slowly and soundly.

Cooperative Wholesale Society of America

The Cooperative Wholesale Society of America took over an earlier movement started by the American Society of Equity. Besides assisting in the formation of retail cooperatives, Equity had helped to start four wholesale buying organizations—Equity Cooperative Association of Montana (with some 20 stores and 75 grain-marketing associations), Puget Sound Cooperative Wholesale Society (owned by a group of half a dozen cooperatives), Equity Cooperative Exchange at St. Paul (with elevator associations in the Dakotas, Minnesota, and Montana, and a number of store cooperatives in Minnesota), and the American Cooperative Association in Wausau, Wis.

Although trade-unionists, as well as farmers had helped to found the American Society of Equity, its cooperatives were mostly farmers' organizations handling groceries, coal, and farm implements.[20]

The Equity wholesales became members of the Cooperative Wholesale Society of America (St. Paul) when that body was formed in 1917. The new wholesale had both marketing and purchasing departments. Findley A. Bennett, organizer of the Montana Equity wholesale, became president and general manager.[21]

The wholesale then began to organize new cooperatives, using methods very similar to those used by the Right Relationship League.[22]

By January 1920, it had 28 affiliates with between four and five thousand members.[23] These included 17 cooperatives in Minnesota, 6 in North Dakota, 3 in South Dakota, 1 in Montana, and 1 in Iowa. The majority were farmers' organizations.

Tri-State Cooperative Association

The Tri-State Cooperative Association, Pittsburgh, Pa., was organized at almost the same time as the wholesale at St. Paul.[24] The coal miners and their unions were strong supporters and some of the unions even invested union funds in the capital of the wholesale.

The first warehouse was opened at Monesson in July 1918, but early in 1919 operations were transferred to Pittsburgh.

The wholesale started with a nucleus of 12 stores in the immediate vicinity of its warehouse. These had already been buying together. Their combined patronage was insufficient, however, and the wholesale began to organize local associations and branches, the latter being operated on the chain system, with centralized control. By mid-1918 there were 23 branch stores, and Tri-State was supplying 44 cooperative stores in Pennsylvania, Ohio, and West Virginia, with an annual business of $2 million. The next month the number was reported to have risen to 56, with over 7,500 members. Salesmen and a force of organizers were bringing in new capital at the rate of $600 to $2,000 per week.

All the branch stores were owned jointly by all the members, and all were managed by the wholesale, assisted by local committees. All were required to buy through the wholesale, except such goods as it could not supply. Associations already established could become branches by accepting Tri-State stock in the amount of their assets, or affiliate (retaining their independence) by purchase of $200 of permanent stock.

The apparent success of this organization deceived even the experts. *Cooperation* (Cooperative League paper) stated in October 1919 that it was the organization of branch stores that "practically saved the Tri-State and made it the powerful organization that it is today."

Chapter 12.—MOVE FOR A NATIONWIDE WHOLESALE

Formation of National Cooperative Association

The organization of a national cooperative wholesale into which the five existing regional consumers' wholesales (with 348 retail members) would merge was authorized by the Cooperative Congress of 1918.

Accordingly, the National Cooperative Association was incorporated on April 21, 1919.[1]

Dalton Clarke became manager of National in June 1919 and immediately started a stock-selling campaign. A branch warehouse was opened in Hoboken, N. J.[2] on October 1 of that year and one in Seattle 12 days later. In Chicago the association leased a 5-story building on October 28.

The regionals that had been expected to merge with National showed great reluctance to do so.[3] The existing independent associations, also, either held off or failed to join in sufficient numbers to support the elaborate superstructure that had already been erected.

The central organization then began to organize patronage in the form of new branch stores operating on the chain plan. Each branch warehouse had its local retail chain.

The steel strike that began in October 1919 furnished some needed patronage for the wholesale, also. It was arranged that National in Chicago and Tri-State in Pittsburgh should do all the buying for the strikers' commissaries. The first shipment of goods to a local cooperative store (in Gary, Ind.) took place early in November.

During the next several months optimistic reports were issued, telling of the increase in number of affiliates, endorsements (and even capital subscriptions) by labor organizations, and earnings on business.

The first annual meeting of the wholesale, held in March 1920, was told that 167 stores were either already in operation or were being organized—59 in the Seattle, 29 in the Chicago,[4] 58 in the Pittsburgh, and 21 in the New York district. President Clarke reported that at least some of the regional wholesales were expected to "merge as branches within the next year."

At this meeting the word, "wholesale," was added to the organization's name, so that it became National Cooperative Wholesale Association.

Seven months later, only two wholesales—Pacific Cooperative League and Tri-State—had joined National, and they had come in as independent affiliates, not as branches. Tri-State appears to have been a firm supporter; in 11 months its region was reported to have contributed $190,000 to National.

The Cooperative League v. National

The Cooperative League had at first been officially noncommittal regarding National's methods. An article in the October 1919 issue of *Cooperation* pointed out that the plan of National was based on "unimpeachable principles" but was "peculiarly American in its working methods."

Beginning the next month, however, both in letters to the wholesale and in its magazine, the League warned against National's top-down methods and the opening of warehouses before business volume warranted. It noted the reluctance of the wholesales to affiliate, reports of misrepresentation by National's agents, and distrust among the members.

National's officials countered by saying that its organizers were mainly educators and teachers and calling Dr. Warbasse a theorist with no practical knowledge of the cooperative movement. The chain-store plan was claimed to be founded not only on the most successful experience in the United States but also on European practice. This last (incorrect) statement was reiterated in many subsequent statements during the ensuing months.

Action at Cooperative Congress of 1920

The 1920 Cooperative Congress, held in Cincinnati, November 11-14, disclosed the deep and widening rift among cooperative leaders on the question of the new wholesale.

The League and its supporters would settle for nothing short of true Rochdale cooperation, with grassroots control. National, Pacific Cooperative League, and others advocated centralized control and promotion on the chain system. They pooh-poohed the "orthodox" stand of the League. Between these two extremes were those (like John Walker) who favored Rochdale cooperation "in principle," but believed American conditions required modification of it.

President Warbasse fired the opening gun, with the statement that, although great progress had been made since 1918, not all of the growth was sound. The movement needed, among other things, national unity, education, and joint buying by neighboring associations as a starting point to the evolution of a wholesale.

After some heated exchanges, the regular program was set aside temporarily and the meeting became in effect a trial of both the PCL and National.

There were charges of "frenzied finance," "fast and loose use of funds," and even (in the case of PCL) misappropriation of money. In defense, Ernest Ames of PCL complained of "unwarranted interference" by Dr. Warbasse and his supporters, favored combining education and business in one organization, and even went so far as to say that he thought it was "a lot of nonsense to talk about these Rochdale principles."

John Walker, although satisfied by Ames' answers to the charges, defended Dr. Warbasse, saying it was his duty to raise his voice if in doubt. In the cooperative movement, he said, one can not wait for proof of ground for suspicion, because the organization may be destroyed in the meantime.

The upshot was a resolution condemning National. Its delegates were unseated. Mr. Ames and the other PCL delegates were accepted, in the absence of first-hand witnesses from PCL territory.

The congress recommended that the associations of each district form a collective-buying unit, with a view to the ultimate formation of a national wholesale. It endorsed the League's action in advising cooperatives not to affiliate with PCL, as long as it remained under the present management and methods.

"Hereafter, no society carrying on questionable methods will be seated in a national congress of the League."

One signal and constructive step taken by this congress was the adoption of a constitution making the League a permanent organization. Thereafter, instead of being composed of both individuals and cooperatives, it would accept as voting members only cooperative associations.

Chapter 13.—COLLAPSE AND REVIVAL IN WHOLESALING

End of the National Wholesale

By late fall, 1920, the end of the whole National network was near. The Seattle branch had closed its doors on August 15. The Hoboken warehouse was placed in the hands of a receiver on December 17, and the Chicago warehouse followed on January 18, 1921. Fifteen months later it was reported that National's obligations would be settled at 1 cent on the dollar.

The Chicago retail organization—National Consumers Cooperative Association—continued in operation for about 2 months after the closure of the warehouse. In the New York district, several stores, including those at Lehighton and Perth Amboy, N. J., withdrew from the chain and took up operation under local control. They survived for several years, finally going out of business in the middle 1920's.

Fate of the Other Wholesales

Cooperative Wholesale Society of America

The Cooperative Wholesale Society of America was in trouble as early as mid-1920. By November the association had ceased warehousing and was acting merely as a brokerage agency. It went into receivership in January 1921; and the stockholders voted unanimously to disband.

The wholesale was a completely top-down organization. The stores were organized on the chain system, with local boards that rarely functioned. There was no educational work. Nearly everything—organizing, purchasing, accounting—was done from headquarters in St. Paul. Success was declared to be guaranteed. Glowing reports of success were published; mistakes or failures were not mentioned.

When the organization got into difficulties, therefore, there was no solid underpinning of either local confidence or local success on which it could fall back. What faith there had been originally was undermined by dissension and suspicion.

Tri-State Cooperative Association

At Tri-State, even though the stores were not patronizing the wholesale as had been expected, all had been well on the surface as long as new money was pouring in. Complaints on service were received in such volume, however, that the organization campaign was suspended, pending reorganization for greater efficiency. As the flow of new capital ceased, the wholesale began to feel the pinch.

At the 1919 convention, many delegates were "extremely hostile and acrimonious."[1] There had been no financial reports to the members, no interest on capital, and no returns on patronage.

The wholesale and its members had already felt the stresses incident to the coal and steel strikes. The local cooperatives extended credit and then, with their capital frozen in accounts receivable, could neither discount their own bills nor pay the wholesale. Before they had recovered from this situation, the railroad strike occurred.

This was the final blow. Unemployed workers moved away to find work, and membership and volume fell. Those remaining either withdrew such of their capital as was redeemable, or ate it up in credit.

The wholesale went out of business early in 1921, and all the local cooperatives in the Tri-State group were also gone by 1930.

Penn Central Cooperative Association

In the meantime another cooperative movement—also of miners—had come into being in Pennsylvania, under the sponsorship of United Mine Workers' District 2. By February 1921 there were 27 stores of all degrees of success, each separately incorporated and autonomous.

A federation, Penn Central Cooperative Association, with headquarters in Clearfield, Pa., had been organized in October 1920. It had attempted no wholesaling but had begun to do joint buying under the management of T. D. Stiles, an officer of District 2. By May 1923 it had 18 affiliates.

Although this was a more soundly conceived movement than that of Tri-State, the strikes, the depression, and sharp controversy between the manager and John Brophy (another District 2 official) over some of the policies of the association proved too much. Penn Central went out of business shortly afterwards.

The local cooperatives lasted for varying periods. As far as can be determined, none now survive.

Pacific Cooperative League

The Pacific Cooperative League's report to the U. S. Bureau of Labor Statistics for 1919 showed 9,208 individual members, a wholesale business of $1,399,000, assets of $480,618, and a net worth of $392,586.

Signs of trouble.—The bankruptcy of the Seattle Consumers' Cooperative Association and National's branch warehouse there, with which Ernest Ames had become involved, was accompanied by much ill-feeling in that region, a good share of which was directed toward him. And since the 1920 Cooperative Congress, PCL had been in a state of more or less open warfare with the national League.[2] The cooperative and union leaders in California rallied to Ames' support, however, with a unanimous vote of confidence in his management.

Certain operating and administrative difficulties began to be revealed in a series of circulars sent by PCL headquarters to the stores: unfulfillable promises causing "an unlimited amount of time, explanation and unnecessary work" for the home office; poor daily reports from the managers; and insufficient patronage of the wholesale. (PCL territory was admittedly so large as to make impossible the adequate servicing of all the stores.)

By spring, 1921, the Pacific League was reported to have in California, Arizona, and New Mexico 47 cooperative stores with 15,000 members and an annual business of about $4 million. Only about a fifth of the business was being channeled through the wholesale, "because of distance." During the year ending April 30, PCL had distributed $58,000 to the members in "savings and profits."

By this time PCL's liabilities exceeded the assets by $74,000, and the creditors were pressing for their money.[3]

As the whole system gradually became more and more centralized, the individual members grew more and more dissatisfied. It was charged that their wishes were disregarded, that the local branches were kept isolated from each other and communication discouraged, that funds collected at one place were diverted to another and that the capital was usually a step behind the needs.

PCL, on its part, claimed that the overexpansion had been "most strenuously fought" by the officers but was forced on them by "the clamorous demand for cooperative stores." The managers persistently violated the rules and in nearly every instance were supported by local "directors" (Ames' quotes). "Now, at last, we are compelled to enforce control and management of the business entrusted to us," otherwise either the creditors or the State authorities would take away the business.[4]

Mr. Ames said, significantly:

> "We mistakenly developed too much freedom by a laudable desire to encourage local autonomy. For the last several months, we have been steadily and critically hindered by the possessors of power *reluctantly given* [author's italics] to remedy the conditions described above."[4]

These words must have had a peculiar sound to cooperators who knew that in the cooperative movement "power" derives only from the members; it is not conceded, reluctantly or otherwise, by officers or employees.

Reorientation and final collapse.—In swift succession, a drive for $50,000 in new capital was launched and local thrift clubs were organized, as well as a new body, Pacific League Cooperative Stores, to act as operating manager of the whole PCL chain. Three men—Ames, Todd (a PCL director), and Dobbs (assistant to Ames)—were named as trustees of the Stores and were to be given control of 51 percent of the total stock, or in other words complete control of the whole organization.

These, however, were the last desperate measures devised to keep afloat a craft that was already sinking. On February 17, 1922, the State Commissioner of Corporations revoked the League's charter, and 10 days later Mr. Ames petitioned the court for a receivership. He was arrested on charges of fraud, preferred by the El Paso, Tex., grand jury, and extradition to Texas was requested but refused. Mr. Ames then left California.[5]

Thus ended dismally the movement that had seemed so promising.

The finances of the PCL and the local stores were so intricately involved that most of the latter were engulfed in its debacle. A few, stronger than the rest—such as those in Los Angeles, San Bernardino, San Diego, and Whittier—survived for several years.

During the later 1920's the only consumers' cooperatives in California were a few remnants of the earlier Rochdale movement—at College City, Dinuba, and Hollister—and several cooperatives that had never joined in any organized movement. Among the latter were the Fort Bragg Cooperative Association and the New Madera Consumers Cooperative Association, both still active at last reports.

Central States Cooperative Wholesale Society

Last days of the American Plan.—October 1920 proved to be the peak of expansion of the Central States Cooperative Wholesale Society. Even though 15 new stores were organized before January 1921, market conditions were undermining the whole system.

The wholesale's board and management had the task of holding the branch stores together and keeping the wholesale above water. In this they succeeded for a time. They even obtained another $150,000 from the United Mine Workers.

The 1921 convention met in September, with all outward manifestations of wholesale prosperity, even though in the past year the cooperatives had gone through "the most serious depression" since the Civil War. The reports of President Walker, of the secretary-treasurer, and of the District 12 auditor all indicated large savings, the figure running as high as $250,000 (in the treasurer's report). (Actually, an audit in January 1923 by a professional company showed losses at the close of 1920 of $243,000, or two-thirds of the wholesale's capital. In 1921 there was an additional loss of $90,000.)

Total wholesale sales to 69 American Plan stores and about 20 of the 100 independent associations for the year ending July 1, 1921 exceeded $2½ million.

Disagreement and friction between the central organization and the stores increased in 1922.

Reorganization on orthodox basis.—In July Manager McKechan was succeeded by John Nummivuori (then manager of Cooperative Central Exchange).[6] Allen W. Warinner of Brookfield, Mo. was chosen as chief accountant.[7]

The worst blow came on July 14 when two creditors brought suit, charging bankruptcy. District 12 might have come to the rescue, once again, but the miners were on strike and an injunction by Judge Landis tied up all its funds. As it could not help, the Federal court appointed a receiver.

In the interval before the Central States' 1922 convention, the coal strike was settled and District 12 signed as guarantor of the $100,000 outstanding in merchandise accounts. All loan certificates were turned in and canceled, and the receivership was lifted.

The annual meeting adopted a plan of reorganization on the Rochdale basis, thus fulfilling Dr. Warbasse's prophecy of 2 years before. It also voted that the deficit be written off by cancelling all outstanding share and loan capital and issuing new stock valued on the actual net worth.

In the meantime, the new management was left to do a business of $100,000 monthly, with practically no money. District 12 helped by paying an $85,000 note due to an East St. Louis bank, and later canceled $177,000 which it had advanced for merchandise. Thirty stores had been closed during that year and it was evident that many of the other 40 would have to be closed also.

Thanks to the generosity of District 12, the new stock was issued at 35 percent of the former face value. Branches were organized into independent stores wherever local interest was sufficient; elsewhere either the union took over the store or it was closed.

By the end of 1923 the American Rochdale Plan had lived its span. Peter Moerth of Staunton, who had been opposed to the American Plan from the first replaced John Nummivuori as manager, when the latter resigned.[8]

Unfortunately, it proved to be impossible to increase the wholesale volume to the point of being self-supporting. At the end of 1925 it was decided to discontinue business. From the educational department was organized, in April 1926, the Central States Cooperative League.

Under the leadership of A. W. Warinner,[9] a new publication, *United Consumer,* was started, an aggressive educational program was undertaken, and a plan for collective buying got under way in October 1927. Thus began a long pull upward that eventually evolved into full-fledged wholesaling again.

The American Plan history is notable for several things—the presence of an "angel" in the form of District 12 and its locals, which had advanced upwards of three-quarters of a million dollars; the most substantial and consistent support of cooperation by organized labor seen up to that time; the spectacle of cooperative officers concealing facts and deliberately manipulating figures to hide the true situation from the members; and finally, the belated recognition by the members that shortcuts such as the American Plan were inferior to true Rochdale cooperation.

New England Cooperative Wholesale Society

The New England Cooperative Wholesale Society (Boston) organized in July 1919, did joint purchasing of groceries for about 40 affiliates and about half a dozen other cooperatives that were not members. Waldemar Niemela served as manager.[10]

This association, unlike most of the others previously described, was not a business failure. With the falling apart of its largest customer, United Cooperative Society, because of political differences, in 1921, its business dwindled. It liquidated voluntarily in 1923.

Causes of Failure of Wholesaling

The wholesales that failed had certain attributes in common. The Cooperative Wholesale Society of America, Tri-State, and National had all undertaken warehousing when the local cooperative development was sufficient to support only collective buying. Having once incurred the heavy expense of maintaining warehouses, the leaders were more or less forced by circumstances to promote the formation of new groups to furnish the business needed by the wholesale. The contagion of this move spread to Central States Cooperative Wholesale Society and Pacific

Cooperative League, as the urge for rapid growth swept the country. Of all the wholesales in the consumer movement, only the New England and Wisconsin organizations resisted the get-rich-quick philosophy, and continued on a democratic, sound basis. And it is significant that only these two did not fail financially.

The leaders of the others found themselves in a whirlwind of activity which they were unable to control, with physical expansion beyond the available managerial ability and with subsequent laxity in record keeping, use of funds, and business practices. Extravagant methods, leakages of one sort or another, the heavy cost of recruiting new members—all these produced expenses outrunning the business volume.

It was probably inevitable, human nature being what it is, that some of the leaders resorted to questionable tactics to conceal the true state of affairs, in the hope that it could be corrected without becoming known. And as long as new capital was coming in, the situation could be—and was—glossed over.

The growing rebellion of members was met by more and more centralization at the top, with less and less grass-roots control. And this, in time, led to even greater member dissatisfaction. Pacific Cooperative League showed the greatest shift from democratic to autocratic methods, but the three others exhibited it in more or less degree. It was a case of great enthusiasm misdirected and gone wrong.

Under normal conditions, it is possible that some of the wholesales in this group might have been saved. But these were not normal times. The end of World War I saw a great deal of social unrest. Unionists, who then comprised the majority of the members of consumers' cooperatives, had their purchasing power reduced by the coal, steel, and railroad strikes occurring in quick succession. Their stores suffered, in consequence, from this cause as well as from the sudden deflation which drastically reduced or wiped out inventory values. All of these factors were reflected in the fortunes of the wholesales.

The cooperative movement, in the loss of these wholesales and their retail networks, sustained a blow from which it took years to recover. It was a pity that so much real devotion and self-sacrifice—shown even by the leaders who went farthest astray—should have been wrecked on the reef of the passion for bigness.

Revival of Wholesaling, 1926-29

Of the regional wholesales that had been expected to become part of a national network, the only one left intact by the end of 1925 was the Cooperative Central Exchange. In Illinois, although the Central States organization was still in existence, the wholesale had been closed.

Cooperative Central Exchange

The CCE had gone along quietly and slowly during the cooperative boom period, although seriously hampered by lack of sufficient capital. It felt no direct effects of National's failure. The sudden deflation and unemployment were serious in Exchange territory, but the wholesale managed to operate in the black in 1921 and its volume sagged only slightly. It even added an auditing department in that year, under the direction of H. V. Nurmi. Eskel Ronn, bookkeeper, was elevated to the managership of the wholesale when John Nummivuori resigned in 1922. George Halonen became educational director in 1925.[11]

Beginning in 1922, the association's volume of business rose each year through 1930, and each year's operations showed earnings.[12] By 1926 the Exchange, which had started as jobber only, was doing wholesaling.

In 1925 the Exchange began publication of a mimeographed bulletin, issued about every other month. It became a monthly with the July 1926 issue, under the name *Cooperative Pyramid Builder.* A. J. Hayes became editor in 1928.[13] In 1930, another paper, commonly called the *Finnish Cooperative Weekly,*[14] was begun, under the editorship of George Halonen and, later, Henry Koski.

Farmers' Wholesales

During the consumer wholesales' period of "boom and bust," a farmer cooperative movement had been growing. Two wholesales organized some years before—Farmers Union State Exchange (Omaha, Nebr.) and Associated Grange Warehouse Co. (Seattle, Wash.)—were still in operation. Two new farmer-sponsored wholesales had also been formed: Farm Bureau Services (Michigan), organized in 1920, and Indiana Farm Bureau Cooperative Association (1921).

Farmers Union State Exchange

With the transformation of the Farmers Union State Exchange into a federation of local cooperatives in 1919, the mail-order business with individuals (which had constituted its chief volume) yielded place to dealings with member associations. With the encouragement of the wholesale, the FUSE's retail branches were gradually taken over and operated by local associations formed for the purpose.

The Exchange suffered severely in the sudden deflation of 1921-22. Caught with high-priced inventory, it incurred a deficit amounting to about half the share capital. This deficit was wiped out in 1923 by cutting in half the face value of its shares. Since that time the wholesale has operated continuously in the black.[15]

For a few years the Exchange was a member of the Cooperative League, and L. S. Herron, editor of the *Nebraska Union Farmer,* served on the League board from 1918 to 1933.[16]

Grange Cooperative Wholesale

The Grange Wholesale Warehouse was organized in Seattle in May 1919 as a collective-buying agency.[17] It was this organization that stepped in to salvage the remnants of the Seattle fiasco of 1920 and 1921, when both the local and wholesale movements failed. The whole cooperative movement in Washington was then "entirely without credit." Funds advanced by the Washington State Grange in 1920-24 tided the Grange wholesale over this difficult period, during which it (acting as jobber only) was supplying groceries to some 90 stores.

After the departure of general manager Albert Goss to become master of the State Grange,[18] some of the members became dissatisfied and by 1928 the wholesale had in affiliation only 17 associations.

Four years later the number of patrons had risen to 25, and its accounting department was keeping the books for 20 of them. The depression had a galvanic effect, and within the single year of 1935 membership increased from 42 to 57. A reorganization, begun in 1934, was completed in 1937.

Cautious Expansion

About the middle of the decade of the 20's several new central supply associations were organized, four of which either immediately or eventually affiliated with the consumer movement: Minnesota Cooperative Oil Co., with headquarters in Minneapolis (formed in 1926); Farmers Union Central Exchange, St. Paul (1927); Eastern Cooperative Wholesale, New York City (1928); and Union Oil Co., Cooperative, Kansas City (1929).[19]

Minnesota Cooperative Oil Co.

The Minnesota Cooperative Oil Co., incorporated on September 8, 1926, led a straitened existence at first. It started as a nonstock membership association, without a cent of capital —a circumstance believed to be unique in the annals of wholesale cooperation.[20] Business was transacted at a borrowed desk in an office rented from an independent oil company. Member associations paid in advance for the supplies they ordered. Manager Edwin G. Cort received no salary at first; the minutes recorded that when he made good,[21] the matter of salary would be considered.

Fortunately the business yielded savings, and refunds were declared from the very start. In order to build capital, the 1927 membership meeting voted that until otherwise decided, the refunds should be paid in certificates of indebtedness. (This continued until 1936, when the revolving-fund plan was adopted.)

In the meantime the trading territory of the wholesale had expanded beyond State borders and the association was supplying petroleum products to cooperatives in Michigan and Wisconsin. In 1928, therefore, "Minnesota" was dropped from its name. Another change was made in 1930, when its name became Midland Cooperative Wholesale.

By the end of 1929 the number of members had risen to 40, the assets had been built up to $18,911, and the volume of business (about $270,000 in 1927) had increased to nearly $450,000. Already, on a total business of about $1,100,000, the wholesale had declared patronage refunds amounting to $10,234.

Eastern Cooperative Wholesale

This organization grew out of joint-buying activities started by Eastern States Cooperative League. The wholesale was incorporated in the summer of 1928 and went into operation in New York in March 1929, with Adolph Wirkkula (manager of the Cooperative Trading Co., Brooklyn) acting as buyer.

During the first 5 years of the wholesale's existence, the number of member associations remained unchanged at 10. Volume increased slightly from 1929 to 1930 and earnings were made. No patronage refunds were returned, however, the gains being used for capital.

Union Oil Co., Cooperative

The Union Oil Co., Cooperative, was incorporated in February, 1929, largely as a result of the efforts of Howard A. Cowden who became its president and general manager—positions that he has retained ever since.[22]

The new wholesale began business in a 2-car garage, in modest circumstances but under what seemed propitious conditions of general prosperity. Eight months later came the stock-market break. Nevertheless at the end of the association's first year, it was able to pay 8 percent on its stock and a 20-percent refund on patronage. It now had 22 members.

Almost immediately it had been forced into production. As its wholesaler refused to supply it with lubricating oil, the cooperative started a small oil-compounding plant of its own in July 1929—an act that headed a long series of new adventures in cooperative production. And thus began one of the most spectacular performances in the history of cooperative wholesaling in the United States.

Chapter 14.—CONDITION OF LOCAL COOPERATIVES, 1920-29

General Cooperative Situation

As early as the end of 1920, the cooperative stores were feeling the effects of the sudden deflation and growing unemployment. The failure of the wholesales in 1920 had disastrous effects on most of their retail affiliates, especially where operated on the chain plan, with all funds centered in the headquarters organization. The death rate among independent cooperatives was also high.

On the other hand only two of the 40-odd affiliates of the Cooperative Central Exchange—surviving wholesale—failed.

The situation varied in different States. Only 13 Kansas cooperatives were reported out of business. The Nebraska movement, also, did more than merely survive; it had only ten failures among 325 associations. Some of its cooperatives went "right through the depression without losing a dollar."[1] In Illinois, 13 of 125 failed. The Pennsylvania cooperative movement was making a fresh start. Many cooperatives failed in New York but the death rate was not believed to be greater than elsewhere; it was just that the records were better and more complete. In Washington State such stores as had survived the general devastation following the Seattle failure were continuing largely because of supervision by the Grange wholesale, and by 1924, a new movement was being built there.

New Cooperative Associations

Even while many cooperatives were going out of business, others were being formed. Most of the new associations were stores. A new line, however, was that of petroleum distribution.

We have already noted the three gasoline stations of the Farmers Union Cooperative of Mitchell County in Kansas, which were in operation as early as 1913. The next recorded activity was a department of the Farmers Union Elevator Co. at Hazelton, N. Dak., opened in 1920. The elevator was closed in 1928, but the oil department was continued in operation and incorporated as the Farmers Union Oil Co. in June 1934.

The first associations to handle petroleum products exclusively—all organized in 1921—were the Cottonwood (Minn.) Cooperative Oil Co., Casco (Wis.) Cooperative Oil Co., Manawa (Wis.) Farmers Cooperative Oil Co., and New London (Wis.) Farmers Cooperative Oil Co. All of these pioneers are still active.

The oil associations were nearly all successful from the beginning, made large earnings, and as a group have had probably the lowest death rate of all forms of distributive cooperation. There are several reasons for this: (1) The simplicity of operation of a business with only a few lines, as compared for instance with the many hundreds of items carried in grocery stores, (2) the extremely wide profit margins in the early days (the margin has narrowed considerably, largely as a result of the cooperatives' entrance into this business, but is still substantial), and (3) the added earnings received from petroleum wholesales, some of which now not only operate refineries but also produce crude oil.

Another new type of business was the distribution of dairy products for the benefit of the consumers. The first in this field was Franklin Cooperative Creamery Association, started in 1920 by striking milk-wagon drivers in Minneapolis, when they were locked out by their employers. Harold I. Nordby, one of the organizers of Franklin, became its first president and also its general manager from 1924 to 1932.[2]

Patronage refunds were discontinued by Franklin in 1924, when the annual meeting voted that thereafter the earnings available for such distribution be used for some social or public purpose.[3]

This cooperative has been a million-dollar business since 1922.[4] Over the years, however, the number of members dwindled steadily, from 5,260 in 1925 (the peak number) to 3,340 in 1946. (It has since risen to 3,600.) As the membership declined the association took on more and more the aspect of a workers' productive association. By 1939 all the directors were employees (who were also stockholders). The non-employee shareholders have always far outnumbered the employee members[5] and could, if they desired and were sufficiently interested, change the complexion of the board. Membership apathy is probably the reason for the fact that, as of November 1953, only one director was not also an employee. Thus the association has been directed by persons who may represent the worker rather than the consumer viewpoint.[6]

On the other hand, there is no doubt that the presence of this cooperative has acted to keep down the retail price of milk in Minneapolis.[7] Also, Franklin has been one of the chief proponents of coordination of cooperative activity, was a member of the Northern States Cooperative League, and has been a faithful adherent of the Cooperative League almost since its own inception.

Following Franklin's example, striking milk-wagon drivers in Cleveland, Ohio, organized the City Cooperative Dairy in 1920. It was in financial difficulties from the first. Franklin lent it $6,000 and even gave the services of its manager for a while. He pulled it up into the black temporarily, but it declined again after his departure and went out of business in 1926. More successful was the Consumers Cooperative Dairy in Astoria, Oreg., started in 1927 by a group of Finns. It is still in operation.[8]

Among the other types of cooperatives being organized in this period were bakeries and even some service organizations, such as burial cooperatives and a cafeteria association later described.

Cooperative Bakeries

Bakery associations had been organized on the eastern seaboard as early as 1908. Of these, quite a few were started by union bakers (especially in plants making Jewish breads), either in time of strike or lockout or as a protest against conditions in the bakeries in which they worked.

The first bakery association of record was a Jewish cooperative, started in 1908, which lasted only a short time. Several others, organized in Massachusetts in 1911 and 1912 were likewise unsuccessful.

With the outbreak of the First World War in Europe, war conditions and rising prices in this country led to a number of new cooperative bakeries, again mostly Jewish. At that time, the bakers were struggling against conditions that "made the trade a hell for its workingmen."[9] The cooperatively owned bakery appeared to be an instrument for bettering the situation, and bakeries "began to spring up on all sides."[9]

So great was the interest in bakeries that the Federation of Jewish Cooperative Societies devoted most of the discussion at its 1920 convention to this subject, and in 1921 six associations formed the Conference of Massachusetts Bakeries, for mutual assistance. This Conference immediately affiliated with the Cooperative League.

Lack of educational grounding and business ability were killing the associations about as fast as new ones started. Then, the deflation of 1920-21 acted as a brake on the development of bakeries and none were formed from 1922 through 1924. There were still, however, 25 to 30 bakeries in the East and perhaps 14 or 15 others throughout the country, operating either as independent associations or as departments of a retail store business.

In spite of their high fatality rate, the bakeries had had a good general influence. Wherever a cooperative bakery appeared, it had resulted in raising the level of both wages and working conditions. Unionists recognized this by becoming members. Without exception, all the bakery employees belonged to unions. Wages were reported to be about a third higher than those in nonunion shops against which the cooperative bakeries had to compete.

Every year the Jewish cooperative bakeries made contributions to philanthropic causes, regardless of whether the year's operations had shown a gain or a loss; rarely were refunds paid on patronage.[10] In the textile strike of 1922, six Jewish bakeries in Massachusetts contributed 170,000 loaves of bread to the strikers' food kitchens although the strikers were strangers to them and of alien nationalities and races. In the 1924 silk strike in Paterson, N. J., the local cooperative bakery was reported to be the "mainstay of the strikers' committee." In the railroad strike the Los Angeles Consumers Cooperative League (lone cooperative bakery in the West) gave bread to strikers.

The Finns, who had several cooperative bakeries (usually in connection with a cooperative store) showed the same devotion to causes and the same readiness to support federation and cooperative unity among the associations as did the Jews.

By 1936 there remained only nine associations (in Massachusetts, New Jersey, and New York) whose enterprise was a bakery. (Seven other cooperatives were operating a bakery as one department of their business.) The 7 reporting all antedated 1921, two having been formed in 1917, one in 1918, one in 1919, and three in 1920. The average age for the group was slightly over 18 years. In three of the associations the members were Jewish; in the four others the predominant nationality was Polish, Lithuanian, Italian, and Finnish.

As the above indicates, the successful bakery associations were unusually long lived. Three were especially so: (1) Polish Cooperative Bakery Association at Adams, Mass., organized in 1916, reorganized as a joint-stock company in 1948 because of operating losses, after 32 years as a cooperative. (2) Purity Cooperative Association at Syracuse, N. Y. (1917), was in operation for 32 years, also, before dissolving in 1949. (3) At the end of that year the only bakery association left in the United States was the Purity Cooperative Association at Paterson, N. J., organized in 1905. It was still in operation at the end of 1954.

Records could be found for only 34 bakery associations known to have been organized through 1954. Of them, 18 were in Massachusetts, five each in New Jersey and New York, two each in California and Michigan, and one each in Connecticut and in Ohio.

No new cooperatives of this type have appeared in the past 20 years and none are likely. Bakeries nowadays are mainly unionized, and the conditions that gave rise to the early cooperatives have been largely overcome. It is probable that only ones opened in the future will be departments of other businesses.[11]

Cooperation in Last Half of Decade

By 1925 the consumers' cooperatives were on the upgrade, more than holding their own in point of membership, "real sales," capital, and reserves. In that year 72 percent of the reporting cooperatives had earnings, averaging 3.9 percent on sales. Although many of them preferred to put their earnings into the business to build up the operating capital and reserves, patronage refunds in the amount of over three-quarters of a million dollars were returned—an average refund (by the 40 percent of reporting associations that made refunds) of 3.8 percent on sales (29.3 percent if figured on capital).

"It is doubtful if private business operating in the same line of business can excel such a showing, especially when it is considered that this return is in addition to interest paid to the members on their capital investment."[12]

Many adverse circumstances were affecting the cooperative movement during the twenties, however. Organized workers had become greatly disillusioned with cooperation because of the failure of so many of their stores; and members were inclined to blame the "idea" rather than their own mistakes.

Also, unions had to deal with increasingly serious problems of trade-union organization. Union membership had declined as unemployment increased during the depression, and some of the unsuccessful strikes had been followed (as in coal mining) by open-shop operation. The labor leaders' thoughts naturally became engrossed with these problems and they had less attention to give to the fostering of cooperatives.

Other factors were the depressed condition of agriculture, the large number of bogus cooperatives whose fraudulent operations mulcted the wage earners of millions of dollars, differences of opinion between industrial workers and farmers which militated against joint action in cooperative enterprises, and the increasing difficulties in the cooperative movement itself arising from ideological differences—between those who looked upon cooperation merely as one part of the labor movement and dedicated to the class struggle, and those cooperators who opposed identification of the cooperatives with any political or class movement. This last problem became acute during the final years of the decade and was resolved only after it had split the cooperative movement (especially in the Great Lakes region) from end to end.

The Coolidge "prosperity" period that began in 1925 gave the country a sense of well-being. Consumers had little interest in the small savings possible through cooperation. Buying on the installment plan was general. Members of cooperative stores also were demanding credit, and this was reflected in an unfortunate increase in the accounts receivable and a noticeable rise in operating expenses.

In the four years, 1925-29, nearly 600 associations went out of business. The greatest mortality was in the Middle West, but there were severe losses in Pennsylvania and Washington also. Certain southern States (Alabama, Florida, Louisiana, Mississippi, and South Carolina)—never strongholds of cooperation—dropped out of the picture altogether.

An encouraging feature was the rapid development of the very profitable oil cooperatives in the Midwest, with wholesale supply associations in Illinois, Minnesota, and Nebraska.

Chapter 15.—THE PSEUDO-COOPERATIVES

Organizations masquerading as cooperatives were not unknown even in the early days. The Grangers in the 1870's had to contend with profit merchants who represented themselves to be Grange stores, in order to cash in on the popularity of the Patrons' cooperatives. In the early 1880's a joint-stock organization in New York City also tried to exploit the cooperative idea. Prof. James Ford noted in 1914 that the "usual crop" of pseudo-cooperatives had come to notice in that year.

Not until the First World War, however, did such associations reach any significant number. Then the intense interest in cooperation throughout the country gave rise to innumerable fake schemes promoted by unscrupulous persons desirous of exploiting the situation for their own benefit. The Cooperative League was kept busy investigating and exposing them. This was one of its greatest contributions to the cooperative movement in this period.

Among the fakes were three in Minneapolis that cost the city's workingmen more than $250,000.

Another was the Glynn System of retail stores in and around Buffalo, N. Y., and its companion wholesale, United Consumers of Buffalo, in 1921. This was a "promoted" chain of 14 stores, controlled by four men who sold nonvoting shares to individuals. Promotion work was carried on in 10 or more cities, the procedure being first to get into the good graces of the Central Labor Union in each city and secure its endorsement. Extravagant promises were made of goods sold below current prices, high patronage refunds, and local autonomy. Actually, none of these benefits materialized. The promoters took $5 of each $20 membership certificate sold; also a commission was collected on all goods handled by the wholesale. Between $70,000 and $100,000 was collected in "memberships."

An investigation disclosed gross mismanagement, and organization expenses running as high as 33 percent. The organization was insolvent by midsummer of that year and went into bankruptcy late in September. By this time the promoters had disappeared. The principal organizer—"an ardent friend of labor for many years" and a sincere man—was left to face the irate membership and the creditors. In the process he lost his life savings and was reported at the end to be penniless.

By 1922 spurious schemes had become so numerous that the Cooperative Congress of that year took note of them. A committee reported such schemes to be a problem of first magnitude, and estimated that they had collected from consumers at least 15 million dollars in the past three years. Not only had this money been lost, but they had shattered confidence in the cooperative movement wherever they had occurred.

The largest of all—and the most reprehensible—was the Cooperative Society of America, in Chicago, the intricate financial manipulations of which, during the 20's, cost the working people of that area many millions of dollars.

Cooperative Society of America

The Cooperative Society of America was built on the remains of the National Society of Fruitvalers, organized to promote a chain of stores in Chicago, which went into receivership in December 1918. Its 5,000 certificate holders were then given the opportunity to exchange their certificates for those of the Cooperative Society of America.

The latter was formed on February 20, 1919 as a common-law trust (like its predecessor), in the name of Edith Parker, and the security was the same as in the Fruitvalers—a tract of 10,000 acres "of doubtful value" in Muskegon County, Mich., owned by her.

The deposition establishing the trust gave the three trustees, of whom her husband (Harrison Parker[1]) was one, absolute power, subject to no checks whatever.

The society, represented to be "an equal partnership of people without any partnership liability," claimed to operate on Rochdale principles. Its literature described in glowing terms the cooperative movements abroad—especially in Great Britain. The English volume of business and monetary benefits gained for the members were reported, with the inference that the same methods were practised by the Cooperative Society of America and the same benefits could be expected from its operations.

The actual practices of the organization were as far from the Rochdale principles as it was possible to be. The holders of the beneficial interests had no vote, no voice in the formulation of policy, and no participation in the operation of the business; in fact, practically no rights of any kind.

A chain of 916 stores was planned, with 300 or more "members" each. The Rochdale Wholesale Co. was formed in January 1920 to operate them. A large force of salesmen, estimated variously at 1,400 to 1,800, was put into the field.

By September 1920 the society claimed that 41 stores were in operation in Chicago (especially among the immigrant population) and 21 in other places. Quotas had been reached in 16 additional districts. A month later it was reported that 40,000 people had bought beneficial interests and two-thirds of the total issue had been sold.

There were immediate evidences of opposition—by the Chicago Federation of Labor and other labor organizations in Illinois and other States into which CSA salesmen had penetrated; by the Rochdale cooperative movement headed by the Cooperative League[2]; and by the CSA members in court actions and receivership petitions (dismissed on technicalities that did not touch the real problems involved and thus permitted Parker to claim "victories").[3]

Financial Operations

When the attacks against the society began to be made, the original trustees were replaced by others. In mid-February 1921, the society was reorganized under the name, Cooperators of America. Mr. Parker was again chief trustee, and was given practically unlimited powers and authority to issue any number of beneficial interests at $50 each. Shares of the Cooperative Society of America were exchangeable for these, share for share.

By summer, the society's agents were selling certificates not only throughout the Midwest but even in New York. At the end of September the Great Western Securities Co. (possessor of the exclusive right to sell the certificates) was reported to have collected nearly $17 million, of which it had retained as its commission $8,700,000 (or over 50 percent, instead of the 20 percent allotted under the trust agreement). Its financial statement showed assets of only about $4½ million. The accounts receivable were later found to be practically worthless.

The Cooperative Society of America reached the peak of its expansion in October 1921. At that time it had a controlling interest not only in the chain of about 200 grocery stores, but also in plants manufacturing food products, canned goods, candy, gum, and meat products, as well as in creameries, insurance, and banking companies. With total claimed assets of $32¾ million, it had a deficit of over 8½ million.

The grocery operations were going badly. The wholesale supplying the chain of retail stores was poorly managed, as were the stores also. This fact, keen competition, and the price drop in 1921 together produced an operating loss for the year of over $451,000.

The Rochdale Wholesale Co., in which over $1,600,000 had been invested, and which had lost $800,000 on its own operations and about $1 million on those of the retail stores, was sold late in 1921 for an estimated $817,000.

Later Court Action

Early in August 1921, Judge Kenesaw Landis[4] entered an order restraining the society from selling any more of its certificates.

The first real court test had begun on August 2, with a bankruptcy suit brought by some of the certificate holders. The CSA had virtually gone out of business by February 1921, but had continued to sell beneficial interests at $75 each until the issuance of the restraining order, six months later. Evidence showed that 81,000 persons in Chicago and vicinity had bought certificates, but only $2,600,000 had been paid in to the credit of CSA. The rest had been kept by the Great Western Securities Co. owned by Mrs. Parker.[5]

The court found that "evidence of fraud and insolvency" was "overwhelming." A receiver was appointed in October.

Meantime, the New York office of the society had closed, anticipating action in a court case brought by cooperative organizations there. In Iowa nearly $50,000 worth of certificates had been sold to unsuspecting investors. Activities in Wisconsin, where the society had planned to raise $5,000,000, were restrained by court order.

In Illinois CSA appealed to the U. S. Circuit Court of Appeals and was upheld, the court ruling that the holders of beneficial interests were not creditors. The assets were returned to the society in March 1922. The court selected Seymour Stedman (Chicago attorney) as chief trustee, but Parker was still on the board.

New Attempts at Reorganization

Under this leadership a new approach was made. A mail-order house was purchased and discussion groups were organized, with the idea of developing patronage and speeding up installments on beneficial-interest subscriptions.

This venture was short-lived and in 1923 the mail-order concern admitted it was bankrupt. Two months later, Harrison Parker resigned as trustee.

After another reorganization, announced in 1925, it was claimed that there were 25 member clubs, that the certificates (down to $2 in value in 1923) were up to $39, and that the 1923 deficit of $9 million had been reduced to $5 million. The membership was estimated at 90,000 and it was claimed that 30,000 of them were supporting the reorganization plan. The Peoples Life Insurance Co., a subsidiary, was stated to have policies in force aggregating $6 million.

By 1929 the City State Bank (a CSA subsidiary) claimed to have deposits of nearly $5 million. The trustees stated that debts had been reduced to $25,000. They began to promote another subsidiary—Randolph Drug Co.—to act as central purchasing agency for both drugs and groceries.

The whole network, however, was no more cooperative than before.

Early in 1929, the trustees were haled into court in the matter of the City State Bank, at the instance of the Illinois Bank Commissioner, for "years of fund juggling," receiving deposits while insolvent, and making unsecured loans to the CSA. The bank examiners closed the bank in mid-November, its charter was revoked, the organization was dissolved and deposits were refunded. Harrison Parker was arrested on charges of swindling, in March 1930.

Three years later the outcome was still in doubt, for Parker had covered his tracks with great care. The people who had trusted him and had invested money in his schemes had lost all their investment. As far as I have been able to learn, Harrison Parker got off scot free from this situation.[6] One beneficial result, however, had been the amendment of the State law to make less possible henceforth the improper use of the common-law trust form of organization.

The Moral of the Tale

This sad tale points the moral of how easy it can be to lure hard-earned money from credulous people with high-pressure salesmanship and promises of big returns.

Where honest cooperative leaders, who would make no rash promises, could barely raise the very minimum necessary for their projects, the CSA enticed from 11 to 16 million dollars from poor wage earners (especially the foreign born). And most of this was collected in a time of economic hardship! The more fantastic the promises, the faster the money came in. The very size of the operation seems to have dazzled the investors.

The cooperative movement in this country has never seen such an intricate and dishonest financial manipulation or one on such a scale. The National Cooperative Wholesale Association fiasco heretofore described pales into insignificance beside it. At least National was promoted by honest persons who did not themselves benefit in a pecuniary way and who genuinely believed in cooperation, however mistaken they were as to methods. The Cooperative Society of America was from start to finish a cynical attempt to exploit the pathetic eagerness of the working people for some panacea for deflation and hard times, by a group of congenitally dishonest promoters.

Chapter 16.—THE COOPERATIVE LEAGUE DURING THE TWENTIES

The 1920 Cooperative Congress adopted a constitution transforming the League into a national educational body, Cooperative League of America,[1] thus marking the end of the old League—"a temporary organization." The plan adopted provided for district leagues with local autonomy. Local associations were to be members of the appropriate league and could affiliate directly with the national League only if there was no area organization.

The League neglected neither the labor movement nor the farmers. Of the 15 directors on its board, 4 were representatives of labor unions, 2 were from farm organizations, and 5 were representatives of local or regional cooperatives. It must be said, however, that in these early days membership on the League board meant comparatively little. The directors were so widely scattered geographically that it was next to impossible to hold board meetings between the biennial congresses. The League's affairs were therefore in practice carried on by the staff and the directors from the eastern States.

The membership of the League at the end of 1920 was reported as 290 associations (with 91,000 members), and 916 individuals without voting rights. The "member" associations were not yet financing the League; it was relying mainly on voluntary contributions.

During this time the new national organization was carrying out its task as monitor of the cooperative movement. It cautioned local cooperatives not to allow the withdrawal of share capital or to overstock on inventory,[2] and advised them not to affiliate with nor to contribute any money to a wholesale or any other organization without ascertaining its soundness from the League. In May 1922, the League moved into its own building at 167 West 12th Street, New York City.

In 1922 the Federation of Jewish Cooperative Societies of America, formed in 1916, proposed to the League that the latter take over the Federation's functions. After consideration, the League agreed to establish a Jewish department, with a Jewish secretary. This arrangement was ratified by the membership of the Federation at a meeting on June 11, 1922, and the Federation then went out of existence.

A legal department had already been established (1921), under the direction of Harry Rappaport, to promote more and better cooperative laws, give legal advice to cooperatives, and hunt down and expose bogus schemes. During 1922, it was finally able to get the New York cooperative law amended, to authorize the formation of cooperative federations. The League then incorporated under that law, under the name, Cooperative League of the United States of America (Association, Inc.).

The third biennial congress, held at Chicago on October 26-28, 1922, accepted delegates only from affiliates and was therefore the first to be really representative of member associations. The total League membership then numbered 289 associations, with 82,000 members and a combined business estimated at $35 million. Five area leagues had also been formed by that time—for Missouri, Ohio, Chicago, Cleveland, and New York.

Dr. Warbasse reported that most of the affiliates had joined simply by paying a $1 registration fee—no dues. This was permitted because "we feel that we must first get all societies into the League. When that has been accomplished we shall then have a league of societies. The value of the League should steadily impress itself upon the member societies and in the course of time there should be no question but that they would adequately finance the League."

Much stress was laid on the necessity for improving and expanding cooperative educational work, both in informing members and patrons and in providing technical training for managers and other employees.

The committee on promotion of cooperation by trade-unions, consisting of 13 representatives of various labor organizations, urged the State federations of labor to form committees on cooperation.

The need for good State cooperative laws had long since been recognized, and one of the first acts of the committee on legislation was to draw up a model cooperative statute, copies of which were sent to every State Attorney General, to legislative reference bureaus, to prominent labor leaders, and to teachers.

This congress adopted the now-familiar "Circle Pines" seal, showing twin pine trees surrounded by a circle.[3]

The year 1923 was notable chiefly for the publication of Dr. Warbasse's book, *Cooperative Democracy,* revised several times since then and still recognized as the authoritative philosophical work on the consumers' cooperative movement in the United States. In it he discussed the philosophy and principles and accomplishments of the movement and its relation to the State, to profit business, to agriculture, and to the labor movement.

In 1924 an Accounting Service, under the direction of Werner E. Regli, was started. Although the primary purpose of the new service was to assist cooperatives, it also served liberal, nonprofit organizations. The League's Employment Service, begun in 1917, was still in operation.

The League's secretary told the 1924 Cooperative Congress, held in New York November 6-10, that there had been no increase in number of cooperatives since 1922, except for agricultural marketing associations, credit unions, and housing associations. However, many of the cooperatives already organized had been strengthened.

This congress elected a standing budget committee to prepare an annual budget and "devise ways and means by which its [the League's] constituent members shall be made to bear their proportional share of the burden" of running the League. It also favored the formation of a health committee, to join with the Workers' Health Bureau in formulating a code to give "maximum health protection to workers in cooperative enterprises."

Cedric Long became League secretary in 1924 and served in that capacity until his death in 1931.[4]

The League had 333 affiliates at the end of 1924, with 50,000 members. By that time it was issuing two monthly magazines[5] and had published and was distributing 59 pamphlets on various phases and problems of cooperation. In addition, during the preceding 2 years it had carried on a voluminous correspondence giving information and advice, had sent out speakers, and had conducted two training schools dealing with store management and administrative problems.

Congress of 1926

When the 1926 Cooperative Congress was held in Minneapolis, November 4-6, widespread dissolutions had reduced the membership to 132 cooperatives with 64,700 members.

Four committees were created by the meeting: (1) to study and make recommendations on cooperative insurance, with a view to the League's entering the field,[6] (2) to draft recommendations on health and safety standards for cooperative employees, (3) to work out a uniform system of accounting for cooperatives, and (4) to formulate a plan for a national correspondence school.[7]

The constitution was amended to admit farm organizations as fraternal members.

Congress of 1928

By this time the situation with regard to the Communists (described in detail in a succeeding chapter) had become so serious that President Warbasse questioned the advisability of even trying to hold a congress in 1928. Nevertheless, the meeting was held as usual—in Waukegan, Ill., October 29-31.

The treasurer (Mary Ellicott Arnold) was able to report that an essential part of the League's activities was being financed by the constituent associations.[8] In this congress, as in all the congresses while Miss Arnold was treasurer, one feature was her success at charming pledges of money from the delegates present—on behalf of either themselves or their associations—to help meet the current deficit.

The chief evidence of the growing Communist threat was a draft resolution that would have abolished the traditional political neutrality of the cooperatives. It failed because of the abstention from voting of the Communist delegates from Superior.

At the end of 1928, the League membership included the Northern States Cooperative League with 88 member associations (and 50,000 members), Central States Cooperative League with 14 members, and Eastern States Cooperative League with

25. The total membership of the League—140—included in addition some associations in arrears, those with no district league, and a few buying clubs not paying dues.

The Decade's Record

The League ended the decade, and its first 13 years of existence, with a rather impressive record of achievement, especially considering the condition of the consumers' cooperative movement and the small funds at its disposal. The national body had made some progress toward becoming a really democratic and representative federation of consumers' cooperatives; its advice, literature and speakers were gaining respect among the cooperators and doing much to keep the movement headed in the right direction; it was steadily increasing its contacts with organized labor and the farm organizations and gaining their good will; and its congresses were enabling representatives of cooperatives from all over the United States to become acquainted and exchange ideas and experiences, as well as to explore cautiously the possibilities of expansion into other fields such as insurance. It and the cooperative movement, were, however, being increasingly threatened by a Communist faction.

Chapter 17.—DISTRICT COOPERATIVE LEAGUES

Following the authorization of formation of area leagues by the 1920 Cooperative Congress, several such organizations were formed.

The first was the Ohio District Cooperative League, November 1920, with Thomas J. Donnelly (secretary-treasurer of the Ohio Federation of Labor) as president. It never had a full-time worker and made little progress. Upon its dissolution in 1926, its territory was incorporated into that of the Central States Cooperative League.

In December 1920 the Missouri District Cooperative League was started, with A. W. Warinner of Brookfield as secretary, but was "destroyed by the deflation of agriculture which began in 1921."

Then, in quick succession, were formed the Greater New York Cooperative Union (February 1921), the New Jersey District Cooperative League (March 1921), the Cleveland Cooperative League (early in 1922), and the Northern States Cooperative League (March 1922). No further action occurred until 1925, when two additional federations came into being—Eastern States Cooperative League (February) and Illinois District Cooperative League (July). The Illinois body was succeeded by the Central States Cooperative League when the latter was organized in May 1926.

By 1928 all were out of existence except the Eastern, Northern, and Central States leagues, described individually in the following pages. All of them were affiliates of the national League, but retained their local autonomy.

All of the leagues were nonstock associations supported by dues from affiliated cooperatives, by income from various services and the sale of pamphlets and other printed material.

The leagues carried on general educational work in the theory and practice of cooperation, gave information and advice on cooperative problems and organization procedures, issued pamphlets on cooperative subjects, and furnished articles for the press, speakers for meetings, and instructors for cooperative schools and institutes and other interested groups. One important activity was the giving of short courses for employees and managers of cooperative associations.

Eastern States Cooperative League

The Eastern States Cooperative League, with headquarters in New York City, was organized in February 1925, to act as educational body for cooperatives in New Jersey, New York, and New England. (Later, after the wholesale was formed and its territory expanded, the league's jurisdiction was enlarged accordingly and included associations as far south as northern Virginia.) One of its first activities was to hold a cooperative institute, in August 1925, which combined instruction and social events.

Only 7 of 175 cooperatives in the eastern territory had joined the league by the end of its first year. A year later the number had risen to 12; nearly half were bakeries. The league was already buying certain supplies for 14 cooperatives.

By the end of 1927 the league had 29 affiliates with 16,000 individual members. Only 5 or 6 of the associations were then using the collective-buying service (several of the bakeries had gone out of business), but some goods were being bought under a co-op label. Money earned through the buying service was retained to help finance the new wholesale (Eastern Cooperative Wholesale) that was incorporated in the summer of 1928. Another league activity was the publication of a monthly paper, *The Cooperator.*

Cedric Long, executive secretary of the Cooperative League of the USA, and his successor, Oscar Cooley, served also as secretary of the district league. In 1933 Leslie E. Woodcock, manager of Eastern Cooperative Wholesale, was elected as secretary of the league, a position that he continued to fill until 1946. "States" was dropped from the league's name in 1936.

In 1947 the league amalgamated with Eastern Cooperative Wholesale, each becoming a department of a new organization, Eastern Cooperatives, Inc.

Northern States Cooperative League

The Northern States Cooperative League was organized in March 1922,[1] with headquarters in Superior, Wis.,[2] and a territory covering Michigan, Wisconsin, and Minnesota (later extended to include Montana and the Dakotas).

Educational work was begun immediately, under the direction of the league's secretary, V. S. Alanne, with training schools and, later, correspondence courses.[3]

Northern States Cooperator, a bimonthly, began publication in August 1925 and continued until 1928.

A department for collective buying and an auditing service were started in 1927, but the former was discontinued in the following year.

Depression caused the league to grow and its activities were greater than ever before. Of its 29 affiliates in 1933, 12 were in Minnesota, 7 in Wisconsin, 4 in Michigan, 4 in North Dakota, and 2 in Montana. Its actual strength was greater than these figures indicated, however, for one of the members was Central Cooperative Wholesale with 99 local member associations; another (admitted in 1933) was the Farmers Union Central Exchange (St. Paul) with 172 members. In the 5-month period ending in February 1934, 17 new members joined, in addition to 2 fraternal members.

The year 1934 was one of considerable progress. A branch of the auditing department was opened at Jamestown, N. Dak., to serve cooperatives in the Dakotas and Montana. Through league efforts an amendment was obtained to the Minnesota cooperative law, bringing it into better conformity with Rochdale principles; and cooperatives were exempted from the State tax on chain stores. A new insurance organization promoted by the league, Cooperators' Life Association, was chartered in October 1934.

The first check on league activities came in the 1937 convention, when the delegates voted that the organization should not compete with, or duplicate activities of, its member associations. Also, for several years the league members had tended to use its educational services less and less. The wholesales were doing their own employee-training work. A change in the requirements of the Minnesota State law, also, made it necessary to change the auditing arrangement and engage the auditors as individual contractors, rather than as league employees.

Cecil R. Crews[4] became executive secretary of the league in 1938. The league was reorganized that same year, and in January 1939 it became a federation of wholesales and federations. Local cooperatives were members through affiliation with these central bodies; only if no such federation existed in the region could they join directly. Authority was given the league to carry on services, such as auditing and installation of uniform methods of accounting, but commercial activities were prohibited.

The new arrangement did not work out very well, and the 1939 fall board meeting voted to liquidate unless the members provided better support. As it became clear that this was not forthcoming, the league was officially dissolved early in 1940, but its charter was retained for possible future use.

Central States Cooperative League

The Central States Cooperative League, formed from the educational department of the defunct wholesale of that region, went into action in May 1926. Its office was then moved from East St. Louis to Bloomington, Ill.

The new league had to meet very adverse conditions. Not only was it handicapped by the failure of the wholesale but economic conditions in the coal fields were bad. Miners' cooperatives were either going out of business or struggling along on budgets that allowed little or no margin for the support of an educational federation.

Thanks chiefly to the efforts of A. W. Warinner, its secretary, the league managed not only to survive but to grow. By 1929, in addition to its general educational work, the league was furnishing auditing service and its printing plant (begun as a single mimeographing machine in Mr. Warinner's basement) was serving both the league and the members, at cost.

In 1929 the first summer school was held, combining educational and recreational features. In the summer of 1933 the league directed six cooperative summer schools for the Indiana Farm Bureau Cooperative Association.

At the league's 1930 convention it reported 18 member associations with 6,780 members and an annual business of over 25 million dollars. Several associations in Ohio (including the big miners' cooperative in Dillonvale) had joined. Of the league's 18 members, 11 were in Illinois, 6 in Ohio, and 1 in Indiana. (Later, the league territory was extended to include lower Michigan.) More than 100 commodities were being bought jointly.

The convention of 1931 endorsed the league's current policy of trying to assist and expand existing cooperatives rather than start new ones. In the fall of that year the league began to buy canned fruits and vegetables from a California cooperative cannery. By this time the joint buying had been dignified by the name, Commercial Department, and the latter at the beginning of 1933 became the sales agent for co-op label goods obtained through Central Cooperative Wholesale at Superior, Wis.

The original 18 members had been mostly small struggling stores in Illinois mining towns. The slow decay of the mining industry wiped out these stores one by one. By 1928 five of the original group were out of business, reducing the membership to 13, at about which level it remained until early in 1933. Then the depression and the accompanying interest in cooperation caused a "most phenomenal growth." By the end of 1935 the league (then in Chicago) had as affiliates 32 of the 51 cooperatives in its area, and membership applications were coming in at the rate of 1 every 10 days. The Cooperative Wholesale was in process of organization, also, and started operation on March 1, 1936.

In 1939 the league undertook its most extensive program, with the leasing of a camp (with 45 buildings) in Barry County, Mich. There the league conducted a series of eight summer schools and institutes, attended by some 200 students, in addition to cooperative campers using the camp's recreation facilities.

At the end of 1940, the league forfeited its separate identity and merged with the wholesale, each becoming a department of the newly created Central States Cooperatives, Inc., which went into operation on January 1, 1941.

The Role of the Leagues

The leagues at first filled a real need. Most of them were formed when little or no educational work on an area basis was being done and when member interest and information was at a low ebb. When the regional wholesales began to be concerned with the practical business training of their managers and employees and to offer such courses themselves, part of the leagues' reason for being disappeared.

Ultimate merger with the regional wholesales in the Eastern and Central States areas into an over-all organization which supposedly would carry on both education and commercial business was, in my opinion, of doubtful value and success. This was one of those moves that seem logical but do not always work out. The tendency is for the businessman to overshadow the educator and for the commercial aspects of the operation to gain ascendancy. Advertising is likely to take the place of real educational work.

Chapter 18.—COMMUNIST MOVES FOR CONTROL, 1921-50

Much of the cooperative development in this country has been fostered by ardent adherents of one political party or another, and in the early years cooperatives often became involved with organizations having economic or political aims or both.

In perhaps the majority of the very early cooperatives, the Rochdale principles were either not known or followed. Toward the end of the 19th century, however, the tenets of the Pioneers came into greater observance. Possibly for that reason—and also undoubtedly because few of these later cooperatives were prompted by organizations with other aims than cooperation—few of the associations of that time had any political tinge, as far as can now be ascertained.

After the turn of the century, members of the Socialist Party became intrigued with cooperation, sometimes more as a possible instrument for influencing people in the direction of Socialism than in cooperation for its own sake. Many cooperatives were organized by Socialists, especially in the East.

In the Midwest the social and political clubs of the Finnish immigrants, along with the natural clannishness of the Finns, were a great source of the cohesiveness that helped their cooperatives to success, in the face of hard times, unemployment, and social discrimination. They were also a source of occasional, and very deep, divisions that took their toll among the cooperatives.

Rise of the Communists

The Bolshevik revolution in Russia caused a split in the Socialist Party in the United States, with one section declaring in favor of the Communist ideology. In Massachusetts, this resulted in the break-up of the United Cooperative Society (formed by the merger of a number of Finnish cooperatives in Massachusetts and New Hampshire). The Communists then tried to gain control of the units, but had little luck. They even attempted, without much success, to set up rival organizations (one, in Fitchburg, limped along for about a year and then closed). In Maynard their bid for both domination and appropriations to promote the "class struggle" failed.

The Communist faction gained control of the (Finnish) Cooperative Trading Association in Brooklyn, N. Y., and held it until the end of 1928.

Among the Jews, too, certain cooperatives had come under Communist influence. Communists also formed several new ventures, among them a large housing project in the Bronx and grocery and meat markets to serve the residents there.

The ideological differences had soon begun to be reflected in the congresses of the Cooperative League. In the 1924 congress, Red delegates tried, unsuccessfully, to get through a resolution urging recognition of the Bolshevik Government. Two years later a Communist-sponsored measure that would have condemned the traditional political neutrality of the cooperatives was introduced. Among the proponents of this resolution were the delegates from the Cooperative Central Exchange, wholesale at Superior, Wis., most of whose affiliates were associations of Finnish membership. Leader of the CCE group was Eskel Ronn, general manager of the wholesale,[1] who had become a Communist sympathizer. An appeal by Dr. Warbasse to Mr. Ronn resulted in the CCE delegates' abstention from voting, with the result that the resolution did not pass.

The congress voted, instead, a resolution proclaiming the cooperative movement to be part of the general labor movement and seeking the cooperation of "all workers' movements for the benefit of the exploited toilers."[2]

The League board, alive to the seriousness of the situation, later passed a resolution declaring that the cooperative movement was best promoted by freedom from religion, politics, and class connections, and that it was therefore the judgment of the board that publications of organizations connected with the League should not contain matters contrary to this principle.

Both the national League and the district leagues were having trouble because of the divisive effects of the Communist controversy. The conservative members were considering withdrawal, and others who might have joined refrained from doing so because they did not want to become associated with a radical group such as they feared the organized cooperative movement was becoming. There was also the question in the Northern and Central leagues whether, if the Communist-dominated associations withdrew or were expelled, the rest were financially strong enough to support the leagues by themselves.[3]

One countermeasure was a referendum among League members on a motion to exclude from Cooperative Congresses all discussion (1) of Communism, Socialism, and other political or economic theories, and (2) of the attitude cooperators and the cooperative movement should take toward other political and economic programs and movements. The referendum, announced at the 1928 congress, resulted in 208 votes for exclusion and 42 votes against.[4]

At the end of 1929 the 2-year-old (Communist and Jewish) Prolet Cooperative Restaurant on Union Square in New York City suddenly went into bankruptcy, an event noted with grim satisfaction by the conservative element in the Jewish community in that city.[5]

In Detroit the Consumers Cooperative Exchange, started by Communists in 1928, dissolved in 1931. In the same city the Workers Restaurant (1927) went Communist; it closed its doors before 1936. But a non-Communist restaurant, Detroit Workmen's Cooperative, was still operating in 1954.

The Situation in CCE-Land

The Lake Superior district had been one of the first to feel the effects of the Communist upsurge. The Finns who formed the core of the cooperative movement there had been largely Socialist in their politics. Oppressed for centuries in their own country and thrown in upon themselves in this one because of differences in language and customs, they had formed their own cooperatives and social and political clubs and had their own newspaper, *Työmies.*[6]

The paper wielded an enormous influence. Its readers believed implicitly in what was reported and said editorially in its columns. Its political coloration had originally been Socialist, but after the split in that party it veered more and more to the left, and by 1922 had become frankly Communist. Probably the majority of its readers followed its lead.

By 1929, however, the more conservative CCE cooperators—and even some of those who had previously favored Communism—had become revolted by the increasingly brazen demands of the Communists. Relations between the Party and the cooperative wholesale became more and more strained as time went on. *Työmies* continually carried broadsides against Eskel Ronn and George Halonen (educational director of CCE)—both of whom had by now changed their minds about Communism.

The last straw was laid on when the Party demanded $5,000 from the earnings of the wholesale and, later, that regular contributions be made at the rate of 1 percent of total sales. It was even suggested that the money should be charged to "legal advice," to keep the members from knowing. With this, the majority of the board discovered once and for all that they were cooperators and not Communists.

During the winter of 1929, Matti Tenhunen (who had been president of CCE from 1918 through 1927) and Henry Puro were summoned to Moscow to explain the situation in the CCE area. On their return, they began actively campaigning in behalf of the Communist Party. For the next five months, *Työmies* assailed the wholesale unremittingly, and Ronn and Halonen especially. The CCE board had, in the meantime, expelled from its membership Tenhunen, Oscar Corgan (president since 1928), and Jacob Vainionpaa, when they announced that their first allegiance was to the Communist Party.[7] In this action the board was upheld by a vote of 35 member associations (with 10,400 members) as against seven associations (with 900 members).

The 1930 annual meeting of the Exchange in April 1930 defeated the Communist candidates for office,[8] changed the name of the Exchange to Central Cooperative Wholesale, and referred to the incoming board the design of the wholesale's commodity labels (which for the past ten years had carried the hammer and sickle).[9] The regular "co-op" labels were adopted in 1933.

Action at 1930 Cooperative Congress

By the time of the 1930 national biennial Cooperative Congress, the lines were pretty well drawn in the CCE area, and on the national scene matters were also coming to a head. The factions met at the congress held in Superior, Wis., October 20-22, prepared for a showdown.

Almost immediately after the congress convened, Karl Reeve, Superior district organizer for the Communist Party, was granted time in which to present, as he said, the greetings of the Party. The "greetings" proved to be a blast of invective against Dr. Warbasse, Ronn, Halonen, and others. At its conclusion, President Warbasse, who was in the chair, said smilingly: "The congress has listened to the greetings from the representative of the Communist Party. We may console ourselves that we have not been attacked, for if these are greetings, what would an attack have been?" Eskel Ronn, replying for the League, was heckled by Communist delegates until he demanded to be listened to as quietly as the meeting had listened to Reeve. Thereupon the Communists left the hall in a body (but *Työmies* declared the next day that they had been driven out with clubs!).

With their departure the congress was free at last to settle down to its agenda, and League Secretary Long reported that over the United States as a whole the political differences had become less noticeable than before. He said that the Central States region had "always kept relatively free from political entanglements," and the East, which in 1928 had had an "extremely serious" situation, was now "almost free" of Communist agitation.

The Diminishing Threat After 1930

After 1930 the Communists ceased to be an important factor in the cooperative movement, except in the Lake Superior region. There the contest continued for some years, though on a diminishing scale.

For months after the Cooperative Congress, meeting after meeting was held throughout the CCW area, at which officers and directors of the wholesale explained what had happened and why, and what the current situation was. Eskel Ronn literally wore himself out, and the rigors of this time contributed to his sudden death from a heart attack in 1931.

In some associations open fighting came suddenly and as a surprise, and not all the memberships grasped the actualities of the situation rapidly enough to clean house in time. Altogether, 20 CCE cooperatives (five in Michigan, 11 in Minnesota, and four in Wisconsin) aligned themselves boldly with the Communists. In other cases Communist factions seized control for a time.

Then followed Communist boycotts of the stores loyal to CCE, organization of new cooperatives to compete with them, or opening of branches of existing associations.

The non-Communists also opened new stores in some towns where the Communists had gained control of cooperatives.

A competing wholesale, Workers and Farmers Cooperative Unity Alliance,[10] was also started in 1931, to which (according to its reports to the U. S. Bureau of Labor Statistics) 36 cooperatives affiliated.[11] Its total volume never reached $300,000 in any of its three years of operation, and it went out of business in 1938. Its first manager was Oscar Corgan who was reported to have wavered considerably before finally casting his lot with the Communists.

Left-wing maneuvers at the 1932 and 1933 meetings accomplished nothing.[12] Overtures for business relationships between the Communist associations and wholesale and the CCW in 1935 and 1936 were likewise futile. However, late in 1938, the Communist wholesale having gone out of business, CCW's ban was lifted from certain of the Red-dominated stores to the extent of allowing them to buy from it, since they were not competing with any "loyal" association. It was specified, however, that they must observe the political-neutrality principle and carry on educational work on that basis.

In 1940 the wholesale refused to serve several Communist associations because of their political activities detrimental to CCW. In this group were the stores at Ironwood and Mass, Mich., and Cook and Makinen, Minn. In 1948 the Ironwood association was expelled from the wholesale (and later from Range Cooperative Federation) for persisting in "practices that cast serious public discredit on consumers' cooperation generally and upon CCW and its members in particular."

It is probable that the tactics of the Communists had been aided by the deteriorating economic conditions in the area, that gave a radical turn to the views of the people. Even in 1939, the statement was made that "one-third of rural St. Louis County, Minn. [in which a number of the CCW associations were situated] is a poorhouse," and 80 percent or more of the CCW associations were said to be composed of farmers on marginal cut-over land.

Even as late as mid-1950 a renewal of infiltration tactics was reported. *Työmies* was again fulminating against the CCW, and urging the comrades to take advantage of the cooperative open-membership policy and gain entrance.

Ten of the associations that sided with the Communists were still in existence at the end of 1950 (the others had all failed), but whether they were still sympathetic to Communism I do not know.

Cooperative Resolutions on Communism

The Communist situation had been well in hand for 15 years or more. In view, however, of the public concern over "security," and in view of attempts of certain organizations to discredit the cooperative movement, the board of directors of the Cooperative League adopted the following resolution at its meeting of late August 1948:[13]

"Membership in cooperatives is open to all people of good will regardless of race, creed or economic status. But cooperatives are not called upon to admit to membership either those who actively oppose cooperatives, their methods and principles, nor persons who hold beliefs which render it impossible for them to desire the success of cooperatives as a basic solution to human problems.

"Cooperatives represent the application of free, voluntary democratic methods and principles to economic problems. Cooperatives seek peaceful evolutionary solution of the people's problems by the methods and competitive influence of cooperatives belonging to and controlled by voluntary groups of citizens.

"Cooperatives offer an opportunity for the people to solve their own problems by their own efforts rather than by dependence upon or through the authority of government.

"Both the aims and beliefs of cooperatives and their practices and results are at the opposite pole from those of any form of totalitarianism. In fact, successful cooperatives are the best single available guarantee against the possible growth of a totalitarian movement in this or any other country. Believers in Communism or Fascism will know this and consequently cannot desire the success of any cooperative. Their purpose in attempting to join a cooperative, if they did so, would be to use it for their own propaganda purposes for a temporary period and then destroy it as inevitably constituting, if successful, a barrier against the achievement of Communist or Fascist goals.

"The American cooperative movement has been remarkably free of any such attempted infiltration by totalitarian forces. This statement of policy is issued, therefore, not because of concern over the present situation in cooperatives, but in order that the position of American cooperatives may be crystal clear and that there be no confusion as to the true meaning of the principle of open membership."

A similar resolution was adopted by the annual meeting of Central Cooperative Wholesale in 1953.

Retrospect

To anyone looking back from the perspective of 1954, the events in this chapter present a familiar picture of Communist tactics—the now tiresomely customary invective and abuse, the distortion of facts and outright lies, the devious methods, the behind-scenes intrigue, the alternate gestures of hostility and conciliation, and the willingness of the "comrades" to go to any lengths to obtain advantage, funds, and control for the Party.

The observer cannot, however, fail to be struck by the fact that cooperators were the first to realize the menace and to recognize Communism for what it is, a program aiming at no less than absolute control and to be attained at any cost. Twenty-five years before most of our society woke up to these facts, the directors of the Cooperative League (and other like-minded cooperators) were aware of them and so were able to save the cooperative movement. Since that time there has probably been no segment of our population more alive to the continuing threat or more convinced of the need for vigilance.

Chapter 19.—COOPERATIVES IN THE DEPRESSION

Decline, Offset by New Growth

Late in 1929 came the stock-market "break" that ushered in several years of increasingly serious depression conditions, during which many cooperatives closed their doors.

Cooperatives held their own rather well in 1930 and 1931, although volume of business fell with the decline in member purchasing power and in price level. As the depression worsened, the movement felt increasingly the effects of wage cuts, part-time employment, unemployment, and losses from bank failures. By 1933 (the low point of the depression) the volume of the cooperative stores was down to about half the 1929 level. Thereafter sales began to rise slowly. The business of the retail petroleum cooperatives held up remarkably, never falling below 93.4 percent of 1929 sales, even in 1933. That of the cooperative wholesales continued to rise slowly throughout the depression, practically without a break, and without a single failure, though here and there one sustained a net operating loss for a year or two.

The retail mortality was not so great as in 1921-22, partly because the associations were older and had had time to improve their business methods and build up reserves. Many associations, indeed, were able not only to make ends meet but to make savings returns to the members throughout the whole depression period. In others which could have done so, the members voted to leave the money in the business to insure financial stability.

Even in 1933, over three-fourths of the cooperatives reporting to the Government had earnings, amounting to 5.5 percent on sales. Refunds on purchases by cooperatives furnishing data for the four-year period, 1930-33, totaled nearly $4½ million.

Among the new associations was Cooperative Distributors, carrying on a mail-order business, the idea of which had been endorsed by the 1932 annual meeting of Eastern States Cooperative League. Its board of directors included representatives of cooperatives, labor unions, and other nonprofit organizations. Its manager was E. J. Lever.[1] CD representatives helped to organize buying clubs all over New Jersey, some of which later became full-fledged store associations. By 1937 the association had 8,000 individual and club members in addition to 150 affiliated nonprofit organizations. It operated until 1944, when wartime supply conditions caused it to disband.

Between 1933 and 1936 the retail cooperatives' record was "one of slow, quiet expansion, of the strengthening of both local and wholesale associations, and of increasing emphasis upon educational activities." The rate of progress was very uneven, being "greatest where the sense of cohesion and of a definite social and economic aim was liveliest and least among the scattered associations operating on the 'go-it-alone' policy."[2] The consumers' cooperatives in general reported increased sales in 1934, and another "decided improvement" in cooperative business and earnings in 1935.

During these years a slow change had been occurring in urban cooperation. Previously, the cooperative membership in the cities had been drawn from labor unionists and the foreign-born or those of foreign descent. Now native Americans, especially the "white-collar" groups, began to form or join cooperatives in increasing numbers. Partly this was due to the depression, with its spotlight on ways and means of survival; partly it was due to the publicity received by the cooperative movement from various directions[3] and to the encouragement extended by various agencies of the New Deal. As a result of all these factors, interest in urban cooperation was unusually great.

The Illinois consumers' cooperatives responded also to the stimulus of the formation of a new central supply association in Chicago—The Cooperative Wholesale—and 19 store associations joined it.

The cooperative oil movement expanded rapidly in the Midwest in this period under the encouragement of several new oil wholesales and the program of the Farmers Union. In this period of economic stringency their earnings were a strengthening factor in the economy. Glenn Talbott (then president of the North Dakota Farmers' Union) said that in 1934, when 55 percent of the farmers in that State were on relief, their petroleum associations paid $500,000 in refunds on purchases.

Their effect on the price level was also impressive. Thus, in 1924 (just before the cooperative oil movement got under way in Nebraska) the price of gasoline in the eastern part of the State was 25 cents a gallon, without any tax; in 1937, with the State well covered with cooperatives, the price averaged 20 cents a gallon, including a 6-cent tax. The margin on gasoline in Minnesota in 1925 was 9 cents on a gallon; in 1939 it was about 4 cents. Oil cooperatives reduced the retail price of gasoline in Ohio by 13 percent in 5 years. Their effective competition in Kansas, also, was indicated in the reduction of gross margins in the industry in that State from 37.60 percent in 1930 to 17.56 percent in 1936.[4]

Cooperative Activity in California

There was little cooperative enterprise in California during the late 1920's after the collapse of the Pacific Cooperative League. Toward the end of the decade prices were rising rapidly but wages were good and there was no great incentive toward small savings. The number of consumers' cooperatives in the State declined from 47 in 1921 to 12 in 1925, and to 5 in 1929.

As the depression began and wore on, the attention of the workers was directed elsewhere—into political movements and into self-help associations.

This was the period when the Townsend Plan, the End Poverty in California ("Epic") plan, and production for use were being advanced. Self-help cooperatives among the unemployed sprang up all over the State, but especially in the southern part. The Epic movement advocated combining the self-help and production-for-use features with that of pensions for elderly people. After the defeat of its program in the November 1934, election, some of the Epic supporters turned to consumers' cooperatives as a possible avenue to eventual production for use. Though this latter aim was never achieved, at least the attention of the people was directed to consumers' cooperation.

This accession of interest began to produce new associations. In the 8-month period, September 1934 to April 1935,

50 buying clubs and 30 stores were started. By September 1935, there were 56 cooperatives with a membership of about 7,000. Of these, all but four had been formed since 1934. However, 26 of the contemporary movement had already gone out of existence.

Of the associations reporting in a State WPA study, 41 owed their formation either to Epic clubs or their members and seven had grown out of self-help cooperatives. The group included a number of production-for-use stores, operating on a cost-plus basis (none of which lasted for more than a few years); about a dozen chain stores of The American Unit (half of which were already out of business by the end of 1935); and a few independent stores at all stages of success, loosely federated into the southern division of the California Cooperative Council.[5]

Of the associations organized in the period from 1930 to 1935, the only present survivors are the store association in Palo Alto (1935) and the University students' rooming and boarding association in Berkeley (1935).[6]

These figures point up what had always been the most prominent characteristics of the California cooperative movement—the short period of life, the feeble roots and lack of vitality, and above all else the completeness with which each crop of new associations disappeared.

Self-Help Cooperatives—A Depression Phenomenon

The self-help cooperatives were born of the depression. Composed of unemployed, they turned their hands to anything that promised to bring in food, clothing, housing, or articles of family use. Some of them were thus, in a broad sense, "consumer" cooperatives. Some of them confined themselves to "swap" arrangements, often operating with scrip or "points"; thus, a family could bring any useful articles into the shop, and receive for them credits usable in the purchase of goods brought in by others.

To fill the primary need, food, some groups made arrangements with nearby farmers or market gardeners whereby they received vegetables or fruit in return for work on the land. The units in southern California were especially fortunate in this respect, as the region has a succession of crops nearly the year round.

Gradually the self-help activities expanded and became more or less organized. "Chiselers" (later called by the more dignified name of "contact men") scoured the locality systematically, to locate jobs and supplies. Requirements for articles other than food were met by various barter agreements. Meat—one of the most difficult items to obtain—was sometimes earned by work, sometimes by barter, or by a combination of the two.

In some of the barter schemes as many as six or eight separate transactions might be required in order to obtain the desired article.[7] This, required "an amount of contact work, an ingenuity of planning, and an expenditure of thought and energy far beyond the inclinations and possibly even the abilities of the average person."[8]

The self-help groups, however, included not only the rank and file but also persons of outstanding ability. In the nationwide industrial stagnation of this country's worst depression, leaders as well as followers lost their jobs. It was these leaders who gravitated to the top of self-help units, and their leadership was in many cases of a high order.

One of the great problems of the self-help cooperatives was that of raising cash to purchase such items as salt, sugar, and coffee that were very difficult to obtain by labor,[9] and to pay for the utilities and gasoline needed to carry on the group activities. In recognition of the value of their work, some of the municipalities assisted the units with small grants from relief funds. In other cases, charitable donations helped out.

After the Federal Emergency Relief Administration was created under the New Deal, in 1933, small grants were made to self-help units to enable them to produce needed articles of various kinds. During this phase the units became workers' productive associations rather than consumers' cooperatives. Each group specialized on one commodity.[10]

The first self-help cooperatives of record appeared, almost simultaneously, in Seattle and Salt Lake City, in midsummer 1931. The quick success of these two organizations (Unemployed Citizens League and Natural Development Association) attracted widespread publicity and interest. Imitators sprang up all over the country.

The peak of the barter and exchange movement (operating without any public funds) was reached in the spring of 1933, when there were over 400 units and the active membership was about 75,000. During the following year, when public relief became obtainable, the number declined sharply.

Federal grants for productive purposes began in the fall of 1933 and by the end of the year 33 units had received funds. From this time forward the number of grant units rose, as that of non-grant groups fell. The high point of the production units was reached in mid-1935, when 225 such groups were operating. By this time the non-grant units had decreased to 112.

As the depression was gradually overcome and employment opportunities opened up, the membership of the self-help organizations declined. Naturally, the most able members were the first to get jobs and leave, and the units became increasingly the refuge of the less able, the superannuated, and the downright unemployable. Nevertheless, some of them continued for a long while. At the end of 1938 there were still 140 associations (31 in barter groups and 109 in production units), almost half of which were in California. They had about 5,500 members.

It was estimated in 1939 that since 1931 over half a million families had been affiliated with about 600 self-help organizations in 37 States. These groups, according to the Federal Emergency Relief Administration, had by their activities saved the public over 2¼ million dollars that, except for them, would have had to be expended in relief. (Grants allocated for self-help from August 1933 through December 1935 totaled $3,158,000.)

These cooperatives come into the present story for three reasons: Their early goal was to supply food and household articles to the members; some of them later sold some of their products to consumers' cooperatives; and a few themselves developed into consumers' distributive cooperatives. Among those known to be in the last class were three in California, three in Utah, two in Washington State, and two in Wisconsin.

Three wholesales started under the self-help program later became part of the consumers' cooperative movement:

(1) Wolverine Cooperative Exchange (1935) which had not only a distributive department serving about 25 consumer groups but also a manufacturing department (operated under

the name, Pontiac Cooperative Industries) that tanned leather and made shoes. The Exchange, which was a member of the Central States Cooperative League, could never quite make the grade and went out of business before 1939.[11]

(2) North Pacific Cooperative Wholesale, Seattle (created in 1936 by the State Relief Administration) which in 1937 became a consumers' organization supplying local consumers' cooperatives. It never attained sufficient volume for successful operation and its affairs were wound up in November 1939.

(3) A self-help warehouse in Utah which was transformed into a true federation of local consumers' cooperatives—Utah Cooperative Association—and is alive and prosperous today.

Chapter 20.—COOPERATIVES AND THE NEW DEAL

When the Roosevelt Administration came into office it was primarily concerned with restoring the tottering national economy. Many measures were taken to this end. Cooperatives, as people's institutions, received greater official recognition than under any previous administration. The consumer for the first time was given direct representation of his interest, in his national government; materials were made available to assist him in organizing cooperatives through which to help himself; and consumer and producer cooperatives were even organized under Government aegis. The period of the New Deal was truly an unusual one for cooperative development.

Consumer Representation in Government

One of the early New Deal measures was the creation of the National Recovery Administration. To it a Consumers Advisory Board was attached, and persons were appointed to represent the interests of the consumers. Among them, as representative of cooperators, was Dr. James P. Warbasse.

People were becoming more and more economy minded and from there the next step for many was consideration of cooperatives as a possible source of saving. As a result of their requests to the Board, the U. S. Bureau of Labor Statistics[1] issued a bulletin telling how to organize a cooperative. This, with later revisions,[2] proved to be one of that agency's best sellers.

After the National Industrial Recovery Act was declared unconstitutional, the consumers' advisory work was transferred in February 1936 to the Department of Labor, where it was renamed Consumers' Project.

The Project made several valuable contributions to the cooperative movement during its brief life, among them a compilation of consumers' cooperative laws, a study of standards of legislation and of the status of consumers' cooperative laws, and the draft of a model cooperative law. Its monthly, *The*

Consumer, issued from October 1935 to February 1936 contained information about commodities, cooperatives, and other subjects of interest to consumers.

In 1938 the consumer work was again transferred—to the Consumers Counsel Division in the Agricultural Adjustment Administration. Its publication, *Consumers' Guide,* carried articles on consumer buying standards, consumer group activities, and interpretation of the various farm programs of interest to consumers, with occasional items or articles about cooperatives. The Division went out of existence in July 1947.

Cooperatives and the NRA Codes

Under the industrial codes, a new threat loomed for the cooperatives. The prohibitions against rebates or discounts (regarded as a discriminatory or unfair trade practice) would if applied literally to cooperatives have meant the elimination of the distinguishing feature of cooperative enterprises—the return of refunds on patronage.

After a strenuous protest by National Cooperatives and its members, President Roosevelt issued an Executive order on October 24, 1933. It expressly exempted all "bona fide and legitimate cooperatives," both agricultural and consumer, from such code prohibition, provided the patronage refunds were paid out of actual earnings at the end of the accounting period and not as a discount at time of purchase. Another Executive order, February 17, 1934, ruled that selling through cooperatives, either directly or through an intervening agency, was not a violation of the codes.

Also, on October 12, 1934, the National Recovery Administration issued an administrative order ruling that it was no violation of the codes to pay or allow brokerage fees to cooperatives where such fees were properly paid.

These three measures relieved cooperative fears and insured against discrimination under the codes.

Rural Power Cooperatives—The REA Program

One of the programs of the Roosevelt Administration was that of rural electrification, resulting in many cooperatives for the distribution, transmission, and even generation of electric power. Even before this, however, there had been a few cooperatives for distribution of electricity. As early as 1886 the Colorado Bureau of Labor Statistics reported the existence of a mutual light and power plant at Glenwood. At least 45 electric-power cooperatives predated the REA; practically all of them had been organized before 1930 and some as far back as 1914.

The early associations were mainly in the Midwest (Illinois, Indiana, Iowa, Minnesota, Missouri, and Wisconsin), with one or two associations each in North Carolina and Virginia. In some cases their formation had undoubtedly been hastened by the existence of municipal power plants from which current could be bought at moderate rates.

After the adoption of the new program, the agricultural States began to pass laws authorizing the formation of rural electric cooperatives. Some of the early associations then reorganized as REA cooperatives and obtained loans enabling them to expand.

The Rural Electrification Administration was created by Executive order in May 1935, but not established by law until May of the following year. The law provided for loans to public utility companies, public power districts and municipally owned plants, and cooperatives—but with preference to the last two groups.[3] Loans could be made for construction of distributing plants, generating plants, and lines for transmission of power.

The first Administrator, Morris Llewellyn Cooke, envisioned the bulk of the loan business as being done with the utility companies. Events proved him mistaken. The utilities appeared to be as uninterested in the program as they had previously been in extending their lines to the farmers intended as the beneficiaries of the REA plan.

The REA had been hesitant to take the initiative in the formation of cooperatives, for history had demonstrated that healthy cooperatives could not be evoked by outside promotion. Nevertheless, circumstances compelled it to do so. Although the rural demand was urgent and enormous, most of it was inchoate and formless; the farmers wanted power but were unorganized and had no idea how to go about getting it and no conception of the problems of organization, incorporation, rate calculation, engineering, financing, etc., involved. And it became increasingly evident that the power companies would not be of assistance.

The agency decided therefore not only to provide staff advice and assistance in organization and operation, but to maintain relations with the individual borrowing cooperatives.

Experience not only confirmed the wisdom of the guidance policy but led to its expansion to provide advice and aid at all stages of cooperative development.[4]

By November 1935, seven months after the Executive order was issued, not only had the administrative machinery been organized but loan contracts exceeding $2¼ million had been negotiated with 11 cooperatives, for the construction of 1,940 miles of line to serve 8,286 rural homes. The current was turned on in the first REA-financed project—in Iowa—on December 15, 1935.

During 1936, according to REA's first annual report, more than 25,000 miles of line were erected and "over 110,000 farms received electrical service for the first time." Most of the loans were for financing power lines but, by mid-1937, 11 projects had been allotted funds to build generating plants.

The utilities were shocked out of their complacency by the passage of the Rural Electrification Act of 1936, with its preference to public and cooperative organizations. They then put on a burst of speed, "in an attempt to get the highest-profit-yield rural areas while the getting was still possible."[5] They cut down on their rate and other requirements, made a drive for the "cream" areas, and built "spite lines" through the heart of proposed cooperative territory in an effort to make cooperative development impracticable.

At the same time they opposed the passage of State enabling laws for cooperatives or endeavored to incorporate in them provisions that either "froze" the utility claims to territory they had no immediate intention of serving or otherwise hampered the cooperatives. When associations were formed, the utilities resorted to litigation and other means of keeping the cooperatives from getting into operation.

In spite of all the problems, by the end of April 1940, about $249 million had been earmarked in loans to 614 electric cooperatives, and some 483,000 families were already being served in 42 States.

Progress was halted by the war. For a time even the installation of new lines by existing cooperatives was forbidden, as it would involve the use of copper wire (a strategic commodity). Activity was resumed at the war's end, but on a smaller scale described in a later chapter.

Cooperatives and the TVA

Cooperatives entered only incidentally into the Tennessee Valley program, as its main purposes were the harnessing of the rivers tributary to the Tennessee, and the generation and distribution of power from their waters. The Tennessee Valley Authority, however, in its efforts to improve the economic condition of the people in the valley, gave encouragement to various types of cooperatives.

According to its 1938 annual report, among the cooperatives "assisting in its program" (i.e., distributing current generated at TVA dams) were 19 electricity associations with 3,814 miles of line and 20,911 patrons, several soil-conservation cooperatives, and about a dozen cold-storage associations. TVA had also rendered administrative assistance and even made loans to three area-wide associations; one of these, Southern Highlanders, is still in existence and maintains retail outlets in New York City and other places for the sale of handicraft articles produced in the valley.

Cooperatives of the Farm Security Program

The measures that finally evolved into the farm-security program covered three broad categories: Rural rehabilitation through loans and supervision; three planned suburban communities ("green-belt" towns);[8] and the "homestead" projects (subsistence homesteads, rural communities, and scattered farms). In the third group, the rural projects involved full-time farming, as contrasted with the part-time gardening in the subsistence homesteads.

By June 30, 1941, the FSA had under its supervision the 3 green-belt towns, 178 homestead projects (5 for stranded workers, 25 subsistence homesteads, 73 rural communities, and 75 projects of the scattered-farms type), 58 migratory-labor camps, and 69 defense relocation or housing projects. These were scattered virtually all over the United States, but by far the largest proportion was in the South and "dust-bowl" areas.

Cooperative Activities

From the first, the Farm Security Administration favored cooperative action. In all phases of the program, the participants were encouraged to work together in providing even the simplest services. The cooperatives that resulted were of varied types:

1. Informal service cooperatives. By 1943 some 21,271 FSA loans had been made to about 16,000 such service groups.

2. Rural rehabilitation cooperatives, whose purpose was the provision of goods or services to assist in the economic rehabilitation of the members. Such cooperatives numbered 4,129 by mid-1943. Most of them received from FSA only technical advice, not money.

3. Cooperatives at resettlement projects, numbering 126 in 1940.

Among the above three classes of cooperatives there were, according to FSA estimate, at least 135 that handled consumer goods or provided some consumer service and that therefore fall within the scope of the present history. Enterprises commonly carried on by them were a general store and gasoline filling station.

The consumers' cooperatives were small; nearly half had fewer than 50 members each and less than a fourth had at least 100 members (commonly regarded as the very minimum for efficient operation). Of the total number of members, 66.3 percent were white, 27.3 percent Negro, and 0.2 percent Indian; for the other 6.2 percent the race was not reported. Both white and colored were in membership in 14 associations, in 62 all were white, and in 24 all were colored; 15 associations consisted of Indians only.

As was natural for new businesses, some cooperatives incurred deficits during their first few years. Of these a considerable proportion were able to get on their feet eventually, whereas others had to be dissolved. Some organizations prospered from the beginning. The 1940 business for 104 cooperatives reporting exceeded $2½ million. Forty had a net gain of $172,000 and 64 a net loss of $462,000.

Cooperatives at Subsistence Homesteads

Subsistence-homesteads projects were provided for three groups: (1) Industrial workers in or near towns or cities where employment could normally be found, on at least a part-time basis, (2) industrial groups (miners and lumber workers) left stranded in rather isolated places by the exhaustion of natural resources, and (3) agricultural workers with at least part-time work outside the project.

Altogether 51 subsistence-homesteads projects were developed,[7] most of which were completed in 1935 and 1936, and some of which constituted entirely new communities. In 12 of these, cooperatives were organized either to supply the household needs of the residents or to operate industries for their employment.

Most of the industrial workers' projects were adjacent to employment opportunities. There were nine, however (including those for stranded workers) not so situated, and in which part-time employment therefore had to be provided. This posed a real problem.

It had been expected that private companies could be induced to build factories in or near the projects, but this proved a vain hope. Another attempted solution—factories owned and operated by the Government—was blocked by Congress, which prohibited the use of any appropriations for these purposes.

After several false starts, a combination of cooperative-private arrangements was adopted for the nine projects: The Government advanced loans for the erection of plants. The projects' industrial cooperatives (which held title to the plant and 49 percent of its stock) then leased the facilities to outside companies holding 51 percent of the stock and providing management and directorship.

One such enterprise was a tractor plant at Arthurdale, W. Va., which the industrial cooperative leased to American Cooperatives, Inc. The members of the latter were regional cooperatives that had previously had tractors manufactured in Michigan under a cost-plus arrangement.[8]

Another was at Jersey Homesteads (near Hightstown, N. J.) where seven regional wholesales[9] had representation on the board of Consumers Wholesale Clothiers—an organization for managing the women's clothing factory and distributing its products. (The arrangement was not very satisfactory, for the retail cooperative stores, depended upon as outlet for a considerable proportion of the output, did not provide a sufficient market, and the enterprise had to close down.)

The Bankhead project had only the industrial cooperative. All the others had additional associations to carry on various business activities. Thus, Skyline Farms Cooperative operated a retail store, filling station, farm-supply business, and potato-storage warehouse, besides marketing the farm produce grown on the project. The Penderlea Mutual Association had a store and gas station, and also did marketing. At Jersey Homesteads there were a cooperative store and tea room.

The cooperatives at the five stranded-groups projects undertook a great variety of projects. About 76 percent of the settlers there—939 of a total of 1,233—were members of the cooperatives at the end of 1940.

In the three "green" towns, the participation of the FSA was limited to providing commercial buildings, equipment, and fixtures, for lease. In each town a commercial organization was started and financed by the Consumer Distribution Corporation, founded by the late Edward A. Filene of Boston. It was understood that as soon as possible a genuinely cooperative organization would take over the business, subject to such supervision as was necessary to safeguard the corporation's loan until it should be repaid. By 1942 the transfer to cooperative operation had been made in all three towns.

Liquidation of Resettlement Program

Even as early as mid-1937, formidable opposition to the whole resettlement program had developed, on the ground that the projects and their enterprises were socialistic or even communistic or that they constituted unfair competition with private enterprise.

Pressure for immediate liquidation developed. Congress expressed its disapproval of the resettlement program in several measures cutting off funds for factories, for cooperative membership, for collective farming, etc.

The sale of houses to participants (begun in a small way as early as 1937) was speeded up, and the factories were disposed of in 1945-47. Liquidation of the entire resettlement program was practically complete by the end of 1951. All of the other farm-security programs were continued: Home-management service and loans for *individual* farm ownership, for production and family subsistence, for the provision of water facilities, rural housing, group services, and even to enable the farmers to join *existing* cooperatives. Gone were the collective farms, the rural communities, and the formation and financing of new cooperatives.

No FSA loans were made to cooperatives (except to provide water facilities) after June 30, 1943. By mid-1945, 113 of the 446 cooperatives (all types) to which loans had been made had repaid their loans in full. Those which had not shown "a reasonable chance for success" were being liquidated. Of 264 associations reporting on operations, 183 had made earnings in 1944; the others had combined losses of over $94,000. These figures constituted the last report on the *operations* of the FSA cooperatives.[10]

A year later, 163 associations had completely repaid their loans, and by mid-1947 a total of 212 had done so. Liquidation was going on in 119 cases. All the other cooperatives were making their payments in a satisfactory manner. No later reports of the Farmers Home Administration (successor to FSA) contain information on this point.

Distributive and marketing associations.—With the sale of the homestead and industrial properties, the cooperatives that had been started on the projects, in some cases under "forced draft," had begun to languish. All the cooperatives in the communities for stranded industrial workers had wound up their affairs by 1946. In several of the other industrial-homesteads projects the cooperative distributive associations held out for varying periods[11] and a few were still in operation at last reports.[12]

Cooperatives at migratory camps.—Cooperatives had been organized by the residents in at least seven of the FSA camps for migratory farm workers—five in California and one each in Arizona and Florida—during 1939-41. In the liquidation of the camp program, ordered by Congress to take place when county farm labor authorities so determined or 6 months after termination of World War II, the cooperatives disappeared. They were all out of business by the end of 1947.

Cooperatives at "green" towns.—All three "green" towns had had consumers' cooperatives since 1942. That in Greenhills, Ohio, originally had a meat and grocery store, drugstore, barber shop, beauty parlor, lunch counter, pressing service, and laundry-collection service. By 1948, both it and the association at Greendale, Wis., had lost to higher bidders the leases on some of the businesses previously operated. The Greenhills cooperative since that time has run only a drugstore and tavern. The Greendale association has a gasoline station, auto-repair garage, and tavern, having lost its grocery store, barber shop, and drugstore.

The story of the Greenbelt, Md., cooperative, now the leading nonfarm consumers' cooperative in the entire United States, is that of continuous expansion and success. Its record is the more notable because Maryland has never been an area with any extensive consumers' cooperative activity, and because of the top-down method of organizing.

The enterprise was financed in the beginning by Consumer Distribution Corporation in the amount of $50,000—$10,000 in share capital and $40,000 in a 10-year loan at 5 percent interest. CDC opened a food store, valet shop, drug store, gasoline filling station, barber shop, and movie theater.

The business was run under CDC management from October 1937 through December 1939. During this time the new residents were moving in, and the volume of business grew but slowly. But, by the end of 1939, 311 families (slightly over 50 percent) had joined the cooperative.

The CDC membership requirement having been met, the association began operating as a real cooperative at the beginning of 1940 and assumed the management of all the businesses, under the name, Greenbelt Consumer Services. It has had the advantages of excellent management,[13] wide-awake boards of directors, and a business monopoly in a self-contained community somewhat removed from other settlements.

Its sales passed the million-dollar mark in 1943, at which time its membership had risen to 1,283.

Hardly a year (except during the war) but has seen the opening of a new facility. In addition to the Greenbelt enterprises, it now operates a food store and drug store in Takoma Park, Md., and a "general" store, a service station, and a 24-hour pharmacy in Wheaton—all the last word in equipment and layout.

By the end of 1954 the cooperative had over 5,500 members, 75 percent of whom were Government employees. Its business for the year amounted to slightly over $5,450,000. Some $55,400 was returned on patronage in addition to 5 percent interest on share capital. Ten percent of net earnings was set aside for the employees' retirement fund, approved in 1953.

The FSA Program in Review

Taken as a whole the resettlement and farm-security program constituted, in the opinion of the author, the most hopeful and constructive measure for rural underprivileged people undertaken in her lifetime. Anyone who had the opportunity of following the social and economic rehabilitation of some of this country's poor, especially the agricultural laborers of the South, could not help being impressed with the worth of the program.

True, it was costly in terms of money and possibly sometimes extravagant, but a large part of the cost (especially in house construction) was due to the employment of not-too-efficient relief labor, the use of good materials, and the fact that, as the program was breaking new ground in many respects, it was necessarily experimental. The ideas that did not work out nevertheless had to be paid for.

However, as FSA pointed out, "the resettlement projects were not launched as a real-estate investment." They accomplished their purpose: They had given employment in a time of industrial stagnation, had added to the value of rural communities, and had made "down-and-outers" into useful tax-paying citizens. And the experiments in housing produced "the most economic yet adequate farm home" yet devised.[14]

It must be remembered that to many the very foundations of society appeared to be crumbling, and some economists even thought that for literally millions of our wage earners full-time employment could never be provided in the future. The varying directions and policies that caused so many FSA mistakes and so much of the waste were the inevitable result of the differences in views and objectives of the various forces sponsoring the program and of the lack of definition in the beginning.

Both the rehabilitation-loan program and the housing part of the subsistence homesteads were, in my opinion, a complete success. The subsistence phase did not continue, in most cases, as planned. The program had begun in a period of almost complete economic prostration, with millions of unemployed. During the remainder of the depression, the subsistence gardens furnished a substantial, and much-needed, part of the participants' living. As employment conditions improved, there was a great deal of turnover in the projects and many of the original residents were succeeded by families of higher income level, selected (in accordance with changed policies) rather with a view to their ability to keep up payments to the Federal Government than to assist low-income families. The residents with industrial experience tended to spend a greater proportion of their time in paid employment and less on the subsistence gardens.

Among the cooperatives, the agricultural ones seem to have been quite successful on the whole. In their first 2 years of operation, 21 of 161 grain-marketing associations had already repaid their loans in full. As for the industrial and consumers' cooperatives in the urban workers' projects, even the most ardent cooperator must admit that most of them were not a success, although individual associations expanded and prospered. There were several reasons for this:

1. The cooperatives as well as the projects themselves suffered from the lack, from the beginning, of a clear Congressional definition, almost continual reorganizations of administrative machinery,[15] numerous shifts of authority, and changes in administrative and Congressional policy, with resulting frustration and insecurity for the settlers.

2. The members were poverty-stricken sharecroppers, tenants, and laborers with no previous acquaintance with each other, no knowledge of cooperative methods, unused to working in cooperative groups, and with no idea of how to run a business enterprise or what could reasonably be expected in results.

3. The cooperatives were often promoted by well-meaning, paternalistic Government employees in the Farm Security

Administration who believed sincerely in the efficacy of the cooperative method, rather than resulting from action by the FSA participants to satisfy a felt need.

4. In most cases, since the homestead project was usually at some distance from markets and shopping centers, there was an immediate need for such facilities on the project. The cooperative therefore had to be started before an adequate groundwork had been laid in the form of cooperative understanding.

5. Since the enterprise was financed (and in some cases, overfinanced) by Government funds, the members lacked the incentive to thrift and careful management that would have been present had the money come from their own pockets.

6. The tendency to irresponsibility was increased by the tight controls deemed necessary to safeguard the Federal investment, resulting in the members' inclination to let the Government, therefore, run the whole thing. In most cases, it is doubtful if the majority of the members ever acquired the feeling that this was *their* business.

The whole procedure was in striking contrast to that under the REA program. The latter, it is true, dealt with participants of a higher economic and educational level. But the REA had the advantage of continuous progress, under a single agency, in one well-defined direction. The whole REA plan was built on a foundation of education in cooperative practices and business and technical procedure, gradually diminishing as the individual associations gained experience. This pattern of advice and education, with continuing emphasis on increasing local responsibility, was the key to its success.

Burgeoning in the Sun

Probably never in the history of this country had there been more sympathetic understanding of the philosophy and aims of the cooperative movement on the part of Government agencies and their officials than was manifest in the Roosevelt Administration. The consumer and his viewpoint were, for the first time, given consideration in various ways. Cooperatives were extended preference in the development of electric power for rural areas and were used also by the Tennessee Valley Authority. They were encouraged in all phases of the farm-security program—most of which was rural—and given direct Government loans.

The nonfarm distributive cooperatives received no direct aid or encouragement aside from the three measures that safeguarded their existence, as cooperatives, under the NRA codes. Nevertheless, they benefitted from the friendly climate of the New Deal and from the publicity, whether favorable or not, attendant upon those of its programs that involved the use of the cooperative method. The old-established procedures and philosophies appeared to have failed and the times called for bold new experiments. Cooperation, new to most Americans though old in point of time, thus received its mead of attention along with other ideas, and made the most of it.

The results were new converts to the cooperative "idea," expansion into new lines, and perhaps most significant of all, the evidence of the increasing maturity of the movement shown by the meshing of local associations into central organizations for wholesale supply and service, and by the wholesales' moves into service and production—all described in a subsequent chapter. For the first time the cooperative movement in this country could be said to have become moderately well organized —strongly in some areas, still feebly in others.

Chapter 21.—ENDOWED COOPERATIVE PROMOTION

The Consumer Distribution Corporation

The Consumer Distribution Corporation was organized in June 1935 by the late Edward A. Filene (merchant of Boston), with a capital of a million dollars and with Mr. Filene as president and only stockholder. Herbert E. Evans was vice-president and personnel officer and Percy S. Brown was secretary-treasurer.[1]

Mr. Filene's plan, which he recognized might entail a "difficult promotional job," was to start a Nation-wide chain of department stores that would eventually be taken over and operated cooperatively by associations of local residents.

Functions contemplated for CDC were furnishing top and local management, central purchasing, and informational, public-relations, and other services. It would "assume direct managerial control" over the local department stores for the first 5 years, while local responsibility was being developed. Then ownership would begin to revert to the members. At the end of 10 years it was expected that CDC would automatically come under the complete control of locally owned stores, along with "any funds that have accumulated during this period."

Unfortunately, the plan did not work out just as Mr. Filene had intended. The executive director, Flint Garrison, having studied the program, resigned,[2] saying that a department store was not practical "as an agency of consumers' cooperative activity at the present time." He pointed out that department stores serve mainly people in the upper income levels; that they require a very wide range of merchandise to operate successfully, but purchases from them account for only 14 percent of the average family budget as contrasted with 30-40 percent for food; and that department stores can not be used economically for food distribution.

In the light of this, the program was shelved and the organization undertook, instead, the training of cooperative managers and employees and extension of financial aid to existing cooperatives to enable them to modernize their premises for more efficient operation. In line with this new policy, CDC sponsored (with Rochdale Institute and Eastern Cooperative Wholesale) the formation of the Council for Cooperative Business Training.

The Loan Program

The first loan was made to the CDC organization at Greenbelt, Md., in mid-September 1937, in the amount of $40,000.

Information on the full extent of the loan program is not available. However, at least 34 local cooperatives and 3 regional wholesales are known to have received loans from CDC up to the beginning of 1942. At the end of October 1941, loans outstanding amounted to nearly $184,000; by the end of July 1942 the total had been reduced to about $96,000. In addition, outright grants had been made for educational purposes to Rochdale Institute and to the Cooperative League of the USA through 1940. In 1943 the Good Will Fund (another Filene-endowed organization) appropriated $40,000 for cooperative field work, the money to be under the trusteeship of Central States Cooperatives and Eastern Cooperative Wholesale.

The relatively small success of this phase is indicated by the fact that, of the 34 local associations known to have received loans, 19 were out of business by June 1952 and 4 others by the end of 1954. The amount of possible loss to CDC is not known.

The loan and other activities of CDC were discontinued during the war years of 1943-45.

Department-Store Program

Resuming after peace was declared, CDC took up again Mr. Filene's idea of a department-store chain, although Mr. Garrison's warnings were still valid. It planned to start with three stores, with additional ones later.

The locations chosen were Arlington, Va., Irvington, N. J., and Providence, R. I., and they were to be opened in that order. The reasons for the selection of the last two are not readily apparent, as neither had been the scene of any previous co-operative activity, although Providence had some active credit unions which favored the store project.

The Arlington store was opened in March 1948, in the Shirlington shopping center. The Providence store was opened next, in November. The Irvington store was postponed indefinitely and never materialized.

Shirlington Cooperative Department Store[3]

Although a market survey of local shopping habits in Arlington was supposed to have been made in advance, the merchandise at time of opening was of a type that offended and alienated many of the people who would otherwise have become patrons. The store thus got off to a bad start. It had a CDC-appointed manager, but was operated under a general-management contract calling for a monthly fee of some $2,000—a fact that, by itself, was enough to cancel out the probability of operation in the black, unless volume of sales was very large.

The planned budget submitted by the CDC general manager showed expected sales of about $1½ million per year, an estimated net margin of 5.56 percent, and a patronage refund of about 4 percent. The actual volume ran from 45 to 65 percent of the budgeted amount. From the beginning the overhead was too high in relation to sales. In only 2 of 5 years' operation were earnings made, and then their maximum was about 3 percent; the accumulated loss was over $200,000.

In 1951 and 1952, CDC waived payment of interest on the preferred stock it held, and this made possible the payment of patronage refunds in one year and of interest on the local members' common stock in the other.

There was increasing friction between the local cooperators and the CDC general management.

Just before the 1953 annual meeting, a letter from CDC informed the members that, since the store had not become "in any substantial measure" locally owned, the CDC board had decided to exercise its right to fill four of the five directorships becoming vacant.

At the meeting, the store's president, Glen B. Wall, reviewed the situation. Among his points of criticism were the loss in value of shares, making it impossible to obtain new investors, the early and very expensive mistakes,[4] and CDC'S unwillingness to delegate any real responsibility to the members.[5]

The membership meeting was unable to get any report on the year's operations.[6]

During the next several months, a local committee explored what could be done to save the situation. Nothing came of this, for CDC, after rejecting two cooperative proposals, sold out in August to a Washington department store which planned to operate the store as a branch.[7] There was no loss to the stockholders, for CDC voted to redeem all the common stock—about $63,000.

Rhode Island Cooperative, Inc.

The Providence store moved into a big building erected for it by the Good Will Fund at a considerable distance from the center of the city, on a main highway. This location was selected in the belief that it would become the nucleus of a shopping center. The section failed to grow as anticipated, the parking space was inadequate, and pedestrian traffic was scanty. The patronage was therefore decidedly below that necessary for successful operation.

Late in 1951, after some 3 years' losing operation, the building was sold and the store moved downtown, where CDC had leased the basement and part of the first floor of a building. (CDC absorbed the greater part of the losses—over $600,000 in all—and even purchased the shares of members who decided at this juncture that they wished to withdraw.) Only the clothing, shoe, and appliance departments were retained.

Even this drastic move failed to put the business on its feet, however, and the store was closed and the association dissolved in the fall of 1953.

Program in Retrospect

Thus ended another noble experiment which, with the best of intentions on the part of all concerned—but with some rather appalling errors—simply did not work out.

In both cases initial mistakes got the enterprises off to a poor start. The "expert" management that was supposed to be supplied from CDC headquarters proved not to be so expert after all—and far too expensive. Although the experience in Greenbelt had shown the advantages of early transfer of authority to local people, in neither of the department stores was this done. Providence had no body of consumers' cooperative members to support the store, only credit-union members who ordinarily have little or no sense of kinship with consumers' cooperation and failed to rally around in sufficient numbers.

Arlington (part of the Washington metropolitan area, with thousands of members of various types of cooperatives) also was unable to obtain sufficient volume, as a result of early mistakes, inability to sell the store's worthless shares, and local participation limited to advice only (not real operation).

It is a pity that such a well-meant program should have ended thus. The department-store experience provided another demonstration that cooperatives cannot be set up from outside, without widespread local participation and control, and hope to succeed.

However, all of the wholesales and a number of the local associations assisted with loans were enabled to regain a sound footing. The loan program therefore may be said to have been beneficial, especially in view of the Greenbelt success.

The closing of the department stores also ended the CDC cooperative program, as the Filene endowment had been exhausted by that time. The only present activity consists of closing out the few local loans outstanding.[8]

Chapter 22.—LOCAL COOPERATION, 1936-41

By 1936 there were store associations in practically every State in the Union. Their greatest concentration was still in the North Central region, with a smaller growth in New England, the Middle Atlantic States, California, and Washington State. Petroleum cooperatives were most numerous in the Mississippi and Missouri Valleys, with a few in the Mountain States and Texas, almost none in the East. A few bakery associations were still operating in Massachusetts, New Jersey, and New York. Cooperative housing was concentrated in New York City. The South, aside from a group of farmers' cooperatives handling gasoline and fuel oil, had almost no consumers' cooperatives except rural electric-power associations and credit unions.

The retail associations were still small both in membership and in business volume. The 1936 sales of the stores had climbed only to about seven-eighths of the 1929 level, but that of the petroleum associations was nearly 70 percent *above* 1929. Over 70 percent of the retail distributive associations reporting for the year had had net earnings; slightly over 7 percent had losses. Patronage refunds were returned by 38.4 percent of the stores and 62.6 percent of the petroleum cooperatives.

Organized labor was beginning to take an interest in cooperation again, as were also church groups. Farmers' cooperatives were increasingly handling groceries, household supplies, work clothing, and fuel, and thus coming into the consumer group.

The last half of the decade was one of cooperative advance, with the birth rate in 1937 exceeding that of any previous single year and business volume holding up in spite of the "recession." The year 1940 was the "most solidly successful" period in 20 years from the business standpoint, and several hundred new associations were organized.

A modernization campaign, to tackle a recognized weakness —that of unattractive and poorly designed quarters—was sparked by a committee (headed by William Torma) authorized by the 1940 Cooperative Congress. National Cooperatives, the Cooperative League, and the Consumer Distribution Corporation had representation on the committee. With some financial assistance from CDC, the program brought forth great improvements in cooperative merchandising practices and premises throughout the United States.

As the supply situation became more acute, consumers more and more looked toward cooperatives as a source. Most of the new cooperatives were stores—among them stores for the residents of migratory-labor camps. There were also a few among the workers in the National Youth Administration, during the period it was in existence.

Chapter 23.—THE GOLDEN AGE OF COOPERATIVE FEDERATION

The decade of, roughly, the 1930's was a period unparalleled as regards coordination of cooperative activities. Not only was a national wholesale organized, but an unprecedented number of both regional and district wholesales was started, as well as federations to provide specific services or manufacture certain products. There were also in existence, by 1941, numerous noncommercial federations, of which five were Nation-wide in scope,[1] 12 were regional or State-wide, and 23 covered a district, county, or city area. The last group were more or less informal, used for exchange of experience or fostering of joint action, and often meeting only sporadically and rather inactive between times.

A National Cooperative Wholesale

In view of the resurgence of regional wholesaling toward the end of the 1920-30 decade and the many new associations that had been formed, circumstances seemed propitious for another Nation-wide wholesale. However, this time the leaders had in mind, not warehousing but collective contracting for those commodities handled by the regionals in quantity sufficient to provide both savings and control of quality.

At an exploratory meeting called by Howard Cowden in November 1932, it became clear that most of the interested associations wanted an organization that both urban and farmer wholesales could join. The meeting therefore authorized articles of incorporation and bylaws for a general cooperative wholesale.

National Cooperatives was incorporated on February 23, 1933 under the Indiana Corporation Law. It was explained that that law offered more latitude for a general wholesale than would a cooperative statute; cooperative features could be written into the bylaws. Also, voting in proportion to patronage was desired, which cooperative law would not permit.

Five of the organizations at the preliminary meeting were charter members—Central Cooperative Wholesale, Farmers

Union Central Exchange, Midland Cooperative Oil Co., Union Oil Co., Cooperative, and Farm Bureau Oil Co.[2] I. H. Hull[3] was elected president and Howard Cowden secretary.

In order to qualify for membership, a wholesale had to have a volume of at least $100,000 a year and be doing at least 75 percent of its business through cooperatives; must submit a map of its trading territory; and must subscribe for a minimum of two $100 shares of common stock. Each member was to have one vote, plus an additional vote for every $5,000 in patronage of National (but up to 1937 at least, the one-member, one-vote practice was adhered to). A two-thirds favorable vote of the directors was required for admission of new members.

The bylaws provided that members must refrain from soliciting business from affiliates of other members. To form or sell to a cooperative in another member's territory was regarded as "unfair competition." At the 1935 annual meeting the bylaws were so amended that the "competitive" clause bound the members to refrain from soliciting "in any manner" local associations doing business with any other members of National or associations in process of organization by a National member "within the boundaries recognized" as such member's trading area.

Early Activities and Growth

National joined the Cooperative League toward the end of 1934. In 1935 the two bodies formed a joint committee to work for closer coordination between them.

Not until the fall of 1936 did National have an office of its own. When it opened one in Chicago, in October, Ivan Lanto (previously head buyer for Central Cooperative Wholesale) became the first manager.

Electrical appliances had been added to the contractual lines by 1937. At that time the commodities for which purchase contracts were being made were, in order of importance, gasoline and motor oil;[4] tires, tubes, batteries, and auto accessories; radios and electrical appliances; farm equipment; uniforms for cooperative employees; and bindery twine. No food products were contracted for as yet.

A full-time office was opened in 1939 and in the same year Mr. Lanto resigned as manager and was succeeded by Stanley

Colburn. (In 1941 Manager Colburn, in turn, resigned and Toik A. Tenhune[5] became acting manager.) The office of chairman of the board was created and A. J. Hayes (general manager of Central Cooperative Wholesale) was selected to fill it.

In the legislative field, National had been instrumental in obtaining amendments to the Farm Credit Act, first to permit farmers' purchasing (as well as marketing) associations to borrow under the act and, next, to raise from 10 to 15 percent the allowed proportion of nonfarm members. National likewise endorsed the bill for a cooperative law for the District of Columbia, passed in 1940.

During this period the membership had been increasing steadily; now 12 regional wholesales had joined.[6] The organization, however, was still small financially. Its statement, as of September 30, 1941, showed assets of only $67,000; reserves totaled $7,734.

Improvement of Quality

Cooperatives have always been concerned with improving the quality of goods and thus assuring that their members receive the best grade available for the money. This and the elimination of adulteration were among the declared objectives of the Rochdale Pioneers 110 years ago.

Labels for Co-op Goods

Identification of commodities with the cooperative movement through special labels or brand names is a device of long standing in this country. In the first years of the century, the California Rochdale Co., a cooperative wholesale in San Francisco, conceived the idea of having packed for it under its own brand, "Rochdale," such items as extracts, baking powder, syrup, spices, and coffee. This practice was continued after the wholesale was taken over by the Pacific Cooperative League. However, it is believed that little or no attempt was made to control quality; the label was probably a trade device, to attract business and to identify the goods with the cooperative.

It was reported at the 1924 Cooperative Congress that Soo Cooperative Mercantile Association (Sault Ste. Marie, Mich.) was using a "cooperative" label on the bread baked in its bakery, as a means of spreading the cooperative idea. And the Central States Cooperative Wholesale Society, until its demise in 1925, used both union-label goods and its own label as far as possible.

A number of midwestern cooperatives of the current movement also made use of their own labels. Thus, Cooperative Central Exchange (Superior, Wis.) began using labels with red, blue, and white stars and the hammer and sickle in 1921. The first item to appear on its market was red-label coffee. These labels were discarded as part of the repudiation of the Communist influence, in 1930, and an oval-shaped "co-op" label was adopted in their stead. In 1931 the latter was registered at the U. S. Patent Office as a trade-mark for CCE canned and packaged groceries.[7]

In the meantime an affiliate of Midland Cooperative Wholesale, The People's Cooperative Oil Co. (now Federated Cooperatives), at Jackson, Minn., had developed a label for lubricating oil, which it registered in January 1926. Its design, using clasped hands for the hyphen in "co-op," was transferred to Midland Cooperative Wholesale in 1932.[8] In the same year Midland began to use the label on car batteries manufactured expressly for it.

"Co-op" was also being used on the gasoline delivery trucks of Cooperative Services at Maple, Wis., as early as 1930.

Consumers Cooperative Association (then known as Union Oil Co., Cooperative) had likewise registered a co-op label, for use on auto tires, in 1932.

The next step was to include on the label some description of the product in the package or can. It is to be feared, however, that some of the early labels were examples of advertising and puff, rather than of description of tested quality; and that fact was called to the wholesales' attention not only by members but also by persons outside the movement.

The criticism had a healthy effect. Cooperative buyers began to be more exacting in their purchases, and reliability of sources of supply became a greater consideration.

The system of individual contracting naturally made for a great deal of variety not only in label design but also in quality of merchandise offered to cooperators. After the organization of National Cooperatives in 1933, pressure grew for uniformity of labeling and specifications. Accordingly, a series of meetings was held which resulted in the adoption, in the spring of 1939, of uniform labels for the 600 or more items then being packed under co-op labels.

At the same time a set of standards was adopted. Three grades were established: A, top grade, bearing a red label; B, second grade, bearing a blue label; and C, third grade, bearing a green label. On the 28-odd items for which there were Government specifications, the goods had to measure up in each case to the top requirements for the grade.[9] The labels gave in most cases not only amounts but also a description of the contents and their required condition.

The regional wholesales then assigned their label rights to National and it thus became sole trade-mark owner and custodian of the "co-op label." It also owns the molds from which "co-op" tires are made.

Few of the items that carry the label and the notation, "packed for National Cooperatives, Inc.," are actually bought by National. Use of the label is delegated to the member regionals, provided the quality conforms to standards. Practically all label items are obtained from regular manufacturers and suppliers or producer cooperatives, under cooperative specification.

Although there is still room for improvement, it is my personal belief that the labeling and truth-in-merchandise policy of the consumers' cooperative movement is one of its real social contributions.

Regional Wholesale Expansion

The business of the cooperative wholesales held up well after the depression began. Not until 1931 did volume begin to decline, but this continued through 1932, when the lowest point in cooperative wholesale business was reached—70 percent of the 1929 figure. Curiously enough, in 1933 (the trough of the depression) sales began to climb again, and this upward trend continued through 1937, when the volume reached the highest point recorded up to that time. In 1938 a slight decrease occurred in money sales (but not in physical volume of goods), which was more than recovered in 1939.

Net earnings and patronage refunds had shown a slight dip in 1931 and 1932, but in 1933 and 1934 that setback was more than overcome and each succeeding year through 1939 showed a higher level than before. Even during the five depression years, 1930-34, regional wholesales handling consumer goods continued to make refunds on members' patronage, to a total of over $825,000. In the next 7-year period—up to the outbreak of World War II—their patronage refunds exceeded $8 million.

Much of the increased business was due to the increase in number of wholesales. From 8 handling consumer goods in 1929, by 1937 the number had risen to 22. These new organizations were scattered in 12 States. All of them got off to a good start. Several others were not so fortunate.[10]

The wholesales were also developing a variety of services for their members: auditing, advice on merchandising, store lay-out, etc., technical training of managers and clerks, and even management service for ailing affiliates.

Right up to the outbreak of World War II the wholesales went on expanding their services, erecting new headquarters and warehouse buildings, and enlarging all their activities. Their business success had also resulted in attracting as members many new local associations or existing ones hitherto unaffiliated with any wholesale. In 1929, fewer than 400 retail cooperatives had been members of consumers' regional wholesales. By the end of 1941, the 23 regionals handling consumer goods had 3,104 associations in membership. In the same period, wholesale volume had risen from $11 million to $97¼ million.[11]

District Commercial Organizations

In Michigan, Minnesota, and Wisconsin certain business enterprises of less than State-wide coverage had also been organized. These were federal associations supplying goods or services that the retail cooperatives preferred not to carry themselves. They make relatively small, but regular, earnings year after year. Their performance is not spectacular, but they seem to fill a real need in their areas.

They are composed of retail cooperatives. Their memberships in 1951 ranged from 7 to 104. Most of them do a business of less than half a million dollars a year.[12] Their combined volume for 1951 was about $6½ million. Earnings were nearly a quarter of a million dollars, and patronage refunds exceeded $164,000.

Federations for Service

Many of the regional and district wholesales have service departments. In addition, a number of special service federations have been organized. In some cases the service association, although organizationally independent, is a supplement to a regional wholesale.

The membership of the federations consists of local (retail) associations. The single exception is National Cooperative Finance Association, the members of which are regional wholesales; although in nominal existence since 1943, it has never got into actual operation.

As in the case of the district wholesales, the service federations are, with two exceptions, all in the Midwest. They provide a variety of services, such as auditing, funerals, business and tax advice, finance, etc. They are all small. Their total business in 1951 was only $2,517,000. Earnings totaled $57,000 (many of them do not try to earn a profit) and patronage refunds amounted to nearly $39,000. They are owned by nearly 900 local associations.

Federations for Production

Beginning in the middle thirties a whole series of productive federations was formed. Unlike the service associations, the productive federations were in most cases organized by regional wholesales. Generally they were started to produce commodities for which a single regional could not supply sufficient patronage or which it could not finance by itself. They are further described in Chapter 25.

The Cooperative League in Maturity

The Cooperative League began the 1930-40 decade with the congress at Superior, Wis., that exiled the Communists. In the remainder of the session and in the ensuing years a new harmony was attained that more than made up for the loss of the comparatively few Communist-dominated associations.

On December 16, 1930, the League officially launched Clusa Service, with William Hyde as director, to act as broker in obtaining employee bonds and various types of insurance for cooperatives.

League members at the end of the year included 140 associations with an annual business of $18 million.

The attendance at the eighth biennial congress, held in New York City, September 26-28, 1932, was limited by finances. The depression had already been under way for some 3 years, and the local cooperatives and their members were feeling the effects. The League, however, had gained considerably in membership and now included 458 associations.[13]

Cedric Long had died during 1931. For reasons of economy Dr. Warbasse doubled as president and executive secretary during the remainder of the year. Mr. Long was succeeded by Oscar Cooley[14] who served during 1932 and part of 1933. Early in 1934, Eugene R. Bowen was appointed to the position.[15]

By 1934, in spite of adverse economic conditions, the number of League affiliates remained at 450, with an estimated 160,000 individual members. With the accession of National Cooperatives (bringing indirect affiliation of its regional members and their membership), the League represented 1,498 associations and 500,000 individual cooperators.

The congress of that year was held in Chicago, October 18-20. It revealed a considerable increase in participation by farmers' organizations and recognition of certain common interests of producer and consumer cooperatives. The treasurer's report contained the good news that, for 1933-34, for the first time in the League's history, the budget had been met entirely from receipts from the member organizations.

This congress directed the formation of a Cooperative News Service, which was accordingly started before the end of the year.

Broadening of Membership and Coverage

An organization chart, issued in 1933, had shown the membership of the League as consisting of the three district leagues, 6 regional wholesales, 4 retail associations directly affiliated, and 17 fraternal members.

Dr. and Mrs. James P. Warbasse at 25th Anniversary Dinner, 1941

I. H. HULL

HOWARD A. COWDEN

EDWIN G. CORT

PERRY L. GREEN

Of the regional wholesales, only Eastern Cooperative Wholesale was entirely urban and nonfarm in character. All the others were composed entirely or preponderantly of farmers' cooperatives.

This pointed up a membership shift that had been in process since the latter 1920's. Even as late as 1932, the majority of the members of League affiliates were industrial workers. By the mid-1930's a majority were farm people.

Along with this change had gone a broadening of the League's definition of "consumers' cooperatives," tacitly accepted but not specifically formulated. Originally this term—and the League's membership—had included only those cooperatives handling consumer goods, i.e., food, clothing, and other items of family use, or providing consumer services. It had by now been relaxed to include all purchasing done by farmers' organizations, whether of purely family supplies or of goods used in the productive business of the farm.

Internal Differences

The League had long been making friendly gestures toward the agricultural cooperative movement. This extension of definition, however, was largely the idea of the new secretary, E. R. Bowen, and was due partly to his urge to "build faster" both the cooperative movement and the League.

Speaking to the 1934 Cooperative Congress, Mr. Bowen expressed the opinion that previously only "the simple matter of a difference in phraseology" had separated the farmers' and industrial workers' cooperatives. The former used the term "cooperative purchasing" and the latter "consumers' cooperation." According to Mr. Bowen, the phrases meant "one and the same thing. Let us accept that once and for all."

Under the new definition many organizations came in as members that previously could not have qualified. During the next few years several additional farmers' wholesales affiliated. Their influx increased the size and influence of the League, but it also resulted in some dilution of the orthodox Rochdale viewpoint that had characterized the League.

There was now in evidence in the membership some willingness to condone a certain amount of top-down promotion, financing, and control; an emphasis on centralization and the purely business aspects of cooperation; and the placing of somewhat less stress on the cooperative enlightenment of members.

Dr. Warbasse felt it his duty to combat what he regarded as unsound tendencies. Partly as a result of these basic differences, an antagonism between him and the new secretary developed, and a backstage struggle that grew more and more bitter. Both men were convinced of the rightness of their stand and, accordingly, were unyielding. As time went on, the affair also became one of personalities. Factions developed, each side attracting not only adherents on the basis of cooperative policy but also those who disliked or had been antagonized by the opponent.

The League and the Farmers

Nine other regionals had, by the end of 1935, affiliated with the League either indirectly (as a result of their membership in National Cooperatives) or directly, bringing the total to 15.

This was probably the high point of farmer affiliation. To some extent it represented on their part a certain softening of the purely producer viewpoint and an accompanying acceptance of the concept of the farmer as a consumer. In several cases this was only skin deep, however, denoting the attitude of progressive leaders rather than the conversion of the rank and file of their membership.

The 1936 Cooperative Congress, held at Columbus, Ohio, October 8-10, was characterized by Secretary Bowen as having "by far the largest attendance and the largest representation ever recorded at any Cooperative Congress in the United States."

Of the 21 directors of the League, 7 were now representative of the farmers. Prominent among them were the following:

> Howard A. Cowden, of farmer background, who was a wholehearted convert to consumer cooperation and who was instrumental in changing the name of the wholesale of which he was president to Consumer Cooperative Association in 1935.
>
> I. H. Hull, general manager of the Indiana Farm Bureau Cooperative Association, whose acceptance of the consumer viewpoint was concurred in only reluctantly and temporarily by his constituency and finally rejected.

R. N. Benjamin, of the Pennsylvania Farm Bureau Cooperative Association, whose views were also in advance of his followers, but who remained on the League board, as an active supporter, for some time after his organization had withdrawn from membership.

Murray D. Lincoln, then president of the Ohio Farm Bureau Cooperative Association, through whose influence both the wholesale and the Farm Bureau insurance companies were to become great forces in the consumers' cooperative movement in the United States.[16]

The new League viewpoint regarding "consumers' cooperation" was made official in a definition adopted by its executive committee in August 1937: "Consumers' cooperation as defined *in its broadest terms* [author's italics] is understood to include all joint purchasing and production of goods, foods, or services by ultimate users[17] organized on the basis of the Rochdale principles."

Further growth in League membership was reported at the Cooperative Congress of 1938 (held in Kansas City, October 12-14). No member of the League had failed during the past 9 years.

Removal to Chicago, and Other Changes

Removal of League headquarters from New York City to Chicago (a more central location, where National Cooperatives had its offices) had been under debate since midyear. Here again, the president and secretary were at odds, the former being against and the latter for the move. At its November meeting, the board voted to move to that city the executive office and the departments having to do with development, education (except Rochdale Institute), commodities, services, insurance, and finance. The Institute and Bureau of Cooperative Medicine were to remain in New York City.

In June 1940 Clusa Service (League insurance agency) was transferred to become a department of Eastern Cooperative Wholesale, and early in the autumn a "research and information" office was opened in Washington, D. C., with John Carson as director.[18]

The 1940 *Congress*

At the 1940 Cooperative Congress, held in Chicago, October 16-18, the executive secretary reported faster progress than in any two preceding years, but nevertheless headed his address: "Cooperators! Build Faster." The president reported that the League now had 2,175 affiliates with 1,116,000 members.

One of the many resolutions of this congress expressed the gratitude and the "deep and abiding affection" of the cooperative movement for Dr. Warbasse.

Retirement of Dr. Warbasse

The event of 1941 that overshadowed all others was the resignation of Dr. Warbasse as president of the League, after 25 years of service in that office. Tribute was paid to him in testimonial dinners in various parts of the country. He continued in active service on the League board for several years but thereafter withdrew increasingly from active participation in League affairs. The Cooperative Congress of 1944, at which he was chairman of the session on world cooperatives, was the last one graced by his presence.[19]

He was succeeded as President by Murray D. Lincoln, who has held the office since that time.

Decade's Accomplishments

The decade had witnessed in the commercial field the formation of 6 new service federations, 8 new district wholesales, 14 new regionals, and a new Nation-wide supply agency (National Cooperatives).

In addition, not only had the regional wholesales been establishing departments or subsidiaries for the production of such things as lubricating oil, grease, insecticides, and refined petroleum products, but 6 productive federations had come into being. The latter were producing flour, feed, fertilizer, and printed matter.

Here at last could be seen the first outshoots of the reach toward the self-sufficiency that has been the goal of the Rochdale cooperative movement since its inception.

In the educational or noncommercial phase of cooperation, there was no doubt that the League's prestige and influence in the cooperative movement suffered from the backstage struggle for power that divided the board (and to some extent, the movement) into factions. Some farmer organizations that had joined or been attracted by the League's overtures were alienated. Between 1935 and 1941 the number of affiliated farmer wholesales dropped from 13 to 7. The danger was recognized, and some of the League's most earnest friends were seriously concerned.

Nevertheless, the decade had produced a number of gains for the national body. Its membership expanded from 140 associations with 125,000 members in 1930 to 2,175 associations with 1,115,500 members in 1940. By far the greater part of the increase was due to the accession of the agricultural cooperatives brought in through the efforts of E. R. Bowen (though whether all of these had been won over to complete acceptance of the consumer philosophy was open to question).

The tacit broadening of the definition of consumers' cooperation became official with the board action of August 1937 and, perhaps inevitably, the make-up of the League board became overwhelmingly representative of cooperative management and the agricultural interests.

The League was pursuing vigorous programs for students and young cooperators, it continued to favor closer relations with the labor movement (in spite of the recognized conservatism of the farmer members in this regard), and naturally it was also concerned with closer working relations with agricultural cooperatives.

It had finally become a federation of central, not local, cooperatives and, a crowning achievement, it had at last become self-supporting. As a federation of federations, it was extending its influence increasingly to phases of cooperation outside the purely distributive field that had been its main preoccupation for its first 15 years or more. As evidence of its authoritative position as the keystone of the whole consumers' cooperative movement, it now had affiliation (as fraternal or full members) insurance associations, national organizations of the medical-care, students', and credit union movements, and a national recreation association. It had, on the whole, cause for satisfaction.

Chapter 24.—COOPERATIVES IN WORLD WAR II

The Local Cooperatives

For cooperatives, as for other businesses, the onset of war brought new problems arising from wartime restrictions and regulations. The quota system (under which supplies were based on the volume of the previous year) was especially hard on associations whose business was growing. The lack of manpower was also serious for cooperatives, in view of their preference for employees with some knowledge of cooperative philosophy. All during the war one of their greatest difficulties was that of obtaining and keeping trained workers, especially for more responsible jobs.[1]

One of the first results of wartime shortages was the closing of branch service stations by many of the petroleum cooperatives —even those of farmer membership (with larger rations). The strictly urban associations, particularly those on the East Coast where rations were unusually low, were in serious difficulties as volume abruptly dropped below the point necessary to carry the overhead. In the cities, only a few cooperative stations lasted out the war period. Rural petroleum cooperatives diversified into side lines such as groceries, farm supplies, farm machinery, auto and machinery repair, etc.

From the first, the cooperatives advocated and supported Nation-wide rationing, to insure equitable distribution of the supplies available and to prevent hoarding. They also urged consumer representation on all rationing boards, and offered their services in safeguarding the consumer interest. The cooperatives' war support was the more remarkable in view of their previous pacifist stand and their traditional hatred of war. They assisted in drives for war bonds and for needed war materials, and some of their factories worked on war contracts for the Federal Government.

New Associations

In 1942 the cooperative wholesales were trying to discourage the opening of new stores because of difficulties in obtaining fixtures and equipment. Buying clubs were favored instead. Nevertheless in that year an unusually large number of new food markets were opened. A few new petroleum associations were also organized, in spite of the tight supply situation.

World War II also produced two transitory types of cooperatives—those of Japanese-Americans in the War Relocation Camps and of conscientious objectors in the Civilian Public Service camps.

There are known to have been cooperatives in at least nine of the CPS camps: Two in Arkansas, three in California, two in Indiana, and one each in Michigan and Oregon. Most of them were stores, but the residents at Camp Magnolia, Ark., also had a book-buying club. These cooperatives were all started during 1941 and 1942 and went out of existence when the camps closed at the end of the war.

After the Japanese-Americans were evacuated from the West Coast, nine so-called "relocation" camps were built for them.[2] All the needs of the camp residents were supplied through cooperatives promoted and encouraged by the War Relocation Authority. By early 1943 there were 109 such cooperatives. Started without share capital, on credit advanced from various sources, they were supervised by veteran cooperators from the consumers' cooperative movement.[3]

Periods of operation of these associations in 1943 ranged only from 2 to 7 months, but their total business in that year exceeded $10¼ million. The membership at the end of 1943 numbered 40,720, out of a total camp population of 92,451. With the termination of the war, all the residents were released from the camps and the cooperatives were liquidated.

Cities have always been the hardest nut for the American cooperative movement to crack, but in 1945 it appeared that the Chicago cooperators might have the proper approach. There a city-wide association, Chicago Consumers Cooperative, was started. By August 1946, six previously existing associations in the city were reported to have become branches. At its peak the association had 3,200 members and 10 stores in the integrated plan. Almost from the beginning it operated at a loss, however. By 1950 three stores had been closed or sold. At the end of that year, two of the remaining stores (both antedating the city-wide organization) were returned to the local members for revival of independent operation. The third was sold at auction, and the city association went out of business, though still retaining its charter for possible future use. Loss of close ties between members and the organization and insufficient grounding in education were blamed for its failure, though other factors undoubtedly contributed their share.

Business and Finances

In 1942 the retail cooperatives in both the store and oil business showed increases in volume. In fact, cooperative business, in terms of money sales, held up very well all during the war, with each succeeding year reaching a new high.

The regional wholesales were consistently recommending caution, however, since they were aware of the pitfalls of the artificial war prosperity and the uncertainties of the postwar period. That their apprehensions were well founded began to be apparent as early as 1944, when unusually large numbers of cooperatives in the East (especially the smaller ones) reported operating losses.

Business conditions became still more difficult for the food stores in urban centers in 1945. For the whole store group, operating results were the poorest in the 5-year war period, as greater proportions went into the red. The petroleum associations, on the other hand, in 1945 had the largest proportion with earnings and the smallest with losses in the whole period.

Thus began, for the stores, a time of increasing difficulty, culminating in the closure of several hundred small associations during each of the first few postwar years. Indeed, so numerous were the dissolutions that they more than counterbalanced the number of new associations and caused the total number to decline in 1948 for the first time in 25 years.

The Central Organizations

The war period started unpropitiously with an occurrence unusual in the latter days of cooperative wholesaling—i.e., the dissolution of the Consumers Cooperative Wholesale, Los Angeles, in 1942. This was a small organization serving cooperative stores in southern California. It was a victim of supply difficulties and insufficient volume of business.

The other cooperative wholesales, however, throve during the entire interval. Each year from 1942 through 1945, every regional increased its sales over those of the preceding 12 months, and without exception all operated in the black. So prosperous were they that the group was able to return to the members on the 4-year patronage over $23 million.

Up to 1943, National Cooperatives had made no reports as to the volume of business done through it. In that year its volume, reported for the first time, was $4,096,872. This was stated to be "nearly double" the figure for 1942. Sales increased to over $6½ million in 1944 and earnings of $36,524 were made. In that year also, the organization was reincorporated, under the District of Columbia Cooperative Act. The new bylaws omitted the former provision on competition among members.

Expansion continued in 1945, with the beginning of a trade paper, *Co-op Magazine,* in January and the addition of three new departments—for advertising, for architecture and plant design, and for groceries (this last had previously been under a committee of buyers from the member regionals). Sales rose to over $6¾ million, but earnings fell to $7,008. Contracts for the manufacture of a new co-op refrigerator were signed in June. This was to be part of a new program for postwar distribution of electrical appliances, but supply difficulties caused delays in getting it under way.

By September 1942 the work of the Cooperative League had so expanded that the executive secretary had four assistant secretaries—for publicity, Wallace J. Campbell;[4] for legislation, John Carson; for recreation, Ellen Linson; and for education, Jack McLanahan.

The congress of that year, held in Minneapolis, September 28-30, centered its attention on planning for the postwar economy. Committees were authorized, to draw up a 5-year program and to work with planning committees of other groups. This congress also ordered the removal of Rochdale Institute from New York City to a more central location.

The 1944 congress, held in Chicago, October 8-13, celebrated not only the League's 14th biennial meeting but also the centennial of the founding of the Rochdale cooperative movement. It exhibited especial concern over wages and working conditions in the cooperative movement. After the meeting a placement service and employment clearing house was started by the League.

The War Period in Retrospect

In spite of wartime stresses, certain cooperative advances were made: diversification of business by both retail and wholesale associations, many new cooperatives, increased volume and earnings, and widening acceptance of cooperatives as indicated by endorsement by varied types of social, religious, and economic organizations.

On the other side of the ledger were the closing of many branch stores and oil stations for want of supplies and manpower, and, toward the end of the war, and immediately following it, the loss of many small cooperatives that had been kept afloat by price supports and the artificial prosperity of wartime, but that were economically unsound. The last year of the war was especially difficult for the small urban food stores.

The League, which had gone on expanding, gave special attention to the personnel deficiencies that had been revealed by the war. Its congress resolutions were plain revelation of a recognition that, if the cooperative movement was to recruit high-caliber staff, it must provide attractive wages and working conditions, and "fringe" benefits. At the same time, its officers farsightedly began to look ahead into the future and lay plans to meet expected difficult conditions, on behalf of cooperatives both in this country and in the war-ravaged countries abroad.

Chapter 25.—POSTWAR PERIOD, 1945-54

The Immediate Aftermath of the War

Upon the ending of the war, the cooperatives in the War Relocation camps ceased to exist practically at once, as did also in most cases the cooperatives in or near discontinued war plants.

The period was characterized by continued restrictions on civilian travel (necessitating cancellations of meetings); by extreme shortages of certain items while price control was still in effect, which resulted in substitutions and curtailed sales; and by long delays in deliveries of commodities, especially those involving the use of metal.

With the lifting of gasoline rationing, the urban petroleum cooperatives that managed to survive the long drouth of gasoline began to show improvement. Those with repair garages had continued at a fair pace during the war, keeping in driving trim the aging cars of their members. This situation was reversed, however, as new cars needing servicing, but no repairs, began to come on the market.

Membership and business of consumers' cooperatives reached an all-time peak in 1946, with the stores showing the greatest dollar increase in any year since 1942, and the petroleum associations the greatest since 1941. However, the nonfarm cooperatives as a group showed results less satisfactory than those composed of farmers. They were small in membership and seriously undercapitalized, especially considering that they had been in operation for a considerable time (the average was slightly over 14 years). These and other deficiencies revealed later were already beginning to bear bitter fruit.

Structural Changes

Regional and national cooperative meetings had considered recurrently the relative effectiveness of separate organizations for educational and commercial activities, or a single body combining the two.

Until the middle 1930's the American practice had been to form separate organizations, education being carried on by the Cooperative League of the USA and leagues affiliated with it.

As the regional wholesales grew, however, they began more and more to give employee business training, along with background courses in cooperative theory, thus overlapping the district leagues.

In 1938 the Northern States Cooperative League relinquished to the wholesales in its area educational work for and with their local associations. The next year, in California, education and business were combined in two new wholesales, one serving the northern and the other the southern part of the State. (The latter went out of business in 1942 and the former then began serving the whole State. Some years later, when the wholesale was in difficulty, a separate league was again formed, to improve the educational work and bolster cooperative understanding and patronage of the wholesale.)

At the end of 1940, education and commerce in the Illinois-Indiana-Ohio region were merged into a new central organization, Central States Cooperatives, Inc., which took over the duties of the regional league and wholesale. The question of a similar amalgamation between Eastern Cooperative Wholesale and Eastern Cooperative League had been under discussion since about 1937. Finally, in 1946, the annual meeting authorized the consolidation of league and wholesale, under the name Eastern Cooperatives, Inc.

At the national level a proposal for the merger of National Cooperatives and the Cooperative League had been agitated behind the scenes since E. R. Bowen became executive secretary of the latter. He did not originate the idea (shortly after the formation of National in 1933, it was suggested at a League board meeting that the two be combined), but he became its most active proponent.

The merger question did not come up for open membership debate until the congress of 1938 and then only in connection with a proposed revision of the League's bylaws. During the next 6 years proposals and counterproposals were made without result.

In these backstage moves the League's president and secretary were on opposite sides. Mr. Bowen favored combining the two national bodies. Dr. Warbasse favored the continued independence of the Cooperative League, as the capstone of the entire cooperative movement, with the various branches (including the national wholesale) affiliated to it. The League would thus be independent, both financially and organizationally, and free to criticize and suggest on a basis of equality.

In January 1946 the recommendations of a joint committee were adopted calling for (1) a single executive head for National Cooperatives, The Cooperative League, and National Cooperative Finance Association and (2) allocations by the two business organizations of a certain percentage on gross business, for educational purposes.

Less than a month before the 1946 congress, the boards of National and the League unanimously approved a plan whereby National would take over the League's educational duties, in addition to its own current functions; and the League would become an over-all organization for the various branches of the consumers' cooperative movement (distribution, housing, insurance, credit, etc.).

The plan was adopted by the congress after prolonged discussion.

This meant that the League's duties in the future would be mainly in general public relations, research, and compilation of statistics. Regional distributive wholesales would be affiliated with it only through National, which would be a League member. Although offering nominally a wider sphere of interest, actually this would have reduced the League's effectiveness.

Then occurred an event that nullified much of the 1946 congress action. Opposition to *consumer* education, that had been building up among National's farmer members, made itself felt and, as a result, National's board voted to turn back to the League—and the latter gladly accepted—all of the activities that had been transferred (except the training of employees for commodity jobs), with National paying the League for the work.[1] One congress decision was untouched; the League would still be a federation of national federations.

At least for the present, the question of structure thus seems to have been settled in favor of separate organizations for education and business. The present attitude appears to be that of letting well enough alone.

Years of Crisis, 1947-49

Cooperative Retailing

An all-time high was reached in retail cooperative membership and business in 1947, and 10 nonfarm associations had sales for the year exceeding a million dollars each. From the standpoint of operating results, it was the worst year in a long time, and dissolutions (mostly of grocery cooperatives) exceeded those in any 12-month period since the early 1920's.

In 1948 new peaks in total membership and business were again reached. But the "toughest competitive battle in years" materialized as predicted by the wholesales. The supply situation improved, but prices were still unsettled, and net margins were narrower. Nevertheless, operating results (though not entirely satisfactory) were better than in 1947.

The drastic situation in this early postwar period led to some experiments in retailing, none of which had any lasting success. One was the "warehouse-type" unit, situated in some out-of-the way place, handling only a few hundred items, and displaying the goods in the boxes in which they had been received. These first appeared in 1947, among the union-supported enterprises in the automobile-manufacturing centers in Michigan and Ohio. Advantages claimed were reduction in handling costs and in investment in equipment and fixtures, and rapid turnover of inventory. But housewives accustomed to doing all their marketing in one convenient place, with many brands to choose from, did not take to this innovation very long. Declining volume forced most of the units to revert to the usual type of market or close.

Another experiment was the so-called "co-op center," tried in some of the East Coast States. A small location would be found, away from heavy traffic and open only a few days a week. Only members and their friends would be dealt with. A limited line of "co-op label" goods was carried and labor was provided on a volunteer basis. This plan, intended as incubator for full-fledged stores eventually, also failed to "take."

In 1949, for the first time in many years, the total volume of retail distributive business of cooperatives declined, partly because of flagging vitality and dissolutions and partly as a result of a declining price level.

Cooperative Wholesaling

The regional wholesales, in the meantime, had been having their own troubles. Although, without exception, all had shown substantial increases in business in 1947 as compared with 1946, those with grocery departments were already feeling the effects of the situation in that business. In five cases the grocery department, or the entire wholesale operation, had ended 1947 in the red.

Several of the wholesales dealing mainly in petroleum products reached an all-time peak in 1948; but the grocery wholesales' volume decreased as their member associations shrank in number. In two of them the 1948 figure was less than in the previous year.

In 1949, declining volume was reported by a number of regionals, including some with an unbroken record of increase over a long period. A few of the latter even reported operating losses; in this group were two petroleum wholesales which went into the red for the first time in their entire existence. All but four regionals had smaller earnings than in 1948, and in most cases the drop was sharp. Causes for all this were higher operating expenses, price declines, the much more difficult competitive conditions, and the "squeeze" in the petroleum market that led to steep declines in oil-production and refinery earnings (or even losses).

National Cooperatives had difficulties of several kinds. It had a serious morale problem among its employees, an unsatisfactory management situation caused by lack of a clear-cut delegation of responsibility and duties by the board, a cleavage among the directors themselves as to the organization's proper functions, and a worsening financial position.[2]

Volume fell by 36 percent between 1946 and 1949, and heavy losses were incurred. Retrenchment was started. The

Co-op Magazine, begun in 1945, was discontinued at the end of 1947. The work force was reduced. And the educational payment promised to the League had to be cut drastically. By 1950 the financial statement showed black figures again.

Slow Recovery, 1950-54

By Local Associations

Beginning with 1947, the proportion of stores having operating losses decreased steadily through 1950. The oil cooperatives had made a consistently better showing, partly as a result of higher margins on petroleum products than on groceries and partly because of extra income in the form of patronage refunds from their wholesales. (The grocery stores affiliated with the city grocery wholesales, however, not only had no such income but had to write off on their books the decline in the value of their wholesale shares.)

By the end of 1950 the retail situation was showing real improvement. Dissolutions of small cooperatives were still occurring, generally after several losing years, and the picture of urban cooperation was not too good on the whole, but some city associations were pulling up slowly from extended periods of red operation. There were now 15 nonfarm cooperatives doing a retail business of over a million dollars each per year.

In 1951, some small stores continued to disappear, especially on the Atlantic seaboard, but the number of petroleum cooperatives even began to increase. The proportion of both types of associations having losses increased as compared with 1950. As in previous years, the urban associations made a poorer record than the farmer cooperatives.

The situation in the United States as a whole improved somewhat during the next 3-year period. But here and there, cooperatives (like other businesses) were faced at the end of 1954 with problems of declining volume caused by unemployment or short working weeks in the industries employing their members. The associations of farmer membership were feeling the effects of reduced farm income.

As has been evident, after the end of World War II there was a two-way trend in local distributive cooperation: (1) The downhill slide and eventual disappearance of the small and weak associations and even of some that had to all outward seeming been successful and (2) the bold advance and expansion of the larger and more modern cooperatives. In between these extremes were the moderately prosperous associations that had not quite kept up with the times and have been struggling against odds ever since the war's end. Upon the success or failure of this "middle class" will depend, in the long run, the fate of the cooperative distributive movement in this country, for they are its largest portion.

By the Wholesales

Regional wholesale membership in 1950 showed the first decline recorded since the twenties, as a result of the dissolutions of local cooperatives. However, business operations showed a marked improvement, largely as a result of reduced overhead and closing of losing departments. Volume rose, and earnings increased.

The following year both membership and business were up, and earnings nearly doubled as compared with 1950. Nearly $17 million was returned to members.[3]

In 1952 and 1953 the wholesales were caught in the vise of shrinking gross margins and rising overhead incident to the inflation that was in process. However, each postwar year brought improvements or expansion in physical facilities—new buildings and new productive plant or the modernization of that already in use.

National Cooperatives has continued to show earnings since 1950, though volume has declined slightly each year for various reasons: A splurge of buying after the outbreak of the Korean war was followed by a dull period; and sales were naturally affected when, one after another, three wholesales closed their grocery departments.[4] In 1953-54 automotive supplies constituted nearly 70 percent of National's total business. It handles just under 2 percent of all the tires sold at wholesale in the United States; its milking-machine division does about 10 percent of the business in its field.

National resumed payment of patronage refunds in 1951. In 1954, all of the *cash* investment the members had ever made was redeemed—a total of $132,400.[5] Under a "revolving fund" plan $71,200 in preferred stock was returned in the same year.

Centralized Production

In the United States such cooperative production as has been carried on has been chiefly by the wholesales and productive federations. Few of the retail associations have ever gone into this field; the exceptions are a small number operating consumers' dairies, bakeries, or sausage plants.[6]

The first cooperative productive enterprise of a central organization was a wholesale bakery opened as early as 1919. No further production was undertaken for the next 10 years. Then, beginning with a small plant for the compounding of automobile-lubricating oil, the ensuing 15 years were notable for the many and varied productive ventures by central organizations.

The Cooperative League reported that, at the end of 1942, the productive facilities of consumers' cooperatives included 12 oil wells, 92 miles of pipeline, four oil refineries, seven oil-compounding plants, two paint factories, a grease factory, three printing plants, two bakeries, two canneries, a coffee-roasting plant, three flour mills, eight feed mills, 11 commercial-fertilizer plants, a lumber mill, a tractor plant, a serum plant, and about a dozen chick hatcheries.

During the war years productive expansion was so great as to overshadow all other cooperative developments. Progress was especially great in the oil industry. By March 1945 consumers' cooperatives owned nine petroleum refineries (and a part interest in another), nearly 1,400 miles of pipeline, and 420 producing wells.

In 1947 the output of cooperative plants of all kinds passed the $100 million mark. Thereafter the pace slowed again as, in 1947 and again in 1950, the cooperative refineries were caught in a price "squeeze," when wholesale prices for their product declined, while at the same time they had to pay peak prices for the crude oil needed to supplement their own production.

By 1951 the value of cooperative products exceeded $230 million. By the end of the year cooperators owned or controlled over 1,800 producing oil wells, 71,675 acres of leasehold in production, and 332,000 acres of oil-bearing land held in reserve, as well as leases on thousands of acres of timberland and leases on extensive phosphate beds, to supply the fertilizer plants.

New facilities since then have been mostly in the way of expansion or modernization of plants or for the production of farm supplies such as fertilizer. Between 1952 and the end of 1953, over $30 million was spent on major improvements to their refineries alone. A study by the Cooperative League showed 2,857 producing wells in which consumer cooperatives had a "working interest" at the end of 1954. Net crude-oil production from these during the year exceeded 5 million barrels. Over 50.6 million barrels of refined products came from the cooperative refineries in that year.

Leader in productive expansion has been Consumers Cooperative Association, Kansas City, most of whose plants have been pioneers in their respective fields.

National's Experience With Production

National Cooperatives went into manufacturing in 1943, when it bought a plant with facilities for making milking machines, electric water heaters, and dairy-farm accessories, and one for household chemicals and cosmetics. In January 1947 it took over a flour mill in Auburn, Ind., that had been owned since 1933 by several of its members.

National had, however, been outstripped by both the wholesales and the productive federations. Then, at a meeting on August 16, 1946, its board (with representation from 19 regional wholesales) voted that, in future, production on a national scale should be centered in National.

Oddly enough, the announcement of the policy appeared to precipitate a countermovement. Early in 1947, some of the producer-minded members[7] moved to incorporate separately the production of water heaters and milking machines (National's most profitable operation), on the ground that the earnings from these primarily producer items should not be used to finance promotion of *consumer* cooperation. However, opponents of the motion showed that two-thirds of the output in 1946 had been bought by associations that were opposed to the divorcement move.[8] The proposal was tabled at two successive meetings (in March and May) and never thereafter revived.

Because the chemicals plant and the flour mill were operating in the red, both were disposed of in 1948.

As a result, National was left with the manufacture only of water heaters, milking machines, and small dairy equipment. The production department was later moved to Albert Lea, Minn., where a new modern plant was erected in 1952 and a new wing added the next year to house the headquarters office which moved from Chicago in November 1954.

At the peak (1948), the annual output of National's productive departments was valued at $3,389,000. Following the sale of the chemicals plant and flour mill, the volume fell to less than half, or $1,653,800. It rose slightly in both 1950 and 1951, reaching $2,022,000 in the latter year.

Productive Federations

Supplementing the wholesales' plants, there had developed a number of joint enterprises, organized by groups of regionals for commodities that the individual wholesales could not or did not wish to carry on alone. By the end of World War II, these federations were producing fertilizer, printing products, farm machinery, crude oil and refined petroleum products, cedar shingles, and coal.

Most of these ventures were profitable; a few were not.

One in the latter class was the National Farm Machinery Cooperative which grew out of previous, rather unsatisfactory experiences during and preceding the Government's farm-security program.[9] Organized in 1940, by 1943 it had in membership 11 regional wholesales in the United States and two in Canada.

The new business had hardly got under way when its output was diverted to war purposes. (It lost money on its Government contracts, however.) After the war's end the business expanded rapidly, rising to nearly $19½ million in 1949. In 1947-49 nearly a million dollars was declared in patronage refunds.

Sharply reduced demand, heavy expenses for the engineering of new equipment, lack of able management, and unsatisfactory labor relations combined to produce a serious situation which was not overcome even though sales rose to $13¼ million in 1951.

The organization went into voluntary receivership in the fall of 1952 and the plant was sold to the Canadian company that had previously made for it (under contract) part of the machinery it handled.

In the nine years (of a 12-year operation) for which figures are available, the federation had losses in five (totaling $1,015,000) and made earnings (totaling $1,455,000) in four. Upon the sale of the enterprise it was said that the entire investment of the member associations had been wiped out.

Another unsuccessful venture was the International Lumbering Association in Vancouver, B. C., organized in 1944. Its purpose was to make cedar shingles, then in very short supply.

Loss of some two million feet of cut timber by fire and an ensuing long shutdown, in 1946, and a decline in both wholesale prices and demand in 1948 (while production costs remained high) proved to be impossible to surmount, and the association dissolved in 1949.

In its five years' operation it had had operating losses in three (amounting to $107,900) and gains in two (amounting to $46,000). However, it had returned patronage refunds amounting to $92,763. That and the fact that it had assured a supply of good-quality shingles when most needed led one member wholesale to comment that it had not been an entirely unsuccessful enterprise.

In striking contrast has been the experience in oil refining and fertilizer manufacture. In the ten-year period, 1941-51, the fertilizer plants returned to their members $2,369,000 from earnings of $2,720,000.

The National Cooperative Refinery Association was organized in 1943 by five regional wholesales, three of which already had such plants of their own.

Almost immediately there was difficulty in obtaining sufficient supplies of crude oil, and in neither 1943 or 1946 was the refinery able to operate at capacity. NCRA therefore began acquiring production facilities, and by the end of 1951 had 486 producing oil wells, supplying over half of the refinery's total needs. A modernization program, plus the construction of a catalytic cracking unit which went on stream in 1952, raised the capacity of the refinery from 18,000 to 23,000 barrels daily. It owns nearly 350 miles of pipeline.

In its eight years of operation from 1944 to 1951, the association made earnings in every year except two—1945 and 1946—when it lost nearly a quarter of a million dollars, caused mainly because of shutdowns forced by crude oil shortages. Earnings in the other six years totaled $11,428,000.

Besides serving its primary purpose—the supply of refined fuels—it returned in patronage refunds the tidy sum of $10,706,000. On 1952-53 sales amounting to nearly $29½ million, refunds totaled $2,254,000.

Conclusions on Production

From less than $1½ million in 1937, the value of output of plants owned by the cooperative wholesales and federations has risen steadily, exceeding $230 million in 1951. About $93 million of the latter figure represented the product of the federations and nearly $138 million that of the wholesales. The bulk of the manufactures in 1951 was in two categories: petroleum products, crude and refined (60.6 percent), and feed, seed and fertilizer (27.2 percent). No other commodity group accounted for as much as 10 percent. Food products, which had constituted 4.5 percent of the total in 1946, had decreased continuously thereafter and in 1951 formed only 1.2 percent.

As we have seen, cooperatives were sometimes *forced* into production in order to survive.

This was especially true in the production and refining of crude oil, in which departure they encountered many problems in shortages of crude oil, refusal of supplies by some of the major oil companies (which together control over 80 percent of the Nation's crude oil reserves), and pressures between high prices for crude oil and declining prices for refined products.

The competitive situation is especially difficult in the petroleum industry. With a surplus of refinery capacity now general in the industry,[10] competition is very keen and cooperators must do a topnotch job to hold their own. Future prospects also depend to a great extent on obtaining control of oil-bearing land from which to derive supplies of crude oil for the plants.

The value of the productive enterprises has been demonstrated. Although, as has been seen, some of the productive plants were not financially successful, even they performed a valuable service as suppliers in time of need. As a group the productive federations returned over $20 million to their member regionals in refunds on patronage over the 9-year period, 1943 through 1951.

Certainly, if figured on the basis of investment, the return has been high. No data are available as to the amount of share capital of the federations. However, 10 reporting for 1951 had combined assets of slightly over $43 million. They paid back on that year's business $4,469,000, or 10.4 percent on the total assets.

In most cases there is no separate information regarding the productive plants of the wholesales. Their annual reports reveal, however, that generally the factories yield greater earnings than does the distributive business.

In 1942 the productive departments of Consumers Cooperative Association and the Farm Bureau Cooperative Association (Ohio) produced 72 and 70 percent, respectively, of their entire savings for that year. Midland Cooperative Wholesale reported that over 60 percent of its total earnings in 1947 came from either its own plants or those of the federations of which it was a member. Two-thirds of the 1953 earnings of the Farm Bureau Services of Michigan were derived from its processing and manufacturing departments and only one-third from its wholesaling.

In fact, production has ordinarily been so profitable, and the benefits to the members so substantial, that Howard Cowden coined the slogan: "Factories are free for cooperators."

Its meaning becomes clear when it is considered that National Cooperatives' investment in its chemical plant was paid back out of the earnings of 6 months' operation and that in the milking-machine plant in 10 months. The oil refinery of Indiana Farm Bureau Cooperative Association and the jointly owned feed mill in North Carolina were both paid for out of the first year's gains. A similar mill in Ohio, owned by three regional wholesales, paid for itself in 16 months. The oil-compounding plant of Farmers Union Central Exchange paid out in a "short time." Its refinery has "paid for itself many times over in savings" and its cracker unit and modernization program of 1952 were financed out of refinery earnings. The profits from the paint factory of Consumers Cooperative Association paid for all the equipment in the first 5 months' operation. That wholesale reported in 1948 that all its productive enterprises as a whole were repaying, over every 22-month period, all the capital invested in them.

The experience with farm machinery, shingles, flour, and coal has shown, however, that cooperative plants do not necessarily have a ready-made or known adequate market. The capacity of some has exceeded the patronage from the members. In order to attain capacity operation (necessary for black operation) the surplus product has had to be sold to noncooperative buyers.

In future, more and better advance planning of new enterprises is necessary, to be sure of actual need and the likely market. This is now recognized throughout the entire consumers' cooperative movement.[11]

For the productive plants now in operation, it is the belief of this writer that greater coordination, possibly through an intercooperative agency is needed. The cooperative lumber yards in the trading area of certain regionals, for instance, may be insufficient to use all the products of the regionals' sawmills. But it would seem reasonable that those affiliated with wholesales in contiguous regions, not having such facilities, could absorb the surplus lumber, to everybody's advantage. Long hauls and resultant freight costs might interfere in some cases. But I feel sure that more could be done in the direction of intercooperative trading.

Activities of the Cooperative League

E. R. Bowen retired from the post of executive secretary in 1946[12] and was succeeded in 1947 by Jerry Voorhis who has filled the position since that time.[13]

The new executive found himself confronted almost immediately with a serious situation. National Cooperatives was in trouble, as were also several of the other League members; and they were therefore unable fully to meet their obligations to the League. Mr. Voorhis attacked his task with characteristic determination, and things began to happen.

The League's New York office was closed in May 1948 and consolidated with that in Chicago, to which the literature department had already been moved in July 1947; the film department was transferred there in August 1948. This made possible some reduction in staff and in overhead expense.

The bylaws were amended to permit local cooperatives and individuals to join the League as associate members. The regular membership list was swelled by the addition of several wholesales. The bylaw amendments also permitted acceptance of national federations in the various branches of the cooperative movement, as well as any "mutual or nonprofit" organization "subscribing to the fundamental principles of cooperation."

By mid-1948, regular dues income was double that of 1947. The 1948 Cooperative Congress, at the recommendation of the League board, raised the dues of the regional affiliates to 10 cents per individual member (from 7½ cents). By the end of the year, expenditures were in approximate balance with income.

The chief accomplishment of the congress of 1950 was the adoption of the 4-year expansion plan worked out by a committee appointed two years previously. The plan called for (a) a national education and research program under a full-time director, (b) a greatly strengthened legislative program, (c) a broad public relations and information program, (d) closer working relationships among cooperatives at all levels, at home and abroad, and (e) expansion into new fields.

Under this mandate the League began exploring ways to expand and improve the cooperative movement. By 1954 this work had crystallized into a set of annual conferences or institutes designed especially for professional cooperative workers in certain fields: public relations, education, insurance, health, management (regional and local), editors and publicists, and finance.

It had been apparent for some time that, if cooperatives were to hold their own in present-day competition, they must have well-qualified personnel, especially for the top-level jobs, and must make use of expert consultative and technical assistance.

The day of the well-meaning amateur was gone. The entire 1952 Cooperative Congress was geared to this concept. Its theme was "Cooperatives Meeting the Needs of the Present World." Work sessions dealt with better methods of research and of public relations, of training, of education (including publicity and information), and of economic development. Other sessions discussed ways of adapting cooperative techniques to a changing economy and the need for greater coordination of action among cooperatives.

Early in 1952 the League board appointed a committee on organization to examine the League's whole program and procedures in the light of present-day needs, to see whether it was fulfilling its basic purposes in the most effective way. Its report was presented to the congress of that year.

Its definition of the basic program (adopted by the congress) was as follows:

> "The basic purpose of the Cooperative League is to promote, initiate, and protect cooperatives owned and controlled by the people whose needs they serve, to the end that cooperative business enterprise can become an effective balance wheel asserting the general public interest in a just and truly free economy."

The long-range objectives as formulated by the committee (and adopted by the congress) consist of education, public relations, and specific consultative services for the members such as will promote the attainment of the basic program.

The 1954 congress adopted a general statement of policy, setting forth the stand of the organized consumers' cooperative movement on such matters as democracy, world peace, free enterprise, monopoly, health and welfare, conservation of natural resources and taxation.

League membership at the end of 1954 consisted of the following regular members: National Cooperatives and seven regional wholesales, the national federations of the credit union and rural electric cooperative movements, the Cooperative League of Puerto Rico, three insurance groups, two local cooperatives, and a State association of electrical cooperatives. The associate members consisted of three regional wholesales in the United States and one in Canada, five State cooperative councils, the Cooperative Institute Association (New York), an electric cooperative federation, a State credit union league, and an area federation; also a number of local distributive cooperatives and many individuals.

Part III.

COOPERATIVE SERVICES

Chapter 26.—EDUCATION, RECREATION, AND PUBLICITY

Education

In the cooperative movement, it has been said, education is regarded principally "as a means to certain ends, and the ends are an active membership with a clear grasp of current issues and problems, especially in the field of economics; a public informed about the cooperative movement; and individuals receptive to the idea of joining cooperatives."[1]

These three goals are approached in different ways. Education of the members goes on through cooperative papers, pamphlets, speakers at meetings, institutes at which general and special cooperative subjects are presented, neighborhood discussion groups, and programs designed for children and young people. However, education (the very idea of which might repel some people) is sugarcoated with other names and with accompanying recreational and social events.

The public is approached through films and radio, sponsorship of community affairs, participation in and support of local projects for the public welfare, and other means by which the cooperative movement is presented in a favorable light.

It is desirable also that the cooperative managers and employees who meet the public know something of the philosophy and purposes of the movement and be able to answer intelligently questions about them, in addition to having a grasp of the technical requirements of their job. The training of cooperative employees in these respects has not been neglected, though it cannot be said that the movement has by any means fully met the demand for employee training.

The agencies of education in cooperation have been many and varied. They have included the Cooperative League of the USA and its committees and special educational arm, Rochdale Institute; the district leagues (described elsewhere) that flourished in the 20's and 30's; the regional wholesales that supplanted the leagues in education; the women's guilds and youth organizations whose special purpose is the education of women and young people in cooperation, with a view to enlisting their membership and intelligent participation in the movement; the innumerable county or district educational organizations; and, finally, small local groups of members which study and discuss not only cooperative subjects but also topics of general and special interest affecting the general welfare.

With increased emphasis on education came the need for persons trained in the work, and the leagues began to hire full-time educational directors. Beginning about the middle thirties, the wholesales and some of the larger retail cooperatives also added such directors to their staffs. By 1943 half of the local cooperatives in Ohio had full-time educational workers. That State had progressed farthest of all. In Indiana, Texas, and Washington, also, the regional wholesales now had such directors.

Central Cooperative Wholesale was the first to attain a well-rounded program and in so doing earned the praise of E. R. Bowen, who cited it in his report to the Cooperative Congress of 1938. Other regionals whose educational programs have been outstanding are Consumers Cooperative Association, Midland Cooperatives, Inc., and Ohio Farm Bureau Cooperative Association.

Educational Agencies and Their Work

Leader in the promotion of cooperative education is, of course, the Cooperative League of the USA which throughout its entire existence has carried on as its chief function various activities designed to spread the knowledge of Rochdale-type cooperation among cooperators and the general public.

The League had no sooner been organized than it began to issue pamphlets describing the cooperative movement, what it stood for, and what it could do, as well as how to go about organizing a consumers' cooperative. Nearly every issue of its journal carried articles or news items on educational work. As funds permitted, the League provided speakers for cooperative meetings and courses in cooperative theory. The number and variety of courses increased each year.

Its congresses urged the local cooperatives to appoint educational committees for the cooperative education of both members and the community at large and to set aside from earnings funds to enable them to do the job adequately.

The prime mover in this was the League's president, Dr. James P. Warbasse, who believed passionately and preached continually that, for sound development of cooperatives, education must precede business enterprise.

To coordinate the educational activities of the various cooperative bodies, the 1940 Cooperative Congress created a national publicity and educational committee, consisting of the educational director and editor of each regional cooperative association. The committee was divided four years later, with a committee for each group—educators and editors—to permit more intensive and specialized work in each field.

In addition to the three district leagues described in a previous chapter, there have been a great many agencies on a smaller geographic scale. Most of them were not regularly incorporated organizations, but operated informally, functioning for a while and then lapsing into inactivity.

The California Cooperative Council was organized in 1934. Its buying agency evolved into the Cooperative Wholesale Association of Southern California. The Council itself ceased operation on January 1, 1936, because its functions were being duplicated by the educational department of the wholesale.

Early in 1940 the Southeastern Cooperative Education Association (changed in 1941 to the Southeastern Cooperative League) was formed. Grants from the Rosenwald Fund made possible educational work throughout the South and as far west as Arkansas. After the grant funds were exhausted, the league moved to Raleigh, N. C., where it continued to operate, though on a much smaller scale, under the direction of D. R. Graham, chief of the Credit Union Division of the North Carolina Department of Agriculture. It ceased to function late in 1954, but Mr. Graham writes me that he is hopeful of reactivating it in "the not too distant future."

The Cascade Cooperative League (1948), with headquarters in Seattle, also seems to have become inactive.

From time to time many educational federations have been formed for the exchange of experience among the cooperatives in a particular region—usually a natural trade area, a county, or a metropolitan district. Such federations have usually admitted cooperatives of all types, producer as well as consumer. Most of them have been rather short-lived.

Three area consumer federations deserve special mention. One was the New Jersey Cooperative Federation in Trenton. With Jerome Ludlow as its leader and dynamo, the federation was a great stimulator of cooperative activity during its existence. Formed in 1936, at its peak (1942) it had as members 22 cooperatives throughout the northern part of the State. It went out of operation after the end of World War II.

The second was the Philadelphia Area Cooperative Federation which for several years, beginning in the middle 1940's, carried on, under the leadership of Mary Ellicott Arnold, an intensive educational and merchandising program among its 16 member associations in the metropolitan area.

One of the most outstanding to date is the Potomac Cooperative Federation of Washington, D. C., formed in 1944 as successor to the Washington Consumers Club (1935) and D. C. Cooperative League (1937). Its progress has been due mainly to the devotion of its executive secretaries.[2] The association carries on a variety of duties, including promotional and educational work in preparation for the opening of new branch stores in the area; giving advice on legal questions, accounting, taxation, and organization; the preparation of the periodicals of three of its members; and various public-relations chores. As Washington is a Mecca for cooperators from all over the United States and even from abroad, the organization of appropriate tours of cooperatives, meetings, and social affairs in connection therewith forms a minor but significant part of its work. Federal Government agencies call upon the Federation to assist in the cooperative education of persons visiting the United States in connection with the various "exchange" programs.

It had in membership at the end of 1954 the four distributive associations of its area (Greenbelt, Md., Washington, D. C., and Alexandria and Hampton, Va.), and various other types of cooperatives (housing, arts, medical care, rooming, the District of Columbia Credit Union League, and the Council of Cooperative Nursery Schools).[3] I know of no other similar area educational organization with so many years of service behind it or with so wide a range of activity and influence in the consumers' cooperative movement.

Training of Cooperative Employees

The first essay in the technical training of cooperative employees that has come to my attention was the school for cooperative managers held by the Right Relationship League in 1909. Its auditors had been appalled by the ignorance of the managers of the RRL stores of even the rudiments of bookkeeping. The course (apparently the only one it ever offered) was intended as a partial solution to the problem.

Even 20 years later the bookkeeping of the cooperatives could only be termed "primitive." Some of the financial statements submitted to the U. S. Bureau of Labor Statistics, for instance, were models of how not to do it. The need was early recognized by the Cooperative League. Sessions of its congresses of the twenties dealt with cooperative accounting, bookkeeping, and auditing, and the desirability of uniform methods.

Beginning with a bookkeeping course offered by Cooperative Central Exchange in 1918, the wholesales and district leagues nearly every year gave courses in business subjects, and/or history and principles of cooperation. This practice was continued by the new wholesales as they began to appear on the scene in the late 20's and early 30's. By the late thirties, there was evident a general and exceptional emphasis on educational work of various kinds.

Conditions during World War II curtailed the training work considerably where they did not stop it altogether. When the educational program was resumed, the courses were generally of shorter duration than in prewar times.

Rochdale Institute.—The question of a League-sponsored training school had been discussed at Cooperative Congresses since 1932, but it was not until 1937 that such a school was organized under the name, The Cooperative Institute, with Dr. Warbasse as director and Lionel Perkins as registrar.[4]

The first term's offering consisted of 8 weeks of classwork, followed by 8 of field work. There were two distinct departments, one for training executives and the other for training educators.

For both categories of students there was a common core of lectures in the economics of cooperation, history of cooperation, cooperative philosophy and principles, and cooperative organization and management. The course for executives also included bookkeeping, business-management problems, and lectures on the various types of cooperative business (buying clubs, stores, wholesaling, housing, etc.); that for educators, instruction in educational and publicity methods, the functioning of educational committees, youth and women's guilds, and related topics.

Classroom instruction was supplemented by visits to cooperative businesses in and around New York, voluntary work in cooperatives, discussion groups, and other activities. A paper, *Rochdale Cooperator,* was also issued, which at first was written and edited by the students.

The Institute faculty consisted of cooperative leaders, professors in New York City educational institutions, and cooperative executives who gave special lectures.

Thereafter, spring and fall classes were offered, greater and greater emphasis being laid on food-store operation. By the end of 1940 the Institute had trained 250 persons for service in the movement.

Early in 1938 the trustees applied for a charter under the educational laws of New York State. On July 29 a provisional charter was granted, under the name of Rochdale Institute, by the University of the State of New York.[5]

During the war the Institute found itself in a vicious circle of declining revenues and decreasing enrollments (caused by the military draft and the departure of actual and prospective students to take well-paid jobs in defense plants). In 1943 there were only 9 students in the fall general course and 40 in the evening extension classes.

In accordance with a mandate of the 1942 congress, the Institute was moved to Chicago in the autumn of 1944. Dr.

Warbasse and Mr. Perkins both stepped out of their official positions and C. J. McLanahan, educational director of the Cooperative League, was appointed as acting director.

After settling into its new location, the Institute throve for a while. For January 1945 was offered what it felt was "one of the most ambitious nationally coordinated training programs yet undertaken." More than 150 managers from "all parts of the country" gathered at three centers (farm supply at Columbus, petroleum at Kansas City, and food at Chicago) for 2 weeks of intensive training. Twenty weeks of training were offered during 1945—the largest variety of courses and the greatest number of students (228) in its history. Two other important events occurred that same year: The Institute was accepted as an accredited school under the GI Bill of Rights; and it received a permanent charter from New York University.

By this time some of the regionals were contributing to Institute financing, but still could not seem to decide just what should be done about training at the national level. The League was having many troubles of its own and could do little. By 1949 the Institute had ceased to conduct any courses of its own. Of late years its only activity has been the sponsoring of courses with other agencies. RI regards as one of its real accomplishments, however, the inclusion of courses on cooperation at increasing numbers of educational institutions, at secondary and higher levels.

Council for Cooperative Business Training.—The Council for Cooperative Business Training was formed, with a grant from the Good Will Fund, in the autumn of 1939, to give practical business courses for employees and managers of cooperatives. The Council included two representatives each from Rochdale Institute,[6] Eastern Cooperative Wholesale, and the Consumer Distribution Corporation.

The first offering, described as a "lecture discussion course," consisted of a lecture per week for 10 weeks, in the fall of 1939. Others were added as time went on, mainly courses in food-store management.

Most of its courses were held in New York City. In January 1942, however, an 8-week management institute drawing

25 students was held in Chicago, under the auspices of the Good Will Fund.

Attention was thereafter divided between the Central States area and the East. William Torma was engaged as a field man in the drive for greater urban development in the Central States. Eventually this work evolved into the Council for Cooperative Development. The Council for Cooperative Business Training went out of existence on January 1, 1944.

League Training Institutes.—The Cooperative League now holds a series of annual training institutes, developed over a period of years, designed for special groups of cooperative workers. They are the following:

1. A modern management institute for developing management personnel. This school, staffed by authorities in their special fields, covers technical job instruction, management methods, and personnel policies. Educational materials on these subjects are also issued by the League.

2. A summer school at which district educational managers, field workers, and others learn effective techniques for adult education in cooperation. These schools are held on university campuses and are staffed in part from their faculties.

3. A technical institute for editors and editorial workers of all types of cooperatives, in which instruction is given on editorial and other problems—readability, content, presentation, etc. These institutes are arranged in collaboration with university schools of journalism and other departments.

4. A conference for managers of local consumers' cooperatives (mostly attended by managers of the larger associations), held on the home grounds of some successful cooperative. Here the managers receive technical counseling and consult on mutual problems. Subjects include activation of membership, successful financing, employee training, personnel management, store layout, good merchandising practices, etc.

5. A conference for the general managers and finance officers of cooperatives on problems in the finance field, consisting largely of discussion and exchange of experience, supplemented by counseling by outside experts.

6. A conference for personnel of insurance companies, for exchange of experience and discussion of problems. Subjects in-

clude public relations, the human side of the insurance business, policyholder participation, relations with government, etc.

7. A public-relations institute for cooperative directors in this field, conducted in Washington, D. C., and providing for discussions with Government personnel and Congressional delegations on current issues.

General Education of Members and Public

For the building of sound cooperatives, the members must know what cooperation is and aims to do, and what is going on in their organization and in the community. The best results for this are achieved, not by lectures or large meetings, but in small groups meeting in members' homes. Such discussion groups began to be formed in the mid-30's.

In Ohio the program began early in 1937, under the aegis of the Farm Bureau Cooperative Association (regional wholesale). According to its own statement, its "advisory councils" have three objectives:

> "First, to develop a virile functioning local leadership to man the cooperative movement in Ohio; second, to inform members of cooperatives regarding the philosophical, cultural, and practical sides of democratic, economic group action; third, to bring about a thorough understanding between rural and urban consumers of the problems and opportunities in which both are vitally concerned."[7]

In order to get the thinking focussed on a single problem at a time, all councils are supplied with identical discussion material each month. Each group—12 families meeting monthly in the members' homes in rotation—carries out a program of music, business, discussion of the evening's subject, recreation, and refreshments. To the councils are also referred any developments or new enterprises contemplated by their cooperatives. Such "referendums" serve to build up understanding and afford cooperative management the views of members, in advance of action.

In mid-1939, an additional step was taken, with the organization of the council leaders into "county cabinets," for *action* in some chosen line or lines, with a blueprint of specific steps to be taken.

The success of the Ohio program has rested on two things: the discussion materials were carefully prepared at a central place, and the councils know that their conclusions exert a real influence on the decisions of their central organizations.

Similar groups were started by other wholesales, with considerable success. By the fall of 1940, Ohio had 800 such groups, Central Cooperative Wholesale 350, the Eastern area 150, Consumers Cooperative Association 100, and northern California about 20.

After the end of the war the members of the Farm Bureau Federation of Vermont organized 75 neighborhood circles which, it is said, have been especially attractive to the younger families.

At the instance of V. S. Alanne, the Cooperative Correspondence School was started in August 1943, with Central Cooperative Wholesale, Midland Cooperative Wholesale, and Consumers Cooperative Association as sponsors. During the next year Central States Cooperatives, Eastern Cooperatives, and Pacific Supply Cooperative also joined the group.

The curriculum included three courses: (1) Administration of cooperatives, (2) The cooperative employee in food and general merchandise stores, and (3) Consumers' cooperation in principle and practice. Later, courses for employees of petroleum and farm-supply cooperatives were added.

As experience demonstrated that the best results were obtained where there were competent instructors, the work was decentralized and the three original sponsors of the school undertook to provide the study material and supervision. The courses were discontinued upon Mr. Alanne's departure for Finland in 1949. During its existence the school trained almost 2,000 students.

Institutes combining recreation and education have also been utilized to spread the cooperative idea. Their major purpose is to acquaint the cooperative membership with the general theory and practices of the consumers' cooperative movement. The participants range in age from 18 years upwards.

Eastern States Cooperative League was probably the first to hold such an institute. Its initial venture, in 1929, was so successful that it has been repeated each year since then.[8] Both the Northern States and Central States Cooperative Leagues also made use of the institute technique.

During the summer of 1936, over a thousand persons from 30 States attended the 12 cooperative institutes held that year.

Summer institutes are now quite common throughout the consumers' cooperative movement. In the rural districts the winter months are generally those in which the educational work flourishes, as summer is necessarily devoted to work on the farm.

Women in the Cooperative Movement

Cooperatives have always been notably liberal in respect to women. The original Rochdale Pioneers in 1844 admitted women on the same terms as men. In this country, more than 40 years before women were conceded the right of political suffrage, and even before the Rochdale principles were generally known here, the Grangers were admitting them to equal rights in their cooperatives; their 1894 annual meeting passed a resolution favoring woman suffrage.

This tradition has usually been faithfully adhered to in the consumers' cooperative movement and any women who desired to do so could join a cooperative and take part in its proceedings.

Thousands of women have been employed at one time or another in the offices, stores, and other departments of cooperatives. It is not so well known that some have even become officers or managers, not only of city cooperatives but of farmers' associations.[9]

The earliest organized attempt to interest women in cooperatives in this country that I have found occurred in Illinois, where one purpose of the Cooperative Society of Illinois, formed by coal miners in 1915, was to draw the women into the cooperative movement through literature and the formation of women's guilds.

Early in 1921, nearly every local branch of the Pacific Cooperative League (California) had a "women's cooperative league." This development was, of course, killed by the PCL crash, a little later.

Northern States guilds.—In the late 1920's small groups of women cooperators began to organize guilds as auxiliaries to local cooperative stores owned by Finns in the Lake Superior area. In 1929 Helen Hayes began to organize these groups on behalf of the Northern States Cooperative League. By the end of 1936 there were 62 units, with about 1,600 members. Except for three locals—in Mullan, Idaho, and North Chicago and Waukegan, Ill.—all members were in Minnesota, Michigan, and Wisconsin.

The first guilds were all Finnish in membership. The first English-speaking units were organized in 1932 and 1933. Gradually men also were admitted to some of the guilds. Although there had been a slow infiltration of non-Finnish people, Finnish women still constituted about 75 percent of the membership as late as 1936.

In April 1930, twenty guilds in Michigan, Minnesota, and Wisconsin organized the Northern States Women's Cooperative Guild.[10] Helen Hayes was the guild's first secretary.[11] The present (1955) secretary is Vivian (Mrs. Arnold J.) Ronn.

The major functions of the guilds are the cooperative education of the members, and promotion of the cooperative movement in various ways. Guildwomen act as hostesses at co-op food demonstrations, make retail price surveys, and participate in store-evaluation programs. A large part of their work consists of social and cultural activities—sponsorship of educational affairs and entertainments, and operation of summer camps for young people and children. The guildwomen have carried on a continuing camp program since 1930.

Other sections of the country.—Their region is the only one that can boast of guild work carried on continuously since the formation of the first guild. A women's cooperative guild for the Central States was formed in 1939. One for the Kansas-Missouri area had been organized earlier. Neither of these is presently in existence.

In certain other parts of the country, notably Ohio, the 9-State CCA region, and Vermont, the idea underlying the guild movement—to enlist the active interest of women and other family members in cooperation—has been and is being carried into effect through group discussion. In few cases, however, are there separate organizations for the women. But a new association, Pacific Cooperative Women, was formally organized at the end of 1953, after more than 2 years' preparatory work in the territory of Pacific Supply Cooperative.

National guild.—Although considered as early as 1932, it was not until the late 30's that a national guild came into being. Its affiliates were the regional guilds for the Northern States, the Kansas-Missouri, and the Central States areas, and a number of scattered local guilds (four each in Ohio and California, and one each in Alaska, Connecticut, Idaho, and New Jersey). By 1940 the 122 units in existence (in 14 States) had some 3,000 members.

The national guild gradually lapsed into inactivity for lack of widespread and continuing interest and the failure to develop a network of guilds throughout the country to support it. The only present activity at the national level is carried on by the Women's Committee of the Cooperative League (authorized by the 1942 congress). It is now headed by Mrs. Harold Robison (Ohio) who succeeded Mrs. Almer Armstrong (Indiana).

Young People and the Cooperative Movement

In general, cooperative leaders in this country, preoccupied with their own problems, seem to have been slow to recognize that the future of the cooperative movement depends on the influx of new blood from the rising generation, and that the best way to insure conversion to the cooperative idea is to "catch them young" and slip in education in cooperation in the course of activities that are fun to do.

The early history of the cooperative movement gives practically no evidence of realization of this on the part of adult cooperators. As far as I can determine, it was not until after the turn of the century, when the Farmers Union was formed and began cooperative educational work, that any organized program was formed for young people.

Nearly three decades after the birth of this farm organization, another group of cooperators—Finnish men and women in the Lake Superior region—also realized the importance of youth and began to do something about it.

The Northern States Cooperative Youth League was organized in 1930, under the sponsorship of the regional wholesale's educational department. Its high point was reached in 1932, with 50 locals having 2,000 members. Thereafter it declined, partly because of the economic depression and partly (in the opinion of its secretary) because of insufficient interest on the part of adult cooperators.

In June 1937 the league had 33 local units (with 780 members) and 20 individuals in membership.

By the time of its tenth anniversary, in 1940, the NSCYL had units in 40 communities and a membership of over 1,100 young people.

The youth leagues were a war casualty, although the children's summer camps continued to be held in the CCW area all during hostilities. The youth program was resumed in a small way, afterwards, with the holding of youth courses by the wholesale's educational department in 1946. Each year since then courses have been held (with recreational features in conjunction) for high-school graduates intending to seek employment in cooperatives.

About 1938 the Central States Cooperative Youth League was formed. In 1939 it became a department of the Central States Cooperative League and was given a voting representative in that body. This activity was absorbed into the wholesale's work upon the merger of the league and wholesale into Central States Cooperatives, Inc., effective January 1, 1941; but seems to have become submerged since then.

Since 1936 the Ohio program of education and discussion has included summer camps for the children and young people. Cooperative Youth Councils were formed as part of the program. In the councils, although they received some adult guidance, complete responsibility was given to the young people. The youth program was a combination of social and recreational events with discussion of consumers' cooperation, credit unions (thrift), and related subjects. By 1940 thirty camps had been conducted and about a thousand young people had attended.

Consumers Cooperative Association (Missouri) each year holds summer camps for the young people of its 9-State area, in addition to "family" camps for all ages.

Public Relations

The cooperative movement, long a laggard in the matter of public relations, has come to realize the great importance of getting the cooperative idea before the public in a favorable light. In the old days cooperators were engrossed in the immediate, practical problems of running their enterprise, and depended to a great extent on word-of-mouth report and the payment of patronage refunds for community recognition.

Beginning with a year-long publicity and educational campaign (brainchild of E. R. Bowen) in 1941-42, increasing attention has been given to this matter. Present executive director Jerry Voorhis has pointed out repeatedly that the future of the cooperative movement depends on its acceptance by the American people.

In the effort to create a friendly climate in which cooperation can grow and play its part in national and international society, the League has enlarged its extracurricular activities and now takes part in a number of movements.[12]

Indicative of the general cooperative interest in better public relations is the growing number of associations with specialists on their staff, on either a full- or part-time basis. In the eastern States alone, four local associations had engaged full-time directors by the end of 1954. As early as 1945, Central Cooperative Wholesale had a full-time director for radio, advertising, promotional literature, and news service to small papers.

During October—observed for some years as "co-op month"—membership drives and co-op rallies are held and a special effort is made to bring cooperatives to public attention. Favorite media are local festivals and other social events, to which the public as well as cooperative members are invited.

Courses in Educational Institutions

In the 1920's the general interest in cooperation was reflected to some extent on the college campuses. In 1921, 25 colleges and universities (of 33 queried) were giving attention to cooperation in either a separate course or as part of a course on another subject. Fifteen years later 18 colleges had special courses and in 131 cooperation was included in courses on economics or sociology.

Toward the end of World War II, a survey of 133 schools in 37 States revealed that 3 of every 4 (and 6 of every 10 teachers) in small communities were giving some instruction about the cooperative movement. In most cases the subject had been introduced within the past 10 years and was usually taught in classes in the social sciences, vocational agriculture, economics, or home economics. Among 34 land-grant colleges, about half were offering one or more special courses on cooperation, in addition to classes in accounting, business law, etc.

A Wisconsin survey in 1949 disclosed that 58 percent of the teachers questioned had not read the State cooperative law and 37 percent were not familiar with its provisions. A high percentage, however, indicated an interest and belief in cooperatives.

For some years Harvard University, jointly with the New England Cooperative Federation, gave a course in consumers' cooperation.[13] The School for Workers, at the University of Wisconsin, has for many years held a cooperative and labor institute, sponsored jointly with the Cooperative League and the CIO and AFL unions.

In many cases classes in cooperative subjects have been given sporadically, often at the instance of an area cooperative.

The teaching of cooperation has been required by law in Wisconsin in all public schools receiving State aid, since 1935. North Dakota high schools have been offering elective courses in the history, principles, etc., of cooperation since 1937; and the State Teachers' Colleges since 1943.

Recreation in the Cooperative Movement

Far-sighted cooperators have long realized the worth of recreation not alone for itself but in making cooperation a factor in the members' social lives as well as in their bread-and-butter economy. The cooperatives of foreign groups have, perhaps because of their common national bond, been the most successful.

Dinners, dramatics,[14] film shows and social gatherings in connection with the membership meetings, concerts, and picnics are all used as recreational media.

Although much of the recreational work is carried on through women's guilds or committees of store associations, there are also some cooperatives whose main function is social. Thus, several associations own halls or clubhouses used for dramatics, dances, or other social functions. "Play co-ops" buy tickets for theatrical performances, concerts and other entertainments, and sponsor various social affairs.

There are also a number of summer camps either owned by cooperative organizations[15] or leased by them from Government agencies.[16]

The only cooperatively run movie theater that I know of is in Greenbelt, Md. There were reported to be such theaters in Benld, New Athens, and Staunton, Ill., and Newmanstown, Pa., in the 1920's but no details are known about them.

From 1935 until 1954 a cooperative recreation service correlated the projects in the leisure-time field, held regional institutes at various places throughout the country for the training of recreational leaders, and acted as a national clearing house for nonprofit recreational materials and "educational guidance for creative leisure." It acquired copyrights for a number of unique traditional games, and issued a series of folk songs and a bibliography of resource material in drama, music, crafts, and art supplies. The recreational materials are now available through the Cooperative League.

Until the war intervened, the Cooperative League and National Cooperatives sponsored a number of tours to cooperative enterprises in the United States and Canada. The practice was resumed after the war ended and, beginning in 1947, included also tours of cooperatives in Europe. In 1953 the League joined with a number of other groups to form the American Travel Association.[17] Some of the regional wholesales have also sponsored sightseeing trips to the cooperatives in various parts of the United States and Canada.

Media of Publicity

Cooperative Publications

The long-established periodical of the Cooperative League[18] ceased publication at the end of 1943. To some extent its place is now filled by *Co-op Report,* which is just what the name implies—a report to the League members on cooperative developments. It usually contains, also, a short article of general interest and notes on a few individual associations or cooperative events. It also has an insert called "Facts for Managers." The League has also issued six yearbooks (for 1930, 1936, 1939, 1950, 1952, and 1954). In addition it publishes many pamphlets and an occasional book.[19]

The Cooperative League started a news service as early as 1920. In the early days it went mostly to the labor press. Now the *Cooperative News Service* furnishes weekly items of both general and special interest for cooperative papers throughout the country. In shortened form it is also sent, on request, to 102 newspapers with a combined circulation of 4 million and to 238 radio stations. In addition, CNS issues (usually monthly) columns on consumer buying, household hints, and medical advice. Jerry Voorhis writes a semimonthly general column for CNS, entitled "The People's Business." Other periodicals are the *Housing Newsletter* and *Literature-Film Bulletin.*

The Cooperative League endeavors to get the favorable attention of the public by means of press conferences, furnishing articles for encyclopedias and yearbooks issued by a number of private organizations, furnishing data for articles in newspapers and magazines, and through a special monthly service for the religious press, a column on the petroleum industry, a service for radio commentators, and exhibits at union and other conventions.

Between 1950 and 1952 two million pieces of cooperative literature were distributed through the League.

For many years a cooperative press has been in process of development. No daily cooperative newspaper has yet been established, although discussed many times over the years. Virtually all of the regional wholesales (and many of the local cooperatives) have their own papers, issued monthly, semimonthly, or weekly.

A Cooperative Editorial Association was organized in 1953, to work for the advancement of the professional standards of cooperative publications and pool information and techniques. This was a desirable and needed move, for the cooperative papers as a whole are not outstanding from either the journalistic or typographical point of view, though full of information about cooperatives. Some are unattractive in appearance and dull in subject matter. Others are quite appealing to the eye and sprightly in presentation.

One of the best all-round cooperative papers, in my opinion, is *Cooperative Builder,* organ of Central Cooperative Wholesale. It is also the oldest, having begun publication in 1925.

One of the two cooperative weeklies in the consumers' movement,[20] the *Builder* covers not only co-op news but also items on labor, political and economic events, and developments in the international news field. It has special departments for women (news of the guilds, household subjects etc.), youth, the Washington scene (a column supplied by the Cooperative League's Washington office), farm methods, and a question-and-answer column about cooperatives.

The *Builder* has been outstanding, also, for another characteristic—a candor unsurpassed among cooperative papers. Where others tend to ignore or gloss over controversial questions, the failures, or unfavorable developments, the *Builder* brings them into the open, with news items, frank and objective editorial analysis, and subscribers' letters pro and con. This makes for a lively paper and a better-informed membership. All of its editors have followed this policy. The paper itself takes a justifiable pride in its record. It believes, as does the present author, that what happens in the cooperative movement is the business of all the members and that they have the right to know.

Tops from the point of view of education in cooperation is the *Nebraska Cooperator,* edited by L. S. Herron. Mr. Herron can be classed with V. S. Alanne in his devotion to true cooperative method. Higher praise cannot be given.

The cooperative papers rarely accept advertisements, except from cooperatives. They may therefore have a difficult time, and sometimes have to be subsidized. Considerable progress has been made in the past few years in expanding the subscription lists, which helps the financial situation also. The Cooperative League reported in mid-1954 that cooperative papers (including those of the farm cooperatives) were reaching 4.2 million subscribers and those of farm organizations another 3.3 million.

Other Media

Films and radio are other means through which the cooperative message is carried to members and public. Films have been in use since 1939. The League's first talking picture was "Here is Tomorrow," released in January 1942. A few of the regional wholesales and several national cooperative organizations have also issued films.[21]

A Nation-wide membership drive and publicity campaign was launched in October 1941, which continued for a whole year. During it, leading cooperators broadcast over national networks and in a number of radio forums. These were supplemented by many local broadcasts, spotted throughout the period.

After an initial setback in 1942,[22] a series of broadcasts then started in mid-February 1943 and continued for 13 weeks in 36 cities.

Necessarily, most of the radio programs have been presented over the regular commercial stations. A few stations, however, are owned by cooperators. Thus, beginning in September 1937 the Peoples Broadcasting Corp. (an auxiliary of Nationwide Mutual Insurance Co., of Ohio) acquired, in succession, radio stations in Worthington, Ohio, Washington, D. C. (sold in 1953), Trenton, N. J., Fairmont, W. Va., and Cleveland, Ohio. In mid-1953 the corporation was also granted the right to build its first television station, at Trenton.

From 1948 through 1954 another cooperatively owned FM station was operated in the National Capital area.[23]

In 1950 the Nebraska Rural Radio Association, organized in June 1948 and composed of individual farmers and their cooperatives, received its license to build a station, using the letters, KRVN. It began broadcasting early in 1951.

Another avenue of public approach, now more and more being utilized, is that of exhibits at local and State fairs.

The Program in Review

The consumers' cooperative leaders have no doubt about the long-term value of cooperative education for members and the public and the training of cooperative managers and employees. Some of the producer groups may still ignore this phase of collective effort, in the belief that patronage refunds will do the trick, but most of their leaders now recognize the value of educational work in pulling and keeping patronage.

An editorial in *Farm News* (Indiana cooperative paper) late in 1953 cited the findings in a State college survey, that the people with the best understanding of cooperatives are the ones who are the most valuable members and best patrons, and continued—

"Moreover, the understanding cooperators were not merely a shade better patrons, but were very much better. Furthermore, the understanding people helped more in making decisions.

"This is highly significant. It shows that the key to building co-op enterprises lies not in merely doing what the competitive business does and doing it a little better; rather, that key lies in teaching the members and would-be members that the co-op is truly a self-help society, that it is a 'we' project, that the members control it with their votes, finance it with their capital, and give it life with their trade."[24]

As we have seen, the question of the most desirable form of organization for education—whether in combination with business activities or through an independent agency—has called forth a great deal of discussion pro and con.

One of the determinants in reaching the answer has been the matter of financing. Educational activities themselves bring in little or no revenue. The seed of education sown today may not flower for months or even years. It is difficult therefore to demonstrate the value, in concrete results, to practical, "hard-headed" people on boards of directors.

Retail cooperatives in this country have been hesitant or unable to make adequate appropriations for educational work carried on by special organizations such as the district leagues. Accordingly, such bodies have always had a precarious existence, and now nearly all have disappeared.

On the other hand, it is relatively easy for business organizations operating successfully to set aside funds or even to assess member associations when a definite training, publicity, or advertising program is needed. In Ohio, for example, the educational program has been financed through regular contributions of 1 percent of gross retail sales by the local cooperatives. This is favored, rather than appropriations from earnings, because if earnings fail, the educational work ceases.

For the present the question appears to have been answered on the regional level with the combination form under which the wholesales carry on varying amounts of general educational work and virtually all of the vocational training. Most of the wholesales not connected with a general farm organization now have an educational and training program. The Cooperative League functions as the over-all educational agency, besides joining the wholesales in the sponsorship of a number of courses and institutes.

This arrangement, in turn, points to a possible hazard. Cooperators need to be on the alert against the unfortunate tendency that purely business organizations sometimes display —to forget the social aims of the movement and to carry on educational work only to the extent that it serves the business objectives. The educational worker is likely to be overridden in favor of the businessman even in cooperatives.[25]

It has been my observation that when things go wrong and retrenchment has to be made, education is the first to feel the knife and the cooperative paper is sacrificed. Also, when education and business are merged into one organization, the educational work occupies a secondary position or virtually disappears.

This is doubly unfortunate. No cooperative is either safe or sound without cooperatively enlightened, loyal members, and this depends on continuous education. The cooperative paper is the closest and best link between administration and members, a channel of communication that is indispensable in forming the loyalty on which the cooperative must rely for success.[26] As has been said, cooperative education must be "systematic and ceaseless." It is the foundation of all cooperative expansion and without it the cooperative movement becomes merely a business enterprise with no social purpose.

Cooperatives have a long way to go before reaching anything approaching perfection in educating members and informing the public about cooperation, but they are improving rapidly. Chief encouraging sign is the increasingly general recognition of the value and absolute necessity of such efforts. By using cooperative funds in these educational, cultural and recreational projects, cooperatives are also helping their members to a more abundant life.

Chapter 27.—COOPERATIVE HOUSING

The development of cooperative housing in the United States has been limited by the inexperience of prospective homeowners in this field, by their unwillingness to conform to the requirements of true cooperation, by the difficulty of finding financing, by the failure of most housing groups to continue their interest once their own need was satisfied, and by the lack of central sources of technical, legal, and operational knowledge, which would also constitute the continuing and coordinating influence needed to weld the disparate groups into a "movement."

Principles of Cooperative Housing

Genuinely cooperative housing enterprises—i.e., "all-the-way" cooperatives[1]—are characterized by the following:

1. The initiative comes from the group to be housed or from its sponsor.

2. Democratic control (one member, one vote) resides in the membership from the beginning. Responsibility for administration is vested in a board of directors elected by the members.

3. Members receive a leasehold on their dwelling, but legal ownership of the property remains with the association.

4. The member's equity in the association is transferable only with the consent of the association, and never at more than its par value.

5. Surplus accruing from the operations, when not used for collective purposes, is returned to the members in proportion to the amount of their patronage (i.e., their monthly payments).

Not all organizations calling themselves cooperative adhere in all respects to the above principles. Some, although retaining title to the whole property, allow the members to sell their equity for whatever they can get, thus making speculation inevitable. In the "co-ventures"[2] the individual member receives title to his dwelling and may dispose of the property whenever and at whatever price he sees fit. Some associations, otherwise genuine cooperatives, permit subleasing of units at a profit to the member, which nullifies association control of the property.

Beginnings of Cooperative Housing

Cooperative activity with the sole or primary purpose of providing housing is less than 50 years old in this country. The earliest association of record was the Finnish Cooperative Housing Association, "Alku," organized in Brooklyn, N. Y., in March 1916. This veteran organization is still operating as a cooperative.

Cooperatives in New York and Elsewhere

The success of this first venture tempted other Brooklyn Finns and a few Scandinavians to do likewise, and in a few years a dozen or more associations had either built or bought apartment buildings. A few of the non-Finnish groups also bought and remodeled existing buildings. Among them were Consumerized Homes, in the Bronx, of which Hyman Cohn was president, Consumers Cooperative Housing Association, the president of which was Cedric Long (executive secretary of the Cooperative League of the USA), and Beekman Hill Cooperative Association, the members of which were nearly all professional women.

All of the projects named above except Consumerized Homes are still under cooperative ownership.

Several Jewish groups carried on apartment-house projects in the Bronx. Among them was the Farband Cooperative Housing Corporation. Its 6-story elevator apartments occupied only 69 percent of the land—a most unusual circumstance in those days. This association, though never having undertaken any additional construction, is still in successful operation.

Another, United Workers Cooperative Association, started by leasing a single floor of a building in the Bronx, then as the membership grew, took over the whole building, added certain social features and undertook a summer camp.

Beginning in 1925, the association expanded its holdings until it held 6 city blocks of land, all bordering on Bronx Park. It then embarked on a most ambitious housing project, erecting 700 units in 5-story walk-up apartments on two of the blocks, so constructed as to give each room an outside view of the street, park, or interior gardens, and with each room having cross ventilation. Less than 50 percent of the ground space was occupied by the buildings. This must have been one of the earliest groups, if not *the* earliest, to incorporate these features in housing for low-income families.

Its first buildings were financed largely from workers' savings. Unfortunately, down payments were so small as to make the net worth inadequate, and the elaborate community facilities provided (cooperative stores, large well-equipped social rooms, classrooms, gymnasium, library, auditorium, etc.) raised the monthly rental payments so high that the association could not qualify for the 20-year tax exemption that the New York law provided for limited-dividend organizations.

Attempt to retrench came too late. Reorganization (including sale of the cooperative stores), enabled the association to continue in operation for some years. Although management of the project had been returned to the members by 1931, the depression prevented sufficient recovery and by the end of 1941 all the members' equity was gone and the association had to dissolve.

This group was one of those that had accepted the Communist philosophy, and was one of the most vociferous and extreme in that respect. It is regrettable that its real contribution—good-quality housing for workers—was obscured in the impracticality and unwisdom of its social and political program.

One of the few housing ventures outside New York City in these early years was an experiment carried out in Milwaukee, about 1921, under the leadership of the Mayor, Daniel W. Hoan. It made use of a type of financing probably unique in this country, although fairly common in Europe. Briefly, the plan provided for participation by cities and counties through their investment in the preferred stock of housing enterprises organized under a State law of 1919. It involved no subsidy or expense to the taxpayers.

Only 105 dwellings of the 3,500-unit project were built.

The plan had been that the title should be held by the Garden Homes Co., with the residents merely holding a lease on their houses. So many of the tenant-owners became dissatisfied with this arrangement that the law was amended in 1923, to permit the giving of fee-simple title to the tenants with the right to sell at whatever price they could get. With these changes the cooperative character of the plan was lost. As far as known, though the law is still on the statute books, no other project was ever undertaken under it.

In the middle 1920's, also, two cooperative apartment hotels were erected in Washington, D. C., by and for unattached women employed by the Federal Government. Both are still in operation, though in neither case have the members ever had any sense of being part of the general cooperative movement.

Pseudo- and Semi-Cooperatives

One or more of the cooperative principles had been discarded or ignored by many of the housing associations. Judged on the basis of strict compliance, the Cooperative League said it rated less than a dozen of the 40-odd associations as cooperative in all respects; "perhaps two dozen others" were on the "border line between Rochdale cooperation and unrestricted speculation." Outside New York City there was at that time not a single "genuine cooperative housing organization."[3]

Housing as an Auxiliary Operation

Toward the end of the twenties, two interesting projects were undertaken in New York City. One was sponsored by Consumers' Cooperative Services, operating a chain of cooperative cafeterias. Using the surplus accumulated in its business operations, the association helped to finance a 12-story apartment building, with 66 apartments, in lower Manhattan. The residents, many of whom were members of CCS, formed a cooperative to own and operate the building. The project got started just as the depression began, had difficulty in obtaining occupants except on a rental basis, and suffered a high turnover caused by unemployment and removals to other neighborhoods and cities.

The association was able to meet its first and second mortgage obligations and operate within its income until 1935, but could not meet the requirements of the third mortgage or the interest on the common stock held by CCS. A reorganization in 1945 left CCS the principal stockholder, and on January 1, 1946 the housing cooperative dissolved and CCS took over the building as a subsidiary. Since that time all apartments have been on a rental basis, and there have been no member-owners.

The Amalgamated Projects

The other development was the initial activity of what has proved to be the leader and dean of cooperative housing projects in the United States and one of the most successful from both the cooperative and the financial point of view—the Amalgamated buildings, sponsored (but not financed[4]) by the Amalgamated Clothing Workers of America.

The first buildings, with 303 units, were completed in 1926 and 1927; 192 apartments were finished in 1929; and 115 in 1931-32. All of these were in the Bronx. In the meantime, a sister organization, Amalgamated Dwellings, Inc., carried on a project in lower Manhattan, for 236 families, completed in 1930.

The structures covered only half or less of the ground areas. The remainder was given over to gardens, walks and landscaped areas. The buildings in the Bronx had an unusually fine location, being bordered by park areas on three sides.

The first project was only well under way when the depression struck. The concentration of the greater part of the members in the needle trades—which were especially hard hit—and the compactness of the colony presented peculiar difficulties. By the end of 1932, some 60 to 70 percent of the members were out of work. On the other hand, occupational and racial ties gave the group a solidarity that other associations of more diverse make-up lacked.

Contributions from the more fortunate families, rent reductions in 1930 and again in 1932, extension of credit by the cooperative store, and other measures enabled the association not only to pull through the depression successfully, but by 1936 to return $30,000 to the tenants in patronage refunds on the monthly payments they had made in that year.

The cooperative was assisted by much advice from the New York State Board of Housing at the beginning. It has also had, throughout its existence, the benefit of the high-caliber leadership and technical knowledge of A. E. Kazan, its president and general manager, who conceived the plan in the first place and who has carried all the projects through to completion.

Periods of Depression and Recovery

Two new housing associations were started in 1930 but neither got into operation. Among the existing cooperatives, only the Amalgamated was able to begin any new activity.

During the depression some of the apartment cooperatives failed because so many of the members were unemployed (and delinquent on payments) that the associations could not meet their own obligations.[5]

It was not until 1936 that any new expansion occurred in cooperative housing; four new groups were formed in that year.

Among them was the Wisconsin Cooperative Housing Association, in Madison, Wis., composed chiefly of State and University personnel. Its project, Crestwood, situated on 75 acres of land just west of the city, was begun in 1938. The association had intended to operate as an all-the-way cooperative, but difficulties with the FHA forced it to become a co-venture. Land for the single-family dwellings was sold to the members who then carried forward their own negotiations. Being then outside the city limits, the association had to finance new water and sewer systems. In 1940, using funds supplied by an anonymous lender, the association itself erected three houses. Altogether 50 or more houses were constructed in the community.

In St. Paul, Minn., the Cooperative Housing Association built 27 houses on the co-venture basis in 1940 and 6 more in 1941. A companion organization in Minneapolis—also a co-venture—constructed 87 houses. In New York City the Amalgamated group carried out its fourth project (a 2-story, 48-unit building) in 1941. These were the only housing cooperatives active during the two "defense" years.

With the entrance of this country into the war, all civilian housing except that carried on by the Federal Government ceased.

Mutual Housing

After the defense housing program was started, eight projects built under the Lanham Act were earmarked for "mutual" or cooperative ownership after the war's end. To this number were later added the three "green towns" and several hundred permanent Federal housing projects.

By the time the war ended, residents' associations had been formed in six of the Lanham Act projects, and had been given operation of the projects on sort of a probational basis. In two others, negotiations for purchase were begun.

In 1947 the Government announced the discontinuance of the sale of public housing to mutual associations, except for cash. (Previously, purchase had been permitted on a 10-percent down payment, with the Federal Public Housing Administration holding a long-term mortgage.) This requirement was lifted in 1948 and by the end of the year, mutual housing agreements had been concluded with the FPHA for eight wartime projects with over 5,500 units, and negotiations were in process for three others with 830 units.

The outbreak of hostilities in Korea early in July 1950 again blocked mutual purchases until the spring of 1951 when they were resumed on instructions from a Senate committee. In the sale of the projects, preference was commonly given first to residents, second to nonresident veterans, and third to nonresident nonveterans. An amendment to the Lanham Act, in May 1950, provided for sale with no down payments, 45 years in which to amortize, and interest at 3 percent.

As of mid-1950, mutual associations had concluded purchase contracts for 25 projects, containing 9,627 dwellings.[6] Eight others were bargaining for the purchase of 5,141 units. Two years later, it was announced that a mutual had been successful in buying Pennypack Woods, in northwest Philadelphia. The transfer included 1,000 dwellings, 6 stores, and a community building. In 1954, residents of Lincoln Heights (near Cincinnati, Ohio) purchased that 350-unit project.

Most of the mutuals have been content simply to administer the property they bought. The only exception known to the author is the Greenbelt (Md.) Veterans Housing Corporation. Its purchases (made at different times) include about 1,600 dwelling units, 2 small apartment buildings, and several hundred acres of undeveloped land. By the beginning of 1954, plans were taking shape for four new housing projects on this land.

In probably the majority of the mutuals, the residents would have preferred to continue to rent from PHA. Many finally joined the cooperative because the only alternatives were to vacate (if they refused to join the mutual) or to allow the whole property to be bid in by some realtor, in which case there was no doubt that rents would be considerably increased. Only the desire for moderate-quality housing at bargain rates—and they *were* bargain rates—persuaded some. The cooperative feature of title vested in the association, with leases to the members, were accepted by such reluctant members because there was no alternative (this being one of PHA's conditions of sale).

The insufficient cooperative base in some mutuals has been attested by the failure of some or all of the other cooperative enterprises undertaken (such as cooperative store, gas station, etc.) in certain "mutual" communities. However, the concentration of prospective members in large groups does undoubtedly provide the opportunity for cooperation in many directions, if the residents can be persuaded of its value.

Postwar Activity

Removal of controls on the use of building materials in October 1945[7] stimulated a widespread revival of cooperative housing organization. And the Amalgamated leadership started the Sidney Hillman Houses, a slum-clearance project on the lower East Side, providing accommodations for 762 families, in which the buildings occupied only 30 percent of the land. Continuing its patronage-refund practice, in 1944 the association returned nearly $30,000 on rental payments in its older buildings, and in 1945 one month's rent, totaling $26,000.

By the end of 1946, housing cooperatives were being formed all over the United States, especially among returned veterans having building priorities and the advantages of Government loans and guaranties. Types of dwellings planned ranged all the way from apartments to single-family houses on city lots and subsistence homesteads with several acres of land. In some cases the housing association was a co-venture intending only to develop the site, leaving the subsequent processes to the individual members. In others, the association was to contract for the building of the houses, then give fee-simple title to the members. In only a comparatively few was the all-the-way method adopted; most were co-ventures.[8]

In the New York area alone there were over 50 active housing cooperatives in 1946. However, although some of the new associations had been in existence as long as 2 years, only one had progressed to the stage of actual construction. Setbacks were reported everywhere. One difficulty was the various technical and legal problems to which, as amateurs in the housing field, the cooperators did not have the answers. Others were newly imposed restrictions on the use of building materials, uncertainties as to prices, and problems of financing and insurance.

All controls on building were removed in June 1947. Although continued high prices of materials and construction were still a deterrent, a few projects were able to get construction under way during the year. By the end of the following year 13 young housing cooperatives had 571 units completed or under construction, out of a planned total of 1,767.

Some cooperatives that had bought land had been halted by high prices, financing, legal difficulties, etc.

Some progress was made in 1951. Several new associations were formed and a few others began building. Among the new projects were those of several labor organizations (i.e., the Electhester, Harry Silver, and East River projects, sponsored by the electrical workers, men's and women's clothing workers, meatcutters, and others).

Cooperatives and Government

Until the early thirties, such accomplishments as were made in cooperative housing had little or no assistance, even in the form of permissive laws. The regular cooperative laws were generally drawn for agricultural marketing or retail business and were not suitable for housing. None of them provided financial aid, although they did usually require conformity with cooperative methods.

Some cooperatives were able to benefit under State limited-dividend laws passed in the latter 1920's to stimulate housing of all kinds and under the redevelopment laws enacted during the 1940's to assist in slum clearance and the construction of new housing of good quality in blighted areas.

Cooperative Experience with FHA

The Federal Government began to encourage the building industry with the creation of the FHA system of insurance of mortgages in 1934. Under this program the Government relieved the builders and lenders of risk, while leaving them the profits. Although the law did not specifically so provide, under FHA procedure only profit enterprises were found eligible for insurance. Any cooperative groups that had the temerity to apply for insurance found that in the end, if they were fortunate enough to be granted insurance at all, they somehow had been shorn of their cooperative aspects in the course of the proceedings.

This is not to say that this result was the consequence of any special animus against cooperatives at that time; rather, it was probably due to the stereotyped routines of FHA and lenders, neither of which had any knowledge of cooperatives (but were probably suspicious of the cooperative method, if only because it was new). In any case, FHA had the excuse that cooperatives were not mentioned in the housing law, as among the beneficiaries of FHA insurance.

This latter omission was remedied in 1948, when amendment (f) to Section 207 of the National Housing Act added cooperatives to the groups eligible for insurance. No regulations for the handling of cooperative applications were issued, however, with the result that between 1948 and mid-1950, only five associations actually received insurance under the amendment; three of these were mutuals on whose property the Government itself held the mortgage.

The obstacles faced by cooperatives were graphically, though not fully, revealed in a study (limited to genuine cooperatives) made in 1950 jointly by the U. S. Bureau of Labor Statistics and the Housing and Home Finance Agency. The problems included those with which every builder has to deal: the finding of land, overcoming or adjusting to zoning or building regulations, installing utilities, and working out satisfactory relationships with architect, contractor, and labor.

There were others, however, encountered only by cooperatives, such as those arising from the presence of nonwhites in the cooperative membership (or simply the interracial policy enunciated in the bylaws, even though all the actual members were white), and covert opposition by various local groups. Some cooperatives, applying for financing, met no open discouragement. Their applications simply remained "pending," with no decision for or against, until it finally became obvious to even the most hopeful that no progress would ever be made.[9]

Opposition by the HHFA prevented disclosure, in the official report,[10] of the actual extent of the hindrances found by cooperatives in their effort to get financing and insurance. Some of the experiences revealed to BLS investigators were heartbreaking, and a good deal of this could be traced to FHA offices themselves. Although the national headquarters at Washington ostensibly sets FHA policy, it became evident during the study that for all practical purposes the local offices were autonomous. Most of their staff came from the construction or real-estate industries and had no understanding of or love for cooperatives. In one region a top official openly declared that no cooperative would get clearance from him.[11]

The usual tactic of FHA, as of the lending agencies also, was that of delay. Weeks, sometimes months, would elapse between the time of application and the date of initial action.[12] Then one or two objections would be raised and referred to the cooperative. When these had been met, another delay would ensue and other objections would be taken, one or a few at a time. In this way, many months or even a year or more would elapse, during which some members inevitably lost heart and withdrew.[13]

Practically every current association covered in the study had experienced a definite lack of cooperation and what seemed to be discrimination of one kind or another and in greater or less degree, in its relations with FHA.[14]

Time lags were one of the most discouraging conditions for cooperatives. This was a period of great housing shortage, when returned veterans were founding new families and needed shelter. Associations that started with large memberships and long waiting lists found them melting away as month succeeded month and no tangible results eventuated. A great deal of energy and time of officers and committeemen, that should have gone into the project itself, had to be spent in explanations and in enlisting new members. The cooperatives that succeeded in completing their projects were able to do so only because of the devotion and persistence of their (unpaid) officers.

Other unfortunate results of time lags were the continuously increasing costs of materials and labor (that in some cases finally raised the house cost beyond the members' means) and the continued outlay for carrying costs and other current expense.

Data collected in the study showed intervals of up to 4 years between the date of formation of the association and completion of the first dwelling. The wonder is that these cooperatives had any members left at all by that time.[15]

Section 213 *Program*

Unsuccessful attempts were made in 1949 and 1950 to get inserted in the housing law a section authorizing direct Government loans for cooperatives and nonprofit organizations, to provide dwellings for "middle income" families. President Truman's message to Congress early in 1950 proposed a cooperative program for middle-income housing, and the budget submitted contained a suggested appropriation of $50 million for it. This was eliminated in the course of Congressional consideration.

Instead, a provision (Section 213) was added to the housing act on April 20, 1950, authorizing FHA to insure mortgages on property held by either co-ventures or all-the-way cooperatives. The furnishing of technical service and assistance in organization and in the "planning, development, construction, and operation" of cooperative projects was also authorized.

In compliance with the new legislation, FHA created the Cooperative Housing Division under the supervision of an assistant commissioner. Its staff included a legal advisory section, a technical advisory section dealing with land planning and architecture, and a management advisory section.

Regulations were issued, a "kit" of materials and forms was assembled for the guidance of groups applying for insurance, and a "co-op" man to deal with cooperative applications was established in each of the 70 local FHA offices. The regulations prohibited builders (or others benefiting from the project in

V. S. Alanne (left), and L. S. Herron
Outstanding educators in the American cooperative movement

A. E. Kazan, leader in co-op housing in New York City

Dr. Michael A. Shadid, founder of Community Co-op Hospital, Elk City, Okla.

Edward A. Filene
Patron of credit unions

Roy F. Bergengren
Credit union leader

Filene House, headquarters of Credit Union National Ass'n, Madison, Wis.

a pecuniary way) from acting as incorporators or officers of cooperatives.

Unfortunately, in their zeal to make a showing of housing stimulated by the new program, the FHA officials in charge of it failed to adopt a definition that would have limited the benefits under the section to organizations conforming to accepted cooperative standards. It seems reasonable to suppose that the intent of Congress, in adopting the amendment, was to benefit real cooperatives. If that body's interest was merely in getting more housing built, all it needed to do was to extend the life of Section 608.

Within FHA there seems to have been a division of opinion between those interested in getting more housing under way (of whatever kind) and those who favored genuine cooperatives. The former group prevailed, with the result that FHA accepted not only projects with real consumer sponsorship but also those sponsored by profit builders.[16]

There was a rush to take advantage of the program. At the end of the first 6 months, 202 applications for insurance had been received, covering 27,252 planned dwelling units. They were about equally divided between all-the-way associations planning to build apartment houses and co-ventures planning individual houses.

The builders, having now exhausted the rich ore in Section 608 (which expired in the spring of 1950), were examining this new program and finding it good for their purpose. They therefore moved in on it, and from that time forward genuine cooperative housing receded farther into the background, and builder-sponsored projects took by far the lion's share.

By the end of 1951, applications for insurance had been received for 62,554 units, with a total estimated cost of over $593 million. Some of these were later withdrawn. As of the end of the year the active case load was 258 projects, with 37,579 units. Of these, 38 projects had been accepted for insurance, and insurance commitments had been issued for 24 others—representing a total of 12,140 dwellings.

In spite of a continuing shortage of mortgage money, applications increased. The first 9 months of 1953 showed a larger volume than was received under any other FHA housing program and about twice that in the same period of 1952. Seventy percent were in co-venture (i.e., "sales" type) projects and 30 percent in all-the-way ("management" type) projects.

The cooperative program, including provisions for direct loans to cooperatives (introduced by Representative Javits), encountered rough going in Congress in 1953. In conference, the position of FHA assistant commissioner, to head up the cooperative work, was eliminated, and the total personnel reduced to about half a dozen people, in spite of the fact that applications pending totaled $104 million. As a result, the cooperative work was reduced to a section in the Multi Family Housing Division of FHA.

As of June 30, 1954, nearly 30,000 units in 234 projects had been insured under Section 213. Most of them were apartment houses (largely in New York City). Single-family homes had been insured in about 30 States. Among the Section 213 projects were 45 for Negroes, with 1,575 units.

Developments in 1954

Cooperators have many criticisms of the 213 program as it has been developed. But some strictures have also come from within the Government itself, notably from William F. McKenna, a special investigator appointed by the HHFA Administrator in 1954. He charged, regarding the builder-sponsored projects, that "the cooperative and nonprofit character of these ventures was almost wholly fictitious." He said they excluded the home-owner "from effective participation in the co-op's affairs until all contractual arrangements were made and the mortgage loan proceeds fully obligated." Some of them kept control of the land through leaseholds, thus establishing fat "annuities" for themselves, based on inflated land values set by FHA.

Many revisions of policy and procedure in order to safeguard the cooperative character of the program were recommended by him, by an 8-member consumer-interest advisory committee appointed early in 1954, and by cooperative housing leaders. However, the 1954 law passed by Congress contained only two of the recommendations; it provided for a 1-year builder warranty on all construction, and required sponsors of projects to certify actual costs to FHA.

The 1955 act authorized the Federal National Mortgage Association to make prior commitments for $50 million in Section 213 mortgages for which private financing could not be found; restored the position of Assistant Commissioner for Cooperative Housing and increased the staff to provide technical assistance; raised the project ceiling from $5 to $12.5 million; reduced to 8 (from 10) units the minimum project size allowed for cooperative projects; and authorized use of Section 213 financing for mutual housing associations in the purchase of Government-owned developments.[16a]

In the fall of 1954 FHA issued a new regulation requiring that attorneys, architects, and management specialists hired by housing cooperatives under Section 213 be independent of the builder-sponsors. The purpose of this was to insure that the loyalty of these technicians would be to the membership, not the builder. This opened the way for increased utilization of the two cooperative housing-service federations—United Housing Foundation, and Foundation for Cooperative Housing.

Role of the FHA in Housing

In the beginning, FHA requirements undoubtedly operated to raise building standards. In the long run, however, its minimum standards that must be met in order to receive insurance have tended to become maximum standards as well.

Cooperative and other housing has long suffered from this acceptance of mediocrity and the discouragement under FHA procedure of any new ideas or experiments. Projects for dwellings of "modern" style almost invariably found it difficult or impossible to get FHA insurance. This was publicly recognized by Guy T. Hollyday, who served briefly as FHA commissioner early in the Eisenhower Administration, and by his successor, Norman P. Mason.

As various critics have pointed out, FHA has in practice been operated as sort of adjunct to the building and lending industries. Its personnel has come in the main from them and has reflected their points of view, and the FHA program has therefore been conducted openly for their benefit, not that of the home owners. The 1954 hearings on Section 608 (passed to encourage construction of rental housing) revealed, in many cases, overvaluation of the project at every stage beginning with land acquisition, insurance by FHA on these inflated values, sales of the mortgage (i.e., "mortgaging out") by the builders at from 110 to 150 percent, and pocketing by them of windfall profits running up to several hundred percent or more.

Cooperative Program in Review

The projects under Section 213 may be divided into three classes: (1) Genuine, nonprofit, consumer sponsored and controlled enterprises; (2) "'management type," builder-sponsored projects that (although initiated by builders and involving profits to them and no voice in construction for consumers) may, if the residents desire, evolve into real cooperatives for managing the property, and (3) co-ventures, "sales type" builder-sponsored projects that have no cooperative feature of any sort.

In 1950 the FHA described the advantages of the Section 213 program as follows:

To members of the cooperatives—(1) savings from the acquisition of low-cost undeveloped land and the elimination of the "speculative profit usually realized in site improvements," (2) veterans' preference to the entire cooperative membership if 65 percent or more are veterans ("no other FHA-insured mortgage financing at this time provides this liberal feature"), and (3), for members of cooperatives that build apartment houses, equity increased each month, no arbitrary rent increases, monthly payments lower than current rentals in the locality, and elimination of the usual landlord's profit.

To builders and lenders—(1) elimination of many of the risks of speculative building, (2) financial arrangements, "with little or no risk to the builder," made in advance, (3) no sales or advertising problems, (4) financial obligations widely distributed among the cooperative members, and (5) economic stability arising from good housing at lower monthly costs.

The present writer believes that the financial and other advantages to the builders and lenders have outweighed those to the purchasers. In builder-sponsored projects it is doubtful if the speculative profit has been removed (as FHA has claimed) from land development, site development, or even the building construction.[17] The purchaser does, I believe, receive housing as good as or better than that built under Section 207 and at lower cost, and has the advantages of lower down payment, lower interest rates, and a long period of amortization.

In terms of housing per se, then, the Section 213 program has been of considerable benefit, for it has undoubtedly increased the supply of dwellings. Certain other aspects are more open to question.

Section 213 was supposed to have inaugurated a "new deal" for cooperative housing, with FHA assistance instead of opposition. However, all of the cooperative applications are processed as part of the regular routine of the local offices and must still run the gauntlet of FHA personnel of conventional outlook.

The top management of FHA's cooperative program has been sympathetic to cooperatives. Warren J. Lockwood, under whose direction as assistant FHA commissioner the program was carried on until his retirement in 1952, was, I am sure, convinced of the value of the program. His mistake was his failure —fundamental to the whole operation—to discriminate between the true and the false and thus exclude the builder projects. C. Franklin Daniels, his successor pro tem was saddled with a system the policies of which he had no part in formulating, and was so hamstrung by lack of funds and personnel that he could do little or nothing to make the program effective from the cooperative standpoint.

Encouraging features are that the original "kit" of informational material was revised and improved, and that in 1955 the position of Assistant Commissioner for cooperative housing was restored and the technical staff increased again, so that the outlook is somewhat better. And this prospect was still further enhanced by the appointment of Dwight Townsend of Consumers Cooperative Association (Kansas City) in October 1955, to head up the cooperative housing work.

Nevertheless, as was pointed out in the 1954 hearings, the fundamental question still remains to be settled: Whether the 213 program is to be used to "encourage true cooperatives or merely to enable promoters, whose motive is one of profit, to capitalize" on the program under the pretext of helping the "eventual cooperative owners."[18]

Federation Among Housing Cooperatives

The need has long been evident for some central body, or bodies, to supply the technical, legal, and operational knowledge and guidance such as is provided by the HSB of Sweden for housing associations in that country.

In the United States two intended national associations have failed for lack of support. The National Cooperative-Mutual Housing Association (1946) was succeeded in 1950 by the National Association of Housing Cooperatives. Thanks largely to the help of the Cooperative League and its Washington staff, the federation was able to serve as Washington representative of the mutual housing groups and render real service in their relations with the Federal Government. It gave legal and technical advice and issued a monthly newsletter. It became dormant after a year or two. Its newsletter, *Co-op Housing,* was taken over by the Cooperative League and is now issued by it in Chicago.

No further national coordination seems likely in the foreseeable future, barring the unexpected appearance of an "angel" to subsidize it. Groups that have finished their original projects usually are either unwilling or unable to pay for assistance to others; those in the throes of construction have no money to pay for the support of a central organization (or, too often, even to patronize it, if fees are attached). The Cooperative League has given such assistance as it can, but is in no position to carry the financial burden, even if its members (mostly distributive cooperatives) were willing for it to do so.

Federation over a small area having a fairly large number of housing cooperatives appears to be more feasible at this stage, and some progress has already been made in New York. There the United Housing Foundation was formed in 1950, as well as an operations subsidiary, Community Services, Inc., organized under the State limited-dividend law. These two organizations have sponsored several apartment projects in Greater New York.

A second federation, Foundation for Cooperative Housing, was formed by some of the first organization's members who split off from it on a question of policy. It developed a master plan for the cooperative development of the unused land in Greenbelt, Md.

The major purposes of the foundations are to offer advice and aid to existing cooperatives; to help organize new associations on a sound basis; to act as clearing houses for information on cooperative housing; and to develop effective methods of project management, and good public relations.

In the New York area, also, the Section 213 projects have formed two groups for mutual action, one consisting of the presidents of 33 projects and the other called the Coordinating Council of Section 213 Cooperatives. The two groups have represented their members in both local and Congressional hearings.

Appraisal

In terms of dwelling units provided, the results of cooperative housing up to mid-1950 (when the Section 213 program went into effect) were not very impressive in the total housing picture. Based on cumulative records kept by the U. S. Bureau of Labor Statistics since 1918, it appears that 8,723 dwellings had been supplied for members on either an all-the-way or co-venture basis.[19] Considering all the financial and other difficulties, this is not a *poor* record, either.

As the figures of FHA's cooperative section do not distinguish between consumer-sponsored and builder-sponsored projects, it is impossible to say how many additional homes have been provided on a genuinely cooperative basis under Section 213. (But the acting director said they are "negligible" in comparison with the total.)

The 1950 Government survey found that among the cooperative savings to members were those on land development, reduction in loan-service costs when the association acted as collection agency, lower maintenance costs, lower insurance costs where blanket mortgage was used, and savings by self-help and volunteer labor. Cooperative houses had the advantage over speculative houses in "design and quality rather than in price" —in other words, the cooperative member got a better house for the same price.

When, as in cooperative housing, the dwellings are built for living and not for profit, better site utilization and project planning are possible. Savings can be made by use of dead-end streets, the "super-block," and other features of good community lay-out, with shorter sewer lines and utility connections, savings on roads of lighter construction, and greater safety. Maintenance economies are possible in large projects through the employment of one or more full-time all-round workers, in the place of sporadic short-term hirings by individual families for specific jobs. Elimination of the cost of vacancies (because cooperators are usually permanent residents) is another source of saving.

The cooperative housing colony can be made the basis of a better way of life. It can impose standards of maximum occupancy. As co-owners, all the members have a common interest in maintaining a high level of community well-being. In such a compact group, also, many collective activities are possible.

Few of the older housing associations in this country have made use of such opportunities. Among the exceptions are the Amalgamated residents in New York City, who have undertaken, especially in the Bronx, many community activities, including a monthly paper which goes to residents in the Bronx and downtown projects and Hillman Houses.

All-the-way cooperatives, by their very nature and membership, are the ones in which community awareness and cooperative spirit are most commonly found. Most of them are apartment-house projects. Few of the groups building detached houses ended as all-the-way cooperatives, even though that may have been the intention in the beginning. Among the consumer-sponsored co-ventures, also, some have developed a remarkable community spirit and sense of "togetherness."

The Section 213 program is too new as yet for predictions as to the degree of community life and participation in the builder-sponsored projects. However, in the New York area some projects have organized cooperative nurseries and credit unions and most of them issue bulletins and hold meetings and social affairs. Much more can be done if there is organized effort.

Forging a cooperative housing "movement" requires able and devoted leadership. But such have been the hardships in carrying out housing projects that 9 of every 10 officers interviewed in the Government study told the investigators they would never willingly undertake another project. Thus, with few exceptions, additional cooperative housing must look for new leaders, not those who have already been through the mill. It seems a pity that such ability and know-how should be lost and that new groups must start from scratch. It is to be hoped that, as experience is gained and Section 213 cooperatives become more numerous in given areas, the officers will increasingly recognize the advantages of collective action in their own interest and go on from there into the wider field of general cooperative development, following the New York example.

Financing and insurance continue to be problems. Increased appropriations for advance mortgage commitments on cooperative projects and for provision of technical assistance would ease the situation. Tapping of additional non-Governmental sources of funds (such as those in trade-union pension and welfare plans, credit unions, charitable foundations, insurance organizations in the cooperative movement,[20] etc.) should be explored. Already, some steps have been taken toward use of such sources.

It is the author's belief, however, in view of the continued resistance to cooperatives by the conventional lenders, that the fullest potentialities of cooperative housing for moderate-income families will not be reached until some self-sustaining system of low-rate Government loans, like those in Europe, is established.

Chapter 28.—MEDICAL AND HOSPITAL CARE

Voluntary plans for the provision of medical or hospital care or both were known as early as the middle of the nineteenth century. The development of this form of cooperation has had several phases: Mutual-aid societies, organized on a nationality basis, beginning about 1851, voluntary plans for industrial employees, starting about 1885, plans operating under labor-union auspices, beginning shortly after World War I and continuing with increasing momentum to the present, and voluntary plans allied with the cooperative movement, beginning in 1929 and steadily though slowly developing since that time.

Early Plans

Plans of Immigrant Groups

Immigrants to the United States made use of the cooperative method in medicine more than half a century before native Americans thought of it. Few associations of the mutual-aid type, based on a single nationality, are formed today. However, the early ones have been strikingly persistent, as well as outstanding in the membership loyalty they have inspired. California and Florida furnish noteworthy examples.

French immigrants started their own plan, La Societe Francaise de Bienfaisance Mutuelle in San Francisco in 1851. By 1852 they had their own hospital, still active after more than a century. In the same city the German General Benevolent Society was formed in 1854. The next year it opened a hospital in an old rented building. The name of the organization was later changed to Franklin General Benevolent Society. The Franklin Hospital, also still active, has always operated on a prepayment basis for both hospitalization and medical care. A similar French hospital operated for some 25 years in Los Angeles.

The nineties produced in Tampa, Fla., the "centros" that are now the core around which revolve not only the social and cultural life of the city's Latin colony but also a whole series of welfare activities (including a complete medical program in two cases) for more than 23,000 persons.

The first was the Centro Espanol, organized in 1891 by Basques from Spain, who had worked as cigar makers in Cuba until driven out by a depression. Their association was followed by others of Italian, Cuban, and Spanish membership and by two auxiliaries for women and children.

Of the five centros presently operating, only two provide direct treatment. The others pay cash benefits. One of the latter pays hospitalization benefits for up to 90 days in any calendar year, besides paying a pension of $30 per month to members totally incapacitated through loss of limbs, insanity, or accidental blindness.

Three associations (L'Unione Italiana, Centro Espanol, and Delegacion del Centro Asturiano) own their own cemeteries and provide free undertaking, burial service and cemetery plot. They also have their own dispensaries, at which some or all of the medicine is free.

Each of the last two associations also has its own hospital. Espanol has its own staff of salaried physicians, as did also the Asturiano until at least the mid-30's. Then, because of embroilment with the medical profession (which was beginning to take action against all plans not doctor controlled), the Asturiano dropped this practice. Today the member engages the doctor of his choice, the association then reimbursing him; any local physician may practice at the cooperative hospital. The Espanol has continued to maintain its own staff but (although a member of the American Hospital Association) has, because of this, never been able to win AMA accreditation; and its doctors are refused admission to the county medical society.[1] Thanks to a court case won by the cooperative, its doctors are admitted to practice in any local hospital.

As the dues (about $2.50 per month) are insufficient to support the medical plan, the two hospital associations find additional income through a wide and varied social program. Each has a clubhouse (Espanol has two), with canteen, game rooms, classrooms, theater, etc., at which social, educational, and cultural events are held throughout the year.

All five organizations are democratically controlled, each member having one vote only. Elections, at which the large boards of directors are chosen, are said to be as important and exciting to the members as are the community political elections.

The centros have the advantage of a devoted loyalty that requires years of good service to develop—a goal aimed at but rarely achieved in such measure by most cooperative organizations. Tho their membership consists of relatively low-income families, their cooperative program enables them to meet, without outside assistance, the financial drains of illness and death, besides insuring for their members a degree of health, recreation, and culture rarely found at their income level.

Other Plans

There was at least one labor-union plan in this early period, a contract plan initiated by coal miners at Streator, Ill. Agitation began about 1885, when the doctors in the locality began to raise their fees for house calls to $2 (from $1). The local miners' union negotiated a contract with three doctors who agreed to attend "any number of families" for $1 per family per month. A year later, hundreds of families were reported to have joined the plan, and the latter was "working to the entire satisfaction of all."[2]

In 1914 the Joint Board of Sanitary Control in the women's clothing industry of New York City established a health center after long agitation by the International Ladies' Garment Workers' Union. In 1919 nine locals of the union took over its operation and it became the Union Health Center. In 1926 membership was thrown open to members of all labor unions in the city. This organization, still operating successfully, was the first of the medical-care centers by and for unionists of which I have found record. Such plans expanded markedly in the 1930's and at an even faster rate since the end of World War II.[3]

The Stewart's Creek Community Association, organized in Surrey County, N. C., in 1922, was reported to have hired a doctor and apportioned his salary and office upkeep among the members. Complete medical service cost $15 per family per year.

Developments in the Thirties

Elk City Hospital

In 1929, Dr. Michael M. Shadid[4] took the lead in the organization of the Farmers Union Cooperative Hospital in Elk City, Okla., with a starting membership of 12 families and no capital. His intention was to organize the hospital "without injury to existing vested interests in hospitals," but his offer of purchase, made to three local physicians, was rejected because "they were making more money than they could under any cooperative arrangement."

So great was the local need that 500 families were soon enrolled, $11,000 was raised, and erection of the first unit of a hospital was begun.

Notwithstanding almost continual hostility from organized medicine (later discussed), by the end of 1936 the association had nearly 2,500 participants and owned a 3-story building with 75 beds, laboratory, and clinical facilities. A bequest in 1951 enabled the cooperative to pay off the mortgage on the hospital. In 1953 the hospital was air conditioned. The hospital's school for practical nurses was the first to be accepted by the State board under a new State law.

With the exception of certain specific charges, all treatment is on a prepayment basis, with monthly dues varying according to the size of the family.

In 1952 the association had 1,698 families as members.

Other Plans for Medical Care

Three additional medical-care cooperatives had been formed by the end of 1936, all providing care under contracts with physicians: (1) San Diego Beneficial Society, formed in 1933, most of whose members were local office workers, (2) Economy (Ind.) Mutual Health Association (1936), limited to residents of Economy and vicinity, and (3) Wage Earners' Health Association, St. Louis, organized in 1936 by a group of social workers and with membership limited to persons earning not over $300 per month. The only one of these still in existence is that in St. Louis, the members of which obtain service through a contract with the Labor Health Institute.

In the latter 1930's two urban organizations were started—the health cooperative at Greenbelt, Md., active from 1938 until May 1950, and Group Health Association in Washington, D. C. The latter was sponsored by the Home Owners Loan Corporation which, concerned about the working time lost by its employees through sickness, advanced $40,000 to start a clinic on a cooperative basis. The new group operated independently of any control by the HOLC but at first served only employees of that agency. Later, membership was thrown open to all white Government workers, then to all white residents of the District, and finally (in 1946) racial restrictions were removed.

GHA began operations on November 1, 1937. By the end of 1943, it had increased its membership to 3,566 and had opened its own pharmacy.

Cooperative League and Medical Care

Even before the formation of the Cooperative League, its president (a distinguished surgeon) had written many articles on cooperative medicine. But not until 1936 did the subject appear on its congress agenda. The next year the League created a Bureau of Cooperative Medicine,[5] to help organize and develop health associations on the four principles of group medical practice, preventive medicine, periodic payment, and consumer cooperative control.

Nearly every subsequent congress has included medical care in either a regular session or in a sectional meeting.

War and Postwar Developments

Insurance Against Expenses of Illness

Cooperative insurance plans are usually of two kinds: those paying fixed cash benefits for the risks covered, and those reimbursing the patients' outlay for services at a specified percentage of the agreed charges for various types of treatment.

The oldest health insurance organization connected with the cooperative movement is Group Health Mutual of St. Paul, Minn. It was started in 1938 for a few of the credit unions and a group of cooperative employees. It began with 306 members and a capital of just under $16,000, most of which had been borrowed from a credit union.

Membership grew slowly at first, but by mid-1941 it had over 100 local member groups throughout Minnesota, with some 9,000 members. Following an arrangement with the members of the many cooperative creameries for a check-off of GHM dues from the check owing to them for their cream, membership doubled in 1943, and almost doubled again in 1944. In 1945, other members began to come in on a group basis, from municipal employment, labor unions, and industrial firms. By the end of 1953 it had about 120,000 members in 41,084 families.

When Group Health Mutual began, it was the only organization writing health insurance in the State of Minnesota. It was also the first to introduce (about 1950) insurance for catastrophic illness. The whole range of medical and hospital risks is now covered, so that the members have a wide choice of policies. New services include loss-of-income insurance for farmers (over 85 percent of the members are rural people) and life insurance.

In the early future, it plans to make available direct service in the Twin Cities of Minneapolis and St. Paul. An auxiliary, Group Health Medical Services, was organized to own hospital and medical facilities.

The association is licensed to operate in Minnesota, Wisconsin, and Washington State.

GHM has taken a leading part in education and promotional work for prepayment direct service. According to its general manager, George W. Jacobson, Group Health Mutual has contributed through the Cooperative Health Federation of America between 30 and 40 thousand dollars toward building the cooperative health movement. This is a record equalled by no other cooperative organization in the health field.

Such generous expenditure has been made possible through the dual structure through which the group operates. The business organization is Group Health Mutual. But each policyholder must also belong to a companion body, Group Health Association, and pay dues to it amounting to 10 cents per month. In 1954 a total of $70,000 was budgeted for educational work.

GHM sponsors many conferences, provides nine scholarships of $500 each for students in medicine and nursing, and has played an important part in the drives for State and National legislation. It was one of the charter members of the Cooperative Health Federation.

In Ohio, in addition to the main lines—life, fire, and auto insurance—Nationwide Insurance (formerly Farm Bureau Insurance Cos.) has been writing health and accident insurance since 1942. The companies have pioneered in coverage of rural population, aged persons, and dependents.

A new plan, already providing $10,000 in medical care for each employee of the Mutual Service Insurance Cos. of St. Paul, will, it was announced, be made available to the general public on a group basis in the 7-State area served by the companies.

Contract Plans

Some of the plans that operate under insurance laws conclude contract arrangements with physicians or groups of physicians, to whom they pay fees for their policyholders based on a set schedule of charges for specific treatment.

Most of the contract "agricultural health and medical associations" formed under the New Deal went out of existence upon the liquidation of the farm security program. Some of the survivors announced in 1953 that they intended to form a national association. One of these, Southern Oregon Health Service (with 2,100 families and 10,000 participants in 1954) became the twentieth regular member of the Cooperative Health Federation a little later.

Another contract plan was that of Group Health Cooperative (now Group Health Insurance, Inc.) of New York City, organized in 1939. Two of the organizers were Dr. Kingsley Roberts (director of the Cooperative League's Bureau of Cooperative Medicine) and Winslow Carlton. At first the plan offered comprehensive care. Because of inadequate income and wartime shortage of doctors, benefits were cut in 1944 to surgery, hospital care, and maternity care. This plan had 90,543 policyholders at the end of 1953.

The largest of the contract plans is Health Insurance Plan of Greater New York. It has contracts with groups of physicians, who give HIP policyholders direct medical and surgical treatment. No hospitalization is provided, but all employee groups insured are required to carry some kind of hospital insurance.

Started in 1947 under the sponsorship of Mayor Fiorello LaGuardia, for municipal employees, HIP has expanded its field and now accepts residents of the whole metropolitan area. It writes group insurance only. At the end of its 8th year of operation, March 1, 1955, HIP had 420,000 participants (about 5 percent of the total area population) and a thousand family doctors and specialists participating in the plan. The association has a special pension fund for participating doctors. It is an affiliate of the Cooperative Health Federation. Its only opposition has come from organized medicine.

A similar plan proposed for Milwaukee, Cooperative Health Insurance Plan (CHIP) had received its charter by the end of 1954.

Direct-Service Plans

During the war, most of the plans for direct service were stymied by shortages of doctors, nurses, and technicians and by building restrictions. Three hospitals, however—at Mooreland, Okla., Amherst, Tex., and Hardtner, Kans.—did manage to get into operation.

In 1944 occurred several fruitless attempts at organizing for medical care. The one exception, at Two Harbors, Minn., took over a building formerly run as hospital for treatment of railroad employees. When it was condemned unless extensive remodeling was done, a drive for funds for a new hospital and clinic building was begun. After an 18-month contest between the cooperative and a rival organization, an agreement was reached for a new body to be called Lakeview Memorial Hospital. The jointly owned hospital will be built on one of the three lots owned by the cooperative, the latter will operate a clinic on the second lot, and the third will be reserved for any group that may wish to build a clinic. Any licensed physician may practice in the hospital.

Many labor, cooperative, and farm organizations joined in the formation of Group Health Cooperative of Puget Sound in Seattle in 1946. The regional wholesale, Pacific Supply Cooperative, also spent some $15,000 in helping to get the cooperative under way.

GHC took over the hospital and staff of a hospital previously operated as a doctor-controlled organization. In August 1952 a new clinic building was also purchased in Seattle.

By January of the following year GHC had in membership 8,430 families (representing 24,203 persons). In addition, 7,634 persons were served through industrial and individual contracts, and some 2,500 others were patrons but not members.

A separate organization, Seattle Group Dental Cooperative was started in July 1953, with service on a fee basis, at cost. By the end of its first year it had 301 families in membership. A patronage refund amounting to 4.82 percent was made.

Group Health Cooperative also has its own pharmacy. A branch clinic was opened at Renton in 1955, replacing a previous one started in 1948.

In the meantime, across the country, Group Health Association in Washington, D. C., had increased its membership and patronage and had bought a 10-story building, enabling it to bring together for the first time all of its departments.

Participants in its medical program at the end of September 1954 numbered 20,069 and those in the dental department 5,761. Operating income amounted to $1,007,854 in 1953-54, thus raising it into the select million-dollar class of nonfarm cooperatives.

A change of policy in 1954 made possible the acceptance on a group basis of members of union health and welfare funds and other employee groups.

Thanks largely to the interest created by the passage of a permissive law in Texas in 1945, that year and the three years following were notable for the number of new hospital associations. Fourteen were formed in 1945, 32 in 1946, 16 in 1947, and 11 in 1948. Several of these were as far west as Idaho and Oregon.

After some of the easy enthusiasm wore off, the organizers began to realize the size of their problem: the difficulty of raising the large funds necessary to build and equip the hospitals, the opposition of the medical profession and local businessmen, and (in some cases) the unsuitability of the town's location for obtaining the large membership base needed for efficient operation. As a result, a considerable number of projects were dropped during the next few years, without having made much progress.

Others persevered and by the end of 1947 at least 20 cooperative hospitals were open, 3 associations had buildings under construction, and several of the older cooperatives had enlarged their facilities. At least 30 others were in process of organizing. By this time Texas was far in the lead, with 30 associations chartered. Minnesota had 7 cooperatives and Oregon 5.

Altogether, 101 cooperative hospital associations had been chartered by the end of 1948. In 29, the cooperative features or the entire project had been abandoned, because of inability to raise sufficient capital, local opposition, disinterest, or other reasons.

By the end of the next year 31 (of 38) clinics were in operation and 32 (of 52) hospitals. Three other groups had buildings under construction. Clinics were active in 11 States and the District of Columbia and hospitals in 11 States.

In Arizona the Casa Grande Valley Cooperative Community Hospital went into operation in 1953—the only cooperative hospital in the State. Early in the same year a drive for a hospital in the Santiam Valley of Oregon had culminated in the erection of a 34-bed modern building at Stayton; local cooperators were assisted by Hill-Burton funds. Another project, at Deer Park, Wash., denied Federal help, nevertheless, after 7 years of effort, finally resumed construction of its building, financed by membership fees and members' gifts.

A completely remodeled clinic was opened for service in the spring of 1955 by Arrowhead Health Center in Duluth, Minn.

Federation of Voluntary Plans

Several steps were taken in the late 1930's to weld the scattered groups into a movement.

In 1939 the Cooperative League convened a meeting of representatives of medical groups, in New York City. As a result of its deliberations, the Group Health Federation of America was chartered in February 1940. It was superseded in 1946 by the Cooperative Health Federation of America, of which eight medical-care cooperatives were charter members.

By mid-1953 the Federation's member plans were serving "at least 802,000 members and subscribers"—50,000 more than in the preceding year. With the admission of Co-op Medical Services Federation of Ontario, Canada, in November, the Federation became an international organization.

The Federation's purposes are the promotion of (1) the people's right to operate in the field of medical economics, (2) health-promotion measures as well as the treatment of the sick, (3) prepayment plans for comprehensive medical care, both preventive and curative, (4) group practice, (5) the highest quality of medical care, and (6) democratic consumer or lay control of the business and economic aspects of prepayment plans (but with all professional matters left to the medical staff).

This agency helps in organizing new health groups, aids in legislative work, and sponsors an annual institute and convention. It issues the *C. H. F. A. Information Letter* and a *Health and Welfare Newsletter* for union officers.

The organization is now recognized as the representative and spokesman for democratically controlled cooperative and group health plans throughout the country. Its 1954 annual meeting was told that its membership now includes almost every type of voluntary plan.

Enabling Legislation

Cooperators have had an uphill struggle to obtain the passage of permissive legislation for cooperative medical care. Attempts to secure an enabling law in Wisconsin, begun in 1937, finally culminated in a law 10 years later, not the least noteworthy aspect of which was that the State medical society had by that time ceased to oppose it. In Oklahoma and Minnesota, in spite of long effort, cooperators still have not been able to obtain legal authority for cooperative medical-care associations.

General overhaul of the New York cooperative law in 1951 included a new section authorizing the furnishing of hospital (but not clinical) service and the payment of cash indemnities for medical or dental care.

After a fruitless try in 1949 a law was obtained in Illinois in 1951 that authorized the formation of voluntary health services by 5 or more residents of the State, with participation open to any doctor or dentist on mutually agreed terms. In the meantime, however, a cooperative hospital at Staunton, after standing idle for 6 months in 1950 because it could get no medical staff, finally had to drop its cooperative features.

In Texas the medical society had pointed out, after the hospital at Amherst was organized in 1940, that there was no State law for it. Passage of the cooperative hospital law in 1945 was obtained only by acceding to the society's proposal to limit the effectiveness of the law to towns of 2,500 population or less.

While cooperators were battling for the few legislative gains noted above, authority for doctor-controlled plans was voted in one State after another. By 1950 such laws were in force in 23 States.[6]

They prevent the consumers or users of medical care from establishing plans. Further, they usually cover very limited service (generally only surgery and obstetrics), whereas consumer-sponsored plans aim for comprehensive service. They have operated to block the associations that labor organizations and rural groups were organizing, and in some cases even group practice by physicians as well.

Several attempts—notably by Senator Hubert Humphrey of Minnesota—have been made to obtain laws encouraging voluntary nonprofit plans by loans or otherwise. None has been successful.

Cooperatives and the Medical Profession

One of the darker chapters in the history of medical-care cooperation has been the unfortunate relationships with organized medicine, which has never become really reconciled to any but the traditional fee-for-service system. Its few concessions have been made grudgingly and usually only after defeat in the courts.

For a long time the American Medical Association resisted any kind of voluntary health protection. During the thirties it modified this attitude, but only with the proviso of monopoly control by doctors.

The AMA does not thus describe its position, of course. According to its own statement, the principles enunciated in 1934 (10 in number) were adopted to encourage its constituent societies "in undertaking such experiments as offered promise of providing good medical service to all sections of the population."[7] However, the No. 1 principle was that all features of any plan were to be under the control of the medical profession.

In 1939, the AMA said, defensively, that the profession has shown a willingness to experiment in the social field "to as great a degree . . . as in the scientific field."[8]

Attitude Towards Cooperatives

Consumer-controlled plans have been the particular object of anathema. In addition to the fact that they are guilty of the cardinal offense of membership control, the AMA has taken the position that they deny the patient a free choice of physicians, and do so for the benefit of the association's panel. It has also declared that cooperative medical-care plans cannot really claim to be Rochdale organizations because they do not return patronage refunds.[9] The AMA therefore concluded that cooperative plans were "nothing more than contract-practice arrangements" and that it must oppose them just as it opposes "other *unethical* plans [my italics] or activities that threaten the welfare" of the patients.[10] Just what there was in either cooperative or contract plans to threaten the patient's welfare was not spelled out.

In general the AMA attitude has been that the health needs of the Nation are adequately met under the old methods.[11] A possible exception might be those families in need of public assistance.

Some, temporary, relaxation of the AMA attitude occurred in 1949 when the AMA recommended to the State and county medical societies that they "recognize" cooperative plans that met 20 specific conditions. However, in 1954, the "acceptance program" was discontinued because it was "extremely difficult" to conduct on a national level.

Below that level, the attitude of the medical societies has varied considerably, some clinging to the old ideas and some willing to go along with certain new ones. The most stiff-necked resistance seems to have occurred where doctors' group plans had to compete with consumer-sponsored plans, thus lending credence to an oft-expressed lay opinion that it was not "ethics" but, rather, economic factors that bothered the doctors.

A study made by the Farm Credit Administration disclosed that, as a result of professional opposition, some cooperative plans had to give up the prepayment feature in order to get a doctor to serve them.[12]

There is evidence that individual physicians and some medical societies disagree with the AMA stand. The Iowa and South Dakota societies have indicated a willingness to approve medical-care cooperatives and accept their staff into membership. Here and there doctors have spoken out in favor of voluntary, consumer-sponsored plans. There are probably many others who are sympathetic (or at least do not disapprove) but hesitate to take an open stand in opposition to the official position. Disciplinary measures, used by the profession to maintain medical standards and to prevent unethical practices, have also been utilized to check experimentation in methods of paying for medical service, and to hold in line physicians who might be inclined to join the staff of a cooperative.[13]

The cooperative movement naturally believes that the voluntary plans have great potentialities, if the legislative restrictions and the obstructive tactics of the medical profession can be eliminated.

Court Cases and Other Overt Action

The medical profession's lawsuits against cooperatives have usually been based on one of two grounds, i.e., that they are actually engaged in the insurance business without having complied with the insurance laws, or that they are practicing medicine in violation of the prohibition against corporate medical practice. Collateral or secondary charges have included unprofessional or unethical conduct, low-quality care, advertising for members, etc.

Cases brought by the cooperatives against medical societies have alleged (1) conspiracy to monopolize medical treatment in the area, and therefore to put the cooperative out of business, (2) discrimination against its medical staff by refusal to admit the cooperative doctors into membership in the society, and (3) intimidation, to prevent doctors from accepting employment with the cooperative or acting as consultants.

The cooperative hospital at Elk City, Okla., was engaged in an almost continuous battle with the county and State medical societies from its organization in 1929 until 1952. The doctors' tactics included two unsuccessful attempts to have Dr. Michael Shadid's license revoked; disbanding the county society (of which he was a member) and then reorganizing without him; refusal of membership to out-of-State physicians if known that they intended to practice at the cooperative hospital; refusing to admit the cooperative doctors into membership; establishing competing hospitals; pressuring the Federal Resettlement Administration into reneging on a contract with the cooperative hospital for the treatment of farm-security clients; a lawsuit (unsuccessful) charging the hospital with corporate practice of medicine, soliciting business through advertising and agents, and "fleecing the public"; lobbying for a State law specifically forbidding corporate practice of medicine; trying to get the hospital's doctors (including their medical director, Dr. Fred Shadid) drafted into the Army;[14] and marshalling forces to defeat first an initiative petition (backed by the cooperators) and then a cooperative hospital draft bill.

As the hospital's founder, Dr. Michael Shadid, said:

> "Their fight on us has been vicious and bitter. They have fought us with misrepresentation, vilification and abuse. They tried again and again to blackmail us. They planted spies in the hospital in the persons of doctors and nurses and threatened us with death and other calamities. Their efforts to date have been fruitless."[15]

Finally, wearying of the long struggle and determined to resolve it once and for all, the hospital brought suit in 1950 against the Beckham County Medical Society, charging a boycott and other injurious practices, and asking for damages and a restraining injunction. Dr. Shadid said that the real issue at stake was whether "the patients [are] the property of the medical profession or is medicine here to serve as an instrument of public health".[16] The case was finally settled out of court in April 1952, on a basis assuring medical-society membership for the cooperative doctors and providing other community benefits.

In Washington, D. C., Group Health Association brought suit in 1937 for a declaratory judgment to clear up its legal status. It was upheld by the U. S. District Court for the District of Columbia which ruled that, since an individual could contract for a physician's services, there was no reason why a group of individuals could not do the same with a group of physicians.

A case brought a few days later by the U. S. Department of Justice charged the American Medical Association and the District of Columbia Medical Society with violation of the antitrust laws by (1) threatening expulsion of doctors taking employment with GHA, and (2) excluding GHA doctors from Washington hospitals. In a countersuit, three members of the District Medical Society sought to enjoin GHA from engaging in the "practice of medicine." A decision against the AMA and the society was carried to the U. S. Supreme Court which found in favor of the cooperative in a unanimous decision on January 18, 1943.

In Seattle, Group Health Cooperative of Puget Sound in 1949 brought charges against the King County Medical Society, several hospitals and the King County Medical Bureau (a doctor-run service organization). The charges were the usual ones—monopoly, boycott of GHC doctors, disciplinary action against them, and refusal to admit them into membership. An adverse decision was appealed to the State Supreme Court which on November 15, 1951, decided unanimously in favor of the cooperative. The defendants were enjoined from excluding GHC doctors from membership, from any intimidation of staff or private consultants, and from exclusion from King County hospitals.

In 1954 a similar case involving the Complete Service Bureau of San Diego[17] and the county medical society was finally terminated with a decision by the State Supreme Court, upholding the cooperative on all counts.

As a result of all this court action, the Seattle cooperative hospital had by 1948 been placed on the AMA "approved" list, and cooperative hospitals in Texas had been admitted to the State hospital association. Three years later, the staff of the Seattle and Elk City associations had been admitted to membership in the respective county medical societies. In Elk City, by mid-1953 a cooperative staff member was even serving as vice president of the county medical society and another had become the delegate to the State association from the Elk City area. Evidently, once the artificial barriers were down, the profession could see some good in the cooperative doctors after all! In Seattle, however, "the reception we get is still cool."

How Direct-Service Plans Work

In the opinion of Dr. Shadid, dean of the cooperative medical leaders, the requisites of a successful medical plan are the following:

1. It must be supported by a dues-paying system, thus removing the plan from the possibility of fee cutting by competing local physicians.

2. The dues should be as low as consistent with the "best services obtainable."

3. The plan should have a sufficient membership base (2,000 families as a minimum) to support both a clinic and a hospital.

4. Dues should be compulsory, and membership should be canceled for nonpayment (after a period of grace). Initial membership fee should be high ($50 to $100, payable in installments), so that the member will feel that he has an investment he cannot afford to lose by cancellation.

5. The staff should consist of competent, well-paid doctors receiving a yearly bonus in addition to salary, and having a voice in administration.

Nearly all of the existing plans meet these requisites. There is, however, no uniform plan of *operation.* In fact, there are almost as many variations as there are plans, each association having adapted itself to local circumstances and needs.

The greatest number of existing associations have hospitals. Some also give clinic treatment at the hospital, and a few also make home calls. If only a clinic is operated, hospital care for the members in local hospitals is usually provided at somewhat higher dues. (If the member is traveling in other parts of the country, reimbursement for necessary hospital care while away may also be arranged, in some plans.)

Most of the direct-service hospital plans are in rural areas, both because the greatest need (and dearth of facilities) was there, and because of the limitations imposed by some enabling laws. Two of the clinics, and practically all of the contract and union health and welfare plans, are in the industrial centers and large cities.

The prepayment system, calling for periodic dues, is the one generally favored. The dues vary widely, depending on the number of persons in the family and the range of services provided. Usually dues are payable monthly.

The prepaid dues cover most of the cost of treatment. For special items, and for surgical operations, x-rays, etc., additional charges may be imposed on the patient, but these are at considerably lower rates than those currently charged in the community.

Largely because of limited facilities, some plans serve members only. Those that treat nonmembers commonly do so only on a fee-for-service basis. The practice is defended on the ground that the nonmembers have contributed nothing toward building the capital or the organization, and could come in as members if they were willing to pay the membership fee.

The cooperative attends to all the business and nonprofessional aspects of the operation—recruitment of members and staff, provision of facilities and working supplies, making of appointments, collection of dues, etc. Each member has a single vote, and the membership is the final authority on matters affecting the operation of the enterprise as such. The policies are determined by the board of directors, elected annually by the members. Various committees, for membership relations, complaints, education, expansion, etc., may assist the board.

The day-to-day operation of hospital or clinic is under the direction of a manager or administrator.

Invariably the professional aspects—diagnosis, and treatment of patients—are left to the medical staff, without interference by the association or its officers. This branch of operation is headed by a chief of staff or medical director. Patients may choose the physician they prefer, from the association's staff.

Physicians are compensated in a variety of ways: (1) Straight salaries, possibly with some additional bonus at the end of the year, (2) a specified percentage of the total association income, the division among the individual physicians being left to determination by the medical group or by the medical director, or (3) capitation (i.e., in relation to the number of patients treated) and possibly an additional share of any association earnings at the end of the year.

Present Situation

In spite of the would-be reassuring statements of organized medicine as to the need and provision of medical care, the facts revealed in numerous studies are anything but favorable. They show that only a small percentage, even of families with some kind of medical insurance, have anything even approaching complete coverage; that only a small part of family outlay for medical care is covered by insurance; and that many families are in debt because of the cost of care. Even a family with some kind of insurance may not be able to get direct service if there are no medical or hospital facilities in the locality.

Preliminary data on an official study of 299 voluntary plans of health protection estimate a total coverage by them of 9 million persons.

As for the cooperatives, in 1951 there were estimated to be 30 cooperatives with contract arrangements providing medical service for 25,400 members, and 55 associations providing direct medical service in their own health centers for 110,000 members. Counting family dependents, the total number of participants would be three or four times these figures. The above do not include plans (such as Group Health Mutual, HIP, etc.) which provide cash benefits or care through insurance. Neither do they include the nonprofit (but not cooperative) plans of individual labor organizations or those operated for industrial employees under collective agreements with employers. There are probably as many as 10,000 labor welfare programs in the United States. Of these, some 3,000 are large operations; the others are small, and limited to a single company or local union. Part of the program consists of health insurance, covering nearly 10 million workers.

The aggregate coverage of all these kinds of voluntary plans is considerable but still small compared with the need. The union plans are expanding rapidly, and cooperative medicine at a slower pace. Many of the union plans are deficient in that they do not provide care for dependents. The cooperatives are handicapped by the fact that, since they are supported entirely by the members' dues (which must be fairly high in order to provide comprehensive care), they attract in general only the middle-income families. Lower-income people feel that they cannot afford to join. Those at the higher levels have no need for the advance budgeting that is the cooperatives' main attraction.

Both the need and the great gap still to be filled are widely recognized, but there is great difference of opinion as to the means by which the health of the nation should be improved.

The cooperative movement naturally favors, above all, voluntary consumer-sponsored nonprofit organizations, but recognizes that complete coverage of the population under such plans is a forlorn hope, especially since the cost of complete medical care (even under nonprofit plans) is so high as to bar lower-income families from participating. The movement therefore does not oppose national compulsory insurance, if provision is made for the continuance and encouragement of voluntary plans of various types.[18]

Some of the direct-service cooperative plans also believe that the Eisenhower proposal for voluntary health insurance would encourage expansion in the membership of cooperative plans in places with numerous Government employees.

Evaluation and Prospects

The most fundamental problems faced by the cooperatives are those already mentioned—lack of enabling State legislation, opposition by the medical profession, and finances. Others include difficulty in attracting a sufficient membership to make the plan financially feasible, long delays in getting operations under way,[19] and difficulties in obtaining doctors, hospital administrators, and other technical staff.

Some problems have been caused by the cooperatives' own mistakes, and cooperators are the first to admit it. Here and there local groups have suffered from their own inept public relations, from unnecessary antagonizing of local physicians, from one-man leadership or failure to include among the leaders high-caliber people representing the various segments of the community. In some cases high-pressure methods of salesmen or organizers have alienated the very people from whom their support had to come.

Underestimation of amounts needed to finance the building and equipment of the medical center has produced a continuing difficulty in some places. Some of the groups—especially the hospital associations—made the mistake of setting their rates too low for successful operation.

One disadvantage with which the voluntary plans have had to contend lies in the fact that the more favorable risks (i.e., younger people and those with higher incomes) are slow to join and quick to leave. The poorer risks are the most likely to join and stay. This adverse selection may cause a difficult financial problem for the plan, besides burdening it with the undue amount of medical attention demanded.

Circumstances in favor of the cooperatives have been community recognition of local need for the facilities and services the cooperatives strive to provide; the fact that the prepayment system allows the members to budget their medical and hospital costs in advance and ensures care even for catastrophic illnesses; and the fact that preventive work can be done through education of the members, and their early visits enable the staff to catch ailments in their first (curable) stages. Thus, the cooperatives improve the quality as well as the quantity of medical service, besides operating to raise the general health level of the members.

They also provide distinct advantages for the participating doctors.[20]

It seems hardly likely that the voluntary consumer-sponsored plans can ever attain a very large percentage of population coverage. Passage of Federal legislation providing for direct loans for buildings and equipment for nonprofit associations would do much to encourage the expansion of cooperative plans. In any case such plans will have rendered a real service by acting (as in the rural power industry) as a yardstick by which to measure the effectiveness of other plans as regards costs and benefits.

Chapter 29.—POWER AND TELEPHONE SERVICE

War and Postwar Periods

The REA Program

Wartime necessities prevented REA progress until the cooperatives demonstrated the need for additional power to make possible the production of food for the armed forces and the civilian population. Then began the extension of electricity to about 20,000 farms per month.

Some 800 electric cooperatives were in operation by the end of 1944. Nevertheless, only slightly over 40 percent of the farms in the United States had been electrified. Expansion during 1945 was still not enough to meet the postwar demands. In spite of this, beginning in 1946, Congressional action so reduced the REA appropriation that the program suffered badly.

Of 1,008 REA borrowers at the end of 1946, 929 were cooperatives, 59 were public agencies, and the rest were commercial power companies. By that time there were only two States—Connecticut and Rhode Island—that had no REA lines.

Five years later the number of electric cooperatives had increased to 986 and they were serving nearly 3½ million patrons. Gross receipts in that year were estimated by the REA at $254.8 million.

Assurance of sources of electric energy through the building of generating plants and transmission lines had become increasingly important, since Federal agencies were no longer being given funds for these purposes. If the cooperatives were to obtain power from Federal dams, they therefore had to build their own plants and lines. The dangerous shortage of power during and after the war speeded up the granting of such loans, and in the 5 years, 1944-48, the yearly average was 4 times that in the previous 8-year period.

Telephone Cooperatives

Cooperative or mutual telephone associations were known as early as the 1890's. The earliest of which there is a present record was the Holt Mutual Telephone Co., at Lanesboro, Minn., organized in 1893.

Over 700 cooperative or mutual telephone associations were organized in the United States between 1900 and 1909. In Minnesota alone the number rose from 56 in 1900 to 590 in 1911. The cooperative service had many shortcomings as measured by city standards, but as one student pointed out, by 1914 the rural telephone associations had "become one of the most powerful influences in rural betterment."[1] The decade from 1910 to 1919 was also fruitful in the formation of telephone associations.

Considering their legal handicaps (many were formed before the passage of cooperative laws) there was a surprisingly high degree of conformity with cooperative principles. Few, however, had any concept of themselves as part of the general cooperative movement. The exceptions were usually in places where cooperative stores or other enterprises were in existence. Few of the organizations conformed to the patronage-refund principle. Their rates were so low that most of them had no surplus from which to make refunds.

By 1936 almost no new associations were being formed. Some of the cooperatives' facilities were in bad shape, and the bookkeeping of many left a good deal to be desired. In the next few years, some associations went out of business or were sold to private companies. To the disinclination of the latter to serve unprofitable country districts was added the wartime shortages of needed items, the unfortunate effects on the cooperatives of deteriorating facilities, the departure of the younger men into the armed services, and loss of membership through the death or departure of the older members.

Before the war's end the Rural Electrification Administration was pointing out that there were fewer telephones in rural areas than 20 years previously. It suggested a tie-in of power lines with telephone systems.

Telephones under REA.—Although bills for Government assistance for rural telephone cooperatives, similar to the REA plan, were introduced in Congress as early as 1945, it was not until 1949 that such a system was authorized.

The State legislatures thereupon began to enact legislation to permit local organizations to take advantage of this new Federal measure.

By 1951, the telephone companies had begun the same kind of tactics used by their fellows in the power industry, and in several States bills were introduced that would either make it impossible to make use of the Federal law or would bind cooperatives by severely hampering restrictions. In other States they succeeded in blocking bills authorizing the formation of telephone cooperatives.

In Indiana the first loan to a telephone cooperative was made in the spring of 1953, against the bitter opposition of the commercial telephone companies. Their arguments, the cooperative's president commented, were almost identical with those used against the REA cooperatives 20 years earlier.

With the change to a Republican Administration, after the election of 1952, a change in viewpoint was reflected in the recalling and re-editing of a film previously issued, that showed farmers how to go about organizing a telephone cooperative and getting a Federal loan,[2] and a statement by Ancher Nelsen, new REA Administrator, that new telephone cooperatives would be countenanced only as a last resort and that the loan preference to existing organizations (specified for 1 year in the 1949 law) would be "continuing policy."

Each year, however, showed a rise in loans. During the 5 years ending October 28, 1954, loans amounting to $200 million had been made to 300 telephone systems (of which 162 were cooperative), to serve 437,000 farm homes, 230,000 of which had previously had no telephone service.

Federations of Cooperatives

The need for unified defense against the attacks of the power companies early led to the organization of State federations of REA cooperatives. It was a charge, made during the fall of 1941, of hoarding of precious copper wire by the cooperatives, that resulted in federation on a national scale.

Cooperative leaders, in Washington to protest this charge and to present their case, agreed on the need for a national organization to protect their interests. Thus, the fourth attempt to organize nationally was successful, and the National Rural Electric Cooperative Association, with membership open only to electricity cooperatives and public power districts, was formed in March 1942. Clyde T. Ellis, a former Congressman from Arkansas, was chosen to act as executive manager, a post which he has filled ever since.

The national organization proved its worth from the first. In 1944 it obtained a reduction in the interest rate on Federal loans from 2.6 percent to 2.0 percent and an extension of the amortization period from 25 to 35 years. In 1943 it opened a fire and casualty insurance agency, estimated as saving local cooperatives at least $150,000 per year; this department also offers group life, accident and health insurance for cooperative employees and their dependents. In 1949 it started a Nation-wide retirement plan for employees of rural electric cooperatives.

The national association has watched developments in Washington and has been able to head off new attacks from various directions. With each success it has grown in power and effectiveness. Its increasing membership has given added authority and weight to the testimony and actions of its representatives.

The association keeps its members informed through a monthly magazine, *Rural Electrification.*

Its 1954 convention brought together 5,675 delegates representing a consumer membership of 3,555,000 persons in 42 States. Its 937 member cooperatives constitute 92 percent of the total number of power cooperatives in the United States.

Telephone cooperatives that have had loans from REA formed a national federation in 1954. This, the National Telephone Cooperative Association, said that it would work closely with the NRECA.

Cooperatives and the Power Companies

The rural electrification program was undertaken only after generations of neglect of rural needs by the power companies. The latter did not, however, wish to see other agencies enter the field, and so interposed their full weight against the REA program.

In the early days of the program their efforts were directed toward preventing cooperatives from getting into operation. This was done by filing with the State commission notice of "intent to serve" the cooperatives' planned areas (thus, in many cases, succeeding in blocking issuance of a charter to the cooperative); by luring away from the cooperative those farmers whose property was so located that it could be served profitably; or by running "spite lines" into the most thickly settled portions of the area intended to be served cooperatively, thus "skimming off the cream" and leaving only the sparsely settled (unprofitable) portions to the cooperative.

The early reports of the Rural Electrification Administration and its magazine were full of such moves by the utilities. Occasional instances occur today, but are less frequent.[3]

Other tactics were to bring pressure to induce going cooperatives to sell out to the power companies, or to force the cooperatives to defend themselves in costly lawsuits.

Much of the present effort goes into trying to reduce REA appropriations, to prevent loans to cooperatives for generating plants and transmission lines, and to influencing the official administrative policy regarding cooperatives. None of these efforts had paid off very well until the change of administration in 1953. Since then the companies have also made great play with charges of "socialism."

Cooperatives and the New "Partnership"

How the New Policy Operates

President Eisenhower has said repeatedly that he favors "local" initiative and that his new power policy is that of a partnership between Federal, State and local government on the one hand and private power on the other. Let us examine how this has worked out in his administration.

Ancher Nelsen, former Lieutenant-Governor of Minnesota, was named REA Administrator. He immediately announced his sympathy for the cooperatives—as seemed likely, indeed, in view of his past membership in one. However, his official statements and actions began to belie his announcement almost immediately. During his entire first year in office not a single loan was made for cooperative generating and transmission facilities. He said it would be his policy rather to "encourage existing facilities to expand to meet area needs."

The great majority of farms in the United States are now electrified. But a big task still remains. The demand for current has grown to such proportions that the present REA lines are becoming overloaded. To build the much heavier lines that are needed, Government loans will be necessary. They will also be required for constructing transmission lines to carry power from dam sites to the REA distribution centers, for generating plants (REA cooperatives still purchase over half of their power from commercial companies), and for additions to existing facilities. It is essential therefore that adequate loan funds be provided.

But only the alertness and insistence of REA's congressional friends have prevented a progressive deterioration of the program. Each year since 1953 the budget submitted by the administrator has called for less money than in the year preceding, and each year the program has been rescued in Congress. Apparently the lesson still has not been learned, for the budget request for 1955-56 was 77 percent below the appropriation for the previous year.

Meanwhile the REA had abolished its co-op advisory service, saying that the cooperatives themselves could handle the organization, business operations, board responsibilities, and employee training that the service had advised upon.

The U. S. Department of the Interior, through whose Bureau of Reclamation many dams have been built, and which has supervision of the operations of the various power administrations, is also the administrator of conservation programs designed to protect the public interest in the country's resources. It is essential, therefore, that the officials in charge of such an important series of programs be in sympathy with the objectives.

Unfortunately, the new Eisenhower appointees lost no time in indicating that their sympathies lay in other directions: the announcement by the Department of the Interior of Government withdrawal from power projects and the encouragement, instead, of "local" agencies,[4] the substitution of 20-year for 2-to-3 year contracts for power,[5] and announcement of intention to raise Federal power charges to the level of those of the power companies (thus ending the role of the cooperatives as a yardstick for measuring the reasonableness of the utilities' rates).

Atomic energy has more potential for future peacetime power than any other source known. It is an immensely valuable resource developed entirely with the taxpayers' money. Naturally, in view of its value, the predatory interests are eyeing it with the greatest interest.

The Atomic Energy Bill submitted to Congress in 1954 was so flagrantly careless with this great public asset that many public-interest groups, including cooperatives, appeared at the hearings in vigorous protest.

The law, as finally passed, authorized the AEC to build full-scale atomic plants but only "to demonstrate the feasibility of nuclear power"; provided for 5 years of compulsory sharing of patents among the licensed companies and 40-year renewable licenses for private industry, cooperatives, and nonprofit enterprises to operate atomic plants; and gave cooperatives and public bodies preference on such licenses and on power generated by AEC plants. Already, however, the developments in 1955 indicate that cooperatives must exercise unceasing vigilance if they are to obtain their rights under the law.

Other manifestations of the new policy were the allocation of choice dam sites to power companies, administrative rulings that cost the Government many millions of dollars in taxes and tax write-offs, the ill-fated Dixon-Yates contract, and others.

Reaction of Cooperatives and Others

Although the REA, the TVA, and the whole power program have been under practically unceasing attack, the assaults on the various sectors of the public domain have not been allowed to go without protest.

Cooperatives registered their opinions and suggestions in the various hearings. Congressional representatives from the region that has benefited so greatly from the TVA plan spoke sharply in congress and elsewhere, as did also progressively minded members of Congress from other States.

J. E. Smith, president of the National Rural Electric Cooperative Association, set forth the cooperative point of view in an open letter to President Eisenhower after the latter's speech at McNary Dam in Oregon. In the letter Mr. Smith said in part:

> "You are further quoted as saying 'The true issue posed to us is a Federal monopoly of power[6] as against public or regulated private power, freely chosen in each instance by the citizens of the area, with the Federal Government drawn in as a cooperating partner where this seems necessary or desirable.' We do not believe this to be the issue at all. The real issue is whether our hydroelectric resources are going to be developed to their full efficiency, and whether, when developed, the people, the farmers, the urban citizens, commerce and industry are going to get the benefits or whether the benefits must be siphoned off through power-company toll gates. That's the issue."[7]

The cooperatives are also very much concerned about the future development of atomic energy for peacetime uses. They feel that, under the Atomic Energy Act and the attitudes and procedures of the AEC, the cards are stacked in favor of turning over to the industrial giants the results of the taxpayers' 12-billion-dollar experiments. As the cooperators see it, the whole "partnership policy" means in reality the relinquishment of public assets, developed by the people's money, to private profit.

They believe, however, that as a public-interest group they have the right and duty to participate in the atomic-energy program. Accordingly, several proposals for cooperative atomic plants have been made.

The Situation in Review

The regulation of public utilities on the State level has been a complete failure—which is why the power companies favor it as against Federal regulation. Some form of competition is necessary, which the cooperatives and public power districts provide. Until their advent, the utilities had a monopoly. It is significant that the commercial wholesale rate for power never fell below 1½ cents per kilowatt hour until after the REA cooperatives began to build generating plants.

In the States where electricity cooperatives are under public service commissions, they must always prove that any service proposed by them will not compete with companies already in operation and will serve the "public convenience and necessity." Since State commissions are notoriously accessible to organized pressure, some cooperatives have suffered under commissions heavily weighted in favor of commercial companies.

At the national level, it can be asserted without question that the REA program has been a real success. No cooperative loan has ever had to be foreclosed. A few associations might be in arrears at any given time, but as a group they were always paid up in advance of current obligations, and three have already paid out their loans in full, far ahead of schedule. Untold millions of dollars have been saved to consumers through their operations.

As of mid-1954, only 7.7 percent of the 5.3 million farms in the United States were still without electricity. The cooperatives now supply electricity to more farms in the country than all other distributors (commercial and public) combined—51 percent of the total. This electrification of rural areas can be credited directly to the REA. If some farms are now supplied by commercial utilities, it is only because of the competitive effect of cooperative activity. The 5 million farms now electrified would still be using kerosene lamps and manual power if they had depended on the initiative of the profit companies.

The telephone program has made such progress as was possible under the administrative restrictions imposed. But four times as many loans are being made to commercial companies as to cooperatives and under the curtailed loan and educational-service program the latter have not had the sound counseling enjoyed by the REA cooperatives.

From the people's standpoint, the TVA likewise has been a great achievement. It has developed the resources, attracted new industries (thus increasing employment), and at the same time raised the level of living, in the whole Tennessee Valley. Its power is a bulwark of national defense and made possible the development of the atomic bomb. It has created worldwide prestige for the United States; the "TVA idea" is being used in developments in Africa, Asia, Australia, Europe, and Central and South America.

The future of the power cooperatives, in the Valley and elsewhere, will depend to a great extent on whether official policies will be such as to insure their fair share of hydroelectric and atomic power and thus permit their continued growth; or whether, through refusal of generation and transmission loans, and licensing practices, they will be turned over to the non-existent mercies of their enemies, the utility companies. Coopera-tives know that the utilities wage a battle unremitting and none too scrupulous. The actions of the power companies have proved that they are "taxpayers" only to the extent that they cannot avoid such levies through fast depreciation write-offs and other devices; that, in their view, subsidies are not bad when they themselves receive them; and that Government assistance is socialistic only when extended to others than themselves.[8]

Certainly, the consumer and nonprofit organizations will do their utmost to protect cooperative interests. The future will show whether this will be sufficient.

The discouraging feature of the present situation is that the Government agencies, supposedly serving all the people, now appear to be working mainly for certain interests only, and their officials have said as much, directly or indirectly. Under the current policies, about the best the cooperatives can hope for is to hold their own, possibly having to admit to a certain measure of defeat here and there.

Chapter 30.—INSURANCE

In the insurance field, most cooperatives operate on the principles of mutuality, rather than the accepted Rochdale tenets. In the beginning, and for nearly 100 years, "mutuality" in insurance meant that each policyholder was a member of the association; losses were prorated among the members and assessments were levied to cover them. Each member was therefore a direct guarantor of all the others.

Even as late as 1936, over half of the insurance associations were still operating on the assessment plan. This was possible because most of them were quite small; many (if not most) of the associations were doing business within the confines of a single township or county where the members knew each other; and the association was able to judge whether an applicant for insurance was a good moral risk.

The larger companies, though forfeiting this intimate knowledge of policyholders, attained financial safety by spreading the risk over a broad area. However, the larger the field of operation, the greater the difficulty of insuring actual membership control of the operations of the organization.

Insurance Mutuals, 1735-1860

Mutual insurance companies were in existence, in one form or another, as far back as the fifteenth and sixteenth centuries. The first English mutual insurance association, the Amicable Society, established in 1705, clearly influenced the development of mutual companies in the North American colonies. The formation of the most successful mutual insurance company in the colonial period—the Philadelphia Contributionship for the Insurance of Houses from Loss by Fire—may be traced directly to the Amicable Society.

The first insurance association organized in the United States, however, the Friendly Society for the Mutual Insuring of Houses Against Fire, was patterned, rather, on the methods of the Friendly Societies of Great Britain. It was organized under royal charter in Charleston, S. C., in 1735. This pioneer was ruined in a fire that swept the city in November 1740.

Twelve years later appeared the Philadelphia Contributionship, formed in 1752 under a deed of settlement and with the assistance of Benjamin Franklin (who later became one of its directors). It adhered strictly to the principles of mutuality. This organization is still in operation, retaining both its mutual form and its original name.

In the period from 1787 to 1799, trade and commerce grew in unprecedented fashion and 29 companies to insure their risks are known to have been formed. Of these, 8 were clearly mutuals and concerned themselves with general fire risks. Two mutuals organized in 1794 are still active—the Baltimore Equitable and the Mutual Assurance Society Against Fire on Buildings of the State of Virginia.[1]

Numerous mutuals were formed during the period 1800-36, following the success of the pioneer societies. In the first 10 years of the new century, 57 charters were granted to insurance companies of all types, as compared to 29 before 1800. Between 1810 and 1820, only 36 were issued, chiefly because of the unfavorable effects of the War of 1812 and the increased risks.

Fire and Life Insurance

Mutual enterprise made the greatest headway in the field of fire insurance, spurred by the passage of State laws prohibiting the chartering of foreign companies.

It was the great fire that swept the city of New York on December 16, 1835 that gave the mutuals their greatest gain over the commercial stock companies. The fire, one of the worst in the history of the city, devastated the business section and the claims for losses wiped out all but three insurance companies. The danger of concentrated risks in large cities was immediately recognized, especially by the rural people who were in reality underwriting in their premiums the more hazardous conditions in the cities and crowded areas. Within the next 2 years, 44 mutual charters were granted in New York State, the majority of which were in small towns and villages.

These small mutual companies made some valuable innovations. In order to guard against false claims (notably in arson cases), they adopted the plan of insuring property only up to two-thirds of its value. To their vigilance in reviewing claims and their activity in doubtful cases was attributed in great measure the great body of insurance law that began to take form.

With the rapid spread of mutual companies in New York and other States, enabling statutes became necessary, and New York led the way with its act of 1840.

Whatever faith remained in stock companies disappeared when a second fire occurred in New York in 1845, destroying some $6 million worth of property.

The next few years consequently witnessed the incorporation of more mutual fire-insurance companies, especially between 1835 and 1850. Among them was the Mutual Life Insurance Co. of New York (1842). This organization—still active—claims to have been the first successful life-insurance company in this country. It was followed by similar companies, all in existence today.[2]

The companies departed from the strict mutual system in several respects: They adopted the plan of collecting premiums in advance, returning any surplus to members. Membership control became diluted and in some cases lost, as many companies began to issue nonparticipating policies (i.e., policies carrying no voting privilege). Use of proxy votes enabled trustees to perpetuate themselves in office. Thus, many of them forfeited all claim to mutuality except in name. This is now true of all the biggest "mutual" companies. It is in the specialized fields of insurance that the strictest adherence to mutual principles is now found.

The Farmers' Mutuals

The Civil War resulted in the consolidation and growth of industrial enterprises and urban centers. From this time forward the commercial insurance companies confined themselves to risks within those fields.

Previously, cities had represented the more dangerous conditions. With the development of urban fire-fighting companies and means of fire prevention, the situation was reversed and farm and rural areas became relatively more hazardous. Farm buildings had always been particularly liable to damage from fire arising from the use of lanterns in winter and from electric storms in summer and autumn when the barns were filled with grain. The farmers therefore experienced continual difficulty in obtaining insurance, and by 1870 this was one of their worst problems.

It was the Grangers who first attacked the problem of farmers' insurance in an organized and effective manner. At one time Grange insurance companies flourished in practically every State in which the order existed. In fact, over a fourth of the farmers' mutuals in operation in 1920 had been formed during 1870-79, the period when Grange activities were at their height.

To the success of the Grange mutual-insurance companies can be attributed the further growth of farmers' mutuals in the two succeeding decades. Of 1,884 farmers' mutuals in existence in 1920 for which the date of organization was available, 25.7 percent were formed in the decade 1870-79, 17.7 percent in 1880-89, and 23.9 percent between 1890 and 1899.

These mutuals, for the most part, insured fire risks in a single township only. The entrance fees, ranging from $3 to $15, were used to accumulate reserve funds.

The first laws distinguishing between farmers' mutuals and those of the general type resulted from the efforts of the farmers themselves. By 1890, practically every State in the Midwest and several in the South had mutual insurance laws specifically for farmers. Vermont was the only State in New England to follow this example, and it waited until 1915 to do so.

Farmers' mutuals did not long confine themselves to fire insurance. Before long they were also insuring against windstorm and hail. By 1921, it was estimated that the mutuals were insuring 40 percent of the total insurable farm property.

Although some of the mutuals failed, most were successful, and some extremely so. Their cost was so low that the old-line companies practically ceased to solicit the farm business. Victor Valgren, insurance expert for the U. S. Department of Agriculture, estimated that between 1875 and 1910 the mutuals had been the means of saving the policyholders about $20 million, including interest on savings from lower premium charges.

Today the West and Midwest continue to be the stronghold of the farmers' mutual companies, especially those operating on the township basis.

Present-Day Insurance

Farmers' Insurance Organizations

A number of States still have Grange insurance organizations, and a few of these date from the heyday of Grange development.

Although later in the field, the Farmers Union and the Farm Bureau have also gone into the insurance business. Most of their organizations have been sponsored by State branches of the national organizations and usually confine themselves to a single State.

The National Farmers Union, however, has two companies which do business on a wide scale. That farm organization went successively into the writing of life insurance (1938), fire and windstorm insurance (1944), and automobile and casualty insurance (1945). The National Farmers Union Life Association by the end of 1953 had 47,113 policyholders and nearly $60 million in insurance in force. The National Farmers Union Automobile & Casualty Insurance Co. had 116,700 policies (each covering one family) in force. Both companies write insurance in 20 States.

A Nebraska association, Farmers Union Cooperative Insurance Co., dating from 1918, writes fire, windstorm, and hail policies on farm properties, in addition to automobile insurance.[3] Its 1954 report showed $183.7 million of insurance in force.

There are Farm Bureau insurance companies in a number of States, but the largest are those with headquarters in Columbus, Ohio, and these also have links with the consumers' cooperative movement.

The Ohio Farm Bureau Mutual Automobile Insurance Co. was started in 1926 with $10,000 from the local farmers and a loan from the State Farm Bureau. Eight years later this company furnished the capital to start the Farm Bureau Mutual Fire Insurance Co., and in 1936 the Farm Bureau Life Insurance Co. It had also helped with the initial financing of the wholesale, Farm Bureau Cooperative Association.

The companies had 2,900,000 policies in force by the end of 1954. Assets reached $219 million. They paid $5.3 million in taxes during the year. The automobile company is now the second largest auto mutual in the United States and the fourth largest company (of all kinds) writing automobile insurance. This position was attained while doing business in only 13 jurisdictions.

This is one of the fastest growing cooperative groups in this country.[4] They long ago abandoned membership restrictions. Under the leadership of Murray Lincoln they have also swung increasingly into the urban consumers' field, and by 1954 some 80 percent of the business was being done with nonfarm policyholders. It is the policy of the companies to obtain the sponsorship of the local cooperatives and other "people's groups" before entering a new territory. The sponsors, in turn, receive contributions for educational work, based largely on attendance at cooperative meetings.

Policyholder participation is obtained through a delegate system. Local policyholders elect advisory committees, which in turn elect district representatives and they again elect regional representatives. The latter present their ideas and suggestions about insurance needs and procedures at national meetings.

Although the companies have grown steadily, geographical expansion has been hampered by the similarity in name with farmers' insurance associations in some 20 States, thus making it impossible to get State charters there. In September, 1955, therefore, the name of the companies was changed to Nationwide Mutual Insurance Co.

These companies and those of the National Farmers Union lend some of their surplus funds to local cooperatives. The Farmers Union organizations reported in 1951 that they had never "lost a penny" on a cooperative loan, although "in dozens of instances the loan made the difference between having a cooperative and not having one."[5]

Insurance and the Consumers' Cooperatives

The subject of insurance has been discussed in cooperative congresses since 1926, and endorsement was given to certain associations (desirous of aligning themselves with the cooperative movement) which met Cooperative League standards. Among them were the New Era Life Association and the Workmen's Furniture Fire Insurance Association.

The New Era (later changed to Michigan Union Life Association) had been organized as a fraternal benefit society in Michigan in 1897, by men who believed in all types of cooperatives. Cooperative principles were stressed in all its literature from the first. It was chartered only for Michigan, but by 1936 it had policyholders (with policies issued by mail) in 40 States, 5 Canadian Provinces, and Europe.

The association had by then evolved into a mutual, with every policyholder having a single vote in the election of delegates to a biennial meeting at which the management was elected. No proxies were allowed. Mr. E. E. Branch was president of the association for many years.

An increase in the premium rates, necessitated by the change to a legal-reserve basis, and the loss of policyholders during the depression caused such financial difficulties that the association was no longer able to operate independently. It was taken over by the Maccabees about 1939.

The Workmen's Furniture Fire Insurance Co. of New York was organized, without capital stock, in 1872. Its policyholders were voting members who, on joining, paid a deposit (constituting the association's capital) of 90 cents for every $100 issued to them in insurance. It had no salaried agents or solicitors; member satisfaction was relied upon to spread the word. It had a single premium rate for all risks wherever located.

In the early 1930's it reorganized (under an amendment to the New York law for which it was responsible), substituted "Mutual" for "Furniture" in its name, and began to do business in other States. By 1937 it had over 68,000 policyholders and more than $87 million of insurance in force in 9 States. This organization is still in operation (1955).

An insurance-brokerage agency, Clusa Service, authorized by the 1930 Cooperative Congress, was formed on December

16, 1930 and began business in the following January. It purchased fire, automobile, and life insurance and employees' fidelity bonds for local cooperatives. It continued as a department of the Cooperative League until June 1940 when it was transferred to Eastern Cooperative Wholesale under a trusteeship arrangement.[6]

The Mutual Service Cos.—By the end of the 1930's there were in Minnesota and Wisconsin six insurance organizations connected with the cooperative movement—two writing life, two fire, and two casualty insurance. Five of these were under the auspices of the two regional wholesales or the district league. There was no overlapping of territory, thanks to an understanding between the wholesales. The sixth was the American Farmers Mutual Automobile Insurance Co., started in 1919 by a group of German farmers in and around Lake Elmo, Minn.

In 1941, a joint-management plan for all six was adopted, with a new organization, Cooperative Insurance Services, to act as manager and administrator. Later, a series of mergers, extending over a period of years, finally resulted in the formation of three associations—Mutual Service Casualty Insurance Co., Mutual Service Life Insurance Co. and Mutual Service Fire Insurance Co.[7]—to take the place of the previous six.[8] The companies still operate under a single management.

Under the joint program the local cooperatives affiliated with the sponsors acted as insurance agencies for the writing of policies until 1943, when the annual meeting voted to allow individuals also to serve as agents.

Local cooperatives, township mutual insurance societies, electricity associations, and credit unions—to the number of 475, each with a single $10 share—hold Mutual Service common (voting) stock. They are therefore the controlling members of the program. Each has one vote which is cast by its delegate at the annual meeting.

Insurance in force exceeded $85 million by the end of 1954. Assets totaled $20.1 million.

Cooperators' Life Association pioneered in 1938 in group policies insuring the lives of members of local cooperatives, based upon age and the amount of their previous year's patronage of the cooperatives. This type of policy still continues to be issued, and was added by the National Farmers Union Life Association, also, in 1947. Many store cooperatives in the Midwest now carry this kind of insurance.

Health insurance.—Because of their long-term aims and of their intimate relationship with the provision of medical care, certain insurance associations writing health policies or providing services through a combination of insurance and contract medicine were discussed in the chapter on medical care. Some of the associations discussed here also write policies for accident and health or surgical insurance, but these are not their main lines of business. Among them are the National Farmers Union Life Insurance Association and Nationwide Insurance.

Credit Union Insurance

The credit-union movement has its own insurance association,[9] the CUNA Mutual Insurance Society, organized in 1935. Its original purpose was to insure the lives of credit-union borrowers and thus prevent losses when borrowers died, but it now also writes policies for individual life insurance and insurance on savings. It likewise makes mortgage loans on members' homes: at the end of 1953 some 27 percent of its assets were in loans of this kind. Since all of its business is done by mail and no sales commissions are paid, its rates are unusually low.

Headquarters are in Madison, Wis.; there is a branch office at Hamilton, Ont. Thomas W. Doig, long-time credit-union leader, was the association's general manager until his death in December 1955.

Under its procedure, area membership meetings are held in each State and Province in which there are CUNA policyholders. A biennial meeting is held in Madison.

At the beginning of 1954, CUNA Mutual ranked 36th in insurance coverage among the 625 largest insurance companies in the United States. It had 11,695 credit unions covered by loan insurance, had 14,014 individual policyholders, and had insurance in force of $1,476,000,000. (For other data on this association, see Chapter 31.)

The Texas Credit Union League (Dallas) also has an insurance organization, the Members Mutual Insurance Co., that writes automobile insurance. At the end of 1953 it had 13,000 policyholders and over a million dollars of insurance in force.

Coordination in the Insurance Field

Although the township mutuals had almost as many plans of operation as there were associations, they recognized the value of federation. In the period 1879-81 they organized State-wide associations in 4 States, and 8 others by 1900. By 1937 there were such federations in 27 States. The National Association of Mutual Insurance Cos. was formed in 1896. It receives considerable financial support from urban and general mutuals, but is primarily a farmers' mutual organization.

National Insurance Conference

The insurance associations connected with the distributive cooperative movement have never had a formal national organization, though meetings toward that end have been held. In 1946 the Cooperative League sponsored a conference aimed at coordinating insurance activities on a national scale. Five insurance organizations immediately joined the conference,[10] and since then 10 others have been added.[11]

The conference meets yearly for discussion of common aims and problems and exchange of experience.

Conclusion

With one exception, the present insurance organizations are incorporated under either mutual insurance or general insurance laws. The exception is in the State of Utah which has the only cooperative insurance law (for life insurance only) in this country. Under its terms, members have one vote only, proxy voting is prohibited, and earnings may be refunded on patronage (i.e., on amount paid in premiums). Such provisions insure democratic control where the cooperative territory is small enough to make possible the members' attendance at meetings.

The township and county mutuals in other States have no difficulty in this respect, either. But the problem of genuine membership control has always plagued the larger organizations, and as we have seen, various methods have been adopted to insure membership participation and direction.

In probably no other field thus far entered are the opportunities for savings through cooperation so great as in the writing of insurance. The low rates of the mutuals speak for themselves. The assets amassed by cooperators' patronage of their own organizations make possible financial assistance to other types of cooperatives also—through loans for business enterprises, for home ownership, and other purposes.

The farmers' mutuals were forced into insurance by the prohibitive rates of the commercial companies. They then found that necessity had opened up a gold mine, with an apparently inexhaustible vein.

Chapter 31.—BANKING AND CREDIT

By far the largest group of cooperative associations in the credit business in this country consists of the credit unions, which have attained a truly phenomenal growth in the past 20 years. There have also been a few organizations that were in reality banks, but almost none exist today that are entirely cooperative.

Banking

Cooperative Banks[1]

After the failure of the only bank in Johnson County, Kans., a cooperative bank was started in 1883 in Olathe (home of the Johnson County Cooperative Association, an early Grange cooperative). Twenty years later the Farmers Union and several labor unions in Oklahoma promoted the Cooperative Bank & Trust Co., in 1908, the stock of which was to be sold only to members of labor organizations and of the Farmers Union.

In 1928, Senator Smith Brookhart introduced in Congress a bill that would have authorized the formation of cooperative banks, but it failed to pass. However, three States had already enacted such legislation—Arkansas (1921), Nebraska (1921), and Iowa (1927). One bank, the Cooperative Bank of Newell, had been opened in Iowa, but as far as can now be ascertained none was organized under the Nebraska law.

In Arkansas, limited bank functions were permitted under the general cooperative law,[2] and at least 19 associations were organized to do banking. None of them carried the word, "cooperative," in their names, however. They were put out of business by a new law of 1937, passed at the instigation of a hostile bank commissioner who had previously tried, unsuccessfully, to prevent the issuance of new charters. Any cooperative bank in a town with a State or national bank had to go out of business within 18 months. This killed them all.

Labor Banks

Organized labor had from time to time debated the desirability of labor-owned banks. A resolution to establish a series of such banks was rejected by the AFL convention of 1904. Similar resolutions were considered without action in 1914 and 1918. In 1915 the annual meeting of the International Brotherhood of Locomotive Engineers authorized the organization of a labor bank "when conditions warrant," and that of the Amalgamated Clothing Workers of America authorized one in 1920.

Consideration crystallized into action shortly after the second Farmer-Labor Conference (in February 1920), when the first labor bank in the United States was started. It was the Mt. Vernon Savings Bank, sponsored by officers of the International Association of Machinists, in Washington, D. C. The bank opened on May 15, 1920.

Six months later the Locomotive Engineers Cooperative National Bank went into operation in Cleveland, Ohio. New banks followed in swift succession—2 in 1921, 4 in 1922, 8 in 1923, 9 in 1924, and 6 in 1925. Five new banks were added in 1926, but one went out of existence in that year.

By the end of 1926, therefore, 35 banks were in operation in 20 States. The largest group (16) consisted of those started by the railroad workers either singly (locomotive engineers, railway clerks, railroad telegraphers) or as joint enterprises. That year represented the peak both in numbers and in resources ($126,849,000). The movement began to decline in 1927 and by mid-1932 only 7 were still in operation. The Bank Holiday finished 3 of these.

The failures were attributed to unsound methods, business ignorance, incompetent management, and ill-advised loans and investments.

The four survivors were the Amalgamated Clothing Workers' banks in Chicago and New York, the Union National Bank of Newark, N. J., and the Telegraphers' National Bank of St. Louis, Mo. They had combined resources of slightly over $18 million (the lowest point ever reached). Assets began to climb immediately, but the number of banks continued at the same level until September 1942, when the Telegraphers' bank went out of business. The next year the number rose to 4 again, when labor unions acquired a controlling interest in the Brotherhood State Bank of Kansas City, Kans.

In 1954 the United Mine Workers purchased the National Bank of Washington, D. C., raising the total to five. As of the end of the year the five had combined assets of $373.2 million.

The labor banks as a whole were not genuinely cooperative, although several of them had the word "cooperative" in their names and some started with certain cooperative practices, such as limited dividends on share capital, safeguards on the sale of stock, and sharing of earnings with the savings depositors. But, beginning about 1925, the trend was away from the cooperative method.

Finance in the Consumers' Cooperative Movement

The problem of obtaining the wherewithal to finance cooperative enterprise has been perennial. Lack of adequate financing has been a prime cause of failure of cooperatives, and has been recognized as such since the earliest days. Hardly a congress of the Cooperative League that has not devoted at least one session to the subject of finance of one kind or another.

At the 1938 Cooperative Congress, President Warbasse urged the cooperatives to consider steps to make the movement financially independent. Three of the regional wholesales took action in that direction. In 1937, 1938, and 1940, Midland Cooperative Wholesale, Farmers Union Central Exchange, and Central Cooperative Wholesale each launched a finance association. These have all met with moderate success.

The Indiana Farm Bureau Cooperative Association (then affiliated with the Cooperative League) in 1939 bought a controlling interest in the Citizens State Bank at Beech Grove, Ind. Its first year's experience "definitely established the feasibility of cooperative banking." The members and patrons of the bank were drawn largely from four classes—cooperative wholesales, retail cooperatives, credit unions, and nonprofit organizations. The board of directors included one director from each group.

The idea of a national cooperative credit institution to be the repository of cooperative money has often been broached, and was finally authorized by the 1940 congress. The National

Cooperative Finance Association did not, however, materialize until 1943. It has never been able to get off the ground because of insufficient capital. The League board declared to the 1954 Cooperative Congress that either the association should be dissolved or energetic measures should be taken to get it under way. It should no longer be continued in limbo.

Credit Unions

Credit unions constitute the most rapidly and solidly built development in the history of consumers' cooperation in the United States.

Their purposes are twofold: To promote thrift by providing the opportunity to save in small amounts, and to use this money to make loans at moderate interest for "purposes which promise to be of benefit to the borrower." Small "character" loans (originally not over $50, but now in most cases allowed up to several hundred dollars) may be made on no security but the integrity of the borrower. Larger amounts require tangible security or signatures of "co-makers."

Characteristics of Credit Unions

Credit unions operate on the following principles:

1. Membership open to all persons of good character, who have a common bond or community of interest with the credit union group.

2. Membership fees low, and shares of small denomination (usually $5), so that no one need be debarred from membership by reason of poverty.

3. Democracy in government, with directors and committees elected by and responsible to the members.

4. One vote per member, irrespective of the number of shares owned. No proxy voting.

5. Loans to members only, and preference given to the smaller loans, on the ground that the need of such borrowers is likely to be greater.

6. Loans to directors and committee members generally prohibited, to prevent diversion of funds or abuse of office by such persons.

7. Loans made only for urgent needs or for productive or other purposes that promise to be of benefit to the borrower.

8. Amount of loan based, not on the member's investment in the association, but on his needs and character.

9. Loans at low rates of interest, and interest payable only on the unpaid balance.[3]

10. Dividends payable on all fully paid shares of stock. This (specified in the credit union laws) was a departure from Rochdale practice. Now, however, a few laws (including the Federal law) permit not only interest or dividends on capital, but also patronage returns on interest paid.

Administration is vested in a board of directors (from which officers are chosen), a credit committee to pass on loan applications, and a supervisory committee which has general oversight of the finances, auditing, and even over the board and credit committee if wrongdoing is suspected (such cases are carried directly to a special membership meeting). Officers and committee members (with the exception of the treasurer who may receive a small annual payment) serve without pay. Overhead expenses are low.

Early Development

Certain citizens petitioned the Massachusetts Legislature in 1870 to authorize the formation of credit unions patterned on those in Germany. A bill was introduced and received favorable committee reports in both houses, but failed to pass. Nevertheless, lack of a law did not deter a few hardy souls, and at least five credit cooperatives, on the order of building and loan associations, were formed without incorporating. One dated from 1892. There were unincorporated associations that antedated credit union law in other places also—in California, New Jersey, New York,[4] and Utah—as well as in some postoffices.

The first cooperative credit association in the United States to receive legal status was St. Mary's Cooperative Credit Association, formed by French-Canadian cotton-textile workers in Manchester, N. H., which was granted a special charter on December 16, 1908.[5]

The Massachusetts credit union law was approved on May 29, of the following year—the first such law in the United

States. By 1919 nine States had such laws. Four (those of Massachusetts, New York, North Carolina, and Rhode Island) were good; the others were so defective as to be inoperable.

To North Carolina goes the honor of being the first State to provide official encouragement and assistance in organizing. Its Superintendent of Credit Unions, appointed in 1915, also conducted an information bureau, supplied office forms, and gave advice on operating problems. Nearly all the credit unions in North Carolina—all rural—were attributable to the work of the State credit union office staff.

By 1919, credit unions had been organized in North Carolina for 13 groups of Negro farmers, as well as for white groups. These associations put great stress on thrift; most of their energies, however, went into the collective purchase of farm supplies. Such a combination of services is quite common abroad, but is almost never found in credit unions in this country.

Altogether, by the end of 1922, a total of 254 credit unions had been chartered in 5 States—123 in Massachusetts, 2 in New Hampshire, 84 in New York, 43 in North Carolina, and 2 in Rhode Island.

Credit Union National Extension Bureau

The credit union movement, as we have it today, owes its existence to the idealism, vision, and money of Edward A. Filene, retail merchant of Boston, and the work and unflagging devotion of Roy F. Bergengren. Many hundreds of others helped to spread the idea throughout the country. But these two gave the inspiration and leadership.

The Credit Union National Extension Bureau was founded in 1921, at Mr. Filene's suggestion, and was financed by him. Mr. Bergengren became then—and remained for some years—in his own phrase, its "one-man band."

The two men agreed that the major objectives of the Bureau should be, in order of timing and importance: (1) Passage of credit union enabling laws, (2) organization of local credit unions as soon as a State law was obtained, (3) increase of associations to the point where (4) self-sustaining State leagues could be formed and, eventually, (5) federation of these leagues into a national organization.

The first 3 years were mainly exploratory and were spent in developing techniques, making personal contacts for future work, beginning publication of a monthly, *The Bridge,*[6] and issuing the first of four textbooks (all written by Mr. Bergengren) on the organization and operation of credit unions.

Passage of State laws was obtained only after much preliminary work, and not without resistance from organized bankers and money lenders. The three simple words, "get the laws," required 13 years of hard labor.

Once having obtained a law, the organization of credit unions was the next step. This proved unexpectedly difficult because of opposition from industrialists (the obvious place to start associations was in industrial plants),[7] from personnel men (who should have known something of the workers' credit problems),[8] and even in a few cases from State supervisory officials who regarded credit unions as just another "headache."

However, the chief crusader was no longer alone. One by one, he had discovered new talent, men and women who took up credit union work with an almost religious enthusiasm.[9] Fortunately, also, there were at the head of the Department of Service Relations of the U. S. Post Office Department two men in succession who were favorably disposed toward credit unions—Henry Dennison and his successor, Louis Brehm. With their encouragement, it was possible to organize credit unions among postal employees in the various States as soon as laws were obtained.[10] These were an entering wedge and with them to point to, the going was easier elsewhere.

Although there was continued opposition from the vested interests,[11] by the end of 1929 credit union legislation had been passed in 32 States and improvements to existing laws had been obtained in several others.

Credit Unions in the Depression

Up to 1931, over 85 percent of the total credit unions in operation had been organized by the Extension Bureau or persons whom it had enlisted. There were now 1,500 credit cooperatives, or more than three times as many as in 1925.

The depression killed some associations, especially in industrial plants (if the company went out of business, that of course removed the "common bond" on which the credit union charter was based). On the other hand, even in some of the industrial plants that shut down for long periods the credit union managed somehow not only to keep going but to collect on loans outstanding.

There appear to have been no panics among credit unions such as were causing the runs on banks. Banks had been failing right and left, and this posed added problems for credit unions whose funds were in them.[12] But even the Bank Holiday (March 6-15, 1933) failed to halt the credit unions. In one way or another, they managed to get along without the banks during that period. A Princeton University study revealed that 93.6 percent of the credit unions survived the crisis—a record in pleasing contrast with that of the banks and even of the building and loan associations.

It can therefore be said with truth that the depression experience demonstrated the fundamental soundness of the credit unions as a financial institution. I believe they are also unique in that, although some went out of business, so many new ones were coming into being—even in those lean, desperate years when the average worker's family had hardly two nickels to rub together—that the total number rose from 974 in 1929 (at the height of the so-called "prosperity period") to 2,016 at the end of 1933 (the trough of the depression). Credit union loans in 1933 totaled nearly $28¼ million.

By January 1, 1934, laws had been placed on the statute books of 39 States. That year saw the capstone placed on the Extension Bureau's work, with the passage of the Federal Credit Union Act and its signing on June 24, 1934.

This law made it possible to organize credit unions not only in States without credit union legislation but also in those where unsatisfactory provisions or official procedures or attitudes made the Federal jurisdiction preferable to that of the State.

National Federation

By 1934 it was felt that the time was ripe for national federation. The Credit Union National Association was therefore formed and started work on March 1, 1935. This had been preceded by long educational work among the State and local associations.

All of the legal and organizational work up to that time had been done under the direction of the Extension Bureau, with the bills all paid by Mr. Filene—to the tune of nearly a million dollars. Now it was planned that the whole system should go onto a self-supporting basis.[13] The new federation (with Mr. Filene as its first president and Mr. Bergengren as managing director) was to be a combine of State leagues and receive support from them in dues based on their membership.

Actually, the superstructure was formed before the foundation had been completed, for there were in existence only six State leagues. In order, therefore, to put in the proper underpinning the organization of State leagues began in real earnest. Between 1934 and May 1937, leagues were formed in 35 States and joined the national association, bringing its total membership to 41.

The program of the Credit Union National Extension Bureau had now been carried out, and shortly after the formation of the association the Bureau shut up shop, making over to the association all its assets. National headquarters were moved to Madison, Wis.

In 1937 the credit union movement was saddened by the sudden death of Mr. Filene while in Europe on a trip. During the rest of the year memorial meetings honoring his memory and pledging the movement to continue his work were held all over the country. After the end of World War II, a headquarters building was erected (financed by contributions from credit unions and their members all over the United States) as a memorial to their great benefactor, Edward Filene. The cornerstone of the building was laid by President Truman in May 1950.

CUNA became an international organization in fact when the credit union league of Nova Scotia joined it, in 1936. Not until 1939, however, were its bylaws amended to permit the affiliation of leagues outside the United States. Since then eight other Canadian Provincial leagues have affiliated, in addition to the league in Jamaica. In 1954, there were 58 State and Provincial leagues in its membership. After the war's end, offices were opened in Washington, D. C., and Hamilton, Ont.

Mr. Bergengren retired in 1945.[14] He was succeeded by Thomas W. Doig of Minnesota, and Mr. Doig in turn (in 1955) by H. B. Yates of Dallas, Tex.

In its capacity of national coordinating and educational organization for the credit union movement, the Credit Union National Association and its auxiliaries issue a great deal of educational materials and pamphlets for use by the local associations, describing the movement, its aims and accomplishments, and dealing with the insurance and other central activities.

The Credit Union National Association became the 28th member of CARE (Cooperative for American Remittances Everywhere) in November 1953. CUNA has also launched its own World Extension Bureau—an organization to promote the formation of credit unions abroad.

Insurance.—The matter of insurance had long been considered. As early as 1930, some of the credit unions began to act as agents for the mutual savings-bank life-insurance system in Massachusetts. Many had also adopted the plan of having their loans insured, with the premium paid by the borrower in each case. This had never been greatly favored, however, and in 1935, with a loan from Mr. Filene[15] the CUNA Mutual Society (later renamed CUNA Mutual Insurance Society) was formed, with Earl Rentfro of Missouri as manager.

The insurance society was successful from the day it opened its doors. By the end of its first year it was operating in 30 States. During its first decade, notwithstanding its low rates, it returned to its members over a quarter of a million dollars in dividends on premiums, besides paying some 13,000 claims. Its report for 1953 showed insurance in force amounting to nearly $1½ billion. Ever since its organization the association has received the highest insurance rating—A plus (Excellent).

In 1936 it shifted from insurance of individual loans (with the premium paid by the borrower) to blanket coverage of all an association's outstanding loans, with the credit union paying the cost. It also began to issue insurance against permanent total disability. In 1938 it invented a "share insurance" policy (paid for by credit unions from earnings) under which the member's savings—in the form of share capital in the credit union—were insured, up to a maximum of $1,000. In the event of a member's death, an amount matching the amount of his share capital would be paid to his family. The association now also writes both individual and group insurance.

When the national association's bylaws were amended in 1939, to permit it to extend jurisdiction to Canada, the insurance society also received a license to do business there.

Supply business.—Since 1928, the Extension Bureau had been furnishing credit unions with accounting forms at great savings. By the time the national headquarters was moved to Madison, the supply business had grown to about $60,000 a year. In 1936 the CUNA Supply Cooperative was organized. It deals in bookkeeping and accounting forms, ledgers, deposit slips, and other supplies used in credit union offices.

At the end of 1954 the CUNA Supply Cooperative had 56 members (54 State and Provincial leagues, CUNA, and the insurance society). Its business for the year ending February 28, 1955 was $549,000.

Accelerated Growth, and Wartime Decline

The passage of the Federal act in 1934, with attendant organizing assistance from the Federal Credit Union Division, brought into being a great many new associations. It also seemed to have had a galvanic effect on the older, State-chartered movement, for the number of those associations also began to grow at a pace considerably faster than before, even though not so fast as the Federal credit unions.

The known total of 5,440 credit unions at the end of 1936—in 48 States and the District of Columbia—had an estimated total membership of 1,210,000. They had served some 1,035,000 borrowers during the year, lending them over $112 million. Slightly over a third of the associations (with about a fourth of the members) were under the Federal act; the others had State charters. Total capital amounted to $62.6 million and net worth exceeded $52 million.

The same year also saw the veteran credit union State of Massachusetts, which had hitherto consistently held the lead in number of associations, give way to Illinois. Massachusetts was still out in front as regards assets and annual amount of loans made. It relinquished its superiority on membership and loans in 1939 and on assets in 1940. Since then, Illinois has had undisputed leadership on all counts.

In 1941, the last year of peace before Pearl Harbor, the number of credit unions in the United States rose to 10,042. By this time they had 3.3 million members and had accumulated assets of nearly $322¼ million. Loans that year exceeded $362¼ million.

The 1943 annual meeting of the Credit Union National Association authorized the formation of a national credit union bank. This has not yet materialized, though a few steps into central banking have been taken.[16]

The period of World War II (with shortages of the higher-priced consumer goods customarily bought on installments and its Regulation W, restricting credit and installment buying) had an adverse effect on credit unions, reducing their business materially. Employers were crying for workers, wages were high, money was plentiful, and loans were not needed so badly.

Not many credit unions failed because of these conditions, but there were "altogether too many voluntary liquidations" of associations that were fearful they could not last and so went out of operation while they were still in the black.[17]

Up to 1942, each year had shown credit union development and business exceeding those of the previous year. In 1942, for the first time in recorded credit union history, both membership and loans declined. The associations were rolling in money, but business was off. Members were still borrowing, but in fewer numbers, in smaller amounts, and for a narrower range of purposes.

The decline in membership and loans continued through 1943, and the number of associations also fell in that year. Between 1942 (when a peak of 10,099 associations was reached) and the end of 1945, over 1,200 credit unions liquidated voluntarily or otherwise; about 500 of these were small new Federal credit unions.

In 1945 a 3.1 percent drop in total membership occurred. The next year this decline, under way since 1941, came to an end with an increase of nearly 6 percent as compared with 1945. Loans showed one of the greatest relative increases ever recorded. Not until 1947, however, did the credit union business reach and pass the prewar level, rising to nearly $456 million. The number of associations was still below the peak of 1942.

Postwar Developments

Not until 3 years after the war's end did the credit union movement recover entirely from the war-induced slump. In 1948 the membership, business, assets, and earnings were at an all-time high. An unusually large amount of earnings (over $12 million) was put into reserves, raising the combined total to almost $43 million. In spite of this, dividends on capital soared to $13½ million—the highest on record. By 1950 the number of credit unions also had passed the prewar level and stood at 10,581.

In 1951 the assets of credit unions in the United States passed the billion-dollar mark for the first time, rising to $1,198,402,000.

By the end of 1953, there were 13,674 credit unions under Federal and State charters, divided as follows:

	Number	*Members*	*Assets*
State charter	7,096	3,380,121	$1,040,874,593
Federal charter ...	6,578	3,255,422	854,232,007
Total	13,674	6,635,543	1,895,106,600

There are now credit union laws in all but 4 States (Delaware, Nevada, South Dakota, and Wyoming), as well as in the District of Columbia and Puerto Rico. The existence and worth of State laws is of course no longer as important as formerly, for the Federal act can be utilized in all of them. In 1946 its jurisdiction was also extended to cover the Canal Zone.

Recent legislative activity has consisted for the most part of liberalizing amendments to laws already operative. These have raised the ceilings on secured and unsecured loans, reduced reserve requirements, etc. Massachusetts amended its law in 1948, to permit credit unions to establish retirement systems for credit union employees, becoming (I believe) the first to do so.

Administration

The administration of the Federal law and supervision of the associations incorporated under it were originally vested in the Federal Credit Union Division of the Farm Credit Administration. The section was transferred to the Federal Deposit Insurance Corporation in 1941. It was again shifted—to the Federal Security Agency—in July 1948, its status being raised at the same time to that of a full-fledged bureau, with a new name, Bureau of Federal Credit Unions.

During all this period the Federal credit union work had been under the benevolent guidance of Claude R. Orchard. To his contagious enthusiasm and interest, during his 19-year tenure, can be attributed much of the remarkable development of the Federal credit unions.[18] When Mr. Orchard retired in June 1953, he was succeeded as head of the Bureau of Federal Credit Unions by J. Deane Gannon, previously supervisor of credit unions for the State of Wisconsin.

Credit Unions and Consumers' Cooperatives

One of the oldest credit unions in Massachusetts—Workers' Credit Union of Fitchburg (most of whose members were also members of the local Finnish cooperative store)—made a long-term loan for the construction of one of the cooperative apartment buildings erected by the Finnish colony in Brooklyn, N. Y., in the late "teens." In 1938 it advanced a loan to a Finnish distributive association for an addition to its bakery. This credit union, incorporated under the State law in 1914, is still active and one of the largest in the State. In June 1953 it had 3,456 members and assets of nearly $5 million.

Beginning with 1924, each Cooperative Congress has included the subject of cooperative credit, presented by a speaker (usually from the credit union movement) or at a work session. Until 1939, however, the relationship between the credit unions and the distributive movement consisted largely of these occasional opportunities for exchange of ideas. In March of that year the Credit Union National Association affiliated with the Cooperative League as a fraternal member; it became a full member in 1951. CUNA Supply Cooperative is now also a member of the League, and CUNA Mutual Insurance Society was one of the charter members of the League's Insurance Conference. Cooperatives began in the early 1930's to organize credit unions among their members.

Several of the regional wholesales also actively supported the organization of credit cooperatives in connection with their member associations. In 1941 alone, local affiliates of the Farmers Union Central Exchange organized 35 credit unions; by this time there were also 47 credit unions in members of the Indiana Farm Bureau Cooperative Association. The credit union idea, however, has never really "caught on" among the farmers. Possibly this is because they have access to other sources of credit, largely Governmental, such as the production credit system and banks for cooperatives.

Credit union development has therefore continued to be mainly urban and industrial.

At the end of 1953 there were 564 credit unions with over 275,000 members operating in connection with distributive and other cooperatives.

The Umbrella for the Rainy Day

Of all the types of cooperative financing, the credit union has been by far the most successful.

It has the advantage of simplicity of operation, combined with the sale of only two commodities—credit and thrift. The credit union movement has been built on the firm belief that most people are inherently honest and that ordinary people's abilities are much greater than they realize. It used to be commonly accepted that only bankers understand money and its uses and control. The experience of thousands of credit unions has disproved this. The ordinary men and women who never managed anything larger than their own pay envelopes have demonstrated repeatedly their capacity to manage a credit and thrift institution whose business may run into the hundreds of thousands of dollars in a year.

The insignia of the credit union movement—"the little man" who holds over his head an open umbrella (the credit union) which shields him against the rainy day represented by hard times, illness, death, and other troubles—is an accurate and graphic picture of the credit union function and its clientele.

In less than half a century of credit union history in this country, the "average American" workers who are the members of credit unions have accumulated for themselves nearly 2 billion dollars in resources. They also, in the 28-year period for which there are records (1925-53), made earnings from which they returned to the members the tidy sum of nearly $225 million in dividends on share capital. When to this is added the incalculable sum of interest saved in lower rates, one gets some idea of what the credit unions have meant to our people in hard cash.

No one can place a value on the benefit to morale, self-respect, and family happiness which is their greatest accomplishment.

The progress has been made without either public loans or subsidy. No credit union officer has ever suggested that any such be made. The operating funds have come entirely from "ordinary" people and are lent to the same type of people. All that the credit unions ask for is a fair field and no favors, and no outside interference however well meant.

They therefore did not take kindly to President Eisenhower's proposal for Federal insurance of credit union share capital.[19] The enormous credit union funds have been safe thus far with insurance provided through the CUNA organization, and the cooperative officers openly expressed apprehension that it would result in Government attempts to dictate loan policy. Credit unions emphasize the human element in all their dealings, and bank-type supervision and regulations would soon squeeze this out.

Chapter 32.—OTHER SERVICES

The other services have too long been neglected by cooperators. The main deterrents have been, I think, preoccupation with the distributive and related aspects of cooperation, and the fact that no one of the services forms any great proportion of the total family budget. In order, therefore, to attract a volume of business sufficient for profitable operation, a very large membership is necessary, especially if the cooperative is to operate under union conditions (as it is assumed it would). Possibly when cooperators finally recognize the savings to be made from providing their own services on a nonprofit basis, the solution will lie in the organization of "federal" associations, as among the funeral cooperatives. Under such an arrangement the local cooperatives of various kinds in a given area combine to form an association, of which they are the members. Their individual members then become eligible for service from the new association, on payment of a small fee, and this automatically supplies the necessary broad patronage base.

The consumer service associations described in previous chapters constitute by far the great majority of the existing service cooperatives. Those remaining—funeral, water-supply, eating and rooming, cold-storage, and other scattered types—total only about 600, with about 155,000 members. Their combined annual business amounts to about $17 million.

Rooming and Boarding Associations

Finnish Cooperative Boarding Houses

One of the interesting developments of the years immediately preceding and following the First World War was the formation of cooperative boarding houses by unattached Finns.

By 1925 there were 68 such organizations; of 64 for which there are present records, 25 were in Minnesota, 24 in Michigan, 3 in Illinois, 2 each in Massachusetts, Washington, and Wisconsin. and 1 each in Idaho, Montana, New York, Ohio, Pennsylvania, and Wyoming. Thirty-four percent had been organized between 1911 and 1914, 40 percent between 1915 and 1919, and 26 percent from 1920 through 1925. I can find no record of any Finnish boarding house organized after 1925.

A few were out of existence before 1929, but the great majority were killed by the Great Depression and the "recession" in the late thirties. A number were still in operation as late as 1951, but only two were still cooperative. These were the Home Cooperative Club, Nashwauk, Minn. and the Workers Cooperative Club of Superior, Wis.

Student "Living" Associations

Mention has been made of the college book stores, few of which now have democratic control (though many return "dividends" on purchases). Another type of student organization is the cooperative "house" providing shelter and usually meals also.

Aside from the chief benefit of bringing down the cost of room and board, the student organizations have several important values: They provide practical training in household operation and management and the collateral activities, as well as business training in thrift, buying, bookkeeping, making reports, and direction of others; they promote high scholastic standards; they tend to develop a spirit of independence, resourcefulness, and self-help, and to make the individual adaptable and tolerant of others' views; and they provide lessons in democracy and citizenship.

One student cooperative, the Independent Club, serving meals only, was in existence in Detroit as early as 1926, but it was not until the Great Depression that the student houses began to develop.

The idea seems to have taken hold almost simultaneously in many scattered places. At least one eating club each is known to have been started in 1932 at the University of Wisconsin, Bethany Biblical Seminary (Chicago), and Eastern Illinois State Teachers College (Charleston); and there was a rooming house each at Cornell and the University of Michigan. A host of similar organizations appeared on many campuses in 1933.[1]

Some had a religious aspect. Among them were the dining clubs at Cornell and at the Universities of California, and Oregon, the Methodist, Baptist, Congregational, and Catholic eating clubs at the University of Wisconsin, and the Latter Day Saints' dormitory association at the University of Idaho.

These associations continued to expand until the Second World War. By 1941 the 150-odd "living associations" had an estimated membership of nearly 10,000 students. They were handicapped by insufficient capital and by continuous changes in membership, but their savings were great.[2] During the war, closures of the men's houses were offset to some extent by new associations for the girl students.

A considerable revival occurred at the war's end which continued through 1949. Thereafter, membership and associations declined again as students were called into service in the Korean war.

The largest student co-op is that at the University of California, at Berkeley, with 905 members. It owns eight houses and a central kitchen. The cooperative at the Los Angeles branch of the same university has four houses, accommodating some 200 members; the University of Washington cooperative, at Seattle, 12 houses and about 350 members.

Federations.—Some campuses had up to a dozen "living" cooperatives. In most places having a sufficient number of associations, food and household supplies were bought jointly. Also, by 1941, councils of student cooperatives had been organized at the Universities of Chicago, Michigan, Missouri, Texas, and Wisconsin.

Conferences of delegates eventually led to the formation of four regional leagues for education and exchange of ideas—Midwest Federation of Student Cooperatives (1938), for associations in Illinois, Indiana, and Michigan; Pacific Coast Student Cooperative League (1939), for California, Oregon, Washington, Idaho, and Montana; Central League of Campus Co-ops (1940), for Iowa, Kansas, Missouri, and Texas; and North Central Federation of Campus Cooperatives (1946), for the Dakotas, Minnesota, and Wisconsin.

The National Committee on Student Cooperatives had been organized in 1935 by representatives from student cooperatives in 11 States, at a 3-day seminar sponsored by the Federal Council of Churches of Christ in America. Its work was carried on almost singlehandedly by the voluntary labor of its secretary William Moore, divinity student of Illinois. After his departure, the committee languished. It was formally reorganized at the 1940 congress of the Cooperative League of the USA, with a member from each of six regions. The committee was superseded in 1946 by the North American Students Cooperative League, which all four regional leagues and the Canadian Student Cooperative League then joined. (But the Pacific League dissolved at the end of 1950.)

The new national body had plenty of moral support but very little income. At the end of 1953 fewer than 25 (of "530 known" associations) were paying dues to it. With some intermittent help from the Cooperative League and National Cooperatives, it limped along until June 1954, when death stared it in the face. The Cooperative League thereupon arranged to take over "the executive functions," with the student league continuing to publish *Co-ops in Action.* By mid-1955 the league was able to report that it was again on a "firm financial footing."

Houses for Aged

Similar to the students' cooperative living associations was a group of nine cooperative houses in the State of Washington, organized with the encouragement of the State Department of Social Security for elderly persons receiving public assistance. They were started in 1938 to 1940, with the idea that by pooling their small relief incomes, unattached men and women could live better and more comfortably, as well as more companionably, than would be possible alone.

They gradually disappeared until by April 1955 only two were left, both in Bremerton. One houses 12 elderly men, and the other seven women.

One reason for the continuance of these two after the others died may have been that each has local sponsors who act as trustees, give over-all guidance, and provide continuity despite membership turnover.[3]

Restaurants and Cafeterias

In the whole history of consumers' cooperation in this country, records now remain for only 18 associations the sole or chief business of which was that of providing meals for members.[4] Most of them were formed during the decade of the 1920's, but one, the Coffee Club of San Diego (a "temperance" organization), was reported in mid-1898.

Scandinavians started the temperance cafe, "Idrott," in Chicago, which operated from 1913 to 1939. Another group of the same nationality ran a semicooperative store, bakery and restaurant in Seattle during the cooperative wave of the 20's. The Workers Cooperative Restaurant, opened by Brooklyn Finns in 1921, merged with the cooperative store, Cooperative Trading Association. That organization in turn dissolved in the fall of 1955.

There were also cooperative restaurants run by Russians in Chicago, Gary (Ind.), and Detroit, this last being a Communist casualty. The other two, Gary Workers Cooperative Society (1925) and Russian Cooperative Restaurant in Chicago (1922) were still in operation at last reports. The failure of the Communist Prolet Cooperative Restaurant in New York has already been noted.

Others currently operating are: International Cooperative Restaurant started by Russians in Detroit in 1919, the two restaurants of Detroit Workmen's Cooperative Association (1922), and those run by employees of Consumers Cooperative Association at Kansas City, Mo. (1937) and the personnel at the State capitol in St. Paul, Minn. (1935).

Only one of the present associations is large. It has been among the select "million-dollar" cooperatives since 1947. This, most prominent of all, is the white-collar Consumers Cooperative Services (1920) in New York City. It has no nationality lines in either membership or patronage.

CCS was organized by a group of socially minded women, among whom were Mary Arnold,[5] Mabel Reed, Dorothy Kenyon,[6] Mary LaDame, and Ruth True. Starting with one cafeteria, the association opened additional ones in the financial district of the city and was operating 11 by the end of 1935. Its membership then totaled 4,500.

This association has always taken the larger view in things cooperative. It was one of the charter members of Eastern Cooperative Wholesale. In the mid-1930's it assisted the wholesale and Eastern Cooperative League with funds for organizing new cooperatives, and later lent money to pay the salary of a technical fieldman. CCS used some of its accumulated surplus in an apartment-house project already described in Chapter 27.

The grocery business was entered in 1944; by the end of 1945 CCS had four grocery stores, but the number of cafeterias had declined to seven. For the fiscal year ending March 31, 1946, it reported the largest volume in its 26-year history—$1,373,424—and an increase in membership from 5,536 to 7,130.

The grocery-store venture did not turn out as planned. Several of the stores had been in trouble when taken over (from existing cooperatives) by CCS, and the latter was unable to put them on a paying basis. By 1952, all but one, in Greenwich Village, had been closed, as well as three more cafeterias. Consequent diminution of the cafeteria sales led to the discontinuance of its bakery, which had operated for many years.

The cooperative's peak membership (8,291) was attained in 1947-48 and its peak business ($2,049,839) in 1948-49. The grocery volume forged ahead of the cafeteria volume in 1953-54. The 1954-55 business showed an increase over the previous year, reaching $1,252,650. A patronage refund of 1½ percent and 4 percent interest on share capital were paid.

Funeral Associations

The first recorded association to provide undertaking and burial services for members came into being in 1915 at a time when prices were rising and cooperation was in the air again. It was logical and fitting that the pioneer association should be that of coal miners, for that occupation was even more hazardous then than now, the death rate was high, and the cost of burial was a tremendous burden on the miners' families. Further, they suspected that they were providing unduly high profits for the local morticians.

So the miners' local at Harrisburg, Ill. in 1915 voted to assess each member $1 and use the money to start the Cooperative Undertaking Association. In 1921 similar associations were started in Christopher, Marion, Royalton, and West Frankfort, and in 1923 at Gillespie—all in Illinois.

The funeral associations were not, however, genuine cooperatives. They had no separate membership that controlled the funeral business. The operation was a union affair, though nonprofit.

In 1921 a group of farmers in Vienna, S. Dak., formed the Community Burial Association. No more organizations of the kind were formed in that State until 1928. In the meantime, however, beginning in 1924, farmers of Dutch descent in southern Minnesota and northern Iowa caught the idea. And from then on, through 1939 in Iowa and 1937 in Minnesota, each year saw several funeral cooperatives organized. The farmers in South Dakota had in the interval formed five more associations. But the funeral homes at Marion and Royalton, Ill., had gone under as a result of the depression in the early 1920's and unemployment and strike in the coal fields.

It is hard to believe that this second group of scattered associations arose from anything except spontaneous action, for most of them were in places without other types of cooperatives and with no contact with the general cooperative movement. Exceptions were the two associations in Nebraska, organized in 1932 and 1935, which were composed of members of the Farmers Union.

Altogether, 43 associations had been chartered by the end of 1939. A few cooperatives were formed in the period 1940-42, but the war stopped further expansion. Five had already gone out of business and a sixth had merged with the association in a neighboring town.

By now all but a few of the active associations were of farmer membership, and this has continued to be true of the new associations until the past few years.

The cooperatives had also made another discovery, that the undertaking business depends on the death rate, and farmers are rather long-lived as a class. It was hardly feasible to kill off the members in order to increase business volume! Therefore, in order to attain a sufficiently wide membership to produce business in practicable volume, the new associations had begun as early as 1928 to organize for service over a whole county or even several counties. By the end of 1939, there were five active associations serving one or more counties in Iowa, eight in Minnesota, two in South Dakota, and one each in Nebraska and Wisconsin.

A third type had also made its appearance—that formed by joint action of several contiguous cooperatives (usually store associations). This at one stroke assured funds and a very large membership (up to 5,000 or more) from which to draw patronage. A variant development dated from 1939 when cooperative stores began to open funeral homes or take over those of local burial associations.

Most of the associations have their own funeral parlor and hearse, employ their own funeral director and embalmer, and provide a complete funeral. The others arrange a contract with the local undertaker; a few of these buy the caskets (a wide-margin item) themselves.

Before the end of 1936 the Iowa and Minnesota funeral cooperatives had each formed a State federation, and in 1944 those in Wisconsin also federated. These bodies are legislative watchdogs and serve as a medium of exchange of experience.

The burial cooperatives have not had things all their own way. In the early 1930's a suit by the Minnesota undertakers' association to prevent the issuance of a charter to the "federal" Northland Cooperative Burial Association at Cloquet was decided in favor of the cooperative only after a long period of controversy. In Wisconsin a favorable ruling was finally obtained from the State Attorney General relative to a 1939 law prohibiting solicitation of business by licensed funeral directors or embalmers, which the cooperatives feared might be construed to prevent their seeking additional members.

For 15 years the Iowa undertakers agitated against the cooperatives and tried in one way or another to put them out of business. One favorite method was seeking unfavorable rulings or court actions by the State Attorney General. After a series of defeats,[7] the undertakers apparently gave it up as a bad job and no further action has occurred since 1946.

As of the end of 1953 there were 38 cooperative burial associations[8]—28 providing complete funeral services, 3 buying caskets, and 7 providing burials under contract with a local mortician. They had some 30,000 members and a business for the year estimated at nearly $700,000. This did not include the volume of funeral departments of cooperatives in other lines of business, for which separate figures were not available, nor the two cooperative burial associations of federal type having 25 local cooperatives as members and doing an annual funeral business of about $50,000.

Nearly a third of the total associations chartered have gone out of existence. However, the remaining ones are among the longest-lived cooperatives today, with an average duration of over 21 years. Included in the survivors are the three pioneer miners' associations in Illinois.

Practically no new funeral associations are being formed. The only new ones since the end of World War II have been two contract plans sponsored by labor unions—CIO auto workers in Detroit (open to all unionists and cooperators in the area) and AFL and CIO unions in Greater St. Louis.

The value of the burial cooperatives, in terms of money savings, has been demonstrated beyond doubt. They try to set their charges at a level that will just cover expenses of operation and a small amount for replacements and reserves. The patron thus gets his "dividend" immediately, in the form of much lower prices. (Data obtained in the 1930's showed the cooperative average to be about half that charged by their competitors.)

Studies of the undertaking industry have shown that the major cause of the prevailing high prices is too many entrepreneurs and the uneven distribution of volume. The large establishments (forming 10 to 25 percent of the total) do 50 percent of all the business. The other half is divided among the other 75 to 90 percent of the morticians. But the industry has shown practically no elimination of the "marginal" establishments through competition, indeed, the evidence is that most of the larger places keep their charges as high as those of the smaller ones.

Here, it would seem, is a promising field for cooperative enterprise, provided two conditions are met: a sufficiently large membership to furnish an economic volume of business, and education of members away from the mistaken idea that extravagant and elaborate funerals are necessary to show respect to the departed.

Other Types

Cold Storage Plants

Toward the end of the 1930's appeared a new type of consumers' cooperative—that providing refrigerated locker space for members' foods. These associations were an outgrowth of the spread of electric power to rural areas under the REA, and the members were almost all farmers. By July 1940 there were 2,870 rural locker plants, of which a considerable proportion were cooperative.[9]

Cold-storage associations expanded in number throughout the next 18 months, with Illinois the leading State. Some cooperative store associations, also, added a locker plant to their operations. By 1944, these plants stood high among the new cooperatives being formed. At least 15 States reported new plants of this kind during the year.

The rate of organization of new associations began to slow down by 1948. Supply had finally caught up with demand and some of the newer and larger plants were even having difficulty renting their lockers.

It was estimated in 1951 that the 175 cooperative cold-storage associations run for the benefit of consumers had about 90,000 members and an annual business of some $7 million. Only about 14 percent were of nonfarm membership.

Since then, as home freezers have gradually increased in popularity and number, cold-storage locker plants have declined in number and business has further decreased. To some extent this loss has been offset by expansion into other services and the sale of commercially frozen foods.

Laundries and Cleaning Establishments

Only seven laundries serving consumer members and operating on a commercial scale are known to have been formed during our whole history.[10]

All the recorded consumers' cooperative laundries were organized between 1912 and 1920 and, with the exception of one each in Connecticut, Montana, and New York City, all were in the Midwest (Kansas, Minnesota, North Dakota, and Wisconsin).

Not one of these remains today.

Members of the American Society of Equity opened the Chatfield (Minn.) Cooperative Laundry which operated from 1912 to 1929.

In Wisconsin, two cooperative laundries were organized in 1914. The first, at Milltown, had a loss of nearly $500 in its first year, could never get into the black, and closed in 1917. The other at River Falls, was an urban-rural affair, which lasted until 1945 (31 years), finally selling out to two of its employees, with no loss to the members. One wonders whether this was another instance of tired cooperators.

Greenwich villagers opened the Village Cooperative Laundry in New York City in 1919. It encountered difficulties immediately. "Accidentally," acid got into the tubs, destroying large amounts of work in process, the cooperative's deliverymen were waylaid by thugs (reportedly in the pay of competitors), and other "incidents" of various kinds occurred, designed to discourage the cooperators and put their plant out of business. The laundry (consistently in the red) became a department of the big cafeteria organization, Consumers Cooperative Services, in 1923. It was no more successful under this arrangement, and was finally disposed of about 1925.

Two cooperatives were formed in the early 1930's in a related field—dry cleaning. One was a union-supported association, Crystal Cooperative Cleaners, in Minneapolis, which was very successful for a while but finally succumbed in the middle 1930's. The other was the Madison (Wis.) Cooperative Cleaners, started in 1934, which was still doing business (as an agency only) in 1955. At least one store association, Consumers Cooperative Society of Palo Alto, Calif., runs a cleaning establishment as a department of its distributive business.

Water Associations

The cooperative water associations—a very small group—are found in the four States of California, Oregon, Washington, and Wisconsin. Most of them were started to serve small colonies of homes in new suburban developments or too far away from the nearest town to connect with its water system.

The first recorded association was the Maple (Wash.) Cooperative Water Co., organized in 1910. It ceased operation in 1948 only because of connecting with the city water system.

The Parkland (Wash.) Light & Water Co. (1914) is still in operation, as is also the Olivita Mutual Water Co. in Los Angeles (1915). Nine water cooperatives were started during the decade of the 1920's (four in Oregon and five in Washington) of which all but two are still in existence.

It may be said of this branch of cooperation that it is "little, but oh, my!" Even the 10 dissolved associations for which period of operation is known were active for an average of about 11 years, and most of them dissolved only because they finally were able to obtain water from a municipal system. Thirty-three are still in operation. Of 20 of these for which date of organization is known, the average duration (to January 1, 1955) is 23 years. It is a remarkable record, and I know of no comparable one in any other branch of the consumers' cooperative movement.

Unusual Types

Other, rather novel, service associations have included the increasingly popular cooperative nursery schools where the mothers participate in the curriculum; some twoscore flying clubs (whose members jointly owned one or more pleasure planes), which were grounded with the onset of the Second World War and as far as I can learn were not reactivated afterwards; war-born associations to provide transportation for the members to and from work; a watch-repair service; a cooperative residential club for war refugees; an association providing steam heat for the houses of members; and a small cooperative whose members jointly owned a power lawn mower.

It is evident that the cooperative method can be used for nearly everything. The service field presents a wide-open opportunity of which insufficient advantage has thus far been taken.

Part IV.

COOPERATION IN SPECIAL GROUPS

Chapter 33.—COOPERATIVES OF NATIONAL AND OTHER GROUPS

Around the turn of the century cooperatives of a single ethnic group were numerous. They also formed a sizable proportion of the surge that followed the First World War.

Unfortunately, the records for them are very spotty and incomplete, and it is impossible now to determine with any accuracy the actual extent of their cooperative activity. It is very probable that the number of cooperatives actually formed was at least double the number for which there now is information. Many lived and died without attracting the notice of the historians or journalists of their time or without there being any record of the nationality make-up of the association.

The data in the following pages are presented for what they are worth—at best only a rough general indication of the situation.

Racial Groups

Indian Cooperatives

Cooperation among American Indians, though not extensive, is of fairly long standing, but most of their associations have been of producer rather than consumer type.[1]

Minnesota has a fish-marketing association, a cooperative store, and a handcraft-marketing cooperative. The oldest is the Red Lake Indian Cooperative Fisheries Association, at Redby, organized in 1929.

In the early forties at least four cooperative stores were formed among the Navajo Indians in Arizona. Two of these, at Many Farms and Piñon, were still active in 1952.

A store association in North Dakota (at Belcourt), formed in 1946, went out of existence in 1951. In Black River Falls, Wis., the Winnebago Indians have a cooperative that sells their handcraft and operates a grocery store. An Indian association at Ethete, Wyo., organized in the mid-1930's, was still operating in 1951. It was reported in 1952 that, under the leadership of a priest, Indians were running a cooperative store in St. Michaels, S. Dak.; also that some of the Apache Indians had stores.

There are, in addition, many tribal enterprises, most of which are informal and not incorporated. They are not cooperatives in the strict sense, but operate pretty much on a cooperative basis. Thus, in the Gallup, N. Mex., area 20 such groups are in operation. Of these, 8 are trading posts to which every member of the tribe automatically belongs, which buy food and household supplies. Their combined business in 1954 was approximately $130,000.

Alaska also has numerous tribal projects, scattered along the Bering Sea and all the way up to and inside the Arctic circle. The volume of the 48 community stores totals about $1½ million.

The Alaska stores have their own federation—a true cooperative, which purchases the supplies for them, besides assisting in the marketing of native products (ivory carvings, fur pelts, whale oil, etc.). It is the Alaska Native Industries Cooperative Association, to which 33 of the tribal stores belong. It also serves 15 other (nonmember) tribal stores as well as 4 individually owned. In 1954 its volume of business was in the neighborhood of a million dollars.

This development is taking place under the guidance of the Alaska Native Service, of the U. S. Bureau of Indian Affairs. The program also provides training in business, bookkeeping, etc., for the natives.

Negro Cooperatives

The origins and demarcation of early cooperative activity among the Negroes are obscure, as their historians have used the term "cooperative" loosely to cover all kinds of joint activity or collective enterprise. Thus, in 1907, W. E. Burghardt Du Bois listed 103 Negro distributive "cooperatives" in the United States, most of which were probably joint stock companies. Only 6 of the total had the word "cooperative" in their names. In Virginia there was a "combine" of stores—at Keysville (dating from 1889), Evington (1896), and Nameless (1899). In Elizabeth, N. J., in 1907, the Negro pastor of Shiloh Baptist

Church led in the formation of what appears to have been a genuinely cooperative store.

North Carolina had cooperatives, though not of the consumer type, among the Negroes as far back as 1910. A number of credit unions were also formed during 1918 and 1919.

A study made in 1917, covering "economic cooperation" among the colored people in Georgia, included few organizations of the Rochdale type. Of 1,907 businesses covered in the statistics, only 39 had members or stockholders (such as real cooperatives would have) and there was no indication how many of the 39 were actually cooperative.

There are records now for only 77 organizations known to be cooperative and of Negro membership. The largest groups were in the Midwest (31), East (23), and South (17).[2] Of 61 for which year of organization is known, 26 were formed in the latter thirties, and 24 between 1940 and the end of the war. None formed prior to 1935 remains. Nine (organized between 1935 and 1945) were still alive at last reports.[3]

The earliest known association was the Northwestern Family Supply Co., in Baltimore, which was in existence from 1894 to 1896. Between the turn of the century and 1930 there are records for only 6 Negro cooperatives.

The early years of the thirties saw three new associations—in Buffalo, N. Y. (1931), Philadelphia (1931), and Gary, Ind. (1932). In Gary, the Cooperative Trading Association was composed mostly of laborers in the steel mills, and had been preceded by a discussion group and a buying club. A vigorous program of education, in cooperation with the adult-education system of Gary, went on for over 18 months.[4] Then from supposed earnings (actually there had been a loss) patronage refunds were paid. Though undercapitalized, the association had opened two stores and a gasoline station. By August 1937 there was a deficit of over $2,000 and the second store and service station were closed. Business continued to decline and the cooperative dissolved in 1941.

In 1936, at least eight Negro cooperatives were started (in Missouri, New York City, Ohio, and Wisconsin). All are now out of business. The People's Cooperative Association, with a store in Milwaukee, was still operating when visited in the fall of 1954 but was in a declining condition. It appears to have gone out of existence since then.

Red Circle Stores Association, in Richmond, Va., started business in June 1937, across the street from a chain store that had always refused to employ Negro employees. Three months after the cooperative opened, the chain hired a colored clerk, then started a price war. Several wholesalers came to the rescue of Red Circle and sold it goods at cost. The chain store went out of business in June 1940, while the cooperative expanded until it had four stores and a membership of about 1,250. However, inability to obtain personnel and supplies during the war cut its volume in half and by the end of 1950 it had closed its branches. The original store operated for about 2 years more.

Several new cooperatives appeared in the early 40's, one of which (in the Altgeld Gardens housing project in Chicago) was described as "the largest Negro-owned store in America." It later merged into the citywide cooperative there, resumed independent operation after the latter's failure, but itself dissolved about 1952.

The only Negro store cooperative known by me to have been organized since 1944 is Cooperative Enterprises, New York City, started in 1945 under the sponsorship of the Church of the Master. Beginning operations in a basement, it moved to a corner street-level store early in 1953. It was still active at the end of 1954, with a membership of 250 families.

From 1934 through 1944, Negroes had organized 91 credit unions under the Federal credit union law. Of these, 81 percent were still active in 1944 (the proportion for all Federal unions was 74 percent). Although of smaller membership than the national average and less well capitalized, the Negro credit unions' bad-loan losses averaged only 0.09 percent of total loans made, as compared with 0.13 percent for the whole group.

The leadership in many if not most Negro associations has come from the better-educated people within or even outside the group. In certain cases the cooperative has been connected with a Negro educational institution or has received encouragement and support from one.

Jewish Cooperatives

Jews started numerous grocery stores, but many of the distributive cooperatives for which there is information were organized to run kosher meat markets or to bake Jewish bread. Of 44 known cooperatives, 20 were bakeries and 10 were meat markets. The Jewish bakeries—fine, socially conscious organizations—were described in Chapter 15.

So numerous had Jewish associations become by 1916 that they formed the Federation of Jewish Cooperative Societies of America. By 1920 it had 27 affiliates, 15 of which were bakeries. The federation went out of existence in 1922, after resigning its duties to the Cooperative League of the USA.

About two-thirds of the known Jewish bakery cooperatives were started during 1918-19. Some went out of business almost immediately, but most of them failed in the depression of the 1920's. Two survived both depressions, only to fail in the post-war squeeze. Oddly enough, the only one presently active is also the oldest of the entire group—the Purity Cooperative Association, Paterson, N. J., dating from 1905.

The great majority of the above were composed of industrial workers, but there were also numerous cooperatives of farmer membership. They were fostered—and assisted financially—by the Jewish Agricultural Society, whose main purpose was to encourage the movement of Jews onto farms. Under its sponsorship were organized purchasing associations, credit unions, and at least one insurance company.

The Jewish people have been outstanding in New York City for provision of housing; their projects were described in Chapter 28. The cooperative store in the Bronx colony of the Amalgamated group is one of the larger nonfarm cooperatives in the United States, its sales having passed the million line in 1953. Its volume in 1954 totaled $1,125,000.

Immigrant Groups

Finns

Of all the immigrant groups, the Finns have probably organized the greatest number of consumers' cooperatives, notably stores and boarding houses. No national group has made a greater contribution toward the sound organization of the consumers' cooperative movement of this country, had a more idealistic concept of cooperation, or more consistently supported the idea of federation. Many cooperators of this nationality have worked unceasingly for the spread of the movement and have made sacrifices for the cooperatives of which they were members.[5]

Five of their older associations are among the million-dollar nonfarm cooperatives.[6] The average age of these five is 47 years. Quite a record.

Possibly their earliest association in this country was an insurance association in Calumet, Mich., said to have been organized in 1878.

The years 1900-09 saw the formation of numerous Finnish cooperatives in New England and the Midwest, among them two of the five big cooperatives above mentioned. In New England many, if not most, of the members were employed in the textile mills. Minnesota miners opened stores in three towns on the Mesabe iron range (Biwabik, Embarrass, and Virginia), all still active. Even as far west as Wyoming there was a Finnish organization, started by coal miners at Rock Springs in 1906, which operated for some 30 years.

The United Cooperative Society at Maynard, Mass. (organized as Kaleva Cooperative Association in 1907)[7] went into the "select" class in 1946, where it has remained ever since, in spite of the closing down of the woolen mills which were the town's main employer. The co-op's 1954 sales totaled $1,438,000; members numbered 2,721. From the time of organization through 1951, the cooperative returned $325,292 on patronage. Its main store has food, furniture, appliances, and home-supply departments. The cooperative also operates a branch store, a gasoline station, fuel department, dairy, and bakery in Maynard, besides a store and gas station in Worcester.

The Virginia (Minn.) Cooperative Society, organized in 1909, passed the million mark in 1950. It operates food, clothing, and feed stores in Virginia. The business in 1954 totaled $1,095,700.

Another Massachusetts survivor from this period[8] is the United Cooperative Society of Quincy (1904), started under the name of "Turva" (Shelter) by granite cutters and shipbuilders.

The next decade, 1910-19, was even more productive of Finnish cooperatives. Among them were 3 in Massachusetts, 15 in Michigan, 21 in Minnesota, 4 in Wisconsin, 2 each in Ohio and Pennsylvania, and 1 each in New York and Wyoming.

By the end of 1917 there were estimated to be 150 Finnish cooperatives, with assets of about $2½ million and annual business of $4.1 million. The number included 35 grocery stores, 3 bakeries, 26 boarding houses (included among the associations described in Chapter 32), 3 publishing associations and 7 cooperative papers. In the summer of that year the Finnish stores in the Lake Superior district organized their own supply association, the Cooperative Central Exchange.

The Finnish cooperatives in nine cities[9] amalgamated in the fall of 1919 to form United Cooperative Society, with headquarters in Boston. At its peak the cooperative association was operating 16 stores, 4 restaurants, 4 milk-distributing departments, and 3 bakeries. It was an inadequately financed association that included an uneven combination of weak and strong units, with the former in effect being subsidized by the latter. This caused some member dissatisfaction. Also, in the spring of 1921 the membership divided on the matter of ideological beliefs (this was at the time of the split in the Socialist Party). As a result, the individual branches became independent associations again in 1922, retaining in all cases the name United Cooperative Society.[10]

Outstanding among those formed in this decade is Cooperative Trading, Inc., at Waukegan, Ill. It was started as a milk route in 1911 by a group of Finnish housewives outraged when the price of milk was raised from 6 to 8 cents a quart. Under the excellent direction of its general manager, Jacob Liukku, this association has grown steadily. Since 1946 its annual business has exceeded a million dollars. Its sales in 1953 amounted to $2,673,000 and its membership stood at 7,421. Part-time employment in the local steel mill where many of the members work cut the 1954 volume somewhat, but membership rose to 8,165. Besides its milk routes covering the entire city, this cooperative operates a service station, sausage factory, egg department, and five food stores. Its membership includes nearly half of all the families in Waukegan.

Another survivor is the Cloquet (Minn.) Cooperative Society (1910). In a town of some 8,500 people, it has 4,262 members. From its organization through 1954 it has returned $1,207,181 on patronage. The cooperative has two stores handling food, hardware, shoes, drygoods, and furniture, a building-supply store, a coal yard, a service station, and an auto-repair garage. Its 1954 volume reached $1,732,989.

The Finnish distributive associations have had a remarkable record for tenacity and longevity. Of the known Finnish cooperatives for which data are available, 7 of the 13 organized between 1900 and 1909 are still active, 32 of 50 in 1910-19, 9 of 17 in 1920-29, and 4 of 9 in the 1930's. This record cannot be even approached by any other national group.

The Finns have not confined themselves to stores. In the twenties there were numerous boarding houses (described in Chapter 32), many social "halls," at least one mutual savings bank (at Superior, Wis., which is still in operation), a number of cooperative newspapers, and an insurance agency. One of their housing associations was the earliest on record.

Massachusetts credit unions include several of Finnish membership.

Scandinavians

Newcomers from Denmark, Norway, and Sweden formed some of the earliest distributive cooperatives in this country. Three associations identifiable as of predominantly Scandinavian membership were organized in the 1880's. Two of these (at Worcester) operated from 1883 and 1884 until 1921. In 1894 a grocery cooperative was organized at Fitchburg, Mass., and four in Minnesota, three of which are still active.[11] In the following decade at least four associations were formed. Two cooperatives, at Escanaba, Mich., and Grygla, Minn., dated from 1910, and the latter is still in operation.

Danes opened a cooperative store in Solvang, Calif., in 1919, which not only pulled through the deflation of the 1920's but paid patronage refunds every year through 1926. Thereafter its business declined, and it went out of existence in 1930.

Two petroleum associations, in Hector (1926) and Hawley, Minn. (1928) are still operating successfully.

There were also several cafes. The "Idrott" in Chicago was mentioned in another chapter. Others were organized in Chicago and Rockford, Ill., and Seattle.

Of four cooperatives formed in the thirties, three[12] are currently active: At Cambridge, Minn., the Isanti County Cooperative Association, formed in one of the worst depression years, 1932, today operates branches in 13 towns. Its business in 1954 totaled $738,000; it has about 2,700 members. Consumers Cooperative Association at Thief River Falls, Minn., organized in 1936, in 1952 made earnings of $25,600 on a business of $529,000.

Danes were instrumental in the formation of the Racine (Wis.) Consumers Cooperative in 1935. It was for a while one of the leading nonfarm cooperatives. Sales in 1951 amounted to $1,698,000; membership totaled 2,450. Then a whole series of unfortunate events—a dishonest manager, inventory losses, changing neighborhood conditions, defalcation by the treasurer of the credit union connected with the cooperative, the failure of a local cooperative housing project, etc.—caused its decline. By the end of 1954, with business at less than a third of its peak level, it had nevertheless been able to get back into the black and was hopeful of the future.

Lithuanians

Lithuanian immigrants were among the early cooperators. In 1898 they opened a store in South Boston. It was out of business by 1913, but in the preceding decade two others had been started in Massachusetts (at Lawrence and West Lynn) and one each in Connecticut and New Jersey. The next 10 years were especially active ones; nearly two-thirds of all the known associations of this nationality were formed then.

Most of the early cooperatives were started because of resentment against price exploitation by Lithuanian shopkeepers, and their "free thinker" remarks that offended the Catholics. From the very beginning, religious questions had been a cause of strife among Lithuanian immigrants, with the Socialists or atheists and the Catholics arrayed against each other. In some cases each group had its own cooperative, in others both were in membership in the same association.

The first true Rochdale association of Lithuanians appears to have been organized in Lynn, Mass., in 1908. Thenceforth, one or more cooperatives were formed each year. By 1920 there were reported to be about 80, of which 25 had already gone out of business. Only 23 associations were left by 1923.[18]

As far as I know, not a single cooperative of predominantly Lithuanian membership is alive today. Not all were failures, however. The cooperative at Nashua, N. H., started in 1922, operated until 1948. It then merged with a social club and closed the store; on final settlement the members received $225 on each $25 share of stock owned.

Czechoslovaks

The earliest Czechoslovak cooperative of which record has been found is the outstanding New Cooperative Co., in Dillonvale, Ohio, dating from 1908. The success of this association was attributable largely to the leadership and superlative management of the late Joseph Blaha. After 4 years' buying-club experience (during which he delivered the members' purchases in a wheelbarrow), a store was opened in 1908. Steady growth followed and in 1923 the $500,000 volume of this miners' enterprise topped that of all nonfarm consumers' cooperatives.

Then began the long labor struggles in the coal fields in 1927 and 1928, and the dispute over the so-called "Jacksonville scale," ending with the importation of nonunion miners from West Virginia and the break-up of the miners' union. Most of the mines closed down for over 2 years, and the others were operating only a few days per week and paying only about $2 to $3 a day. And here the $88,000 reserve accumulated in more prosperous days came in handy, as the reserves did again, later on, when the depression of the 1930's arrived.

The million mark in sales was reached in 1942 and by 1951 the business totaled $2,967,200—an all-time high. Its 1954 sales amounted to $2,212,710. Since 1947 the association has been the second largest nonfarm store cooperative, in point of sales, in the United States (the cooperative at Greenbelt, Md., now ranks first). Since its formation it has returned $653,194 on patronage.

The New Cooperative Co. has food and general-merchandise stores in six Ohio towns and food stores at three others in addition to the grocery store and department store at Dillonvale. It operates its own wholesale and has a packing plant that in 1951 produced more than $320,000 worth of meat products.

In the "teens" Czechs started stores in Chicago and Westville, Ill. The Chicago cooperative operated from 1917 to 1939. The other lasted only a year or two, dying as a result of opposition by the parish priest, who considered it a "dangerous experiment." A steelworkers' store in Gary, Ind. (1919) was a victim of the depression of 1921-22. In Omaha, Nebr., the Workmen's Cooperative Association (1911) dissolved during the Second World War, for reasons unreported. It had been a financial success; all of its annual reports had shown earnings.

The Cooperators Co., in Cleveland (1916) at its peak operated seven stores, but political differences caused its dissolution in 1933. In the same city the Workingmen's Cooperative Co. (1912) is still prospering after 43 years of operation. Mulberry, Kans., had a store of Czech membership from 1920 to 1926. Two others, in Wilkes-Barre, Pa., and Phillips, Wis., went out of existence in 1925 and 1922, respectively.

Italians

L'Unione Italiana, a medical-care cooperative in Tampa, Fla. (already described) seems to have been the earliest Italian cooperative in this country; it was formed in 1894.

Italian coal miners started a store in Herrin, Ill., which operated from 1901 to February 1954. It admitted to membership only Italians from Lombardy, Italy—one of the few cooperatives with restricted membership to attain any great age. Also in 1901, some stonecutters in Barre, Vt., organized a store (and later a bakery department) which was caught in the deflation in 1921. Within the next few years, Italian stores were organized at Clifton and Union City, N. J., and Lynn, Mass. The New Jersey stores were still active at the end of 1954.

The greatest number of Italian cooperatives of record were formed between 1910 and 1919.[14] Of 30 associations, 9 were still in operation in 1951. More associations appeared in the twenties (with five still in operation in 1951); and three in the next decade (no survivors). No Italian cooperative is known to have been started since then.

A number of Italian cooperatives in New England merged into the Workers Cooperative Union in 1921. This fell apart later, and today the only unit remaining is the Workers Cooperative Union at Stafford Springs, Conn. (started in 1911).[15] In 1954 this 43-year-old cooperative moved into its own new, ultramodern building, having such features as air conditioning, terazzo floors, and electric-eye doors. Its parking lot will accommodate about 50 cars.

A meeting of Italian cooperatives in Union City, N. J., in January 1931, was told that there were then at least 24 cooperatives of that national group—in Connecticut, Massachusetts, New Jersey, New York, Pennsylvania, and Vermont.

Other Nationalities

In the 1890's *Belgian* glassworkers, most of whom were anarchists, formed the Charleroi (Pa.) Progressive Association. It operated on the so-called "Belgian plan" of using earnings for insurance and various other social benefits, instead of paying them out to members in patronage refunds. This was an outstandingly successful cooperative for some years. Branches at Uniontown and Monessen, that sapped the strength of the parent organization, were closed finally, but not in time to save the Charleroi business, which was dissolved in 1917.

Textile workers from the *British Isles* had a cooperative store in Fall River, Mass., formed in November 1866, and another in Lowell that lasted from 1876 until the depression of 1921-22. Cooperatives were formed at Lisbon Falls and Sabbattus, Maine, in the 1880's, that were in business for nearly 30 years. Several others materialized in that State and Rhode Island in the early 1900's.

The Scottish coal miners' store at Glen Carbon, Ill., was in operation from 1904 until 1928. That of miners of the same nationality at Gillespie (1913) was, according to Colston Warne, "for some years the pride of the Illinois miners' cooperative movement." Then a succession of troubles occurred which sent it into receivership in September 1923.

Thirteen Englishmen organized what was known locally as the "Johnny Bull" store at Johnston City, Ill., in 1915. Five years later it became a branch of the Central States Cooperative Society. On the failure of that organization, it attempted to operate independently again but was not successful.

One specialty of Americans of *Dutch* descent has been the organization of the burial associations already described. Among their cooperatives have been the funeral associations at Keystone, Pella, and Sioux Center, Iowa, dating from the late twenties and early thirties. Netherlanders also formed a majority in membership of a number of petroleum cooperatives in Iowa, Michigan, and Minnesota, all of which are still in operation.[16] A cooperative grocery store at Zeeland, Mich. (1937) went out of business in 1942.

The earliest organizations of *French* membership of which there is record were the hospitals described in Chapter 28. A store association at Indian Orchard, Mass., formed in 1906, lasted until 1939. French coal miners opened a store in Roanoke, Ill., that was a branch of Central States Cooperative Society until 1923, then became independent, operating until the late twenties. Another store of French membership was that of textile workers in Gardner, Mass., which operated from 1921 to 1925.

German textile workers' cooperatives were also among the early New England associations. Their grocery store at Fitchburg lasted for 56 years, from 1885 to 1941. Another, at Lawrence, operated from 1891 to 1927, with the same manager. Upon dissolution (because of chain-store competition) the store paid a 50 percent bonus on all shares. A German cooperative also was in business for a while, in the early 1900's, in Manchester, N. H. An association dealing in coal and wood was organized in Adams, Mass., with Germans, English, and native Americans as members; it dissolved in the late thirties.

Of the five known associations of German membership formed in the "teen" years, four went out of business within a few years. The fifth, in Newmanstown, Pa. (1919), was still operating early in 1955.

Thus, the known German associations, although few in number, had quite a good record for longevity.

The existence of about 50 *Polish* stores was reported at the 1918 Cooperative Congress, most of which were "more or less failing" for lack of competent management. I can find records for only 33. Of these, the great majority were in Massachusetts, with a few in Connecticut, New Hampshire, New York, Ohio, and Pennsylvania. The largest group was formed from 1910 to 1919. Not one of them survives. Practically all failed during the 1920's. At least two of the associations started in the twenties, however, were still active early in 1955. They were at Auburn, N. Y. (1920) and Turners Falls, Mass. (1927). The Grodno Cooperative Co., at Forge Village, Mass. (1925), was known to be in operation early in 1952.

The Polish group also included two bakery associations, both organized in 1916, at Adams, Mass., and Detroit.

No cooperatives of *Russian* make-up were found before World War I. The war period produced three—a coal miners' association that joined Tri-State Cooperative Association and went down with it, a store on Long Island (N. Y.) that was already in difficulties in the mid-1920's and did not long survive, and the two restaurant associations already described. Two additional restaurants and a few stores were started in the 1920's.

Available records reveal five cooperatives of *Slovenian* membership. Two were formed in 1913 and 1917. The first of these, Slovenian Cooperative Stores Co. (originally called Slovenian Labor Cooperative Co.) was operating two stores in Cleveland at the end of 1954. The other, at Conemaugh, Pa., operated for 10 years and then dissolved. Of two organized in the 1920's, the Slovenian Cooperative Corp., at Gowanda, Pa. (1922) was still alive in 1951. The other, Waukegan and North Chicago Cooperative, started by striking steel workers in 1921, merged with Cooperative Trading Co., Waukegan, in 1948. The fifth association, at Bridgeport, Ohio, was out of business by 1930.

Three *Ukrainian* cooperatives are known to have been established in the coal-mining area around Pittsburgh in the World War I wave of cooperative activity. A Ukrainian cooperative, started in New York City in 1948, is still operating. Another, a "living" cooperative composed of displaced persons, was organized in Philadelphia in April 1952.

Retrospect

The cooperatives based on nationality were appropriate for their time. They served both the economic and the social needs of people transplanted into a new world of alien tongue and ways. They acted as protectors against the price exploitation (sometimes practiced against them by their own nationals) that was all too common.

On the other hand, in tending to set the members apart from the rest of the community, they may have prolonged the period of assimilation and Americanization. The common denominator of nationality or race can also be a drawback to growth. An organization that has the reputation of being run only for any limited group will be at a disadvantage in trying to attract membership and business from the community at large.

Almost no cooperatives are formed today on a nationality or racial basis and it seems unlikely that many will be formed in the future. With the stringent restrictions on immigration, in effect for many years, nationals of other countries no longer come in in the rather indigestible blocks of former times. Today, far from imposing membership restrictions, it is the practice—nay the necessity, for survival—to welcome into the cooperative all elements of the population.

Part V.

RELATIONS WITH OTHER MOVEMENTS

Chapter 34.—LABOR AND COOPERATIVES

Early Unions and Cooperatives

One of the earliest consumers' cooperatives in the United States was a buying club of a local union in Boston; and industrial workers composed the Protective Union movement, though labor unions as such were not involved in its activities. Organized labor entered the scene again with the cooperative programs sponsored in succession by the Knights of St. Crispin, Knights of Labor, and Sovereigns of Industry. Although cooperatives of industrial workers continued to be formed after the turn of the century, almost none had any connection with labor organizations.

Other labor organizations had also taken official notice of the consumers' cooperative movement. Thus, the National Labor Union, organized in Baltimore in 1866, declared at one of its earliest meetings: "We hail with delight the organization of cooperative stores and workshops, and would urge their formation in every section of the country, and in every branch of business." This union, although intended as a national federation of all unions, lasted only a few years, never amounted to much, and as far as the records show never influenced the formation of any cooperative. Its expression of support is significant, however, as being the earliest of its kind on record, preceding even the Crispins, Knights, and Sovereigns.

The American Federation of Labor, which supplanted the Knights of Labor, expressed itself on the subject of cooperation at its 16th annual convention, in 1896, as follows:

> "Whereas from experience we have learned that trade-unionism and cooperation are twin sisters in the onward march of progression, and that, where one exists the other is almost compelled by nature's inexorable laws to follow, and
>
> "Whereas we believe the credit system to be derogatory and dangerous to any community, as it inculcates a careless

method of business, and men too often learn too late the effect of buying without the cash; therefore be it

"*Resolved,* That the American Federation of Labor, in convention assembled, recommend to all affiliated bodies the careful consideration of the cooperative principle as expressed in the Rochdale system of cooperative distribution and production, and wherever favorable conditions exist to give their aid to such cooperative efforts."

In 1904 the Illinois Federation of Labor became interested in the subject and urged a study of cooperation. Early in the next year a district organization of the United Mine Workers was reported to have invested $500 in the new cooperative store at Pittsburg, Kans.

World War I and the Twenties

A special committee recommended to the 1917 convention of the American Federation of Labor the 1-year appointment of a trade-union cooperator to counsel local groups, advised trade-unions not to organize cooperatives themselves but to form committees to work with other citizens in doing so, and invited all locals to contribute to a cooperative fund.

The report of the committee was adopted unanimously by the convention which also passed the following resolution:

"We believe that the American Federation of Labor should assist in establishing, building up and strengthening in every way possible a legitimate organization of bonafide workers in our country and Canada as a part of the great world's cooperative movement, so that after the trade-union movement has secured for the workers the wages they are entitled to for the labor they perform, they may be assured, in spending these wages, that they will get their full value.

"We hold that it is just as essential that a workingman should get $10 worth of actual value for his wages when he spends them as it is that he should get the $10 that he is entitled to for the labor that he performs.

"The cooperative movement is the organization that is designed to protect the workers in their relations with the merchants and the businessmen in the same sense that the trade-union movement protects them from the employers."

The sum of $50,000 was appropriated for promoting cooperation, and a committee of five was appointed, which worked with the Cooperative League for several years. A two-page leaflet was published, setting forth the cooperative principles, advocating consumers' cooperatives for labor unions, and calling upon the Federal Government to encourage cooperation as a way of reducing the cost of living.

In Illinois the State Federation of Labor had begun to include consumers' cooperation on its agenda as early as 1912, and a pamphlet on cooperatives, issued in the following year, was circulated throughout the State.

The Illinois cooperative law of 1915 was the result of the joint efforts of the Federation, the Illinois Mine Workers, and the farmers.

It was largely as a result of the educational work of the Federation that the mine workers began to encourage the formation of cooperative stores. By 1918 there were 65 such stores in the State.

Between 1916 and 1921, labor groups organized stores on an almost unprecedented scale.[1]

Copper miners in the northern peninsula of Michigan, coal miners in practically every coal field (even in West Virgina), iron miners on the ranges of Minnesota, textile workers in New England, and railroad workers from South Carolina to the west North Central States—all had their new stores. In most of these, although the cooperatives had official union endorsement, labor unions as such were not involved in their formation, as was the case in Illinois and Pennsylvania. In Illinois, although the local stores were distinctly miners' stores, they nevertheless were doing a community-wide business. Pennsylvania, on the other hand, was remarkable for its "splinter" tendencies. Nearly every coal town in the anthracite region had its cooperative store. Some had several, each serving some specific nationality group.

In Illinois the miners' cooperatives were headed by the Central States Cooperative Wholesale Society, which was subsidized by the United Mine Workers during its entire existence. The State Federation of Labor, which had endorsed it in 1920 and authorized aid to it 2 years later, in 1923 (when the unsound American Plan was on its way out) ordered the formation of a Bureau of Cooperative Societies in the Federation, to promote "real cooperation" in Illinois. No mention of cooperation was made at its annual meetings thereafter for many years.

The Cooperative League and Labor

The Cooperative League early recognized the necessity of enlisting union support for cooperatives and of directing labor's new enterprises into sound channels. Representatives of the labor movement were always included among League directors. Although some of them were "more or less half-hearted" in their cooperative enthusiasm, there were certain brilliant exceptions. One was John F. McNamee, editor of the *Brotherhood of Locomotive Firemen & Enginemen's Magazine,* who served on the League board in 1921 and 1923. He continually preached cooperation, and it was partly due to his influence that so many cooperatives were organized by railroad workers. Others were John H. Walker,[2] A. P. Bower (vice president of the Pennsylvania Federation of Labor), and Thomas J. Donnelly (secretary of the Ohio Federation of Labor). In addition to serving on the League's committee on trade-unions in relation to cooperation, they were all active in the cooperative movement of their own region.

If the labor men seemed to have lost interest in cooperation during the middle and late twenties, there were good reasons. In addition to the discouragement incident to the failure of so many labor stores, the sudden deflation had brought in its train a series of strikes and rising unemployment. Union officers were therefore increasingly occupied with holding the line on their primary tasks of wages, jobs for members, and even the existence of the unions themselves. Their difficulties were compounded under the depression conditions of the early 1930's when labor-union membership reached its lowest point in many years.

Depression Revival

Depression, however, revived their interest in cooperation. The report of the AFL executive council to the 1937 convention restated its support of cooperation, but enunciated a new doctrine, that cooperatives supplanting private merchants had a responsibility for workers who lost their jobs in consequence. In that year, to assist its members in organizing cooperatives, the AFL issued a pamphlet entitled, *An Idea Worth Hundreds of Dollars.*

For the first few years after its formation at the end of 1935, the Committee for Industrial Organization was too engrossed in organizational matters to pay any attention to cooperatives. However, the second annual meeting of its successor, the Congress of Industrial Organizations, in October 1939, expressed appreciation of the Cooperative League's encouragement of unionization of cooperative employees. A resolution urged CIO affiliates to investigate and take appropriate action for the development of cooperatives. A number of its State organizations passed similar resolutions.

During the next two years the two major labor organizations renewed their endorsement and urged their members to join and participate in cooperatives.

The League meantime had organized a committee on organized labor and cooperation, of which Rev. James Myers was made chairman—a post that he filled for many years.[3] Under the auspices of this committee, many institutes were held in various parts of the country to acquaint union officials with the cooperative movement and explore ways by which unionists could be attracted to it.

World War II and Its Aftermath

During the war the official interest of labor organizations in consumers' cooperation was manifested chiefly in resolutions. But the 1942 AFL convention also directed the appointment of a committee of three to bring about a "reciprocal relationship" in the development of consumers' cooperatives and credit unions,[4] and the 1944 meeting recommended the immediate creation of a Department of Consumers Cooperation within the Federation, with a full-time executive staff. This recommendation was never put into effect.

In 1943 the CIO United Auto Workers created a Consumers' Division, to provide information and active organizing assistance. It was headed by Donald E. Montgomery (previously Consumers' Counsel in the U.S. Department of Agriculture).

The year 1946 marked the beginning of one of the most active periods of labor participation in the cooperative movement. Repeated endorsement was given not only by the AFL and CIO,[5] but also by their affiliates and various independent organizations. Especially active were the CIO auto workers and steel workers, and the former maintained a full-time field worker to inform its members about cooperation.

That year and 1947 were probably the high points of the wave of labor-union interest in consumers' cooperation that had slowly been gathering force for a number of years. From Maine to California labor was stirred by cooperative enthusiasm, partly because of the sharply rising prices of food, after controls were removed. Some of the interest was academic and never translated into action. Nevertheless, new cooperatives were formed in many places.

The cooperatives thus born differed from many of those formed in the enthusiasm of 1918-22 in that (1) they were not of the closed-membership variety, but admitted everyone and generally made great efforts to interest the whole community, (2) they were all of the autonomous, noncentralized type, with no union control even though individual locals may have lent funds to enable them to get started, and (3) the leaders in most cases recognized the importance of adequate capital and sometimes delayed the store opening even as long as several years while raising funds.[6]

A Government study in 1947 revealed that assistance from unions themselves[7] had taken the form of promoting cooperatives in talks at union meetings, holding joint labor-cooperative meetings, endorsing cooperation (or an individual association) in union resolutions, encouraging union members to join and patronize cooperatives, carrying articles in the union papers, helping to organize new associations (through volunteer or hired workers), and in a few cases, even lending or investing union funds in new or established cooperatives.

The study seemed to indicate, however, rather lukewarm labor support, when measured in concrete terms of unionists joining a cooperative and actually making their purchases from it. Although conventions passed resolutions endorsing cooperatives, and labor leaders commended cooperatives[8] and gave space for articles in labor journals, comparatively few union members actually joined and even fewer families bought their groceries at the store.

Probably in many cases the members of the labor-promoted cooperatives had unrealistic ideas of the savings possible through cooperative stores and were disappointed when they did not immediately materialize. Also, as wages were good and employment plentiful, any small cooperative savings were relatively unimportant to them. By 1952 labor interest had subsided to a relatively low point.

In Michigan, by 1954, all the labor cooperatives organized in the postwar years—practically all in urban, industrial centers—had gone out of business. Interestingly enough, however, in nearly every place a credit union, formed by the cooperative members, was still operating successfully. In other sections of the country, labor cooperatives had also flared and for the most part burned out rather quickly. But there were at least two outstanding exceptions—in Virginia and Ohio.

The former, Peninsula Cooperative Association, in Hampton, was a union-sponsored association started in 1947. Fortunate in having excellent management,[9] it was successful from the start. Sales passed the million point in 1951 and since that time the association has expanded its facilities several times.

The Ohio association, Cooperative Enterprises of Akron, was organized in 1949 but did not open its shopping center until the spring of 1952, after intensive preliminary education and fund raising. Its facilities include two supermarkets, drugstore, restaurant, dry-cleaning agency, clothing store, hardware store, and service station. There is also a credit union among the members. The organization was reported to have had some trouble with a group of obstreperous Communists shortly after its opening. This difficulty was overcome and the cooperative is now doing well, partly as a result of certain merchandising innovations that help to maintain member interest.[10]

Council for Cooperative Development

Contact between the cooperative and labor movements has usually been through speakers, committees, joint councils, goodwill tours, etc.

One instrument was the Council for Cooperative Development, formed on January 1, 1944. It was started by Eastern Cooperatives, Inc., Central States Cooperatives, and the Good Will Fund,[11] and financed largely with a grant (continued for several years) from the last-named. It was to conduct research in cooperation and disseminate the resulting information to the movement.

In this program the Council seems to have accomplished relatively little and soon lapsed into inactivity. It was reactivated at a cooperative-labor conference in June 1947, attended by cooperators and leaders from both AFL and CIO unions. The Council resumed operations in 1948, with the sponsorship of the labor organizations,[12] the two wholesales, and the Cooperative League.

The Council has had several phases, but its major purpose has been to stimulate interest in consumers' cooperation in urban areas. Thus it helped to promote the United Housing Foundation in New York City and the Corlears Hook housing project there, the labor-sponsored cooperatives in several Midwest cities (including the Akron cooperative), and has co-sponsored (with Rochdale Institute) yearly institutes at the Wisconsin School for Workers, to train unionists as organizers and administrators of cooperatives.

In 1951 the Council had in nominal affiliation 11 labor organizations, the Cooperative League of the USA, and 2 regional wholesales. Their effective financial support appears rather doubtful in the light of a statement in the 1952 Cooperative League *Yearbook* that the Council was—4 years after reactivation—still in the "experimental stage," and that its program "has become chiefly a lesson that retail distribution by cooperatives must be undertaken only with the certainty of large-scale financing and top-quality management." The Council was not mentioned at all in the 1954 yearbook.

Cooperative Attitudes

The official cooperative attitude has been that of friendliness to organized labor and its aspirations. As far back as 1897, the Cooperative Union of America (a federation of intellectuals, rather than of worker cooperators), passed a resolution expressing sympathy with the aims and principles of trade-unionism, declaring that all its own printing should be done at union shops, and urging local cooperatives to carry union-made articles.

The same sentiments have been expressed by the present Cooperative League many times. It was always aware of the problems of American workers and in accord with their struggle for better wages and conditions through the medium of labor unions. The League's member associations may or may not have carried these good intentions into practice, in the case of their own employees. Over the years, however, cooperatives by the dozens have aided strikers with moral support, cash contributions, or food, or all of these.

Congresses of the Cooperative League, of its various district leagues, and of the urban regional wholesales have time and again affirmed their sympathy for organized labor and the right of workers to bargain collectively. These expressions of support were of special value in the years before the New Deal, when union labor was still waging an uneven battle for recognition.

Unionization of Cooperative Employees

Organization of cooperative employees into labor unions developed slowly in this country. The early history of consumers' cooperation showed many cooperatives formed under the programs of labor organizations. Rarely did the employees of the cooperatives belong to labor unions, but this was because the mechanical "trades" were organized first and no unions yet existed in the retail distributive field where most cooperatives were.

Also, most cooperatives were started on the proverbial shoestring, and all or part of the work was done by unpaid volunteers. In others the manager was often the only paid employee. As associations grew and staff expanded, the personal relationship between employees and the association and the spirit of fair play were depended upon to protect the rights of the workers.

The League congresses have repeatedly expressed favor toward the unionization of cooperative employees. Constituent organizations have taken similar action, but in the expectation that the initiative would come from the workers themselves.

In the twenties, when the majority of cooperatives were urban associations whose members were industrial workers, the League found that cooperative employees generally belonged to unions if there was one in their trade. However, in many of the small towns that had cooperatives no local existed; in these places, also, labor affiliation was hindered by the traditional distrust of unions shown by the farmers who usually constituted the largest group in the cooperative membership. Their attitude was in some cases intensified by the fact that unionization of the cooperative employees (while open-shop conditions prevailed in all the profit businesses in town) meant payment of a wage scale above the average, thus putting the cooperative in a difficult competitive position.

For the most part, cooperative workers who joined labor organizations became members of AFL or CIO unions. But the employees themselves had already made several attempts toward a general union of cooperative employees such as was suggested by Dr. Warbasse at the 1940 Cooperative Congress.

The Cooperative Employees' Union, organized on industrial lines and drawing its membership from employees in northern Minnesota, was organized in 1930. It was refused endorsement at the congress of that year, for fear of seeming to endorse dual unionism (since there already were trade-unions for the occupations in which these employees worked). The union disbanded at the end of 1937. Cooperative members of regular unions tended to regard it as a "company" union, and it was never very successful in getting recognition. Employees of the large cooperatives in Waukegan and North Chicago, whose employees had been members of the union, after its dissolution formed an organization (for themselves only) with the same name. The staff of Cooperative Distributors (a mail-order organization in New York City) formed a Cooperative Workers' Union in 1935. It was abandoned late in 1936 when they joined a local of the AFL Department Store Workers.

There is no doubt that cooperatives in certain cases formed the entering wedge for unionization in their locality. Thus, the warehousemen of Central Cooperative Wholesale were the first in their trade to be organized in Superior, Wis., and its bakers started the bakers' local there. The Racine (Wis.) Consumers Cooperative Association had the first unionized service station and the first fully organized retail store in that city. In Virginia, Minn.—formerly an open-shop town—employees of the Virginia Cooperative Society organized the first retail clerks' local there. Even as late as 1953, this cooperative was still the only local enterprise employing union labor in the hardware, furniture, and clothing business.

The cooperatives, however, began to resist the unions' efforts to organize cooperative enterprises ahead of other businesses, at wage levels in excess of current rates, in order to use them as levers to force up those elsewhere.[13] The recurrent Cooperative Congress resolutions therefore included a new clause—one urging that the labor movement recognize its responsibility not to impose on cooperatives conditions placing them at a competitive disadvantage or making it impossible for them to produce benefits in the form of patronage refunds for the consumers (who include all the workers).

Strikes of cooperative employees have been comparatively few in number. Occasionally a strike has been called against one particular association, to gain wage increases or other benefits. More often, strikes that have affected cooperatives have been general trade walk-outs over a whole area. Quite often when such occurred, the cooperative employees were allowed to stay on the job, with the promise that the cooperative would grant whatever terms were won from the other employers.

Cooperators as Employers

From the days of the Rochdale Pioneers in England, it has been the avowed intent of the consumers' cooperatives to give their workers good wages and working conditions. In the United States the Cooperative League has consistently advocated the payment of wages at union scale level. Its 1944 and 1946 congresses adopted resolutions urging cooperatives to provide attractive wages and employment conditions, and that of 1946 suggested the desirability of a guaranteed annual wage and the establishment of a national retirement scheme for cooperative employees.

Such evidence as is at hand indicates, however, that in practice cooperatives, except in industrial places (where the going union conditions are met) have tended to exploit somewhat their workers' cooperative fervor (especially that of the managers), expecting that the satisfaction of cooperative participation will constitute partial compensation.

In the thirties a Government survey and, later, a private study indicated that this was the case.[14] According to the Government findings, cooperative wages averaged 5 percent lower than those paid by other local retailers and the working day about an hour longer. The cooperatives of farmer membership were the worst offenders in both respects. Both studies found that the cooperatives were more generous regarding paid vacations and sick leave, tenure was better than in private employment, and labor relations were generally good.

"Fringe" benefits have been increasingly provided since then, covering hospital and medical care, with employer and employee sharing the cost.[15]

The larger associations make a practice of promoting employees to higher-grade positions. Many of the cooperatives, however, have only one or two workers besides the manager, and in such cases there is literally "no place to go." The only way for the manager to advance is to transfer to a vacancy in some larger, better-paying cooperative, and the clerks have a chance to rise only when he goes.

This last circumstance, coupled with insecurity as to old age, has been a major factor in employee turnover in cooperatives.[16] Hours and salaries have been lesser considerations.

The social security system has helped somewhat to alleviate the situation, but a general cooperative retirement system is needed similar to those adopted of late years by some of the regional wholesales and larger local associations.

Conclusions

From the foregoing it is evident that there is still some way to go before ideal relationships between cooperatives (especially rural ones) and the labor movement are attained.

Labor organizations for 50 years or more have made official pronouncements in favor of consumers' cooperatives. The difficulty lies in getting resolutions carried into actuality. Too often they represent the attitude of only the officers, adopted as the consensus of the annual meeting and passed with little or no discussion as a matter of indifference or of no objection to most of the delegates.

The rank and file of union members have known little about cooperatives, and those with some knowledge of cooperative history may have looked upon them with some skepticism, remembering the widespread failures of the workers' cooperatives of the 1920's. It must be admitted that the record of the associations of the industrial workers is not encouraging, on the whole. Most of the labor cooperatives of the late nineteenth century were too involved in the economic and political programs of the sponsoring labor organizations to be able to function independently after the latters' decline. In the wave of the 1920's the failures were likely to be blamed on the cooperative method, instead of on the mistakes of management or membership, where they belonged.

Since the 1920's the nonfarm consumers' cooperatives have been largely those of people of the upper middle class—faculties of colleges and universities, people in the professions, junior executives, and the higher-income white-collar workers. They have ordinarily been attracted to cooperatives not primarily because of the possible pecuniary benefits but because of their conversion to cooperative idea. Such people have formed the "hard core" of dependable members in many an urban cooperative, sticking through thick and thin.

But they are not sufficient, numerically, to be able to cover the cities with the network of cooperatives that is necessary for success under present-day conditions. And their cooperatives are not ordinarily situated in the working-class neighborhoods.

The trade-unions are for the most part in the large cities and industrial towns. Their cooperatives are likely to be built around the union or the plant, neither of which is in the area where the members live. The store then has the disadvantage that if the man of the family does the shopping, he must carry the purchases home (which few are willing to do). Also, the location disregards the fact that traditionally it is the wives who do the family marketing; few, even if they have a car, can be persuaded to drive long distances to the co-op when the supermarket or the neighborhood store to which they are accustomed is handy.

Many a labor-sponsored cooperative has started with the official endorsement of all or most of the unions in the locality, but in spite of this *official* support, has failed to rally a sufficient volume of patronage for gainful operation, and finally dissolved.

The expressed interest in cooperation, even backed by hard cash in the form of share capital, fails to be translated into actual patronage in the necessary amounts. I believe this will continue to happen until both the rank-and-file trade-union members *and their wives,* through good programs of education, are converted wholeheartedly to cooperation. In such programs both cooperatives and labor unions should participate. It is at this point, I am convinced, that effort and educational work need to be concentrated. Even then, I think, the best results will be attained in the smaller cities, where one central association with a branch or two will provide facilities convenient to all its members.

The cooperative characteristics that attract the upper middle class—high quality co-op label goods, emphasis on honesty in merchandising, member ownership, and member control over policies—appear to have less appeal to working-class people. (Perhaps a better approach to them would be to emphasize rather, "best buys" in the lower-grade—and lower-priced—but equally nutritious foods.) Workers are undoubtedly interested in savings, but the savings must be substantial, particularly in times of good wages and full employment. But large savings in the grocery business (in which most cooperatives operate) are rarely possible under present conditions.

Even if it were possible to pay big refunds, that *by itself alone* would be an unsound basis on which to recruit cooperative members. A person who joins and patronizes the store for no other reason than the dollars-and-cents return is not likely to remain loyal if the association is unable to pay a refund.

Urban cooperatives (some of whose members are unionists themselves) commonly encourage their workers to join unions, and try to provide good working conditions. A retarding factor has been the fact that so many of the associations have been started on such a small scale, living a hand-to-mouth existence in which their workers necessarily shared.

Cooperators have complained, with some justice, that even when unionists withhold membership and patronage from the cooperative, they nevertheless expect cooperatives to be solidly pro-labor and sometimes accept cooperative support for labor-sponsored measures as a matter of course. Also, as noted, the cooperatives have sometimes felt that unions have tried to capitalize on cooperative good will and exact wages and other conditions not imposed on competitors. These and other arbitrary and apparently unreasonable demands have sometimes tended to alienate associations otherwise well disposed.

Labor groups themselves have not been altogether consistent in practice with what they demand for their members. Strikes of employees of labor unions have not been unknown. And I remember visiting in the Midwest a cooperative to which, although the association sold goods to all the community, only railroad men were admitted as members. They had won for themselves an 8-hour day; their cooperative employees were still (some 8 years later) working 10 hours a day.

Whether the future will show increased practical support of cooperatives by organized workers remains to be seen. The strongest cooperative movements abroad are those which are solidly worker-owned. Such is not the case in the United States. Here, with a few exceptions, the industrial cities (where labor is strong) have been the weakest sector of the cooperative movement. In this country, the farmers are the backbone of the consumers' cooperatives as well as of the producers' movement.

The efforts in late years to bring the labor and cooperative movements closer together in viewpoints have not been without result. Events have demonstrated that expressions of good will are not enough and both parties must really put their backs into it if the consumers' cooperative movement is to be a movement of all the people, industrial as well as agricultural.

Chapter 35.—FARMERS AND THE CONSUMERS' COOPERATIVES

Major Farm Organizations

As has been seen, the Grange was one of the earliest advocates of consumers' cooperation, and there are still many Grange cooperatives. Cooperation, however, is no longer a very important item in the program of the National Grange.

From the time of its inception in 1902, the Farmers Educational and Cooperative Union of America, as its name indicates, fostered cooperatives. Purchasing cooperatives preceded marketing associations in its program, primarily because they yielded a better return on a small investment. Under its guidance, both retail and wholesale associations (State Exchanges) were formed. They are concentrated for the most part in one-crop areas in the Midwest. In 1942 it was claimed that Farmers Union members had more than a thousand cooperative stores, petroleum associations, creameries, marketing associations, burial associations, and credit unions.

The American Farm Bureau Federation, largest of the three major farm organizations, was organized in 1919. It has maintained a consistent aloofness as regards the consumers' cooperative movement, concentrating its attention on increasing the returns of the farmer as a producer. But some of its State organizations, notably in the North Central States, have turned at least part way towards consumers' cooperation.

The Farmer as Consumer

It is safe to say that few farmers place their consumer interests ahead of or even on a par with their producer interests. The volume of cooperative marketing business in this country is far in advance of cooperative purchasing volume.

Nevertheless, during World War II, farmer cooperatives began increasingly to handle consumer goods. This was partly the result of supply shortages that made it difficult to obtain farm and household goods through ordinary channels. In part it resulted from realization of the important share of farm purchases represented by consumer goods. In part it was the result of persuasion by their leaders.

However, the unfavorable experience that some have had in groceries—a low-margin business—has sent them in the opposite direction, to farm supplies and other goods with larger margins of saving. This swing was hastened by the closing of the grocery departments of Midland Cooperatives, Inc., Farmers Union Central Exchange, and Consumers Cooperative Association during the past few years. Nevertheless, farmers bought groceries and meat to the value of $45 million through their cooperatives in 1952-53.

The Membership Question

In many if not most cases farmers have barred or limited nonfarm members in their cooperatives. To some extent this procedure has been necessitated by the State law under which they operate. To some extent it has reflected the policy of their national farm organizations, which naturally tend toward practices that increase their own membership and importance. (Membership and good standing in the sponsoring farm organization are quite likely to be among the requirements for membership in its affiliated cooperatives.) To some extent it has been caused by conditions imposed in Federal income-tax and loan laws.

As the years have gone by, however, many farmers' retail cooperatives have relaxed their membership requirements to admit nonfarm members, either without restriction or up to the maximum permitted by the loan laws. Some of the wholesales also—Midland Cooperatives, Inc., is a notable example—have voted to have open membership. Central Cooperative Wholesale and Consumers Cooperative Association, though largely farmer in make-up, have no membership restrictions.[1]

Open membership has been found to be of benefit to everyone, including the farmers. Thus, Howard Cowden testified in 1939 that 16 associations affiliated with Consumers Cooperative Association (3.8 percent of the total) were nonfarm. The year 1936, he said, had been characterized by a gasoline price war, a drought, and the "most complete crop failure in the history of the country." He said, "Scores of midwestern cooperatives weathered the drought years successfully because they had some nonproducer members and some nonproduction goods for sale."[2]

The principle of open membership is becoming more important with the changing population make-up in rural areas. In Iowa, for instance, a recent social survey disclosed that almost 20 percent of the people living in the country outside of cities are not farmers. To deny them admission to cooperatives means that they must either organize another (possibly uneconomic) cooperative or patronize the farmers' cooperative which then profits by their patronage without extending the privileges of membership.

Farmers and the Organized Consumers

During the first two decades of this century there appears to have been little or no contact between the cooperative movements of the city consumers and of the farmers.

After the Cooperative League was formed it tried in various ways to bring together representatives of the rural and urban cooperatives, to acquaint them with the other's problems, and to foster understanding between them. Actual working relationships between the two movements were practically nil, however, and this continued to be the case throughout the 1920's.

There were several reasons for this situation. The League still defined consumers' cooperatives as those providing *consumer* goods and services. The farm cooperatives were reluctant to align themselves with city organizations, and this aloofness was reinforced, and stiffened with suspicion, during the decade in which Communism seemed to be gaining headway in the urban movement. Also, the farmers were alienated by the extravagant speeches of some cooperators who envisioned the supplanting of capitalism by the "cooperative commonwealth." This attitude of distrust was slow to subside.

Meanwhile, the Communist issue had been met by the official repudiation of Communist theories and policies. The dramatic climax of the long struggle undoubtedly tended to modify somewhat the farmer attitude. Also, into the post of League executive secretary had come E. R. Bowen, who began assiduously to woo the farmer purchasing cooperatives, with a view to bringing them into the league.

New farmer wholesales had been coming into being—a few not connected with any national farm organization, and others affiliated for the most part with the Farm Bureau. The leaders of several of the latter's State federations and of their wholesale purchasing cooperatives began to appear at the Cooperative Congresses and several (notably in Indiana, Michigan, Ohio, and Pennsylvania) affiliated with the League. Here again, it was the leaders, rather than the rank and file, who saw the value of consumers' cooperation for the farmer and recognized the League as the national exponent of that field of cooperation. Other farmer cooperatives on the whole were still wary of consumers' cooperatives except as a market for farm products.

At various times the conservative farm group has expressed the opinion that the relations between the two should be merely those of buyer and seller, and that the consumer leadership is too much concerned with social and economic reform, in neither of which the agricultural cooperative movement is interested.

United Cooperatives (farmers' interregional purchasing and productive organization) which one writer in 1938 confidently expected to become a "powerful constructive force in uniting rural and urban consumers in common cause,"[3] turned on its heel some years ago and has become increasingly isolationist.[4] Its present attitude seems to be that "A farmer is a producer, a capitalist, a manufacturer, and is out after his share of the consumer's dollar. To try to tie [him and the consumer] together is a fallacy."[5]

Among the exponents of the consumer point of view is Murray Lincoln. He told the 1946 Cooperative Congress he believed the cooperative movement to be "the only cohesive force" which could bring the consumers and farmers into "an effective working relationship." Backing up his conviction with action, he brought his organizations, the Farm Bureau Insurance Cos. (now called Nationwide) and the Ohio regional wholesale, Farm Bureau Cooperative Association, into the League fold as members. He himself has served continuously as board member since 1934 and as its president since the retirement of Dr. Warbasse in 1941.

These groups and the Utah Cooperative Association (now affiliated with the Utah Farmers Union) are the only ones with ties to the national farm organizations that are now full members of the League. Farm Bureau Services (Michigan) is an associate member. However, the League has as members a number of other regional wholesales of predominantly farmer membership. These include Central Cooperative Wholesale (Wisconsin), Farmers Cooperative Exchange (North Carolina), Midland Cooperatives (Minnesota), Pacific Supply Cooperative (Washington), and Manitoba (Canada) Cooperative Wholesale.

Still other farmer-owned wholesales may be said to be indirect members of the League, since they belong to National Cooperatives which is a League affiliate. The tie that binds them to National is commercial. Although the list includes six organizations[6] that have been League members at various times, apparently they do not now have sufficient interest in its program to continue membership.[7]

Variant Viewpoints

Generalities are dangerous and need to be qualified by remembering that there are always exceptions. However, it is true that, on the whole, the farmer is basically an individualist, and working with others has not been easy for him. But the hard realities of existence, exploitation by business interests, and above all the solid accomplishments of the cooperative enterprises entered into by the more adventurous spirits have, over the long years, gradually convinced him. Today, by and large, farmers in this country are thoroughly sold on cooperation for economic ends.

The operative phrase here is "economic ends." The average farmer joins a cooperative for what he can get out of it. He is generally not greatly interested in any "philosophy" or "idea," nor in plans for the general betterment of mankind through cooperative effort. Cooperation is a business to him and nothing more. This was recognized by H. E. Babcock, then general manager of the huge and phenomenally successful Cooperative

Grange League Federation Exchange, Ithaca, N. Y. In a speech to the members in 1935, he said:

> "I regard a farmer-owned, farmer-controlled cooperative as a legal, practical means by which a group of self-selected, selfish capitalists seek to improve their individual economic positions in a competitive society.***
>
> "***My ideal 'farmer-owned, farmer-controlled cooperative' has come together to deal with society as it is (rather than to reform it) on the basis of mean, narrow, selfish interest. Not a pretty picture, is it? But it is the only sure basis upon which I can depend upon your cooperation with me in business. So, why not recognize the fact."[8]

It is this frankly materialistic attitude of the farmer cooperatives[9] and their suspicions of other motives that have constituted the main barrier between them and the consumers' cooperative movement headed by the Cooperative League.

Most of the agricultural-marketing leaders are—have to be, under the circumstances—hard-headed businessmen for whom prices, volume of business, and net returns constitute in themselves the desired end. To them, cooperative "education" commonly means measures to increase business volume.

However, as we have seen, there are some (and very influential) voices in the agricultural cooperative movement that have spoken out, expounding the advantages of consumers' cooperation and of closer relationships with the nonfarm cooperatives. These men combine practicality with idealism. Sometimes they have been successful in persuading their organizations to go along with them to the extent of joining and supporting the Cooperative League. Also, the farm groups represented by Central Cooperative Wholesale, Midland, and Consumers Cooperative Association have been strong and faithful members of the League.

This did not necessarily mean that they had made convinced, idealistic consumer cooperators out of all their members. In some cases the action was an indication of the powerful and persuasive hold of the leaders, or of indifference of the rank and file, or at least an unwillingness on their part to make an issue of it. This has been demonstrated in several regional associations which, upon the retirement or departure of a particular individual, have then ceased to pay dues to the League.

The philosophical aspects of the consumers' movement, and its unwavering goal of an improved way of life for all people through cooperation on all fronts, social and economic, are likely simply to annoy the farmer. He doesn't want to "get mixed up" in any such movement.[10] Neither does he care to associate on too close terms with the labor elements, whose influence on the cooperative movement he looks upon with distrust.[11] He is willing to participate with urban consumers' cooperatives in purely business ways, such as direct selling of farm products or even membership in National Cooperatives, for this nets him additional savings.

Nevertheless, over the years a definite relaxation of barriers has occurred at least between the farmers' purchasing organizations and the consumers' cooperative movement as represented by the Cooperative League. This began during the service of E. R. Bowen and has increased noticeably since the advent of Jerry Voorhis. The latter's earnest convictions and moderate attitudes carry weight when he appears, as he increasingly does, as a speaker before the annual meetings of farmers' cooperatives. He is palpably no wild-eyed radical or "long-hair" of the kind formerly associated by the farmers with city cooperators.[12]

Also, the long-time service of Murray Lincoln, one of "their own," as president of both the League and CARE, both of which have had growing recognition from Governmental and other respectable sources, has contributed measurably toward quieting the old suspicions. I see no reason why this gradual process should not continue, to the benefit of both sectors of the cooperative movement.

Chapter 36.—CHURCHES AND COOPERATIVES

As an example of self-help and of what has been termed "applied Christianity," the consumers' cooperative movement has received the endorsement of many religious denominations.

Not only have church meetings and church organizations favored cooperation, but many of the clergy have spoken out in its behalf, beginning as early as 1880.

Official Church Attitudes

Protestant

Among the Protestants, the most sustained approval has come from the National Council of Churches,[1] a federation of thirty-five religious bodies. In 1912 the secretary of one of its commissions, returning from a study of rural European cooperation, commended cooperatives as promoters of thrift, business integrity, democracy, and responsibility among individuals. Thereafter, the Council's favorable interest continued to be manifested in one way or another. Its "Social Ideals of the Churches," issued in 1932, included "encouragement of cooperatives." Its committee on church and cooperatives, created in 1937,[2] was very active in fostering cooperation through interfaith conferences, conferences of church and cooperative leaders, study groups, and many pamphlets on various aspects of cooperation.[3] Its *Information Service* carried many reports on cooperative-church meetings and developments of interest to religious groups.

One of the earliest official Protestant church pronouncements was that of the National Council of the Congregational Churches, in 1925. It declared that "translating the ideals of Jesus into economic relationships" would involve (among others) the encouragement of the organization of consumers' and farmers' cooperatives. A similar statement was adopted by the General Synod of the Reformed Church of the United States the next year. The Methodist Episcopal Church endorsed agricultural cooperatives in its 1928 general conference.

Other religious bodies that passed favorable resolutions within the next two decades were the following:

American Unitarian Fellowship
Church of the Brethren
Council for Social Action of the Congregational Christian Churches
Friends General Conference
Methodist Federation for Social Action
New York East Conference of the Methodist Church
Northern Baptist Convention
Ohio Council of Churches
Presbyterian Church in the USA
Protestant Episcopal Church
Religion and Labor Foundation
Universalist Church

In 1944 the Reorganized Church of Latter Day Saints sponsored six study courses in cooperative leadership.

Catholic

The Catholic Church, in the persons of the Popes and many other dignitaries,[4] has consistently favored cooperative action. Dr. John A. Ryan, of the Catholic University of America, in 1916 praised cooperation as making for "a better distribution of wealth" and said it had "very great educational value."[5]

Three years later the Catholic Bishops' Program of Social Reconstruction stated that establishment of cooperative stores would prove to be more "important and more effective than any Government regulation of prices." Further, it said, this was "no Utopian scheme," but one that had demonstrated its worth.

The Social Action Department of the National Catholic Welfare Conference has long taken an interest in the cooperative movement and has published several pamphlets on cooperation.[6] Rev. Raymond A. McGowan of its staff served on the board of the Cooperative League during the early twenties.

In 1937 a cooperative committee was created in the National Catholic Rural Life Conference. Repeatedly since then the annual meeting of the Conference has expressed its approval of the movement. Its 1939 statement endorsed cooperatives as being completely "in harmony with Catholic dogma and Catholic philosophy of life." In 1944 it issued a booklet in celebration of the Rochdale centennial.[7]

A Catholic conference on consumers' cooperation in 1943 endorsed cooperatives in Catholic schools and colleges, voted for a program of adult education in cooperation, and recommended holding regional Catholic conferences on cooperation.

In 1944 and again in 1946, Pope Pius XII expressed the opinion that cooperation was in conformity with the teachings of Christianity.

Jewish

Jewish religious organizations were rather slow to take a stand on the cooperative movement, but in 1936, the Central Conference of American Rabbis declared:

> "We believe that the cooperative enterprise, when socially motivated and administered, is one means of establishing a social motive of service in the production, distribution and consumption of commodities."

In 1939, also, a report on cooperation was presented to the Central Conference for its consideration. The report pointed out that, "in a world torn by anti-Semitism, the Jewish moral leaders dare not fail to hold an intelligent position" as regards cooperation. It recommended—and the conference adopted—a resolution endorsing the cooperative movement, pledging interest and assistance in furthering its social aims, and urging that the movement receive "serious, favorable consideration" by Jews.

A meeting of 75 representatives of Protestant, Catholic and Jewish faiths in 1945 formulated a 15-point program for rural agriculture. One of the points favored cooperatives "as a means of intellectual, moral and material advancement."

Cooperatives in Religious Groups

The ethical principles of brotherhood, self-help, and social betterment, characteristic of the consumers' cooperatives, are the basis for approval by the churches and churchmen. Although the cooperative method is not in itself religious, it tends to develop a spirit of altruism and brotherhood that is closely allied with religious principle. In this respect it is compatible with many religions besides the Christian and has been so recognized in countries of various faiths.

The 1954 meeting of the World Council of Churches agreed that the proper "mixed economy" should include private enterprise, government-owned businesses, and cooperatives, and all should be welcomed by Christians, as a part of "responsible society."

The interest of the churches in this country received new impetus when Toyohiko Kagawa, a free-lance, Princeton-trained Christian evangelist from Japan came to the United States in 1935, to arouse Protestant Christians to the desirability of developing the cooperative movement. The terrible depression through which the country had just passed had inclined the minds of men, in the church and out of it, toward experiments in new directions. Thus they were more than usually receptive, and Kagawa arrived at the opportune time. His characterization of cooperation as the "love principle in economic action" found ready acceptance with the clergy, and others.

Individual ministers, rabbis, and priests have become active in promoting cooperation and even in helping to organize cooperatives.[8] Some even served on boards of directors or on committees. Such activities, however, are likely to run afoul of the private interests of some of their flock, whose livelihood depends on the profit system. Credit unions supported by churches are usually less open to criticism than cooperative stores.[9]

Most clergy-supported associations, once formed, have made no attempt to restrict membership to the denomination responsible for the organization, but have tried to attract all the elements of the community.[10]

In the United States several hundred credit unions have as their "common bond" membership in a given church or parish.[11] In fact, the first credit union in this country was formed in a Roman Catholic parish in Manchester, N. H. in 1909. Credit unions lend themselves to this kind of limitation, for they ordinarily do not draw from the general community (except in very small places) and need the bond and personal acquaintance that church membership gives them. Membership particularism may be practicable even for distributive cooperation in a community composed wholly or mostly of people of one faith. Ordinarily, however, the opposite is true. Open membership (the Number 1 Rochdale principle), drawing people from all walks of life, is one of the essential factors for the success of a distributive or service cooperative. This has been demonstrated times without number.

Although the Catholics have been most prone to form cooperatives among their members, Rev. Leo Ward, one of their leaders, has cautioned: "No co-op can afford to be merely Bohemian, or merely Polish, or merely Catholic or Hebrew."[12]

Any factor that tends to set the cooperative membership apart from the rest of the community or that makes for division or differences of opinion on matters extraneous to the aim of the cooperative is to be deplored. To be successful the association needs to concentrate on its goal and eschew alien subjects on which the members may not agree. The distributive or service cooperative should draw from people of all faiths, races, and political persuasions and bear in mind that cooperation may be *the one thing* these diverse viewpoints can all agree upon, even though they may differ on particular points of cooperative policy. Once religious or political questions are admitted, cooperation is likely to fly out of the window.

In spite of official church endorsement of cooperatives and that of individual clergymen, the churches of the United States have not been directly responsible for any sizeable segment of the consumers' cooperative movement. And I am not so sure that this is a bad thing, on the whole. The foreign experience indicates that there are dangers in linking particular cooperatives with particular religions too closely. Cooperation should be free of external influences that tend toward its control, or make for division rather than cohesion among the people. Fortunately, the consumers' cooperative movement of the United States has kept free of such entanglements and preserved its neutrality.

Chapter 37.—COOPERATIVES AND PROFIT BUSINESS

Whenever a cooperative goes into business it inevitably becomes a competitor of and an economic threat to local businessmen. In a city one competitor, more or less, means little to the average independent dealer. And the chains are so powerful that only the strongest cooperative could offer them any real competition. They themselves are the particular nightmare of the independent retailer, and in many cases he has met the situation in the only effective way—by combining with his fellows into a wholesale which, as far as it goes, is cooperative.

In the small town the situation is different. With a small total patronage to draw from, every new competitor causes a measurable decline in the volume of existing businesses. It is understandable, therefore, that small-town merchants take a dim view of new enterprises in their line of business. If the newcomer is a cooperative, the reaction is likely to be emotional, especially when it becomes known that the earnings will go not in profits to an entrepreneur but in refunds to the patrons.

Such antagonism is far from being a new development. As far back as the 1860's, merchants in New England went to extreme lengths against the Protective Union stores, cutting prices, blacklisting employees who dared to join the cooperatives, and stirring up dissension among the cooperators wherever possible. The stores of the Grange, which had as one of its announced objectives the elimination of the middleman, were victims of many price wars.

The Farmers' Alliance stores were discriminated against not only by the railroads which charged them higher rates but also by wholesalers and manufacturers, besides having to contend with cutthroat retail competition designed to put them out of business. Some of the early independent cooperatives also suffered from such tactics.

The early distributive movement in Texas was stopped in its tracks by a law of 1885, instigated by profit business, prohibiting the chartering of any new cooperatives.

The files of the cooperative wholesales contain many instances of refusals of other wholesalers and manufacturers to supply them with goods, because of protests from their dealer customers. Price wars were common in the Midwest after the competition of the cooperative petroleum associations began to force down margins in the oil industry.[1]

Students' stores have been prevented from getting into operation, as a result of complaints to the colleges by local retailers, and some have experienced difficulty in getting supplies.

Credit union laws were fought by bankers, by loan sharks battling to preserve high interest rates, by lenders operating under the small-loan laws, and by the building and loan associations. Some of the State bankers' associations are still opposing credit unions.

In the housing field there were numerous individual cases of proved discrimination, of troubles fomented by local real-estate interests, and legal or other difficulties raised deliberately to balk the cooperative project.

Medical-care cooperatives, as was noted in Chapter 29, have had to contend almost unceasingly with the antagonism of the organized medical profession.

In Iowa the funeral cooperatives for 15 years fought a running legal battle against the undertakers, for their very existence.

The formation and operation of the electric-power and telephone cooperatives was opposed in various ways by the commercial companies. Hampering legislation, "spite lines," lawsuits, and lobbying for reduced appropriations for the Federal agencies administering the programs have all been resorted to.

On the other hand, there have been some recorded instances of friendliness and assistance. Thus, the cooperative in Olathe, Kans., was saved from extinction shortly after its formation in 1876 by a wholesaler who came to its rescue. In the same State a cooperative involved in a price war instituted by local dealers, was saved by a wholesaler who extended credit. A Negro cooperative in Virginia was befriended by wholesalers during the course of a price war with a chain store.

As already described in this chronicle, individual businessmen here and there have recognized the value of cooperation and worked actively for it. The benefits to cooperatives of Edward A. Filene's conversion to the cooperative idea have been detailed in Chapters 22 and 32.

Organized Opposition

Until 20 years ago such antagonism as the cooperatives met from profit business was usually local in extent. It is only since about 1935 that organized and widespread attacks on cooperation have been made.

The cooperative press began noting verbal attacks by businessmen in the middle 1930's. This was no accident. The business world, which (except for scattered incidents) had ignored cooperatives as long as they were small, was taking note of the expansion of the movement during the depression and particularly of the development of farmers' cooperatives in grain marketing and oil distribution, with ensuing emergence of large cooperative wholesale associations—a development that was narrowing and cutting into profits.

The Institute of Merchandising Economics was formed in Indiana in 1935, to fight cooperatives.

As the campaign got under way, trade organizations—national associations of insurance agents, hardware dealers, grain dealers, retail clothiers, etc.—began to pass resolutions about this "cooperative menace" and "insidious development" and to cast about for a way to stop it.[2]

So great had the antagonism of organized business toward the cooperatives become by 1940 that Rev. Edgar Schmiedeler, director of the Rural Life Bureau of the National Catholic Welfare Conference, charged that there was "a concerted effort to smear cooperatives" in a "campaign of deliberate misrepresentation."

Harrassment of individual associations was not neglected, while at the same time attempts were made to damage cooperative reputation in the eyes of the public. Pressure was attempted in the usual ways—price wars, cutting off cooperatives' wholesale sources of supply, public statements impugning the loyalty and patriotism of cooperatives, and refusal of credit or loans.

The enemies of cooperation were especially active in areas in which cooperatives were strong enough to provide effective competition.

The legislative approach was common, through passage of restrictive laws, either specifically naming cooperatives or couched in general terms but so phrased as to be applicable only to them.[3] Hardly a year goes by without hostile moves of this sort.[4]

The NTEA

Because of certain small tax advantages formerly accorded to farmers' (not urban) cooperatives under the Federal income-tax law, agitation on this subject has for some years been one of the favorite anti-cooperative weapons.

This began in 1943 with the formation of the organization now known as the National Tax Equality Association by retailers in the feed, hardware, coal, lumber, and grain business, under the leadership of Ben McCabe, Minneapolis grain dealer.

Stating that, through return of (untaxed) patronage refunds, cooperatives were underselling the other merchants by as much as 30 percent, the group announced that its first aim would be to "equalize tax laws between co-ops and private enterprise."

As farmer cooperatives were the only ones having any tax advantages, they naturally regarded themselves as the object of the drive. Following the organization of the National Conference of Cooperatives (later changed to National Association of Cooperatives) in June 1944, to combat the NTEA campaign, State-wide associations of both farmer and nonfarm membership were formed in a dozen or more States by the end of the year. Their purpose was to inform legislators and the public generally about the true situation.

Each year since then the businessmen's association has widened its appeal, to reach additional groups, has carried on fund drives, hired high-powered lobbyists, and trained its guns on Congress to obtain heavier taxes on cooperatives. In its earlier years the NTEA solicited contributions with the advice that they could be charged off in the contributors' tax returns. But this struck a snag when, in 1950, the U. S. Tax Court ruled that such donations were not deductible, since NTEA's chief function was to obtain a revision of tax laws. A similar decision in another case in 1952 was appealed to the U. S. Supreme Court but only resulted in that body's upholding the Tax Court's decision, in 1953.

The NTEA's tax campaign has been broadened in the past few years to include as targets mutual insurance companies, credit unions, and even churches and educational institutions, as well as distributive cooperatives. In 1952 the organization (although touting itself as the champion of small business) also began to attack even the cooperative purchasing associations of small profit retailers, now found in practically every State. Later in the year its representatives attended the political conventions of both parties, trying, without much success, to influence candidates and platforms.

The NTEA itself operates only at the national level, but it has branches or chapters in many States. These are always busy, introducing bills into State legislatures to "take care" of the cooperatives. Taxation is one of their favorite subjects, of course, and many have been the bills they have sponsored, generally in vain.[5]

The latest move was the issuance, late in 1954, of a TV film "Citizen Dave Douglas," a clever job intimating that if cooperatives were taxed as they should be the taxes of all citizens would be considerably reduced, and showing a well-dressed banker type who is represented as a cooperative officer "admitting" that cooperatives have a tax advantage and since they "have a good thing, let's keep it."

Conclusions

The blind resentment of local dealers who see part of their market and livelihood disappearing with the advent of a cooperative is understandable, as are also their efforts to "do something about it." This situation will probably always continue, but can be abated as cooperatives develop a public information and relations program by which misunderstanding can be avoided through acquainting the community with the true nature of the cooperative method. That some of the tactics used in opposition to cooperatives by competitors are somewhat "below the belt" simply indicates the low level of ethics unfortunately characteristic of a part of the business world where anything goes that will get results.

But when organized business begins to take note of and oppose cooperatives on a national scale, it is a sure sign that the latter have been getting somewhere and are providing effective competition. Business spokesmen often protest that they do not oppose cooperatives as such, but only when they get "too big." There undoubtedly is considerable truth in this. If the cooperative movement still consisted entirely of small, weak associations no one would bother about it. Such have no effect on market conditions. The question of course arises, why does *big* profit business complain when cooperative business becomes *big?*[6]

It is only when cooperative competition begins to get powerful enough to affect fat profits and entrenched interests that it draws the fire of profit business. The latter has not been unmindful of the cooperative yardstick on profits in petroleum production, refining and distribution, and in the generation and distribution of electric power, nor of the truly phenomenal progress made by the Ohio Farm Bureau Insurance Cos. and other cooperatives in the insurance business.

A writer of nearly 75 years ago hit the nail squarely on the head when he commented: "The opposition of the retail trade to cooperation may be summed up in two words—it hurts."[7]

However, if the cooperative method is conceded to be acceptable and beneficial when on a small scale, it should be more so as it expands to the point where it can benefit consumers generally, by acting as a regulator to some extent of margins and prices. Distributive cooperatives in this country do not practice the "active price policy" followed by some foreign cooperative movements, which set their prices at what they consider a reasonable level. Here they sell at the current level, nominally set by supply and demand. But the mere presence of a strong, successful cooperative, especially in the smaller places, provides the competition that sooner or later brings down the price level or keeps it from rising.

Even when consumers' cooperatives get big, the charge of monopoly cannot be truthfully brought against them (as it often can against big profit business), for the cooperative is open to everybody and what is universal cannot be a monopoly.

It is wryly amusing and ironic that profit business, which advocates "free enterprise" so continuously and so vocally, is the first to call for laws to reduce free enterprise by curbing anything and anyone interfering with the tendency to take all the traffic will bear; professes to favor competition but keeps demanding legislation to protect it against competition;[8] and opposes privileges only for the other fellow.

These people seem to feel that entrepreneurs already in business have a priority and a vested right. They need to be reminded that the public (including would-be competitors) are also entitled to freedom of enterprise, not merely those already in business.

Chapter 38.—GOVERNMENT AND COOPERATIVES

State Governments

The consumers' cooperative movement in the United States had been under way for some years before it attracted the official notice of State agencies, generally the Bureaus of Labor Statistics. One of the earliest to take note of the movement was the Massachusetts Bureau of Statistics of Labor which began carrying in its annual reports statistics and other information about cooperatives as early as 1875. In Wisconsin also, beginning about 1885, nearly every annual report carried a section or chapter on cooperatives. It was largely through the efforts of Frank A. Flower, Commissioner of the Wisconsin Bureau of Labor and Industrial Statistics, that a State cooperative law was passed in 1887.

The role of the early official agencies was generally that of moral support and dissemination of information only. In no case was promotional or organizing assistance given or loans made. The creation of the Wisconsin Department of Agriculture and Markets in 1919 was a new departure, in that it actively fostered cooperatives. Its staff assisted in organizing, gave advice on legal and accounting problems, and provided auditing service on a fee basis. About the same time a Bureau of Cooperative Associations was established in the New York State Department of Foods and Markets.

Today, only a few States report on cooperatives, and this is no longer the function of State Bureaus of Labor Statistics. Such reports as are made—and these are usually in the Midwest only—are ordinarily those of Departments of Agriculture. North Dakota in 1939 created a Division of Cooperatives in the State Department of Agriculture and Labor which collects and disseminates statistical information on cooperatives.

In Minnesota cooperatives may obtain auditing service from the State Department of Agriculture. In this State, Wisconsin, and several other States the departments and the agricultural colleges have made many studies of cooperatives of all kinds, especially those of farmers.

State laws.—Many of the associations of the Protective Union, Grange, Knights of Labor, and Sovereigns of Industry had to operate without specific legal authorization. If they incorporated, it was under the general corporation act, making it difficult to follow cooperative principles. If not incorporated, members were jointly and severally liable for any debts of the cooperative. This latter was a serious drawback, for it tended to keep out the more well-to-do families which had a good deal to lose if the enterprise failed.

Michigan has the honor of passing, in 1865, the first State law specifically authorizing the formation of cooperatives. Massachusetts followed in 1866, Ohio in 1867, Minnesota in 1870, and New Jersey in 1881. Three States enacted a cooperaerative law in 1887—Connecticut, Pennsylvania, and Wisconsin. In New England (the region which had been particularly receptive to cooperation), even as late as the turn of the century Connecticut and Massachusetts remained the only States with permissive legislation. (New Hampshire still has no such law.)

Some of the early statutes were obtained through the efforts of the Grangers, Farmers Alliance, and other movements above mentioned.

By the end of the century, in addition to the above States, California, Illinois, Montana, and New York had all legislated on cooperatives. Only three laws were at all adequate, however —those of Massachusetts, New Jersey, and Pennsylvania. Wisconsin enacted a new law in 1911 which the Right Relationship League labeled the first "genuinely cooperative law in the United States."

Cooperative enactments—good, bad, and indifferent—were on the statute books of 34 States and Alaska by the end of World War I. Every midwestern State had a consumers' cooperative law. Progress thereafter was very slow and by 1947 the number of jurisdictions with consumers' cooperative laws had risen only to 38, at which figure it remains. Twelve States still lack such legislation.[1]

Fortunately, an unsatisfactory law or the absence of State legislation is not too important now, because of the general applicability of the District of Columbia law.

The State cooperative statutes vary considerably in their requirements. The best ones enumerate the Rochdale principles (in defining a cooperative), require adherence to them by associations incorporated under the act, and lay down general standards for election of officers, membership rights and duties, and business procedure. Among the most adequate are those of the District of Columbia, Minnesota, New Mexico, New York, and Wisconsin.[2]

Occasionally a complete overhaul of a statute is made (as in New York in 1951 and in Wisconsin in 1955). But for the most part the major State cooperative legislative activity nowadays consists of liberalizing amendments.[3]

Federal Government

Presidents have endorsed cooperation,[4] lesser Government officials have taken similar action, and some have even joined and participated in cooperatives. Some Government agencies are charged with certain duties regarding cooperatives (mostly agricultural).[5] For the most part, however, the role of both State and Federal governments was, until the Great Depression, only that of a more or less interested onlooker.

After Carroll D. Wright left Massachusetts to become the first U. S. Commissioner of Labor Statistics in Washington in the 1880's, his friendliness to cooperatives undoubtedly accounted for the many reports on various phases of consumers' cooperation, cooperative communities, building and loan associations, mutual insurance companies, etc., published by his department in the early 1900's.

Systematic studies were also made during the incumbency of Royal Meeker. Of all the Federal agencies, only the Bureau of Labor Statistics has shown a continuing interest in consumers' cooperation. In 1952, however, several parts of its work were shifted to other agencies.[6] The Bureau's present role seems to be that of reporting occasionally the results of other organizations' work.

In the first few years after the passage of the Federal Credit Union Act in 1934, active assistance was given in the organization of credit unions. This has long since been discontinued, but the present Bureau of Federal Credit Unions still publishes educational material on business and accounting methods as well as pamphlets for the use of cooperative educational workers and credit union meetings.

Federal laws.—It was not until the First World War that any Federal laws on cooperatives began to be passed, and these all pertained to agriculture, which was in the doldrums and as a "depressed industry" was regarded as entitled to assistance.

In 1920 Senator Morris L. Sheppard of Texas introduced a bill providing for the Federal incorporation of consumers' cooperatives, with the law administered by a Bureau of Interstate Cooperative Associations in the U. S. Department of Labor.

This was the first of several attempts, all vain, to provide a Federal law for consumers' cooperatives. However, somewhat the same effect was finally obtained with the passage of the District of Columbia law in 1940. By removal of the usual requirement that incorporators all be residents in the law's jurisdiction, the District act was made available to groups outside Washington. Many associations in States with unsatisfactory laws or no cooperative law at all have incorporated under it.[7]

Nonfarm consumers' cooperatives have never had access to Government loans. A bill to establish a Government banking system for them, similar to the farmers' Banks for Cooperatives, was introduced in the U. S. House of Representatives in 1936, but was not reported out of committee, though hearings were held. The Reconstruction Finance Corporation, whose function was to make loans to business enterprises, ruled that only profit business was entitled to its services. Nonfarm consumers' cooperatives cannot qualify under the Farm Credit Acts, and an attempt in 1939 to amend the law to make them eligible failed.

Efforts to amend the housing and public health laws, to allow loans to cooperatives in those fields, were similarly unsuccessful. The housing measure was defeated by one of the most powerful lobbies in this country, that of the real-estate and building interests.

Agriculture has received favored treatment both as a depressed industry and because of the political power of the organized farmers. But so has profit business, and such business should be the last to cry "unfair." Railroads received great concessions in order to get them started. High tariffs for years protected the so-called "infant industries," and continued to protect them long after they had become adult. Profit business (insurance companies, banks, railroads, etc.) was bailed out on a national scale during the Great Depression. Publishers have the advantage of lower postal rates for papers and magazines, and ship operators and airlines receive outright subsidies. All of these have been "justified" on one ground or another. Fantastic "depletion allowances," intended originally for the benefit of small, struggling independents in the petroleum industry, have (because of a poorly punctuated law) been allowed to the giants in the industry also, with the result of untold tax losses to the country and soaring profits to their stockholders. The "depletion" principle has since been extended to the mining industry and from there Heaven only knows where it will go as greedy interests press for similar treatment.

The Tax Issue

Each year since the formation of the National Tax Equality Association, Congress has been importuned to amend the Federal income-tax law so as to impose heavier taxes on cooperatives. At Congressional hearings, NTEA representatives have made much of the so-called tax "inequities" and favors alleged to be extended to cooperatives. Actually, such favors as there have been were applicable only to farmers' cooperatives that met certain requirements as to membership and business with nonmembers. Such provisions were included in every Internal Revenue Act from 1926 through 1950.

Hearings by the House Committee on Small Business in 1945 resulted in a report dismissing the cooperative tax advantages as slight and commending cooperatives as a successful method of combatting monopolistic concentrations and, as such, a healthy addition to the American economy. The same committee, under a Republican chairman in the following session, started out with the conclusion that cooperatives had unfair tax advantages; its hearings were finally called off[8] and no report was ever issued.

Bills to tax cooperatives were introduced unsuccessfully in 1950, 1951, 1953, and 1954.[9] Congress did remove, in 1951, the qualifying farm cooperatives' exemption on unallocated reserves.

The views of the present Administration on taxation of cooperatives, as on several other subjects, seem contradictory. During his 1952 presidential campaign, General Eisenhower expressed the opinion that taxation of cooperatives had already been "well and soundly settled by Congress." Soon after taking office, he announced that the Treasury Department was studying the matter. There it still rested at the end of 1955, the subject having been "deliberately reserved" by him.

The Cooperative League believes that the ultimate recipient of the income, not the corporation through which the income was made, should pay the tax.

The Facts on Federal Taxation

Two factors are involved in the tax controversy—tax "minimization" and tax exemption.

Tax *minimization* involves price adjustment to the cost of doing business—a procedure adopted not only by cooperatives (through the medium of the patronage refund) but by almost every segment of the business world. The courts have held repeatedly that such adjustments are not corporate taxable net income because not retained as property by the business organization (whether cooperative or profit). Cooperatives have not been the only beneficiaries of these decisions; some of the earliest and most effective were rendered in cases involving proprietary companies that had adopted a profit-sharing or discount plan.[10] In almost every line of business today, also, there are joint enterprises run for the benefit of member companies, to which the earnings are returned, the central enterprise not being taxed on them.

This cannot be regarded as "exemption," for the effect of the rulings is to shift the tax burden from the business organization to the patron, to the extent that the refunds increase his taxable income.

Were patronage refunds taxed, the probable result would be that cooperatives would reduce their margins (and the prices to the members) to the lowest level consonant with continued operation. This would result in ruinous competition, for their competitors would have to follow suit or lose out to the cooperatives. (It is primarily to avoid this that the distributive cooperatives follow the practice of sale at current prices.)

As already noted, such tax *exemptions* as have existed were limited to farmer cooperatives, and applied only to the Federal income tax. Some of the farmer associations themselves believed that their removal from the law would not harm them and might even be a blessing in disguise, in eliminating one talking point for their adversaries. Nearly half of the farmers' cooperatives have never bothered to claim exemptions.

Even the farmer cooperatives, however, pay all property taxes, State franchise taxes, excise taxes, social security levies, and every other type of tax and license paid by competing commercial business.

Urban nonfarm cooperatives have never had any exemptions of any kind. They pay all of the taxes noted above, and the Federal income tax on allocated reserves and on interest paid to shareholders on capital stock. Further, they are taxed on the maximum interest payable under their bylaws, even though the actual payment may be at a lesser rate or none at all.

As for the contention that cooperatives should pay income taxes "just like other businesses," 86 percent of all businesses in the United States never pay any Federal corporation tax at all. The reason for this is that they are either individually owned or are partnerships. In such cases, the tax is levied on the individual owner or owners, since they are the ultimate recipients of the income.

The aim of the NTEA, of course, has been to secure the taxation of the patronage refunds that distinguish cooperatives from their profit-making competitors. Members of farmers' cooperatives are required to pay Federal income tax on patronage refunds received on farm products marketed for them by the cooperatives and on farm supplies purchased for their productive operations. Neither they nor the members of the nonfarm cooperatives are required to pay tax on refunds earned by purchases of consumer goods; such are regarded not as income, but as a saving made through collective action—a return of the "overcharge" voluntarily paid by them to the association at time of purchase.

In neither farm or consumer associations (or businessmen's profit-sharing organizations) is the *organization* taxed on the patronage refunds paid. This has been ruled upon by numerous Federal courts and the Federal Tax Court. Invariably they have held that patronage refunds which the organization has a *written* obligation to pay belong to the members and not to the organization.

This principle was not enunciated expressly for cooperatives. Any business that elects to share some of the profits with its customers or members, and says so in writing, receives the same tax consideration.

Tax Situation in the States

An official study of State taxes on cooperatives, for 1940, showed that of 32 States levying income tax, nonfarm distributive cooperatives received no exemptions of any kind in 27. In three States (Kentucky, Massachusetts, and Tennessee) they were exempted if organized under the nonprofit (not cooperative) law. California exempted from tax the savings returned to members on patronage, and North Dakota exempted allocations to reserves. In Wisconsin, cooperatives organized under the State cooperative law had specific exemption from the corporation-income tax; but (in contrast with the situation under the Federal law) their members were required to pay tax on the amounts returned to them on patronage.

There was no exemption anywhere from capital-stock, corporate excess, retail sales, gross-receipts, or gasoline taxes in States having such taxes. Of 21 States having a tax on chain stores, cooperatives were subject to the tax in all except 4.

Returns from reporting cooperatives showed that, in 1940, taxes (Federal, State, and local) accounted for 3.08 percent on sales of the food stores, 2.17 percent on those of the general stores, and 2.24 percent on those of the gasoline stations. Comparisons with taxes paid by profit business in 1938 (the nearest year to 1940 available for them) showed in all these categories of business higher tax payments by cooperatives than by the profit companies.

There has been some change in the State tax situation since 1940, but it has generally been in the direction of tightening rather than liberalizing the tax treatment of cooperatives, as a result of all the agitation by profit business.

Cooperative Political Position

People of all political persuasions can and do belong to cooperatives. This circumstance is the chief reason why one of the Rochdale tenets is political neutrality on the part of cooperatives themselves. With the exception of religion, probably no subject can stir up more controversy than politics. It is because of this that cooperatives try to exclude from their deliberations anything having to do with political parties, platforms, and policies. The members may not be able to agree on them, but they can and do have a meeting of minds on cooperation or they would not join the cooperative.

Rochdale cooperation works through economic measures, toward economic ends. It is not political. Although often characterized by the uninformed as socialistic or communistic, it is neither.

Under true Socialism, all national resources, business, and means of livelihood would be owned and carried on by government. Genuine Communism would go even farther, abolishing private property of all kinds in favor of an all-powerful and paternalistic State. Although both would create a classless society, in both cases the people would have the final control of policies, through their votes.

In contrast, the corrupted "communism" now found in the Iron Curtain countries abolishes actual democratic control, retains economic "classes" through favored treatment of Party officials, functionaries, and members, and turns not only property and national resources but also all the conditions and circumstances that together make up the lives of their people over to a remorseless, ruthless despotism.

Consumers' cooperation in this country has nothing in common with such movements as these, nor any alliance open or hidden with any political party. It is a free, voluntary, nonpartisan economic movement composed of uncoerced men and women who are free to join and participate, or not, as they choose. Cooperative business is privately, not publicly, owned business the purpose of which is the provision of goods and services on a nonprofit basis for the members.

Political "neutrality," as formerly interpreted in this country meant that the movement remained passive in the political scene and sometimes even sat idly by while political measures were taken against it. At best its action was the negative one of defense only. More and more, under present League leadership, the consumers' cooperative movement is coming to see that it is often difficult to distinguish between economic and political measures, and that it is desirable to take a positive stand on many questions directly affecting the public welfare, though perhaps touching on cooperative interests only indirectly. Though nonpartisan in the sense that they identify themselves with no particular party, cooperatives are not now neutral in the sense of being impassive or nonparticipating.

In my opinion this is all to the good. Cooperators constitute the largest, most alert, and best-informed group of organized consumers. Their influence can be a potent one in protecting the consumer interests. But the movement should avoid becoming associated in the public mind with specific political parties. Issues, not parties, should be the criterion for action. Even then leaders should make sure that they really know the views of the members before committing the movement on any question.

Unlike the lobbies of most "interest" groups, consumers' cooperation seeks no special favors for itself. Cooperation is based on self-help and cooperators would not have it otherwise. Such a course leaves it free and independent. As a prominent cooperator recently pointed out, "what we do for ourselves can't easily be taken away from us. What we count on government to do for us can be voted away by others."[11]

Chapter 39.—INTERNATIONAL RELATIONSHIPS

Cooperators and the ICA

Cooperators from the United States were present[1] at the 1895 meeting that authorized the formation of the International Cooperative Alliance,[2] and as soon as it was organized three American cooperatives joined.[3] Thereafter the ICA had in membership one or more associations from this country, the number rising to six in 1902.[4]

It is to be feared, however, that in most if not all cases, affiliation was only a "token" gesture. Few if any of the early United States "members" were prosperous enough to pay full dues or to send representatives to the international congresses.

Before the Cooperative League reached its first birthday it voted to join the Alliance. Thereafter its representatives (usually Dr. and Mrs. Warbasse) were present at every congress. The League did not, however, play an active part in international affairs for the first 15 years or so after it became an ICA member. More general awareness began to be evinced in the early 1930's.

The Second World War halted the congresses. Upon their resumption after the war's end, United States delegations became larger and larger, and their members began to take an increasingly active part.

Greater participation was accompanied by growing ICA recognition,[5] and the United States now has nine representatives on the Central Committee and one (Jerry Voorhis) on the Executive Committee. (Dr. Warbasse held a position on the Central Committee from 1924 until the Cooperative League Congress of 1946.)

In addition to the Cooperative League, the United States cooperative movement now has another member in the ICA—Consumers Cooperative Association—which applied for membership in 1954, since it was no longer a member of the League. Its application was supported by the League itself.

Cooperation in International Trade

The chief American proponent of cooperative international trade has been Howard Cowden whose organization, Consumers Cooperative Association, has been shipping lubricating oil and grease to overseas cooperatives since 1935. Both CCA and National Cooperatives were members of the International Cooperative Trading Agency until its liquidation in 1954, and Mr. Cowden had served on its executive committee since 1946.

In the middle thirties Mr. Cowden advanced the idea of an organization to trade in petroleum products internationally. His proposal, renewed at the meeting of the ICA Central Committee in 1945, was approved, and the International Cooperative Petroleum Association was incorporated on April 15, 1947 under United States law. National Cooperatives immediately affiliated and Mr. Cowden was chosen as its representative on the ICPA board.

Lloyd A. Marchant, who had had 12 years' experience as general manager of the Illinois Farm Supply Co. (a regional wholesale) was appointed general manager of the new association. Headquarters were opened in New York City.

Though its business grew and savings were made from the first, it has been hampered by currency restrictions, which finally caused it to open another office, in London, in 1953.

Membership in that year consisted of 28 national cooperatives in 17 countries. It joined CCA in crude-oil production, and their first jointly owned well came in in mid-1954. Largest customers of the association are the cooperatives in Egypt, Iran, Netherlands, Sweden, and Yugoslavia.

Cooperation in Relief Work

Cooperators' contributions to relief and economic rehabilitation of cooperatives abroad have been channeled through their own Freedom Fund and through CARE.

Freedom Fund.—A drive for the Freedom Fund,[6] begun in the autumn of 1944, netted nearly $93,000, and from it some 16 countries received assistance. As the recipient countries revived economically, relief measures gave way to a broader program that now includes assistance to democratic publications in combatting Communism, financing of consultants, and aid in developing improved technical services for cooperatives and organizing credit associations in countries where usury is common.

CARE.—The Cooperative League was one of 22 relief agencies that united in 1945 to organize the Cooperative for American Remittances to Europe (CARE).

Murray D. Lincoln was elected president of the new organization, a position he has filled ever since. Aided by a Freedom Fund contribution of $15,000 and a 1-year loan of like amount, CARE immediately began shipping packages of food abroad, using cooperatives as distributors wherever feasible. Later, the purely relief program was supplemented by technical books on agriculture, nutrition and home economics; medical instruments and supplies; and plows and small agricultural tools.

By mid-1953, its operations had expanded from serving Europe only to worldwide coverage; 40 countries had received aid through it. Its name had accordingly been changed in 1952 to Cooperative for American Remittances Everywhere. Early in 1955, the emergency in Europe being past, activities there were sharply curtailed. Hereafter, CARE's major operations will be in Asia, Africa, and South America.

Other International Cooperation

Beginning in 1924, nearly every congress of the Cooperative League has included some consideration of cooperation abroad.

Concerned over the plight of the cooperatives in devastated or occupied countries after World War II, the League called a general conference on international cooperative reconstruction in January 1944. Attended by delegates from 22 countries and the International Labor Office, it drew up a 14-point program directed toward the greater use of cooperatives in UNRRA and other relief programs.

Early in 1947 the National Women's Cooperative Guild was authorized to affiliate with the International Cooperative Women's Guild, at League expense.

United States delegates to ICA congresses have taken occasion also to attend the annual meeting of European movements, and their representatives in turn have been welcomed to the League's biennial congresses. Relations with the Cooperative Union of Canada have been continuous and cordial. Other means to promote international good will have included the giving of scholarships for study here, holding of training schools for students from abroad, participation in Point IV, a project for the distribution of farm tools in underdeveloped countries sponsored by the Mutual Service Insurance Cos., and the sending of several hundred cooperative "rainbow flags" to cooperatives in India. Delegates from the student cooperative movement affiliated with the Cooperative League participated in the formation in 1951 of the International Federation of Young Cooperators.

The credit union movement in the United States, through the Credit Union National Association, has established a World Extension Bureau to assist in the promotion of cooperative credit associations abroad and in training foreign students who will then return to do cooperative work in their own countries.

Conclusions

Murray Lincoln was a member of the United States delegation to the 1943 UN Food and Agriculture Conference, and the Cooperative League sent a representative to the UN Security Conference in 1945. It has given wholehearted support to the various UN programs and its congresses always pass resolutions reaffirming this position.

The present League officers believe that it is impossible to overemphasize the value or potential for world understanding and world peace inherent in the development of sympathy and mutual trust between cooperators of different lands. In the opinion of Jerry Voorhis, "It may well prove the most valuable single asset of the free world in the years ahead." The League is always hammering in the fact, also, that development of cooperatives is one practical way to combat Communism.

Through greater participation in the international cooperative scene, through cooperative tours, and other means of acquainting cooperators with each other, through hearty support of the United Nations and its various agencies, and through direct assistance in relief and productive development, the consumers' cooperative movement of this country is playing its part in the world.

New measures for promoting international good will always find receptive ears in the cooperative movement of the United States.

Part VI.

COOPERATIVES IN THE NATIONAL ECONOMY

Chapter 40.—APPRAISAL

Retrospect

In the course of our long historical journey, we have seen recurring waves of cooperation, some impelled by farm organizations and some by labor organizations, as well as some that swelled into being by spontaneous action without organizational support.

We have seen the growth and expansion of the cooperative educational program through the district leagues, topped and directed by the national League, the slow recovery of cooperative wholesaling after almost complete extinction, the remarkable vitality of cooperation under conditions of unprecedented severity during the depression of the thirties, and the equally remarkable expansion both locally and in federations for service and production in the friendly atmosphere of the New Deal.

We have seen how cooperators were the first to suffer from Communist undermining tactics and also the first to recognize the Communist program for what it is; how this political faction was finally expelled, leaving the cooperative movement numerically somewhat less but morally and ideologically sounder.

Surge after surge of new growth has swelled, reached its crest, broken and faded. But each has left a substantial number of survivors, battling their way not only against economic odds but also against the temporary disrepute that has attached itself to the word "cooperative" as a result of the failures and losses involved in each recession of the movement.

In probably no country in the world did the trial and error stage last so long as here. Some associations still come and go on that basis, but there is no longer much excuse for it, what with the aids, experience, and advice now available.

Until the advent of the Cooperative League, there had never been an organized, sustained effort to correlate education or cooperative activities. In fact, there had never been a genuinely independent cooperative "movement." Either the associations had been tied to some fraternal or labor organization with its own program, of which cooperation was only a part, or there was only an aggregation of scattered organizations moving along and making the same mistakes over and over again. There were also the "promoted" schemes that lined the pockets of the promoters at the expense of the workers, others that soared dizzily for a while and then crashed disastrously. Alongside them were the much more numerous little starveling ventures, known only to a few, that limped along feebly for a time and then quietly expired, and finally the few that were a glorious success for long periods.

Not until the formation of the present Cooperative League did any central educational organization succeed in clinging to life for more than a few years. That the League did so can be attributed to the zeal and devotion of its president and staff and the financial support of Dr. Warbasse. Lacking them, national federation would certainly have been much longer in the making and in its absence the development of cooperation in this country might have taken an entirely different (and unsound) direction.

The formation of the League did not abolish cooperative failures by any means. Cooperatives are organizations of *people,* and as long as human nature remains imperfect, they will continue to make mistakes even to the point of failure. Because of the League's work, however, the consumers' cooperative movement has been kept on a more or less even keel, and operating on accepted principles. "American Plans" are not advocated today, nor do we hear of million-dollar schemes to mulct the public in the name of cooperation.

In evaluating the American consumers' cooperative movement, the work and influence of the Cooperative League of the USA can hardly be overestimated. Not only has it acted as a stabilizer in the distributive movement, but it has been the incubator for fledgling national associations in other branches of the cooperative movement—notably for students, housing, and medical care. As its horizons have widened, so has its influence. It is significant that the most stable, prosperous, and progressive organizations in the consumers' cooperative movement are affiliated with it. Moreover, as it has moved out of its previous rather limited and parochial outlook to one emphasizing the welfare of all the people, it has grown in stature and in public acceptance both official and unofficial.

Elements of Weakness and of Strength

Elements of Weakness

There are many points at which cooperatives have made mistakes. Indeed, there is hardly a possible false step that some cooperative has not taken at some time. Some errors arise from the fact that cooperatives are membership associations and subject to the faults of all democratic organizations. Many are not peculiar to cooperatives, but are equally numerous in profit business. But about nine-tenths of all business failures, cooperative and other, are due to human weaknesses or mistakes.

A. Within the Cooperative:

Within the cooperative the shortcomings are generally the following:

1. Insufficient consideration of choice of the cooperative business to be entered, to be sure that it is needed and will command sufficient patronage for success.
2. Insufficient working capital.
3. Underpaid executives and lack of trained understudies, leading to
   a. High turnover of managers.
   b. Inefficient management.
4. Inefficient management, leading to poor business methods as
   a. Inadequate accounting.
   b. Poor buying of supplies.
   c. Lack of proper controls on merchandise.
   d. Poor housekeeping.
5. Unattractive and out-of-date premises.
6. Inexperienced and ineffective board of directors.

   Directors should be selected on the basis of practical qualifications for the job (in business administration, merchandising, insurance, personnel, law, previous successful cooperative experience, etc.).

7. Inertia and lack of vision on the part of cooperative leaders, and failure to keep abreast of modern methods. Failure to plan intelligently. Insufficient use of research and the results of research and analysis in planning.

8. Insufficient patronage by members.

9. Insufficient member participation in association affairs—apathy.

10. Extension of credit, leading to freezing of capital in large amounts of receivables (an extremely dangerous practice, but especially in a declining market).

11. Overemphasis on purely business aspects, to the exclusion of the social, recreational, and philosophical.

12. Lack of adequate communication between administration and membership.

13. Slow action in making decisions (a general fault of all really democratic institutions).

14. Lack of continuing educational work, especially among new members.

Many new cooperative members have never put in a cent of direct investment. They have earned their shares through patronage refunds. Unless and until such members are converted into *convinced, active cooperators,* they cannot be relied upon for loyalty in the pinch.

15. Insufficient effort to enlist the interest, participation, and patronage of the housewives from whom (in the stores) most of the patronage must come.

16. Dissension and factionalism in the membership.

B. Between Cooperatives:

Among the points needing greater attention for intercooperative relations are the following:

1. Fragmentation of effort, and insufficient integration. Many local units are too small for efficient operation.

2. Insufficient coordination of buying, merchandising, and accounting at the local level. Insufficient joint effort in production, sale of products, research, and employee training at the regional level.

3. Lack of support of central organizations by member associations, as manifested in
   a. Inadequate financing.
   b. Insufficient patronage.
4. Slow action in making decisions.
5. Competition for membership and business between cooperatives.

C. In Relation to Employees:

There is margin for improvement in cooperative treatment of employees, as regards—

1. Inadequate wages and salaries, especially for higher-level positions.
2. Lack of adequate, well-defined personnel policy, incentives, and morale-building measures.
3. Lack of well-defined opportunities for advancement.
4. Lack of sufficient provision for employee security in old age.

D. In Relation to Competitors:

In the business field, cooperatives may suffer from—

1. Competitors' use of underpricing, misleading advertising, and "tricks of the trade," to none of which cooperatives can stoop but which are sometimes formidable obstacles to overcome.
2. False reports about cooperatives ("Communistic," "Socialistic," "tax evaders," etc.).
3. Unremitting efforts of profit business in various lines to hamper or destroy cooperatives through legislative or other measures.

E. In Relation to the Community:

For their own sake, cooperatives should take into consideration the following points in relation to the community:

1. Prevalence of mistaken ideas as to the amount of saving possible through cooperation, which unfortunately have sometimes been fostered by unwise claims of cooperative organizers.
2. Unwise propaganda and extremist statements by some cooperators, that alienate public opinion.

3. The cooperative may not supply a felt need, or the community may already have an efficient distributive system. In the latter case the cooperative must be as good as or better than existing business.

4. Aloofness of the cooperative from community affairs, setting a barrier to understanding and local acceptance.

F. In Relation to the Whole Country:

Considerations of national scope—a formidable hurdle in the aggregate—are the following:

1. The comparatively high standard of living in the United States, which makes cooperative savings relatively unimportant in a family's economic picture.

2. General lack of the habit of thrift among the American people, which also tends to lessen the incentive toward saving through cooperatives.

3. The rapid tempo of American life, which makes people unwilling to take on added responsibilities unless they see an urgent need for them.

4. Decreasing social and recreational dependence on community organizations such as cooperatives, even in rural districts, with the advent of movies, radio, television, etc.

5. Geographic distances (with resultant problems of transport and freight rates) which militate against the success of isolated associations and even against intercooperative action except where numerous associations are concentrated in a comparatively small area.

6. The heterogeneous character of the population, with resultant lack of common interests that make for solidarity.

7. Extreme population mobility, causing rapid turnover of cooperative membership and necessitating continuous recruitment and education of new members.

8. In general, lack of effective support by organized labor, which places its main reliance (for improving its living standards) on collective bargaining, and the rank and file of which has not been convinced of the value of cooperation.

9. Appeal of cooperation to the insufficiently numerous upper middle class, rather than to the workers.

10. The prevalence of the materialistic rather than the idealistic in American life.

11. The lack of a strong consumer consciousness in this country.

Cooperative Accomplishments

Among the important advantages and accomplishments of the consumers' cooperatives, it may be noted that cooperatives—

1. Provide a practical education in business.
2. Develop the spirit of self-help and independence.
3. Call forth and make use of the latent abilities and creative impulses of many people, and in so doing provide a deep satisfaction and sense of social fulfillment.
4. Habituate the members to altruistic modes of thought and action.

"[Cooperation] diminishes selfishness and inculcates altruism; for no cooperative enterprise can succeed in which the individual members are not willing to make greater sacrifices for the common good than are ordinarily evoked by private enterprise. Precisely because cooperation makes such heavy demands upon the capacity for altruism, its progress always has been and must always continue to be relatively slow. Its fundamental and perhaps chief merit is that it does provide the mechanism and the atmosphere for a greater development of the altruistic spirit than is possible under any other economic system that has ever been tried." [1]

5. Help to create better and more socially conscious citizens, and thus provide training for citizenship.
6. Provide an example of true democracy in business and of consumer control.
7. Create a collective capital that can be used for the good of all.
8. Act as correctors of unduly high prices, especially in the smaller towns.
9. Have demonstrated in many fields (but especially in production, insurance, credit, and petroleum distribution) their ability to effect substantial savings.

It is doubtful if, over the long run, cooperative grocery stores have usually made the savings expected of them by their members, though individual associations have made impressive records.

10. Assist in a more-equitable distribution of wealth, through the return of earnings to the many instead of the few.

11. Help to keep wealth in the community, instead of draining it away to absentee owners.

12. Aid in improving the quality of goods for consumers.

13. Serve as a genuine public-interest group working for the consumer who is all of us.

14. Help to prevent both inflation and depression, by acting as a brake on prices and as a support of purchasing power.

15. By providing competition, help to counteract monopolistic trends.

16. Being voluntary and democratic organizations depending for their very existence on freedom of thought and action, they form a front-line bastion against all forms of totalitarianism, whether threatening from the left or the right.

Although cooperative resistance is "not by force of arms but by force of ideas,"[5] it was no accident that dictators have made the suppression or capture of cooperatives a primary objective, knowing that, as long as cooperatives were free, they were a menace to any force trying to destroy democracy.

Elements of Strength

All the points noted above, under "accomplishments," are elements of strength heretofore insufficiently utilized by the cooperative movement in its public-relations work. In addition, the movement has certain other advantages, few of which can be claimed by profit business. Among them are that—

1. They can depend on loyalty of employees and often a devotion far beyond the call of duty, for cooperation is more than just another business to them.

2. They have a reservoir of good will and voluntary effort in the membership.

3. They have closer personal relations with the patrons than is possible to the chains.

4. They usually have good relations with organized labor.

5. They have a reputation for quality merchandise.

6. They have a reputation for truth in advertising and merchandising.

7. They need little or no oversight from government because, acting in the consumer interest as they do, they have no temptation to break laws.

Chapter 41.—COOPERATIVE PRESENT AND FUTURE

Present Status of Consumers' Cooperation

The number of both urban and rural distributive cooperatives has decreased by either dissolution or merger since 1944, and very few new organizations are appearing to counterbalance this trend. However, the Cooperative League reports that total membership has risen 40 percent since the end of the war and business about 20 percent. It estimates that 3 families in every 10 belong to some kind of a cooperative, and that 1 family in 7 is a member of a credit union.

As of early 1955, local cooperatives continued to thrive for the most part. Urban cooperation is still weak. This is grounded in many causes, one of which is the prevalence of grocery operation—a low-margin business needing large volume and excellent management.[1] However, each year sees additional urban nonfarm grocery cooperatives gaining entrance into the million-dollar group.

The regional wholesales in the consumers' cooperative movement are all operating in the black at present, including the three urban grocery ones that were in trouble a few years ago. All reported sizable increases in volume as well as earnings for 1954.

Whereas most profit wholesale houses do business only in a city-wide area, all regional cooperative wholesales cover at least one whole State and some several States. The largest region is that of Consumers Cooperative Association which operates in nine States. The uneconomic territory of Eastern Cooperatives, Inc., which at one time was serving thinly scattered cooperatives in 11 States from Maine to Virginia, was corrected by reorganization into three warehouses each covering part of the area.

Overlapping of trading territory will probably persist as long as isolationism, commodity specialization, affiliation with competing farm organizations, and personal ambition continue.

Duplication does not necessarily result in competition, for in some cases the wholesales are serving separate and distinct groups. There have been and still are instances, however, of solicitation of one wholesale's affiliates by another. Competition most frequently occurs where there are both an open-membership and a limited-membership wholesale.

The insurance associations and credit unions are maintaining their steady growth. Established medical-care cooperatives are prospering and expanding both membership and facilities, but few new ones are being formed. With the decision of some labor unions to use part of their union funds to finance new housing developments under Section 213 of the National Housing Act, some progress in genuinely consumer-sponsored housing is noted. This class of housing is, however, woefully in arrears as compared with that sponsored by profit builders. Other types of service are still insufficiently used by cooperatives, with little or nothing to indicate future growth.

Outlook for the Future

Cooperative development will necessarily be influenced and possibly governed by domestic and world economic and political events that no one can foretell. As long as this country continues to be a stronghold of free thought and action, however, cooperatives will have their chance to grow.

The small, unstable and uneconomic associations that sprang up and were cushioned by the artificial wartime economy have already been swept away. Others now poised on the brink between moderate success and failure may follow. It is no secret that in many parts of the country are small organizations—some of many years' standing—that have been caught in the web of modern problems with which they do not seem equipped to cope. With the family car available, consumers no longer confine their purchasing to the small town where they may live; they think nothing of driving many miles where the facilities are good and the selection wide.

Strong believer though I am in local autonomy and in a close and intimate relationship between members and their enterprise, I have reluctantly become convinced that, if cooperatives are to succeed under present-day competitive conditions, modification of rugged independence is necessary. The modification must, I think, be toward coordination of effort and integration with other nearby organizations. Combination for such things as accounting and record keeping, purchasing, merchandise control, and advertising, and in various technical matters, should make possible a much-needed improvement along these lines as well as the employment of well-qualified personnel (especially management) that no small association can afford by itself.

Whether the individual cooperatives retain their corporate identities or merge into an area cooperative (like the large associations found abroad) would be a matter for determination by the members. But I believe that no longer can the small, fiercely individualistic association succeed, and that some yielding of sovereignty is necessary for survival. At the same time, the unhappy experiences with city-wide organizations having a number of branches have demonstrated that the change must be preceded and accompanied by intensive and greatly accelerated education as well as by measures to safeguard membership control and to insure continuance of the individual member's warm feeling of ownership and participation. The administration must not get so far away that the member begins to think in terms of "they," rather than "we."

Interesting experiments in this direction are now under way in the Lake Superior region. Their results will be watched with interest by all well-wishers of cooperation.

Unfavorable circumstances that must be taken into account for the future are the reduction in income (now into the fourth consecutive year) of the farmers who are the largest group of cooperators,[2] and spotty incidence of industrial unemployment affecting the purchasing power of the workers concerned.

An ever-darkening cloud on the cooperative horizon is credit. Virtually everywhere, accounts receivable are reported to be so large as to reach the danger point.

It is my belief that an important—perhaps all-important—factor for the future development of cooperation will be the continuous demonstration of its ability to succeed in business. There are always a certain number of idealists, attracted by the cooperative philosophy, who will join and patronize faithfully even the poorest specimen of cooperative, and find satisfaction in so doing, because they believe in the "idea." In our materialistic age, however, such people are too few to form a base for cooperative development on any large scale, though they are needed in any organization.

There are even those who believe that the day is past when any considerable number of members can be attracted to cooperation through the old philosophical appeals. A survey by the University of Minnesota School of Business Administration disclosed that this belief was general among the managers of cooperatives there. If they are correct, then it becomes ever more important to emphasize the primary factors necessary for business success. Opinions will vary as to their relative significance, but few will dispute that all of the following are of the greatest importance:

1. Adequate financing.
2. Good business management.
3. An effective board of directors.
4. An adequate volume of business.
5. A loyal, informed, and active membership.

Improved merchandising and operating methods, increased volume to reduce unit costs, speed-up of inventory turnover, and reduction of accounts receivable are other factors leading to better financial results. More adequate wages and salaries will attract better-qualified employees and give better results in productivity.

Cooperatives will also benefit from the infusion of new blood and ideas as younger people are drawn into the movement.

It has been demonstrated, time and again, that the over-all progress of individual cooperatives was in direct relation to the amount and quality of educational work done. The best ones had active committees charged specifically with this duty and allocated regular, adequate amounts for its performance. The value of education may be hard to demonstrate to directors intent on business success, for education is often bread cast upon the waters, that returns only "after many days." But it does return—and pay—in the end.

An association that neglects or disdains education may appear to be sound and prosperous, but it will find its patronage dropping off rapidly at the first sign of adversity. The fair-weather members, who joined only because of the patronage refunds they hoped to get, will be the first to go.

The general disadvantages of present-day life in America, for cooperatives (see F in Chapter 40), are beyond the control of the cooperative movement. The corrective measures for most of the *business* faults are obvious, but certain others, particularly those concerning the cooperative's standing in the community, deserve comment.

Cooperatives need better public relations. They have a good story to tell—and a good idea to sell—and they should do both.

They should become, as far as possible, an integral part of the community and participate in its life. This they can do by sponsoring events to which the public is invited, by advertising in the local paper, by contributing to local philanthropies, taking part in local movements, and joining local chambers of commerce. They can enlighten the public as to the real meaning of cooperation by organizing debates in public halls or over the radio, by showing cooperative films, staging plays with a cooperative theme, or inviting as a speaker an outstanding authority in some other field, to speak on some phase of the movement. (He will carry more weight with the average citizen than an avowed cooperator.) Directors and employees can serve on local committees and join veterans' clubs and civic organizations.

In doing these things, the movement will also be attracting some of the new members that must be flowing into the cooperatives all the time, if they are to live and grow. A certain proportion will join because of academic interest, others because of hoped-for refunds.

It is then the cooperative's task to take them and make convinced cooperators of them. This is harder, but can be done. Possible methods include the use of cooperative pamphlets, lectures, correspondence courses, study or discussion groups, panel discussions with the listeners participating, and institutes combining instruction and recreation. The social or recreational approach can also be used by itself. A special effort should be made to reach the women and young people, and to draw all segments of the membership into active work in the association.

I hope to see the day when membership growth will be accorded equal importance with business results, and stressed equally, in cooperative annual reports and in the news items released.

Outstanding associations have proved that it is not impossible for cooperatives to succeed even in the larger cities. It is my opinion, however, that future distributive cooperative expansion there will come through the opening of branches by existing associations rather than through the organization of new associations. Nowadays a city cooperative can hardly expect to start small and expand gradually. Low margins and expert competition will usually kill off the small store before it even has a chance to take root. An established and successful cooperative, on the other hand, can by its very success attract new members and capital for a branch, on a scale impossible for a new organization.

Most new groups, considering a cooperative enterprise, think in terms of a grocery store, because food constitutes such a large proportion of family expenditures. The grocery business is now one of extremely narrow margins, the competition is very keen, well-organized, and efficient, and the cooperative must be equally good or even better, if it is to hold its patrons for the long pull. As Dr. Warbasse once pointed out, "Loyalty is like liberty; it must be earned," and in his opinion good service was the way for the cooperative to earn it.

Associations in rural areas still operate "general" stores that carry a little of everything. Several very successful urban associations (such as Maynard and Fitchburg, Mass., Cloquet, Minn., and Waukegan, Ill.) have regular departments other than food. Full-fledged city department stores are not feasible for cooperators at this juncture, even though they may come to be in the future, for they require at least a quarter to a half a million dollars' worth of inventory to provide the variety of selection to which city dwellers are accustomed.

Theoretically, there are few fields (aside from the heavy industries, transportation, public services, and high-style goods) that are not possible for consumers' cooperation. Actually, very practical considerations limit the cooperative possibilities. Many lines of business offer good savings opportunities. However, the wide-margin lines generally have the disadvantage of slow turnover or of constituting a very small proportion of the family budget. Such lines as drugs, shoes and shoe repair, books, luggage, and electrical appliances, and the barber, beauty, laundry, and burial services are possible only with an extremely large membership or in combination with some other, quick-turning, business. Any headway in them will be made, I believe, either through departments of established associations or through "federal" associations formed by existing local cooperatives whose combined membership will provide patronage sufficiently large for effective operation.

Some progress has been made in production for consumer needs. The range of commodities produced, however, is still very limited (thus far, producer goods predominate). In the petroleum industry and in fertilizer, however, the commodity goes through cooperative channels all the way from the raw materials to the finished product.

Cooperators need to study carefully the present and probable future conditions in any projected new productive venture. As they have found through bitter experience, hard-raised money has sometimes been sunk in productive plants that (although they did not realize it) were already obsolescent. An insufficient market, poor location, unforeseen difficulties of transportation, seasonality, etc., have already wrecked a number of productive enterprises. Production often yields greater savings than are possible in the distributive lines; it can also be a snare for the unwary and the cause of heavy loss.

The rural areas of the United States (except in the South and Southeast) are well represented by distributive cooperatives. Credit unions have their greatest development in industrial places, especially the big cities where distributive cooperation has been least. They show no signs of slowing their fast pace of development since the end of World War II. It is possible that, if credit union members can be attracted to distributive cooperation, they may be a source of future development in that direction.

There are limitless opportunities in insurance and for credit unions. The spread of voluntary plans of prepaid medical care is being hastened through collective bargaining by labor organ-

Main entrance to the modern shopping center of the Consumers Cooperative Association of Eau Claire, Wisconsin

The Eau Claire co-op serves its members with food, furniture, hardware, appliances and many other lines. A credit union does a booming business for the co-op owners.

In December, 1954 the Greenbelt Consumer Services opened America's largest co-op store at Wheaton, Maryland, a D. C. suburb.

The Wheaton co-op has 25,000 square feet of self-service shopping space.

izations; that of *cooperative* plans will depend on legislative action to remove the monopoly now given to the medical profession in many States. It will also be affected by possible Government action looking toward the inclusion of medical care as part of the social security system.

For any substantial development, cooperative housing needs easier access to financing and credit (possibly through Government loans) and the guiding hand of a strong central organization of its own to provide technical, legal, and other assistance. Even with these, genuine cooperative housing will never progress far, in my opinion, as long as the Federal Housing Administration (and especially its regional offices) is in the hands of the cooperatives' enemies, the real-estate and building interests.

Above all, cooperators everywhere might well ponder this: If every member family were filling all of its needs through the local cooperatives, if the local cooperatives were faithfully buying from the wholesale all their requirements that are available through it, and if the wholesales were in turn as faithfully patronizing National Cooperatives and the productive and service federations—then there would be no doubt whatever that the cooperative movement (without any increase in present membership) would soon attain that 10-15 percent of the United States business that would enable it to act as a powerful balance wheel of the economy. And the members, all the way down the line, would benefit through the additional savings that the increased volume would produce, besides receiving the indirect benefits accruing from recognition of the movement as truly representative of the American consumer.

If cooperators would only cooperate to the fullest! Therein lies the key to the whole problem of the slow cooperative growth. But to attain that goal, *convinced* cooperators are necessary—persons and associations willing to exert just the little more effort required—and that, in turn, is again a matter that requires more, better, and continuous educational work.

In the words of Robert Browning—

> "The little more—and how much it is!
> The little less—and the worlds away!"

As for the cooperative aims in general, I can do no better than to close with the following quotation from Dr. M. M. Coady, one of the leading philosophers of the movement:

> "We of the cooperative movement have no desire to create a nation of shopkeepers whose only thoughts run to groceries and dividends. We want our people to look into the sun and into the depths of the sea. We want them to explore the hearts of flowers and the hearts of their fellowmen. We want them to live, to love, to play and pray with all their being. We want them to be whole men and women, eager to explore all the avenues of life and attain perfection in all their faculties. Life for them should not be in terms of merchandise but in terms of all that is good and beautiful. They are the heirs of all the ages and of all the riches yet concealed; all the creations of art and literature are for them. If they are wise they will create the instruments to obtain them. They will usher in the new day by attending to the blessings of the old. They will use what they have to secure what they have not."[3]

FOOTNOTES

CHAPTER 1

1. Johns Hopkins University: **History of Cooperation in the United States,** p. 28.

2. The Worcester store, Protective Union Co. (1848) and the Natick Protective Union (1866) were still in operation in 1913, though not very cooperative. The New Bedford association (1848) lasted until 1914.

3. Massachusetts Bureau of Statistics of Labor: **Eighth Annual Report,** 1877, p. 123.

4. Olsen, Arden Beal: **The History of Mormon Mercantile Cooperation in Utah.** (Unpublished.)

5. But many Mormons are members of present-day cooperatives—in Utah and Idaho, and probably in other States as well—which have no connection with their church.

CHAPTER 2

1. Because there is a substantial literature on the Grange movement, only its broad outlines are attempted here, to save space for other cooperative developments not so well known or so well explored.

2. Buck, Solon Justus: **The Granger Movement,** p. 275.

3. Thus, in Maine the Houlton Grange Store, organized in 1878 with only $140 in capital—all borrowed—is still in existence. The Union Mercantile Co., at Isanti, Minn., was in business from 1897 until 1940. Texas had what was considered as the most successful example of distributive cooperation in the United States. By 1888 the wholesale there, Texas Cooperative Association, was the largest receiver of cotton in the Port of Galveston, and had an insurance department, and a store department well on its way to becoming the largest store business in the South. This promising movement was checked when the 1885 Texas Legislature, at the instigation of the business interests of the State, passed an act prohibiting the chartering of any more local cooperatives. One of its affiliates, however, the Lee County Cooperative Association (1879), at Giddings, was in business until 1940.

At Olathe, Kans., the phenomenal success of the Johnson County Cooperative Association (1876) inspired the formation of 20 to 30 others. It operated until 1934. The same State is the home of the oldest consumers' cooperative in the United States—the Patrons Cooperative Mercantile Co. of Cadmus. Though never very large (its peak business was $70,000 in 1948), the association deserves a medal for persistence. It surmounted the hard times of the 70's, 80's, and 90's, the money panic of 1907, two World Wars, and the depressions of 1921-22 and 1930-35, as well as the loss of its store building by lightning in 1907 and by fire in 1936. Its 1954 operations were reported to have been good and yielding a saving.

4. It was organized in 1889 as the Highland Local of the Farmers' Alliance, and was reorganized under Farmers' Union auspices in 1913, as the Cooperative Mercantile Association. It was still operating in 1953, with 207 members (an all-time high) and a business for that year of $142,062 (the peak in 1951, was $150,223).

5. It is the Patrons Mercantile Co., at Black Earth (near Madison). Much of the credit for its longevity can undoubtedly be laid to the management of Amos B. Thorsrud who was its manager from 1893 (when it was organized) to 1901, and again from 1915 to 1943. Mr. Thorsrud was still alive and active (at 85) when the present writer visited the store in 1946.

The association reached its high point in membership in 1954, with 850 members, and in business in 1951 with a volume of $737,783 (1954 business totaled $544,907). The Black Earth store, visited again in 1952, was well kept and attractive and had a thriving business, some of which came from members and patrons in neighboring towns. Conversation at the store and with cooperators in nearby towns indicates, however, that no educational work is done and there is little real cooperative spirit. The association is not affiliated with any cooperative wholesale.

CHAPTER 3

1. Among the measures advocated as early as 1878 were the establishment of State Bureaus of Labor Statistics, compensation for industrial injuries, the passage of a mechanics' lien law, arbitration of labor disputes, imposition of a graduated income-tax law, and prohibition of the hiring out of convicts to private employers and of the employment of children under 15 in workshops, mines, and factories. By 1887 the organization was also urging the 8-hour day and, equal pay for women for equal work.

In the South its attitude toward Negroes was liberal. It organized many Negro locals there, and quite a few contained both Negroes and whites.

2. The Sovereigns of Industry Cooperative at Silver Lake, organized in 1875, during its first 10 years never failed to pay interest of 6 to 8 percent on shares and 1 to 4 percent on patronage. The stores at New Britain, Conn. (1877) and Beverly, Mass. (1875) were still operating in 1913. The Lowell (Mass.) Cooperative Association, dating from 1876, went out of business in the early 1920's. The Gardner (Mass.) Cooperative Association (organized in 1868 as an independent association) sold out to the Sovereigns Cooperative Association in the same city when the latter was formed in September 1874; the latter operated until 1925—over 50 years.

One outstanding and persistent association was the Riverside Cooperative Association (1875), at Maynard, Mass., which had a 54-year existence, dissolving in 1929. Regarding it Prof. James Ford wrote in 1914: "It is probable that no cooperative store in urban New England has a wider local influence among the English-speaking population of the community than has this association." (**Co-operation in New England, Urban and Rural**, pp. 25-27.)

CHAPTER 4

1. This was about the same plan as was used during the depression of the 1930's by the self-help exchanges, except that the latters' medium of exchange was usually called "scrip."

2. This convention proved to be rather a fizzle. However, a committee presented rather a crude draft constitution for a national organization to be called the American Cooperative Union. Alonzo Wardall and Mrs. Imogene C. Fales were elected president and secretary, respectively. As far as can be learned, this organization never held another meeting or accomplished anything of importance.

Mrs. Fales had been the founder, in 1882, of the Sociologic Society of America, and served as its president until its dissolution about 1890. It was to collect and disseminate information about cooperation and assist in organizing all kinds of cooperatives. It does not appear to have been effective in either.

3. Ford, James: **Co-operation in New England, Urban and Rural**, p. 79,

CHAPTER 5

1. Adams, Thomas Sewall, and Sumner, Helen L.: **Labor Problems**, p. 398.

2. Perlman, Selig: **History of Trade-Unionism in the United States**, p. 53.

3. Bemis, Edward W.: "Cooperation in New England." (In **Publications of the American Economic Association**, 1886, Vol. 1, No. 5, pp. 103, 104.)

4. One of the few survivors of the early days is the Barneveld Cooperative Co., organized in 1895, which now deals in farm supplies only.

5. Among the early cooperatives were the Farmers Cooperative Supply Co. at Newell, started in 1896, that lived until 1930, and Farmers Cooperative Store at Rockwell (1889), still in successful operation; although it has a general farm-supply business, marketing is now its main line.

6. But the Bear Park association came near to closure in 1954 when, because of an operating loss, a motion was made to dissolve. The motion lost by a vote of 24 to 13.

Other early associations were the Clarks Grove Mercantile Co. and the Hanska-Linden Store Co. (at Hanska), which were in operation from 1891 and 1892, respectively, until late in the 1930's. The Eitzen Mercantile Co. (1899) lasted until 1942. None of these were very cooperative in their later years.

Organized in 1894, the Scandinavian Cooperative Mercantile Co., at Two Harbors, is also active but can hardly be termed a true cooperative; voting is by shares and earnings are divided on shares, not on patronage.

7. Mr. Nelson, a large scale manufacturer of plumbing supplies in St. Louis, had previously become interested in the work of the Christian Socialists in England and advocated a somewhat similar program for this country. He established a profit-sharing plan for his employees and led the way for vocational training and welfare work.

Besides influencing the organization of the cooperative at his factory in Edwardsville, Ill., he made an abortive attempt to found a national cooperative federation in 1902. However, the few replies received in response to his "feeler" questionnaire, and the small proportion of them that favored such a federation, convinced him that the time was not ripe.

CHAPTER 6

1. Randall, Daniel R.: "Cooperation in Maryland and the South." (In Johns Hopkins University: **History of Cooperation in the United States**, p. 502.)

2. Cummings, Edward: "Cooperative Stores in the United States." (In **Quarterly Journal of Economics**, Boston, April 1897, p. 266.)

CHAPTER 7

1. The year 1913 saw the formation of the American Cooperative Federation, intended by its organizers to be a "nation-wide federation." E. M. Tousley, of the Right Relationship League (Minneapolis), was on the organizing

committee and helped to draw up its constitution. The federation never functioned, however.

2. Among them were Willis J. Abbott, editor of **The Pilgrim**; B. O. Flower, editor of **The Arena**; Prof. Frank Parsons, Boston University School of Law; Carl Vrooman, regent of the State Agricultural College of Kansas; and George F. Washburn, Boston department-store owner, who was also president of the Commonwealth Club of that city.

3. A proposal to merge the cooperatives of the East and Midwest, through an organization known as The People's Trust, under the guidance of George F. Washburn, was likewise unsuccessful, though it did gain the affiliation of a few associations. It was to have operated on the same paternalistic basis as the Cooperative Association of America.

4. Among the members were A. E. Kazan (later president and general manager of the Amalgamated housing projects in New York City) and Albert Sonnichsen. Mr. Sonnichsen (of Danish descent) had previously been a sailor for 3 years, a prisoner of Filipino insurgents for a year, and a war correspondent in the Balkans for New York newspapers.

5. Sonnichsen, Albert: **Consumers' Cooperation**, p. 153.

6. It operates in every town in the county except one. Facilities include 8 grain elevators, 5 service stations, 5 bulk oil plants, 3 food stores, and a feed mill. An $800,000 county-wide building and modernization program was embarked upon in 1949 which, in the succeeding 4 years, made all its facilities right up to the minute.

Yearly volume runs about $6¼ million. Its earnings in 1954 amounted to $218,911—second largest in its history. The sum of $50,000 in cash was returned on patronage. One of the reasons for its success is the continual emphasis on member education and information.

7. Ernest O. F. Ames in **The Cooperator** (San Francisco), March 1921, p. 70.

8. **Pacific Cooperator** (San Francisco, Pacific Cooperative League), April 1920, p. 50.

9. Dr. James P. Warbasse, in **Cooperative League Yearbook, 1936**, p. 10.

10. Albert Sonnichsen, in Northern States Cooperative League **Yearbook**, 1925, p. 39.

CHAPTER 8

1. Mr. Tousley had been an organizer for the original League (of the same name), an unincorporated body, started in Chicago in 1900 by Edward Keyes and several friends (including Samuel L. Jones, Mayor of Toledo—"Golden Rule Jones"—and Miss Jane Addams of Hull House, Chicago), to organize cooperatives which would buy established businesses. The Chicago league was an outgrowth from two earlier organizations — Associated Merchants, USA, formed in 1896 as joint buyer for profit retailers, and Cooperating Merchants which succeeded it and served not only 430 dealers but also some 20 cooperative stores.

The initial drive disappeared with the death of Mr. Keyes in 1905, although the league went on until about 1908 under the direction of a dentist named Hawk.

2. This office had as organizers Alonzo Wardall (described as a "Civil War soldier") and Joseph Gilbert. Mr. Gilbert had been manager of the Cooperating Merchants Co. Later, he was, in succession, general manager of the Cooperative Wholesale of America (St. Paul), editor of **Midland Cooperator** and conductor of a column of general observations in that publication from August 1933 until mid-1953 when he retired. Mr. Gilbert died January 14, 1956, at the age of 90. For a sprightly account of his life, see **Nobody Owns Us**, by Davis Douthit, Chicago, The Cooperative League, 1948.

Messrs Wardall and Gilbert did not get along well together, and Mr. Gilbert resigned. The office was quietly closed after about 18 months' operation.

3. **Cooperation** (Minneapolis, Right Relationship League), May 1913, p. 298.

4. Mr. Vedder founded the American Cooperative Organization Bureau, operating from Chicago, which promoted stores (under what was termed the "American Rochdale Plan") in a number of places, especially in Michigan. Few of them lasted long. Reports to the U. S. Bureau of Labor Statistics indicated that many of the cooperatives were handicapped from the start by second-rate stores with shopworn merchandise, bought from their former owners.

5. Mr. Tousley told me, in an interview in November 1920, that in his opinion the only way to educate people to cooperation was by "trial and failure." He did not appear to be concerned that each failure constituted another stain on the cooperative reputation and another obstacle against future development.

6. How earnestly the former owners worked for the success of the cooperatives is, of course, open to question. It is of interest that some of the stores that did not prove successful as cooperatives were sold back to the original owners.

7. The author will supply, on request, the names of survivors of the leagues' stores.

CHAPTER 9

1. Mr. Kraus was then manager of a cooperative in West New York, N. J. Later he managed the North Jersey Cooperative Society at Bergenfield, N. J.

2. John H. Walker, president of the Illinois Federation of Labor, gave support by ordering bundle lots of the paper to distribute at coal miners' conventions. A little later the paper also received the subscription list of **Co-operation** (paper of the Right Relationship League) when that publication was discontinued.

3. Sonnichsen in Northern States Cooperative League **Yearbook,** 1925, p. 38.

4. The scale of League operations is indicated by the fact that its receipts for the first 9 months, March through November 1916, totaled $828.95, of which Dr. Warbasse had contributed $600.

Dr. Warbasse was president of the Cooperative League of the USA for the first 25 years of its existence and its financial mainstay for the first 15. He was born in New Jersey in 1866, of Danish descent.

He took his medical degree at Columbia University Medical School and did postgraduate work at the universities of Göttingen and Vienna. After serving as chief surgeon at a large hospital in Brooklyn, N. Y., he became editor of the **New York State Journal of Medicine** and special editor of **American Journal of Surgery.** His book, **Surgical Treatment,** was a classic in its field. In 1919 he gave up his medical practice to devote himself to the work of the Cooperative League.

5. Organizers of the League were Dr. and Mrs. Warbasse, Mr. and Mrs. Scott Perky, William A. Kraus, Emerson P. Harris, Ferdinand Foernsler, Hyman Cohn, Charles F. Merkel, Dr. Louis Lavine, Max Heidelberg, W. J. Hanifin, Isaac Roberts, Peter Hamilton, Walter Long, Mr. and Mrs. Ernest Rosenthal, Rufus Trimble, A. J. Margolin, and Albert Sonnichsen. The first officers were Dr. Warbasse (president), Scott Perky (secretary), and Peter Hamilton (treasurer).

Mr. Harris was later president of the Montclair (N. J.) Cooperative Society and author of **Cooperation, The Hope of the Consumer.**

Mr. Hanifin was still interested in cooperation in the late 40's and was trying (without much success) to promote a cooperative burial association in Richmond Hill (L. I.), N. Y.

Dr. Warbasse said that, during this organization period, Mr. Perky "gave full-time service without compensation. He carried on the executive work, lectured, and gave unstintingly of his talents. Cooperation in this country is under an unending obligation to this pioneer in its service."

6. Katherine de Selding and Mabel Watson Cheel, the latter serving as financial secretary. Mrs. Cheel was succeeded in 1921 by Mrs. Julia N. Perkins, who filled that position until 1938, when she became (for some years) Dr. Warbasse's personal assistant.

7. Mrs. Warbasse, who died February 3, 1945, had been active in liberal movements for many years. Besides her continuous work for the cooperative movement, she was an active woman suffragist, and one of the founders of the New School for Social Research. She was the author of many pamphlets and articles on various cooperative subjects, especially cooperative housing in which she had a deep interest.

8. Among them were: **Cooperative Movement in America,** by Cheves West Perky; **How to Organize a Cooperative Society,** by William A. Kraus; **Destiny of the Cooperative Movement,** by J. P. Warbasse; **Cooperation and Labor Organizations,** by John H. Walker; and **A Baker and What He Baked,** by Albert Sonnichsen.

9. These were, in order of organization, the wholesale of the Pacific Cooperative League (San Francisco), Central States Cooperative Society (Springfield, Ill.), Cooperative Central Exchange (Superior, Wis.), Cooperative Wholesale Society of America (St. Paul), and Tri-State Cooperative Association (Pittsburgh). These are discussed in detail in Chapters 11 and 13.

10. The temporary board consisted of Dalton T. Clarke (Tri-State), Carl E. Lunn (Seattle), John Nummivuori (Superior, Wis.), Charles F. Lowrie, (St. Paul), Duncan McDonald (Illinois), E. O. F. Ames (San Francisco), and K. E. Grandahl (Eastern States Cooperative Society, Boston).

11. Albert Sonnichsen succeeded Mr. Perky as secretary in 1919 and served until 1920. Mr. Sonnichsen had been on the executive committee continuously, and was on the board of directors thru 1927. He died on August 17, 1931.

CHAPTER 10

1. This interest was not new to the American Federation of Labor. As early as 1896, its convention passed a resolution favoring cooperatives. For details on this, and later actions, see Chapter 34.

2. Sonnichsen, Albert: **Consumers' Cooperation,** p. 160.

3. In articles in the August and September 1920 issues of **Pacific Cooperator** (organ of the Pacific Cooperative League), Mr. Ames described the situation from his point of view. No spirit of bitterness was apparent in this rather detached, impersonal account.

The Consumers board, he said, was suspicious of the wholesale but had to buy from it because, by this time, the association had no credit from private wholesalers. Mr. Ames pointed out to its directors that every store was operating at a loss, and urged that several of them be closed. He proposed an assignment of assets to the wholesale, to cover the debt for merchandise. A membership meeting aproved this, but the board refused.

Mr. Ames said that, during his absence in June, the Consumers board discharged both the manager and the new bookkeeper (August Einhaus), and incurred additional debts. On his return, Mr. Ames again asked for an assignment and was again refused. He felt then that he had no recourse except to ask for a receivership, which he did.

4. Ames' testimony in court case.

5. Following are some of the statements made to the author regarding Mr. Ames:

Anna Louise Strong (then a reporter on the **Seattle Union Record**): He tried his best to save the Seattle situation. In desperation he did what was hardly excusable—went out after new money for a failing organization. He took money wherever he could get it, including the life savings of some people. E. B. Ault (editor of the **Seattle Union Record**): Ames was sincere, but resorted to shady practices. He was blamed in Seattle for everything, including what had been done before he came. He had a hard row to hoe, "trying to put life into a corpse," for the movement in the city was already gone when he arrived. As far as Mr. Ault knew, Ames never went out for new members after he found out the condition of the Consumers, but he did take more money from those who were already members.

Walter Huggins (Englishman, who had previously been a director of the Cash Buyers Union in Chicago and later an organizer for the National Cooperative Wholesale Association in Chicago): Ernest Ames was "one of the biggest men in the cooperative movement in this country and Europe." He could do the work of half a dozen men and do it well.

John Worswick (English-born manager of Cooperative Food Products Association): "The worst-hated man in the West." M. L. Sorber (cooperator at whose home Ames had stayed while in Seattle): "We loved him."

6. The Commission's first board of directors consisted of C. H. Gustafson (president of Nebraska Farmers Union), president; L. E. Shepherd (president of the Order of Railway Conductors), vice president; Warren S. Stone (grand chief of the International Brotherhood of Locomotive Engineers), treasurer; Oscar H. McGill (Washington Cooperative Timber Mills), secretary; and Allen E. Barber (International Brotherhood of Maintenance of Way Employes).

The 1923 letterhead of the Commission showed Charles C. Connolly (president of United Farmers of America) as president. There were five vice presidents—William H. Johnston (president of International Association of Machinists), L. E. Shepherd, Herbert F. Baker (president, Farmers National Council), J. W. Kline (president, International Brotherhood of Blacksmiths, etc.), and C. H. Gustafson (then president of U. S. Grain Growers, Inc.). Warren Stone was still treasurer. Frederic C. Howe was director of the committee on banking and credit. The executive board consisted of Sidney Hillman (president of Amalgamated Clothing Workers of America), Grant Slocum (National Federation of Gleaners), Bert M. Jewell (Railway Employes Department, American Federation of Labor), Benjamin C. Marsh (People's Reconstruction League), J. Weller Long (secretary, United Farmers of America), and R. W. H. Stone (president, North Carolina Farmers Union).

7. Later, under the encouragement of some of the union leaders (notably Warren Stone), a number of labor banks were established (see Chapter 31).

8. Mr. Lowrie, of Scotch descent, was born in Iowa. Prior to 1918 he had been, successively, a teacher, a pioneer in the postal clerks' union in Chicago, and a farm owner in Montana, where he became president of the Montana Farmers Equity Union and then president of the Equity Cooperative Wholesale at Great Falls. He later participated in the work of the National Cooperative Wholesale Association.

CHAPTER 11

1. Albert Sonnichsen in Northern States Cooperative League **Yearbook**, 1925, p. 37.

2. Among its directors were Thomas Conyngton, Seth Low, William Church Osborne, and Albert Sonnichsen.

3. Dr. James P. Warbasse, in letter to author, December 2, 1953.

4. The first board of the Pacific Cooperative League consisted of A. D. Clump, Ernest O. F. Ames, R. P. Brubaker, W. S. Vanderburgh, and Clarence E. Todd. Two others were to be elected in November 1914, to serve for 1 and 2 years respectively.

5. Mr. Ames was born July 7, 1887, in Derby, England. He early became

identified with various labor and social movements, and was a member of the Leeds Cooperative Society, a charter member of the Independent Labor Party, and one of the founders of the Brotherhood Church. He assisted in the migration of the Doukhobors from Russia to Cyprus, and then to Canada, and spent several years helping to translate Tolstoy's works into English. Upon coming to the United States in 1907, he immediately joined the cooperative movement.

Dr. Warbasse, president of the Cooperative League of the USA, wrote in 1919, after a visit to California: "This staunch cooperator has put his lifeblood" into the PCL. And a speaker at the 1920 convention of the PCL declared that it was only through Ames' efforts that the organization survived during the first few years. He spoke of the sacrifices and privations of Mr. Ames and his family during this time.

6. The League (as successor of the Rochdale Wholesale Co.) had for some time been a member of the International Cooperative Alliance. In 1919 it became the agent in the United States through which purchases of the English Cooperative Wholesale Society and the Russian Centrosoyus were made.

7. The life spans of those known were as follows: College City, 1901-31; Dinuba, 1905-33; Hollister 1901-29; Le Grand, 1900-26; Madera, 1906-21; Maxwell, 1907-25; and Wheatland, about 1902-25. These seven associations had an average existence of 24 years each. Germantown (about 1910), Healdsburg (1900), and Porterville (1904) lasted until the early 1920's. The California Cooperative Meat Co. (1904) operated until 1924.

8. Later called the Illinois State Cooperative Society.

9. An audit later showed that actually there had been a loss of $1,712, as the manager had failed to take account of many outstanding bills.

10. One historian said that this was apparently the only time during the entire history of the wholesale that it really showed a profit. (Warne, Colston Estey: **The Consumers' Cooperative Movement in Illinois, p. 53.**)

11. It developed later that there was actually a deficit of $40,618, as no depreciation had been allowed for and inventories had been carried at inflated values.

12. Actually, when the local store accounts were taken into consideration there had been a loss of $13,448. Total sales for the year 1920 amounted to $2,309,532.

13. **Cooperation** (New York, The Cooperative League), November 1920, pp. 169, 170.

14. Among the incorporators were Matti Tenhunen and Adolph Wirkkula. Mr. Tenhunen was later involved in the Communist "uprising" (see Chapter 18). Mr. Wirkkula was then at Iron River, Wis., but later was manager of Cooperative Trading Association at Brooklyn, N. Y. He was the first manager of Eastern Cooperative Wholesale.

15. Up to 1936, less than 10 percent of the wholesale's share capital had been paid in cash; 90 percent had been accumulated from patronage refunds.

16. Previously manager of cooperative stores at Houghton and Hancock, Mich.

17. The first technical training course of record was that of the Right Relationship League (a promotion body), which offered a course for managers in 1909.

18. This genial Finn was later head auditor and then general manager of the wholesale. Mr. Nurmi held the latter position until his death on May 26, 1938. He was a director of the Cooperative League of the USA from 1929 through 1936.

19. V. Severi Alanne was born in Finland in 1879 and was educated as a chemical engineer. He had to leave that country (then under the czar of Russia) in 1907, because of his work for Finnish independence. After his arrival in the United States he became, in succession, publisher of a Finnish Socialist paper in Michigan, manager of a coal mine in Wyoming, and research chemist for a New England firm.

His first cooperative job was as full-time educational director for Cooperative Central Exchange, which position he held from 1920 to 1922. He then helped to organize the Northern States Cooperative League, served as educational director for Franklin Cooperative Creamery Association (Minneapolis) from 1925 to mid-1926, then became executive secretary of the Northern States Cooperative League through 1937. He returned to Central Cooperative Wholesale as assistant educational director in 1938. He served on the board of directors of the Cooperative League from 1923 through 1939.

Mr. Alanne has many writings to his credit, including a manual for cooperative directors and a best seller, **Fundamentals of Consumers' Cooperation.** He founded the Cooperative Correspondence School and was its director.

In 1949, he took leave from cooperative work to return to Finland, in order to revise a Finnish-English dictionary first compiled by him some 30 years ago. Characterized by the **Cooperative Builder** as the "dean of American cooperative educators" and by Kercher as "beyond a doubt the most widely and genuinely respected leader in the Finnish-initiated movement," Mr. Alanne has been one of the leading philosophers and teachers in the consumers' cooperative movement of the United States.

20. Equity cooperatives are still numerous in southwest Nebraska, northwest Kansas, and eastern Colorado, with scattered associations in the Dakotas, Illinois, and western Ohio.

21. Practically all the initial capital was furnished by Mr. Bennett, who put in his life savings. Among the other directors were Charles F. Lowrie (treasurer and manager of the organization department), M. W. Thatcher (manager of the auditing department and now for many years general manager of the Farmers Union Grain Terminal Association), and John Nummivuori.

22. Joseph Gilbert noted, in this connection, that—

"Sometimes when a store was organized, the directors would engage the services of the former owner as manager.

"This was in most cases a mistake, for unscrupulous men would often depress the business and then buy it back again.

"Then again shareholders would be disappointed if large savings were not immediately forthcoming, and in many cases dissensions arose among the membership of stores.

"The result was that as fast as new cooperatives were organized others were closing." (In **Midland Cooperator,** February 4, 1952.)

23. Of the 28 associations, all but three were out of business by 1937.

24. Among the organizers of Tri-State was Dalton T. Clarke, whose first acquaintance with the cooperative movement was as secretary of a small association in Washington, Pa., where he was practicing law. He later gave up his law practice to become manager of a small miners' cooperative wholesale in Monesson. Soon after Tri-State was formed, the Monesson organization merged with it and Mr. Clarke became manager of the new body.

CHAPTER 12

1. The first board of directors consisted of representatives of the various cooperative regions: Dalton T. Clarke, Pittsburgh (president), Carl Lunn, Seattle (vice president), Duncan McDonald, Springfield, Ill. (secretary-treasurer), Ernest O. F. Ames, San Francisco, K. E. Grandahl, Fitchburg, Mass., Charles F. Lowrie, St. Paul, and John D. Nummivuori, Superior, Wis.

2. Later this warehouse also openea a branch in Lakehurst, N. J.

3. Central States was kept out by the opposition of its president. Tri-State and Pacific Cooperative League were willing to affiliate but refused to merge. The president of the St. Paul wholesale thought his association should have formed the nucleus of the new National. Cooperative Central Exchange appeared to have adopted a "wait and see" attitude.

4. Dr. Warbasse noted, in his records, that at the directors' meeting of February 15, 1920, Clarke claimed that 80 associations were affiliated. However, the first few Dr. Warbasse visited in Chicago, said by Clarke to be members, declared that they had not joined.

CHAPTER 13

1. **Cooperation** (New York, The Cooperative League), December 1919, p. 188.

2. In mid-1920, open letters to Dr. Warbasse and Henry J. May (secretary of the International Cooperative Alliance, London) were issued by Mr. Ames.

The letter to Dr. Warbasse charged that, without really understanding the PCL or attempting to do so, Dr. Warbasse was attacking it and its methods and trying to create dissension.

The letter to Mr. May expressed surprise at the implication in the Cooperative League's magazine that the International Cooperative Alliance recognized the League as the parent body in the United States. Ames could only believe that Mr. May was not familiar with the situation here. Dr. Warbasse did not head a democratic movement of associations. The Cooperative League, he said, consisted of Dr. Warbasse, his wife, and his employees. The cooperatives he claimed as members had no connection with the League other than the payment of $1 per year, as evidence of "our desire to support his propaganda work and on general principles of friendliness." If any organization had the right to call a convention, it was the National Cooperative Association in Chicago, that "was created as a national body and has begun to function as such." Dr. Warbasse had turned his back on it, his child, because it was unwilling to be dominated by him. He had also, Ames said, publicly objected to PCL's holding its own (19th) annual meeting "without his direction."

3. Interview of author with E. O. F. Ames, April 18, 1921.

4. Ernest O. F. Ames in **American Cooperator** (Newllano, La., Llano Cooperative Colony), February 1922, p. 6.

5. He left an open letter to the attorney for the League's receiver, in which he said that because of the situation and the threats against his life, he had decided not to return to San

Francisco. He had no money with which to fight, and he was sure that any further attempts against him would be more adroit. He was therefore leaving the State for the sake of his family. The last news I had of him was that he had returned to England.

Concerning Mr. Ames there were almost as many views as people expressing them.

T. D. Stiles (mine-union official and president of Penn Central Cooperative Association): Ames was the most practical cooperator he had ever met, but he was inclined to doubt that Ames could ever have succeeded over such a large territory.

Albert Sonnichsen (in the Northern States Cooperative League **Yearbook,** 1925):"His name is still remembered, somewhat battered and blackened, but in a great measure undeservedly so, I think, for if he resorted to questionable methods, it was in the sheer desperation of a man who sees the labors of part of a lifetime on the verge of being lost. He went down in failure, but he went down fighting."

The present writer is inclined to concur in Sonnichsen's judgment. Ames had spent 15 years in working for the development of cooperation in California, with many sacrifices and no material benefits to himself. That he went wrong at the end was a sign of weakness and desperation, but only human. (For other opinions about Mr. Ames, see footnote 5, page 399.)

6. Mr. Nummivuori later served as manager of the Spencer (N. Y.) Cooperative Society, resigning in the early 1930's to go to Russia where he spent several years. Later, for some years, he again managed the Spencer association.

7. Mr. Warinner, a Missourian, had been a train dispatcher. He became interested in cooperation in 1916-17, and managed cooperative stores in Tucumcari, N. Mex., and Brookfield, Mo., before coming to Central States. He had also served for some time as district advisor for the Cooperative League of the USA, his chief duty being to assist local associations that were in financial difficulties. He was a League director for many years.

8. Mr. Moerth, a coal miner of Austrian descent, became active in the cooperative movement as early as 1908, as organizer for the Right Relationship League. He was in succession, manager of the ill-fated Consumers Alliance-National store at Staunton, manager of the Union Supply & Fuel Co. at Staunton (from 1914 to October 1923), and manager of the Central States Cooperative Wholesale Society (from 1923 to mid-1924). He was out of the cooperative movement for several years, returning in 1927 to become manager of the Piney Fork branch of the New Cooperative Co. at Dillonvale, Ohio.

9. Without the self-sacrificing devotion of Mr. and Mrs. A. W. Warinner, it would not have been possible to rebuild the Illinois movement and the Central States society. Sufficient recognition has never, in my opinion, been given to them.

10. Mr. Niemela is a veteran of many years' cooperative experience, including managerships at Maynard and Quincy, Mass., Brooklyn, N. Y., and Norris and Crossville, Tenn. He was president of Eastern Cooperative Wholesale in 1933. In the middle thirties he was advisor on cooperatives for the Tennessee Valley Authority. Thereafter he served in several capacities with Eastern Cooperative Wholesale. Since 1948 he has been manager of the cooperative supermarket of the Amalgamated housing colony in the Bronx, one of the largest nonfarm cooperatives. That organization, A. H. Consumers Society, made earnings of $21,932 on a volume of $1,109,893 in 1954. It has in process another supermarket for the downtown Amalgamated colony, designed for a business of $2 million.

Mr. Niemela has the distinction of one of the longest periods of service on the board of directors of the Cooperative League of the USA—serving a total of 19 years (see Appendix B).

11. Mr. Halonen was born in Finland in 1891 and had one year of university training there. After his arrival in the United States he spent several years in newspaper work, and edited an English-Finnish dictionary. He was a prime mover in the fight against the Communists. Mr. Halonen held the position of educational director of the Central Cooperative Wholesale until 1942, when he resigned for health reasons and moved to California. Returning in 1953, he became assistant editor of the **Finnish Cooperative Weekly.** He died in 1954.

12. During its whole existence, through two depressions and World War II, the wholesale has operated in the black each year.

13. Alvar John Hayes, a native of Finland, had 1 year in electrical engineering at the University of Pittsburgh, graduated from State Teachers College at California, Pa., and taught for 2 years. Returning from war service, he became active in the labor movement. He served as assistant educational director of the Central Cooperative Wholesale from 1928 to 1938 (and as editor of the **Builder** from 1928 to June 1935). He held the position of general manager of the wholesale, succeeding H. V. Nurmi, from 1938 to December 1948, after which he was research director and advisor for local cooperatives on bylaws until 1952, when the wholesale discontinued these services. Then he undertook free-lance work for both the wholesale and the local associations. He died in 1955.

He was chairman of the board of directors of National Cooperatives from 1939 until 1946, when he succeeded I. H. Hull as its president; he served in the latter capacity until 1948. He was a director of the Cooperative League of the USA from 1943 through 1946.

14. Its actual name is **Tyovaen Osuustoiminalehti** (meaning **Workers' Cooperative Paper**).

15. For 26 years the Exchange was under the general management of Cornelius ("Con") McCarthy, until his death in 1947. Wilbur M. Jenny succeeded him.

16. Later, Mr. Herron became editor of **Nebraska Cooperator**, when that paper was started in 1945. The paper has been probably the most consistent educator in, and most untiring exponent of, the Rochdale philosophy of all the regional periodicals.

17. Name later changed to Associated Grange Warehouse Co. in August 1920 and then to Grange Cooperative Wholesale in November 1924.

18. Mr. Goss had previously been a successful farmer and businessman. He had been one of the organizers of the wholesale. From 1925 to 1936 he served on the board of directors of the Cooperative League of the USA, and was active in its congresses. Elected in 1924 as State Grange Master he resigned in 1933, upon his appointment to be Federal Land Bank Commissioner. He resigned this latter position in 1940, in protest against certain official policies. He was elected Master of the National Grange in 1941 and was still in that office at the time of his death, on October 25, 1950. He was also serving on the National Committee on Mobilization of the National Security Resources Board.

19. Others were Illinois Farm Supply Co. and Iowa Farm Service Co. (both organized in 1927) and Minnesota Farm Bureau Service Co. (1928).

20. Up to 1939 only one association (a city cooperative) had furnished any cash capital; it put in $1,000.

21. Mr. Cort, born in St. Lawrence, S. Dak., in 1885, was a graduate of Iowa State College at Ames. Prior to entering cooperative work, he had operated a farm in Chippewa County, Minn., for 8 years and had been agricultural agent for Freeborn County, Minn., from 1923 to 1926. He was secretary of the Minnesota Cooperative Oil Federation (a noncommercial organization), formed in November 1925. Described as having built Midland "out of an idea, an iron will, and sheer bulldog tenacity" (**Midland Cooperator**, July 12, 1944), Mr. Cort was manager of the wholesale from its formation until his retirement in 1940. He was a director of the Cooperative League of the USA from 1939 through 1942. He died on July 2, 1944.

22. Howard Cowden was the son of a Granger in Pleasant Hope, Mo. He had a 4-month course at the University of Missouri College of Agriculture (reward for a prize-winning entry of corn he had raised), taught school for several years, and organized a number of farm clubs and, eventually, the first egg-marketing cooperative in Missouri. This was followed by the organization of a number of others, and in 1920 he joined the Missouri Farmers Association as secretary in charge of organization, a post he retained until he resigned to form the Union Oil Co., Cooperative.

He served on the board of Cooperative League almost continually from 1935 through 1952.

During World War II, Mr. Cowden served on the Advisory Council of the National Petroleum Association. In 1950 he was given an honorary degree of doctor of laws by St. Francis Xavier University in Nova Scotia. In 1952 he was named as member of a committee appointed by the National Petroleum Association.

CHAPTER 14

1. L. S. Herron, in **Cooperation** (New York, The Cooperative League), June 1921, p. 6.

2. A native of Oslo, Norway (1893), Mr. Nordby came to the United States in 1910. He was general manager of Franklin from 1924 to 1932. He was also active in the Northern States Cooperative League and served on the board of directors of the Cooperative League of the USA for a number of years. He was drowned in December 1933 when his car broke through the ice of a lake while he and a friend were on a fishing trip.

3. In 1925 the sum of $175,000 was used to support a child clinic, and this support was continued in 1926. Other uses of earnings have included donations for the city's public parks, folk-dancing classes, archery tournaments, baseball, volley ball, and soft ball competitions, certain arts and crafts work at city playgrounds, a water festival, a circus, a track meet, and contributions for the support of the Franklin employees' band and chorus.

4. In 1953 its volume was $6,800,000 (the highest in its history) and earnings were $211,989. Because prices were cut in 1954, its volume fell to $6,662,736 in that year and earnings dropped to $134,898 (of which $65,399 went for State and Federal income taxes).

5. At the end of 1953, Franklin had 3,600 shareholders, of whom 425 were employees of the association.

6. How far the association has deviated from **consumers'** cooperation is evidenced by the fact that it, six other dairy companies, and a milk drivers' union were fined $3,000 to $3,500 each, early in March 1953, for conspiracy to fix prices. The judge said, however, that he saw "no occasion to put the earmark of criminality" upon the offenders. The companies pleaded "no defense," but did point out that all paid the same for raw materials under the Twin Cities milkshed price and all had the same labor costs.

7. The retail price in the Twin Cities averages about 5 to 6 cents per quart below that in the rest of the country.

8. The associations at Minneapolis and Astoria are the only ones I know of that process their own milk. Evergreen Cooperative (Seattle) and Co-op Dairy Service (Wyandotte, Mich.) are milk-delivery organizations.

Altogether, there are records for only eight consumers' dairy or milk-distribution associations, including those already mentioned. The others were in Denver, Colo., and Greendale and Madison, Wis.

Several store cooperatives (such as United Cooperative Society at Maynard and Fitchburg, Mass., and Cooperative Trading, Inc., at Waukegan) have dairy departments.

9. Report of committee on cooperative bakeries, in **Proceedings of Fourth Congress of the Cooperative League,** 1924, p. 83.

10. But when the Cooperative Bakery of Brownsville and Eastern New York (Brooklyn) went out of business in 1947, the members who were still on the rolls received $63.06 for each $5 share held.

11. Among the retail store associations that currently operate bakeries are Cooperative Trading, Inc., Waukegan, Ill. and United Cooperative Society, Fitchburg, Mass.,—both largely of Finnish membership. Central Cooperative Wholesale (Superior, Wis.) also has a bakery.

12. U. S. Bureau of Labor Statistics Bulletin No. 437, p. 3.

CHAPTER 15

1. Mr. Parker had sold newspapers in San Francisco, worked as a newspaper man, and at 30 years of age was reported to have been manager of the Chicago **Daily Tribune.** Five years later he had become president of the **Chicago American.** For his career subsequent to the failure of the Cooperative Society of America, see footnote 6, below.

2. The Cooperative League commented sarcastically, regarding the society's continual references to genuine cooperatives and the Rochdale cooperative movement: "Its promoters talk cooperation as though the Rochdale Pioneers were their old boyhood chums." The League also charged that the CSA had reprinted one of the League pamphlets as a CSA publication.

3. In response to these claims the State Attorney General in a public statement, early in 1921, pointed out that the legal victories claimed by Parker were merely technical. "Not one of these cases was in any sense an adjudication or judgment on the merits, legality, or qualifications of the so-called stock of the Cooperative Society of America; neither was the legality of the sale of such certificates or so-called stock passed upon by any one of the respective judges."

4. An interesting sidelight was that it had been using the judge's name as a sponsor of the society, without his knowledge.

5. She was shown to have received $1,500,000 on the sale of certificates, in addition to her salary as secretary of the company (paid even though she had been in Europe a good part of the time). It was charged that Parker had also given his wife $2,000,000 in Liberty bonds owned by the CSA, without making any record of it. Meantime, "Mrs. Parker has disappeared."

6. Later he was involved in the fraudulent promotion of a "church" found by the court to be nonexistent, in a mail-fraud case (arising from the "church" promotion) brought by the U. S. Post Office Department, and in an income-tax suit.

CHAPTER 16

1. The first officers of the new League were Dr. J. P. Warbasse, president; A. P. Bower (vice president, Pennsylvania Federation of Labor, and president of Keystone Cooperative Association, Reading, Pa.), vice president; John F. McNamee (editor, **Locomotive Firemen & Enginemen's Magazine,** Cleveland, Ohio), general secretary; and Waldemar Niemela (manager, New England Cooperative Wholesale Society, Boston), treasurer.

2. Mentioned as horrible examples were an association in western Pennsylvania that had "enough shoe polish to blacken all the shoes in Pittsburgh for the next 10 years," and one in Illinois the manager of which had bought a whole carload of brooms.

3. As explained by Dr. Warbasse—

"The pine tree is the ancient symbol of endurance, fecundity, and immortality. Those are the qualities that we see in cooperation. In the Egyptian,

Persian, and Indian mythology, the pine tree and its symbol the pine cone, are found typifying life and the perpetuation of life. The hardy pine symbolizes the enduring quality of cooperation. More than one pine is used to represent the mutual cooperation necessary. The trunks of the pine trees are continued into the roots which form a circle. The circle is another ancient symbol of eternal life. It typifies that which has no end. The circle in this picture represents also the world, the all-embracing cosmos, of which cooperation is a part and which depends for its existence upon cooperation. The color of the two pines and the circle is dark green; this is the color of the chlorophyl which is the life principle in nature. The background within the circle is golden yellow, typifying the sun, the giver of light and life." (In **A Short History of the Cooperative League of the USA**, pp. 15, 16.)

4. Mr. Long was a graduate of Union Theological Seminary (New York City) and was a Congregational minister at Epping, N. H. He was beaten up for publicly espousing the cause of striking textile workers in Lawrence, Mass., and was read out of the church. Later he served as manager of the Lawrence textile local, and as organizer for the Amalgamated Textile Workers Union. He was secretary of the Eastern States Cooperative League from 1925 until his death.

5. I.e., **Cooperation**, and **The Home Cooperator**.

6. Appointed to this committee were Prof. (now United States Senator) Paul H. Douglas and Huston Thompson (then a member of the Federal Trade Commission).

7. V. S. Alanne (then secretary of the Northern States Cooperative League) and Colston Warne (then instructor at the University of Chicago and a member of the League board) drew up the courses. Mr. Warne, now professor of economics at Amherst College, has been for many years president of Consumers' Union (a consumer rating agency). He was also author of an excellent study—used extensively in the present history—of the cooperative movement in Illinois, covering the whole period of the American Plan.

8. The deficits had usually been met by contributions from Dr. and Mrs. Warbasse.

CHAPTER 17

1. V. S. Alanne said that most of the credit for initiating the league belonged to Mr. and Mrs. Edward Solem of Minneapolis. Mr. Solem was then general manager of Franklin Cooperative Creamery Association. He later did field work for the league.

2. In 1925 the league office was moved to Minneapolis.

3. The correspondence courses ceased with the dissolution of the league in 1940 but were resumed in 1943, when the Cooperative Correspondence School was organized, under the sponsorship of Central Cooperative Wholesale, Midland Cooperative Wholesale, and Consumers Cooperative Association. A number of other wholesales later became joint sponsors. The school was discontinued upon the departure of Mr. Alanne for Finland in 1949.

4. Mr. Crews, of English ancestry, received his M. A. degree from the University of Wisconsin while working at various jobs in local cooperatives. On the discontinuance of the Northern States Cooperative League in 1940, he joined the staff of Central Cooperative Wholesale, where he served as educational director until July 1945. He then became field educational director for Consumers Cooperative Association (Kansas City), acting in this capacity until 1952, when he took leave to help organize cooperative schools in Burma under the UN technical-assistance program. Returning from that country in 1954, he joined the staff of the Michigan State Credit Union League.

CHAPTER 18

1. Mr. Ronn, brilliant and exceptionally witty, was born in Finland February 16, 1894 and was brought to the United States by his parents at the age of 7. Family poverty forced him to discontinue formal education after 1 year of high school, but later he had a year in business college. Local industrial employment, blacklisting by one of the mining companies because of activity in the Socialist Party, several years with the Finnish paper, **Työmies**, and service in World War I preceded his employment in the Cooperative Exchange. He began there as bookkeeper, then served successively as head of the accounting department, sales manager, and finally, in July 1922, as general manager—a position he held until his sudden death in 1931. He had been a Cooperative League director since 1925.

Dr. Warbasse, in a tribute to him after his death, declared him to have been a "magnanimous opponent."

2. Dr. Warbasse wrote in his private notes that—

"Communism does not belong in the realm of economics; it is a religious problem and only when viewed as such can it be understood. The Communist method of thought is not influenced by cold facts. Anyone who has attempted to present facts to the Communist mind knows this to be true."

3. The differences carried over into the international field. Delegates to the International Cooperative Congress of 1927 were Matti Tenhunen, Eskel Ronn, Cedric Long, and Dr. Warbasse. The first two spoke at the congress favoring the Russian position. Later Dr. Warbasse wrote to the International Cooperative Alliance, saying that they did not represent the sentiments of the majority of cooperators here, and again (early in 1928) that it was time that the Alliance "purge itself" of the associations under communist influence. Secretary May replied that he agreed, but that at present there were within the ICA membership too many apologists for the Russians for this to be possible.

4. Among the League directors, 12 were for and 4 against the measure.

5. Thus, **Justice** (organ of the International Ladies' Garment Workers' Union) commented that the restaurant was more than a Communist eating place. "It was the most important part of the American Communist movement," and was always surrounded by a crowd of "Communist loafers, ready for demonstrations." The **Garment Worker** (paper of the United Garment Workers' Union) pointed out that at the restaurant it was permissible either to pay or not to pay for meals. The Reds blamed its failure, however, on "hostile business interests," which the paper identified as butchers, bakers, and grocers who demanded pay for the commodities they had supplied the association. Noting that the latter had failed for $100,000, the **Garment Worker** observed that it was "a sizable bust for a purely utilitarian outfit."

6. "**Työmies**" is Finnish for "workingmen."

7. The Communist International even sent a cablegram to the CCE board, trying to induce it to reverse its decision. According to the **Builder** (October 1, 1953), two expellees, Tenhunen and Corgan, later went to Russia and were "purged" there a few years afterwards; nothing had been heard of them since.

During the course of a spot study for the U. S. Bureau of Labor Statistics in 1937, the present writer was told, by the manager of an association having a number of members who had made this pilgrimage, that most of them returned in a year or two, chastened and thoroughly disillusioned. Independent-minded Finns that they were, the regimentation, terrorization, and general "pushing around" that they observed and experienced combined to open their eyes to the real situation. They were, by 1937, among the most loyal and convinced cooperators in the CCW area, the manager said.

8. The **Cooperative News Service** reported years later, in a review of the 1930 situation, that it was Otto Kuusinen, selected by Russia as the head of a proposed puppet government for Finland (and later Soviet Commissar in Porkkala) who directed the Communist moves. Although he was head of the Communist Party for Finland, he was then living in Russia. During the summer of 1930, the account said, he sent his wife and K. Manner to Superior, with credentials from the Commintern, to take control of the CCE for the Party.

9. The wholesale's board of directors had drawn up a statement of the whole situation, which they intended to carry in both **Työmies** and the **Cooperative Builder.** The former refused to print it, and the Communists even tried to burn the edition of the **Builder** that contained the article (the **Builder** was then being printed in the **Työmies** plant). By chance the loyal faction learned of the attempt in time to save part of the edition. In retaliation, cooperators who supported the wholesale were expelled from the Communist Party, and the latter and its members then entered upon a campaign of vilification that the **Builder** said was "unparalleled in its viciousness and terroristic methods." **Työmies** was later expelled from membership in the wholesale.

10. "Workers and Farmers" was later dropped from the name.

11. This figure is questionable, as there were never more than 25 Communist-dominated associations in the area.

12. In mid-1933 the CCW Cooperative Youth League was approached by representatives of the Young Communists League with a view to a "united front." The Youth League replied that it stood for the protection and furtherance of the consumers' cooperative movement. In this respect it had found—"and still finds"—that the YCL and its parent body, the Communist Party, were "violent and unscrupulous enemies." The Communists were reminded that the YCL had publicly declared its intention to destroy the CYL. The latter's officers therefore said bluntly that they did not consider the YCL proposal as having been made in good faith.

13. At the same board meeting five delegates were selected to represent the Cooperative League at the 1948 International Cooperative Congress at Prague, Czechoslovakia. The board voted that, if a Russian-controlled president were elected for the International Cooperative Alliance, the League would withdraw from membership and announce it to the world. This did not happen, however; the president continued to be an Englishman, opposed to Communism.

CHAPTER 19

1. Formerly representative of the International Association of Machinists

and vice president of Consumers' Research.

2. U. S. Bureau of Labor Statistics Bulletin No. 659, p. 25.

3. I.e., from church groups, from the speaking tour made by Toyohiko Kagawa (a Japanese Christian, active in the cooperative movement there), from accounts of cooperatives in Antigonish, Nova Scotia, and from a number of books published here and abroad dealing with cooperation.

4. In its 27 years of operation (through 1954) the Community Cooperative Oil Co., in Marcus, Iowa, has returned nearly a million dollars on patronage. What this has meant to the well-being of this town of some 1,300 people can be imagined. The Cooperative Oil Co. of Alma, Nebr., has made refunds every year between 1925 and 1953, to a total of over $550,000. Savings of the Kanabec County Cooperative Oil Association (Mora, Minn.) from 1927 through 1952 exceeded $650,000.

Even in 1954, the Farmers Union Oil Association of St. Paul, Nebr., returned 15 percent on patronage. The cash refunds of the Cooperative Oil Co. of Olmstead County (Rochester, Minn.) for 1952 totaled $100,294; its cash returns on patronage from the time of its formation in 1930 through 1953 totaled $1,196,644. Another Minnesota organization, Lyon County Cooperative Oil Co., at Marshall, through 1954 has returned $924,598 in cash on patronage since its formation in 1924.

Undoubtedly other oil cooperatives could duplicate or approach these records.

5. One interesting feature of the California study was the finding that the cooperators of the period were "not itinerants or foreigners." Nearly half had lived in the State for over 20 years and over nine-tenths for over 5 years. Three-tenths had been born on the Pacific Coast. Such foreign-born members as there were had come chiefly from England, Denmark, or Sweden.

6. Among the consumers' cooperatives presently active in the State, only four were formed prior to 1930—the grocery stores at Fort Bragg and Madera (organized in 1923 and 1927, respectively), the students' bookstore at Stanford University (1897), and the Olivita Mutual Water Co. at Los Angeles (1915). But two of the present California store cooperatives—at Berkeley and Palo Alto—are in the big-business group of nonfarm cooperatives. In 1955 the latter had sales of $4.6 million and 3,741 members.

7. A typical arrangement was one made by the Unemployed Exchange Association (known locally as the UXA): Members contributed labor in tearing down a building, receiving from the owner (as compensation) building materials salvaged in the wrecking operation. Using these materials, they then built a barn for a nearby farmer. He paid them with live hogs. Various odd jobs for the owner of a local slaughterhouse paid for cutting the meat and smoking hams.

8. **Monthly Labor Review** (Washington, U. S. Bureau of Labor Statistics), June 1933, p. 1240.

9. Butter or margarine was almost never available and was not expected. The worst privation mentioned to investigators in a Government study was lack of salt. This was brought home to the present writer at a Sunday dinner to which she was invited in Los Angeles. The food consisted of carrots, beets, and string beans—all cooked without seasoning. Dessert was a small cull apple apiece. Carrots, it seemed, were nearly always available, and the members said emphatically that they had already had enough carrots to last them a lifetime.

10. The production units were hampered by regulations prohibiting sale of products on the open market (in competition with established business), by the consequent inability to obtain funds for additional raw materials, and by being restricted to the production of a single (almost always "seasonal") commodity. Thus, if they became efficient, as one observer remarked, "they had a surplus of one commodity, with the problem of marketing it—just the disease that was afflicting the commercial system." (Edna Lonigan, quoted in U. S. Bureau of Labor Statistics Serial No. R. 1045, p. 2.)

11. Among its officers were O. Ulrey (professor at Michigan State College, well known for his encouragement of student cooperatives), treasurer, and David E. Sonquist (later director of Circle Pines Camp), director of education and organization. Glenn S. Kies was manager.

CHAPTER 20

1. The Bureau had been interested in cooperation for many years. Its first report on cooperatives was **Cooperative Distribution**, by Edward W. Bemis, issued in 1896 as its Bulletin No. 6.

2. The bulletin was based, originally, on a pamphlet issued by the Cooperative League of the USA. Later revisions incorporated many changes based on ensuing cooperative experience and the suggestions of cooperative leaders. Its latest revision is its Bulletin No. 1024.

3. Up to June 30, 1937, slightly over three-fourths (76.8 percent) of the total projects for which loans were approved were for cooperative associations, 10.6 percent for nonprofit organizations, 7.4

percent for public power bodies, and 5.2 percent for private profit corporations.

4. In 1940 the REA technical service included guidance in organization; assistance in selection of competent technical key personnel, in preparation of plans and specifications for line construction, in securing reasonable wholesale power rates, and in determining feasible retail rates; engineering supervision; short training courses for project superintendents, managers, and bookkeepers; negotiations for quantity prices on certain types of supplies and equipment; utilization demonstrations; and issuance of leaflets and bulletins acquainting farmers with electrical uses and giving advice on a host of operating problems.

5. Person, H. S. "The Rural Electrification Administration in Perspective." (In **Agricultural History**, April 1950, p. 75.)

6. These towns were Greenbelt, Md., Greenhills, Ohio, and Greendale, Wis. Their purpose was threefold: (1) to give employment to unemployed who were on relief, (2) to demonstrate the soundness of planning and operating towns in accordance with certain garden-city principles, and (3) to provide low-rent housing in good physical and social environment, for low-income families.

7. This figure includes some classified by FSA as "communities," some or all of the family units of which were of the subsistence type.

8. For account of this and their later enterprise (National Farm Machinery Cooperative), see Chapter 25.

9. Farm Bureau Cooperative Associations of Indiana, Ohio, and Pennsylvania. Consumers Cooperative Association, Central Cooperative Wholesale, Eastern Cooperative Wholesale, and Utah Cooperative Association.

10. Some of the surviving associations have made later reports to the Farm Credit Administration or the Bureau of Labor Statistics, but these agencies' figures do not give FSA cooperatives separately.

11. The grocery store and tearoom at Jersey Homesteads lasted until just after the end of World War II. The cooperative at Palmerdale, Ala. (organized in 1936) dissolved in 1947, that at Penderlea (Willard, N. C.) in 1949 and that at Hermantown (near Duluth, Minn.) in mid-1953. Among the resettlement projects for rural people, of those known to have had consumer aspects for which data are available, two went out of business in 1944, five in 1945, three in 1946, eight in 1947, five in 1948, and one each in 1949 and 1950.

12. Among them were the cooperative at Mt. Olive, Ala. (organized in 1937), that at Lakeview, Ark. (but doing cotton marketing only), and the Northern Farmers Exchange at Williams, Minn. (marketing grain and purchasing farm supplies).

Among the strictly consumers' cooperatives known to be still active, the year of formation and the year of their latest report to the Government are as follows: Gee's Bend Cooperative Association, Alberta, Ala. (1933) reported 1950; Dyess (Ark.) Cooperative Store Association (1941) reported 1950-51; Mileston (Miss.) Cooperative Association (1940) reported March 1953; and Tillery (N. C.) Community Cooperative Association (1937) reported 1947. Of these four, all but the Dyess cooperative are of Negro membership.

13. Samuel Ashelman, general manager since December 1945, is a graduate of Swarthmore College, who studied cooperatives in Sweden and Denmark. Previous to coming to Greenbelt, he had been a field man with the Tennessee Valley Authority, manager of the Swarthmore cooperative 1938-40, field man for Eastern Cooperative Wholesale 1941-42, and manager of its Philadelphia warehouse from April 1943 to 1945.

Early managers of Greenbelt included Sulo Laakso, Thomas B. Ricker, and George E. Hodsdon.

In 1955 sales rose to $8,916,000 and patronage refunds were expected to reach $106,000.

14. Cooley Committee report (House of Representatives Committee on Agriculture: **Activities of the Farm Security Administration**), p. 1031.

15. The farm-security program was begun in 1933 under the Federal Emergency Relief Administration and the Subsistence Homesteads Division of the Department of the Interior. The duties of these two agencies were transferred to the Resettlement Administration when that body was created by Executive order in 1935, and its duties were in turn shifted to the Farm Security Administration on the latter's creation in 1937. The FSA was abolished in August 1946 and its functions were transferred to the Farmers Home Administration.

CHAPTER 21

1. Mr. Evans was previously professor at Columbia University; later for some years, vice president (for personnel) of the Ohio Farm Bureau Insurance Cos., and now general manager of the Peoples Broadcasting Corporation. Other directors were Roy F. Bergengren (then executive director of the Credit Union National Association), Howard A. Cowden (president, and general manager of Consumers Cooperative Association), James Drury (professor of Marketing, New York University), Mur-

ray D. Lincoln (then secretary of the Ohio Farm Bureau Federation), and Dr. James P. Warbasse.

2. Percy Brown succeeded Mr. Garrison as executive director.

3. The original name, E. A. Filene Cooperative Department Store, was changed because of opposition by the E. A. Filene Sons Department Store of Boston.

4. Hiring a general manager whose experience was in drugs, not in department-store merchandise; extreme overbuying of initial inventory in anticipation of large volume, resulting in unsalable goods; and hiring (on the basis of a single recommendation, of doubtful authenticity) an unsuitable store manager.

5. According to President Wall, "CDC has maintained final authority on all important decisions, it has imposed an iron-clad management contract which insures its control during the 20-year period of the store's lease, and it has insisted both on a substantial vote in the affairs of the co-op and on representation on the co-op's board of directors." (CDC had one vote for each of its $100 shares; local members had one vote each regardless of the number of shares they owned.)

6. The store manager was absent because of illness and the general manager, though present, refused to give the report because of anger over the president's charges.

7. This proved to have been ill-advised, for soon afterwards the purchaser went bankrupt, and it was reported that CDC would finally get only about 30 cents on the dollar. The store was closed and the fixtures sold in the fall of 1955.

8. Letter to author from Miss B. W. Connors (vice president and assistant treasurer of CDC), August 4, 1955.

CHAPTER 23

1. Cooperative League of the USA, Group Health Federation, National Committee on Student Cooperatives, National Women's Cooperative Guild, and Credit Union National Association.

2. The Illinois Farm Supply Co. (which had favored a farmers' organization, under agricultural law) and the Nebraska Cooperative Oil Association did not join.

3. Mr. Hull, a graduate in law of Northwestern University, later became a farmer, served two terms in the Indiana Legislature, and joined the Indiana Farm Bureau in 1926 as manager of the purchasing department. He was general manager of its successor, Indiana Farm Bureau Cooperative Association, from 1927 until July 1946, when he became its president. He served as president of National Cooperatives, Inc., until September 1946. Since his retirement he has written a book, **Built of Men,** describing the development of the Indiana Farm Bureau Cooperative Association.

4. As the member wholesales went into the production of petroleum, grease, and lubricating oil, National's business in them gradually ceased.

5. Mr. Tenhune was born in Michigan in 1907. He was employed as a grocery field man for CCW in 1928, served in its grocery-buying department in 1929, was advertising and circulation manager of the Cooperative Publishing Association from 1930 to 1932, became head buyer of CCW's clothing department in 1933 and chief buyer for the wholesale from 1937-41.

6. Consumers Cooperatives Associated (Texas) and Pacific Supply Cooperative (Washington) had been admitted into membership in 1934; Eastern Cooperative Wholesale (New York) in 1936; The Cooperative Wholesale (Illinois) and United Farmers Cooperative Co. (Ontario) in 1937; the Farm Bureau Wholesales of Indiana, Michigan, Ohio, and Pennsylvania in 1939 (when United Cooperatives—formerly named Farm Bureau Oil Co.—of which they were members, withdrew); Farmers Cooperative Exchange (North Carolina) and Saskatchewan Cooperative Wholesale Society in 1940; and Associated Cooperatives of Northern California in 1941.

7. Letter to author from Erick Kendall, publications director of Cooperative Publishing Association, December 18, 1953.

8. Letter to author from M. D. Zeddies, general counsel, Midland Cooperatives, Inc., November 25, 1953.

9. National's directors adopted on December 20, 1944, a statement of policy on labeling that read in part as follows:

"National Cooperatives will at all times present the consumer's (the user's) point of view—giving accurate, honest and, where practical, complete specifications on the label. When in the user's interest, we shall give the limitations as well as the advantages of a given product. (Cooperatives, being owned and controlled by the member-patrons, are the only merchandisers who can speak in their behalf.)"

10. This group included (1) the Farmers Union Wholesale Cooperative formed by the wholesales of Iowa, Kansas, Minnesota, Nebraska, and South Dakota; (2) Farm Bureau Services, organized in Ohio to carry on a mail-order service in household items, which was discontinued in 1941 because of insufficient volume; (3) Northwest Cooperative Society, Montana, which went out of business in 1942, when the Farmers Union Central Exchange undertook to

serve its members; and (4) Ohio Cooperative Grocery Wholesale, organized by Central States Cooperatives and the Ohio Farm Bureau wholesale, to supply the retail cooperatives in Ohio, which because of war conditions never went into operation.

11. These figures do not include wholesales not in the consumer field, some of which do an extremely large business.

12. The largest are Range Cooperative Federation (with a volume of $2,574,000 in 1954), Fox Cooperative, Inc. ($1,411,000 in 1951), and Trico Cooperative Oil Association ($611,000 in 1953-54).

13. This number included the members of the Farmers Union State Exchange (Omaha), which had joined in 1931 and in whose territory there was no district league.

14. Mr. Cooley, a native of Vermont, had been a member of Consumers Cooperative Services (New York City) and chairman of its publicity committee. From 1932 to mid-1933 he was secretary of the Cooperative League. Thereafter, until July 1935 he was editor of **Cooperative Consumer** (organ of Consumers Cooperative Association, Kansas City), then becoming editor of **Cooperative Builder** until he resigned to join the staff of the Indiana Farm Bureau Cooperative Association where he is its radio and publicity director.

15. Mr. Bowen, a native of Iowa, and graduate of Cornell College in that State, had previously been in private business as vice president in charge of sales in a farm-machinery company and later as owner of a machinery business. Dissatisfied with conditions of profit industry, he became a convert to cooperation through his reading of economics and cooperative literature.

16. Mr. Lincoln organized one of the first cooperative milk-distributing plants in New England in 1916. He was executive secretary of the Ohio Farm Bureau Federation from 1920 until late in 1948. He assisted in the organization of the wholesale, Farm Bureau Cooperative Association (acting as its executive vice president until 1948), and of the three Farm Bureau Insurance Cos., of which he is still president. He was appointed as a United States representative at the United Nations Conference of Food and Agriculture in 1943, and in 1946 on the President's Commission on Higher Education and also as consultant to the UN Economic and Social Council. He has been a Cooperative League director since 1934 and its president since 1941. He has also served as president of CARE (Cooperative for American Remittances Everywhere) since its formation in 1945.

17. But not, it will be noted, **in their capacity as consumers.**

18. Previously newspaperman, secretary to Senator James Couzens of Michigan, and Consumers' Counsel in the Federal Bituminous Coal Commission. He resigned from the League secretaryship in 1949, to become a member of the Federal Trade Commission. He was again designated for the Commission by President Truman, in 1952, but the new Republican Administration withdrew his nomination.

19. He served on the board for several years thereafter and has continued to write on cooperative subjects. His autobiography, **Three Voyages**, was published by the League in the Spring of 1956.

CHAPTER 24

1. In 1944, Cooperative Distributors and Consumers' Book Cooperative, both mail-order associations, were forced out of business by manpower and supply difficulties.

2. At Poston and Rivers, Ariz., Rohwer, Ark., Tule Lake (Newell) and Manzanar, Calif., Amache, Colo., Hunt, Idaho, Topaz, Utah, and Heart Mountain, Wyo.

3. In charge of all was Otto Rossman, head of the Business Enterprises Section of the War Relocation Administration. Mr. Rossman, a veteran cooperator, had previously managed cooperative stores in the Lake Superior area, and Washington, D. C., and served on the staff of Central Cooperative Wholesale.

4. Mr. Campbell, born in Montana in 1910, is a graduate of the University of Oregon, with B.S. and M.S. degrees. He joined the staff of the League in 1934 as assistant to General Secretary Bowen. He served as editor of the **Cooperative News Service** from 1935 through 1945, and was director of the League's New York office from 1939 through 1945, and again in 1948. For 2 years (1946 and 1947) he was publicity director for National Cooperatives. Since 1949 he has been director of the Washington office, besides acting as head of the League's public-relations department.

Mr. Campbell represented the Cooperative League at the founding of the United Nations in San Francisco in 1945 and represented the International Cooperative Alliance at the sessions of the UN Economic and Social Council, 1946-49.

He is author of **Here is Tomorrow;** co-author (with Jerry Voorhis) of **The Morale of Democracy** and (with Richard Giles) of **Helping People to Help Themselves.**

CHAPTER 25

1. This was a new departure for National, which had never before made a direct contribution to the League's educational work. It represented a compromise between the viewpoints of the consumer-minded and producer-minded directors of National.

As to this, **The Cooperator** (New York, Eastern Cooperatives, Inc.) said in its issue of June 9, 1947:

"Several observations are in order: first, the boards of League and National might ask themselves if they are completely sensitive to the will of the broad membership they represent; second, there could be better understanding whether the businesses we are building are ends in themselves, or sinews for extending the cooperative idea; and third, there is obvious need for patience. Not until we agree on the direction we want to go and the worthwhileness of going there will we really have a **movement.**"

2. According to **Midland Cooperator.** (Minneapolis, Midland Cooperative Wholesale), July 28, 1948, National's problems were centered in "two vital questions":

"1. Do the representatives of regional cooperatives serving on the board really want a strong National?

"2. Do they want it enough to surrender some of the regional sovereignty if necessary?

"Evidence is growing that the answer to these questions is sufficiently in the negative to explain most of the troubles over the past 10 years."

The paper said that there had been much talk about the desirability of unity, but the members were not willing to pay the price.

3. Records of the U. S. Bureau of Labor Statistics show that in the 27-year period, 1925-51, the regional and district wholesales reporting had returned in patronage refunds the sum of $105,840,839. The record of some of the regionals is shown below:

	Period	Refunds
Associated Cooperatives (California)	1939-51	$ 41,472
Central States Cooperatives (Illinois)	1937-51	51,643
Farmers Union Central Exchange (Minnesota)	1931-51	18,311,635
Midland Cooperative Wholesale (Minnesota)	1927-52	6,770,751
Consumers Cooperative Association (Missouri)	1929-51	18,601,521
Eastern Cooperatives, Inc. (New Jersey)	1934-51	192,866
Pennsylvania Farm Bureau Cooperative Assn.	1934-51	2,136,112
Central Cooperative Wholesale (Wisconsin)	1917-51	2,248,190
Indiana Farm Bureau Cooperative Association	1934-51	18,440,996
Farm Bureau Cooperative Association (Ohio)	1935-51	7,066,096

4. Farmers Union Central Exchange (1949), Midland Cooperative Wholesale (1952), and Consumers Cooperative Association (1952). Grange Cooperative Wholesale (Seattle) not affiliated with National, quit handling groceries in 1946.

Thus at present the only regional wholesales handling groceries are the following: Associated Cooperatives (California), Central States Cooperatives (Illinois), Eastern Cooperatives, Inc. (New Jersey), Central Cooperative Wholesale (Wisconsin), Farmers Union State Exchange (Nebraska), and Producers Grocery Co. (Missouri). All but the last-named are members of National.

Defection of the wholesales left their grocery members without a source of co-op label groceries. Some of them have since made arrangements for service: 15 cooperatives in the southern Wisconsin territory of Midland are now being served by Central States, and Central Cooperative Wholesale is now supplying CCA's affiliates in the Dakotas.

5. The remaining operating capital consisted of undistributed patronage refunds paid (in the form of preferred stock) during its 20 years of operation.

6. In 1951, 38 retail cooperatives reported manufactures to the total of $11,157,000 (but the greater part was ice cream made in the plant of Franklin Cooperative Creamery Association, Minneapolis).

7. Notably the representatives from Michigan and Washington State.

8. Central States Cooperatives, Midland Cooperative Wholesale, Farm Bureau Cooperative Association (Ohio), Central Cooperative Wholesale, and Eastern Cooperatives, Inc.

9. American Cooperatives, Inc., formed in 1938, was part of the program to provide employment for stranded coal miners at the Arthurdale (W. Va.) subsistence-homesteads project.

The members of American Cooperatives were four regional wholesales—Indiana Farm Bureau Cooperative Association, Farm Bureau Services (Michigan), Farmers Union Central Exchange, and Consumers Cooperative Association—that had previously obtained tractors under a cost-plus contract with a private manufacturer at Battle Creek, Mich. (the first co-op tractor was demonstrated in 1935).

10. In 1953, the Kansas State authorities imposed a 10-day shutdown on the 30,000 producing wells there, for this reason.

11. In some cases cooperators have unwittingly bought facilities that were already becoming outmoded by new technical advances. The first cooperative refineries were acquired with the sole thought of getting supplies for the members. Sufficient consideration was therefore not given to such fundamentals as good location, freight differentials, transportation facilities, technical requirements, and supply of crude oil. As a result, a few oil properties were poorly located, and too far away from their cooperative markets to be economically feasible, and had to be sold.

12. In the same year the League's Accounting Bureau went out of existence, with the withdrawal of its director, Werni Regli, for reasons of health. But two of its staff—the Englander brothers—have continued (as a private firm) to serve cooperative associations all over the East.

13. Mr. Voorhis was born in Ottawa, Kans., in 1901. He attended public schools in six States of the Midwest, graduated from Yale in 1923, received his M.A. degree from Claremont College (California) in education in 1928 and an honorary LL.D. from St. Francis Xavier University in 1953. His employment record is wide, including service as a factory worker, freight handler, European representative of the YMCA, teacher at Allendale Farm School, Lake Villa, Ill., director of the Episcopal Home for Boys of the State of Wyoming, headmaster of the Voorhis School for Boys, 1927-38 (the school then becoming a unit of the State education system). He was a member of the U. S. House of Representatives from 1937 to 1947. He is the author of a number of books: **Morale of Democracy** (1941), **Out of Debt, Out of Danger** (1943), **Beyond Victory** (1944), **Confessions of a Congressman** (1947) and **The Christian in Politics** (1951).

CHAPTER 26

1. Landis, Benson Y.: "Schools in Economic Democracy." (In **Journal of Adult Education**, April 1939.)

2. H. Haines Turner (1937-38), Margaret Gerber (1938-42), Robert St. Clair (1942-43), Helmuth Kern (1943-46), and Walter Volckhausen. Mr. Volckhausen (1947-55) had previously been, in succession, a mathematics instructor at the University of Maryland and business manager of Group Health Association of Washington, D. C. He was chairman of the organizing committee and the first president of Greenbelt Consumer Services.

Upon his resignation, to become assistant general manager of the Peninsula Cooperative at Hampton, Va., Mrs. Kathleen Nash became acting secretary.

3. Soon after the formation, early in 1955, of the Pan American Cooperative (by employees of the Pan American Union), to sell handicraft articles from Central and South America, it also joined the federation.

4. Mr. Perkins was a graduate of the Cooperative College at Manchester, England, and after graduation had continued his studies at Nancy, France. After leaving Rochdale Institute in 1944, Mr. Perkins was in the Relocation Camp program, then in relief work for UNNRA and IRO. In 1951 he was a member of a CARE team in Yugoslavia.

5. Incorporators (as well as the first board of trustees) were the following:
Prof. Arthur E. Albrecht, College of the City of New York.
LeRoy E. Bowman, United Parents Association.
Winslow Carlton, Group Health Cooperative, New York City.
Prof. James Drury, New York University.
E. Stanley Grant, businessman of Phillipsburg, N. J.
Alvin S. Johnson, New School for Social Research.
Horace M. Kallen, New School for Social Research.
Robert L. Smith, Eastern Cooperative League.
James P. Warbasse, Cooperative League of the USA.

6. Although Rochdale Institute had been among the sponsors, during the 4 years the Council was in existence some coldness developed between the Council and the Institute. The latter, first in the field, believed that the Council was overlapping on and gradually usurping its place as educational institution. The Council thought that the Institute's courses were too theoretical.

7. Winemiller, William G.: "Ohio's Cooperative Education Program." (In **Consumers' Cooperation**, New York, December 1937, p. 183.)

8. In 1950 a separate organization, Cooperative Institute Association, was formed to carry on the work. The regional wholesale contributed $500 for a revolving fund and other organizations, notably the Farm Bureau Insurance Cos., also donated significant amounts. Membership is open to both cooperatives and individuals.

9. Among the cooperatives having women managers, that have come to my attention, are those listed below. There are undoubtedly many others.

Garden City (Kans.) Equity Exchange (marketing association, also handling fuel and farm supplies). Manager, building-supplies department: Mrs. Wanda Gercken.

Rolla (Kans.) Cooperative Association (operating a food store, locker plant, and service station). Manager, food store: Elva (Mrs. Carl) Taylor.

Farmers Union Cooperative Association, Vliets, Kans. (grain-marketing association, also handling petroleum products, feed, and farm supplies). Manager: Mrs. Bernice Turnbull.

Andover (Mass.) Cooperative Association (food store). Manager: Mary Angus.

Farmers Co-op Co., Wright, Minn. (store handling food, hardware, clothing, petroleum products, and farm supplies; also cafeteria). Manager: Ellen C. Peterson.

Farmers Union Store, Reeder, N. Dak. Manager: Mrs. Amy Nichols.

Greenwood (Wis.) Cooperative Association (supply cooperative with departments for petroleum products, farm supplies, electrical and farm appliances, hardware, and farm machinery). Manager, appliance and farm-supply department: Mrs. Bernice Clayton.

Kendall (Wis.) Cooperative Services (food store). Manager: Elsie Kiel.

The 1953 president of one of the largest urban consumers' cooperatives in the country, Consumers Cooperative Society of Palo Alto, Calif. (operating two supermarkets, cleaning establishment, gasoline station, and cold-storage plant) was also a woman—Mrs. Dorothy Varian. In mid-1955 Mrs. Hilde Burnbaum was elected president of Group Health Cooperative of Puget Sound, at Seattle, Wash.; and Mrs. Vivian Fikus is president of the Nutley (N. J.) Consumers Cooperative.

10. After the men began to be admitted in numbers, "and Clubs" was added to the guild's name, and the word "women" was deleted. The present name is therefore Northern States Cooperative Guilds and Clubs.

11. Now on the staff of the Colorado Credit Union League. She was succeeded by Esther Benson who served in 1934-35. Later secretaries have been Ida Lauri, (1935-36), Maiju Nurmi (1936-39), Helmi Lake (1939-42), and Ida Lauri (1942-52).

12. Among them are the National Conference on Citizenship, the Adult Education Association, the American Association for the United Nations, and the National Committee for the UN. Also, the executive director reported: "We support and contribute to the Future Farmers of America and the American Country Life Association and attend their national meetings. We support the Crusade for Freedom and Radio Free Europe. We cooperate with the Foreign Operations Administration in many ways. The League is a member of the Film Council of America and Mr. Beall [League director of educational services] is active in its work" (Proceedings of 1942 Cooperative Congress, p. 25).

Wallace Campbell (director of the League's Washington office) is a member of the executive committee of the United States Council for UNESCO and for the Food and Agriculture Organization.

The League has received citations for "outstanding service to the cause of freedom and democracy" from the U. S. Foreign Operations Administration, National Committee for Educational Television, and the Crusade for Freedom.

13. This could be credited to the efforts of the late Ethel Fair of Boston, who was secretary of the federation. A teacher by profession and active in the teachers' union, Miss Fair became interested in cooperation during the depression. She helped to organize the Atlantic Lobstermen's Cooperative. She died early in 1953.

14. A number of plays with cooperative themes have been written for or by and sponsored by the Northern States Cooperative Guilds and Clubs, Central States Cooperative League, Cooperative League of the USA, and others, and an original play, "Day of Faith," was recently presented at the annual meeting of the Michigan Credit Union League.

15. Among them are the camp on the Brule River in Wisconsin, in operation for 25 years, Circle Pines Camp in Michigan, in existence since 1937, the Perch Lake camp in Minnesota, and the Rapidan River camp in Virginia (formerly part of the camp used as a holiday retreat by President Hoover and his cabinet).

16. These include one in Illinois, one at Estes Park (Colorado), and one in the high Sierras in California.

17. Wallace J. Campbell, director of the League's Washington office, is president of the American Travel Association.

18. **Consumers' Cooperation** from January 1935 through 1943. It had previously had two other names—**Cooperative Consumer** (1916-18) and **Cooperation** (January 1919 through 1934).

19. Among the recent League publications are the following:

History of Cooperation, by Emory S. Bogardus.

Your Co-op on a Sound Financial Basis.

Here's How to Tell Your Tax Story (a kit).

So Naturally I Buy at the Co-op.

Cooperatives in the United States.

1954 Co-op Yearbook.

The Cooperative Road to Abundance, by E. R. Bowen.

Guide to Modern Management for Cooperatives.

20. The other is **Midland Cooperator** (Minneapolis, Midland Cooperatives, Inc.).

21. As early as 1939 the Cooperative League and the Harmon Foundation jointly produced a film entitled: **The Lord Helps Those Who Help Each Other.** Films currently in use include the following (in color, unless otherwise indicated):

Produced for the Cooperative League—

Where People Count—documentary report on various types of cooperatives with emphasis on the role of individual cooperators in building them.
What is a Co-op? (Black and white.)
A Trip to Cooperative Europe.
There Were Three Men.
The Goolibah Tree—puppet film for children.
Owners All—cooperatives in Nova Scotia.

Produced for Credit Union National Association—

King's X—how the credit union helps to solve the financial problems of a family. (Black and white.)

Produced for Consumers Cooperative Association—

Forest to Farm—operations of the regional's lumber mill at Swisshome, Oreg.
Beyond the Land—cooperative ownership of "off the farm" facilities.

Produced for Indiana Farm Bureau Cooperative Association—

The Power of Neighbors—development of Indiana cooperatives, especially in the petroleum industry.

Produced for CARE—

To Help Themselves—work of CARE in underdeveloped countries.

22. During "Co-op Week" two major networks and the local stations in Sheboygan and Milwaukee, Wis., refused to sell time for cooperative programs on the ground that they were "too critical of private business' or "too controversial." This provoked a storm of criticism and the introduction of a resolution in the United States Senate calling for an investigation. The networks finally agreed to allow the cooperative broadcasts, provided they contained no criticism of other business or systems of distribution and provided the discussions of cooperative philosophy were confined to "sustaining time" agreed to by the individual stations over which the program was broadcast.

23. It was operated by Cooperative Broadcasting Association, the members of which were the local cooperatives and nonprofit organizations in the area. The station won a number of prizes for its programs. It began with two strikes on it, however. With only an FM channel, it immediately ran into the slump that ensued when television appeared, usurping the commanding place that had been anticipated for FM. Unable to finance an AM channel, it was never able to attract sufficient advertising to get on its feet. It went off the air on October 8, 1954.

24. Quoted in **Nebraska Cooperator** (Omaha, Nebr.), November 1953.

25. Ironically, the latter are sometimes not even aware of the anomalous position that they take. Thus, the manager of one department of a regional wholesale continually admonishes the local associations to "loyally" patronize the wholesale and channel all their purchases through it. Yet, although the wholesale is a member of National Cooperatives, this same manager does not buy his supplies through it nor carry co-op label groceries! In other words, he is asking for a loyalty that his own actions do not warrant.

26. I agree with J. W. Koski (general manager of Central Cooperative Wholesale) who pointed out that they "are our cheapest and best regular salesmen, both of the merchandise and of the philosophy of our people's business." (**Cooperative Builder**, December 10, 1953.)

CHAPTER 27

1. Under the National Housing Act these cooperatives are called "management type" associations.

2. Under the National Housing Act such organizations are known as "sales type" associations.

3. Northern States Cooperative League **Yearbook**, 1928, p. 259.
The League noted also that the "big, profiteering real estate operators" had begun to exploit the cooperative idea for their own advantage. To them it was simply another sales device, under which to unload their holdings at a good profit. Hundreds of such so-called cooperative apartment houses were reported in the fashionable sections of New York City and as far west as Los Angeles.

4. The union acted as guarantor for the first buildings, agreeing to make good any losses incurred. As the association was successful from the first, the union was never called upon to fulfill its pledge. The mere fact of its support, however, undoubtedly eased financing and other problems.

5. The genuine cooperatives compared favorably, however, with the "plush," so-called cooperatives in the wealthy sections of New York City, which failed almost without exception in the years following the 1929 stock-market crash.

6. Two mutuals were composed entirely of Negroes. One of them—

George Washington Carver Mutual Homes, in Arlington, Va.—has attained what may well be a unique record: it has had no turnover in membership among the 44 dwelling owners in the 5 years it has operated the project.

7. They were later partially reimposed.

8. Some "phony" organizations also made their appearance. In these cases, apartment occupiers were suddenly confronted with a choice of buying their units as part of a so-called "cooperative" at higher monthly rates, or vacating. In view of the tight housing situation, this was really a Hobson's choice. It was also an arrangement for realtors to evade rent ceilings; co-owners could legally set their monthly payments at any figure.

The "cooperatives" were formed by the promoters, provided with officers, and then presented to the tenants as a **fait accompli.** Such arrangements reached such "threatening proportions" that early in 1945 the Office of Price Administration issued regulations limiting the conditions under which tenants might be evicted for refusal to buy.

9. One FHA official (himself at least not antagonistic to cooperatives) attributed the leaders' unwillingness to deal with cooperatives to (1) the delays while matters were referred back to the members for discussion and decision and (2) the ample supply of business available to lenders from other sources under simpler arrangements and at higher rates.

10. See U. S. Bureau of Labor Statistics Bulletin No. 1093 (also issued as HHFA Housing Research Report No. 24), 1952.

11. This official, it was revealed in the Congressional hearings in 1954, accepted money and other favors for himself and his wife from builders whose applications he processed.

12. The Amalgamated group, leader in cooperative housing, has made little use of FHA insurance, partly for this reason. A. E. Kazan, its president, told the 1954 Senate investigating committee that FHA delays caused the corporation to drop the idea of insurance on its 1,688-unit Corlears Hook project.

13. In one extreme case investigated by the author, nearly 3 years went by before FHA finally rejected the application for insurance. Its letter of rejection (seen by this author) gave as reason that "neighborhood influences do not indicate sufficient stability of this location for continuing residential use in accordance with the requirements established by the FHA." The objection to this as a valid reason was that when the initial application was submitted, photographs of the site and the surrounding areas had been furnished, as required. Thus, apparently it had taken the FHA office 3 years (during which this point was never raised, though plenty of others had been) to examine the pictures and decide that the neighborhood was not good enough.

This case was also complicated by race prejudice—the cooperative had several Japanese-American, Nisei, families in membership—by local opposition aroused by a neighboring house owner and by real-estate interests, by threats of physical violence, and by attempts to bribe cooperative officers, as well as by active hostility in the FHA office.

14. In fairness to the FHA, it must be said that it is possible its side of the story may not have been fully given. But that was no fault of the investigators. Each was armed with a letter from the FHA director of the cooperative work, explaining the study and its purpose and bespeaking local FHA assistance. It was the general experience, however, when trying to check cooperators' stories at FHA offices, to receive a brusque brush-off. Officials were "in conference," out of town, or otherwise not available; or they refused information. In one office, the investigator was even told that the information desired was given only to builders or lenders (not to another Government office with which its agency was supposed to be collaborating on a study)! The attitude of the San Francisco officials, however, was in pleasing contrast to that of most FHA personnel.

15. In contrast was the experience in Oklahoma where the head of the district office (an official in the American Legion) gave his active support to Legion-sponsored cooperative housing for returned veterans. So speedy was the action there that by the end of the first year not only had all of the 15 associations obtained FHA insurance but nearly all had one or more dwellings completed, and in one case the whole project (20 houses) had been finished. This shows what would have been possible, had other FHA officials been really interested in cooperative housing.

16. According to FHA, in the builder-sponsored projects—

"The initiative for the project has come from a sponsor builder who organizes the nucleus of a cooperative group and through it submits plans to the FHA with an application for a statement of eligibility. Upon receipt of a statement of eligibility (issued to the cooperative group), the sponsor advertises for the members necessary to complete the cooperative. A mortgage is obtained, the insurance commitment issued, the project is built, and then management and control are assumed by the cooperative group."

FHA has justified its acceptance of builder sponsorship by claiming that it "provides expert skill and know-how in the critical organization, planning, and construction stages." Cooperators point out that these are available on a hire basis (and possibly at less cost, finally) and, besides, Section 213 contemplated the giving of advice by FHA itself in these stages of the project.

16 (a) But because of an increase in fees by FNMA to a point exceeding the FHA maximum, no housing cooperative was able to borrow a dollar of the $50 million authorized.

17. Thus, in the 1954 Congressional hearings, one West Coast builder testified that he had made a profit of nearly $1.3 million on an investment of $15,000 on a "cooperative" housing project. In another case, a 2.5-percent service charge (in addition to FHA interest of 4 percent) was levied for merely handling the financing of half of a Los Angeles builder-sponsored project, this yielding a million-dollar fee.

In at least one case the Government has brought suit to recover the excess profits. An anti-windfall provision in the 1954 act will limit builders' profits on future apartment-house projects to 10 percent.

18. Statement of Harry Held, president of the Bowery Savings Bank of New York City, which has financed a number of genuine cooperative projects.

19. An additional 10,915 units were held by mutual associations; they, however, had not built their projects but had merely bought them from the Government.

20. Some of the insurance organizations are already making such loans and at least one cooperative employee-retirement fund is doing so. Also, some of the labor-union benefit plans are reported to be interested in this kind of investment.

CHAPTER 28

1. In the beginning the chief surgeon, Dr. R. M. Winton, had been accepted as a member of the county medical society without question. Later it disbanded, then reorganized, pointedly omitting Dr. Winton from its membership.

2. Illinois Bureau of Labor Statistics: **Fourth Biennial Report,** 1885-86, pp. 456-460.

3. Increasingly, collective agreements between labor unions and employers are providing for health protection of members (and in some cases for service to their families, on payment of dues). It was estimated in 1953 that about 16 million workers were so covered. They are nonprofit but not cooperative, though some of them are members of the Cooperative Health Federation of America.

Some labor groups are served on a group basis in cooperative clinics. Group Health Cooperative of Puget Sound serves a large number of unionists, and Group Health Association of Washington, D. C. amended its bylaws in order to be able to do so.

4. Born into poverty in Syria, Dr. Shadid was educated in a Protestant missionary school. He came to this country in early manhood. He peddled jewelry and trinkets. He worked his way to a medical degree from John Tarleton College in Texas. Then followed post-graduate work, and a year's study in Europe. He built up a private practice first in Missouri and then in Oklahoma. Observing that half of the illness occurred in the poorest families and that only about 2 percent of the money spent for medical care went for prevention of illness, he gradually came to the conclusion that the answer was consumer-owned medical care. This conclusion he put into practice, with the results shown in this history.

In 1946 Dr. Shadid was elected the first president of the new Cooperative Health Federation of America.

5. The executive board of the Bureau consisted of Dr. Warbasse, president; Kingsley Roberts, M.D., medical director; Martin W. Brown, secretary; and Esther L. Brown, chairman of the advisory council. Other directors were Prof James Drury, New York University; Herbert Evans, Good Will Fund; Robert L. Smith, Eastern Cooperative League; and Abraham J. Isserman, counsel for the Bureau.

6. Alabama, California, Florida, Georgia, Illinois (but a "partial" law was passed in 1951), Iowa, Kansas, Kentucky, Louisiana, Maine, Massachusetts, Michigan, Minnesota, Montana, New Hampshire, New Jersey, New Mexico, North Dakota, Ohio, Pennsylvania, Rhode Island, South Carolina, and Tennessee.

7. American Medical Association. Bureau of Medical Economics: **Medical Service Plans,** p. 10. Chicago, 1943.

8. American Medical Association. Bureau of Medical Economics: **Organized Payments for Medical Services,** p. 35. Chicago, 1939.

9. This, of course, is not a valid objection. Patronage refunds are made only from earnings. Many service organizations deliberately set their charges at a level that suffices merely to cover their expenses, so that they have little if any surplus. In such cases the member actually receives his patronage refunds at the time he purchases the service.

10. American Medical Association. Bureau of Medical Economics: **Medical Service Plans,** p. 143. Chicago, 1943.

11. The 1943 AMA pamphlet dismissed the claim that the people need and desire prepayment plans with the statement (again unproved) that "there is no such public demand for prepayment of medical services as advocates

of private and governmental schemes have claimed" (p. 72).

12. In one case, a medical society opposed a cooperative prepayment plan not even in its own country but in another which lacked medical facilities of any kind and had not a single doctor.

The most recent outbursts against voluntary consumer-sponsored medical care occurred in New York where five county medical societies of Greater New York in 1952 charged the Health Insurance Plan with being a monopoly, and also charged one of its doctors with unethical conduct, in that he benefited by its advertising. The charge was dismissed by the AMA Judicial Council, with the words: "Since HIP may lawfully advertise; since the quality of its advertising is not an issue; and since Landess had nothing to do with the advertising, his conduct does not violate the ethic relating to solicitation and advertising."

An aftermath was the introduction in the 1955 New York Legislature of two bills, both aimed at HIP.

13. "The county medical society is the basic unit of organized medicine in this country. A doctor cannot be a member of either his State medical society or of the American Medical Association unless he has membership in his county society. Such membership is important for more than general professional and social reasons. A large proportion of our hospitals will not appoint a physician to their staff unless he is a member of his medical society. Since a hospital staff connection is important to the professional status and financial success of most physicians and is essential to the practice of surgery, deprivation of membership in his medical society will lessen and in some instances largely destroy his livelihood. Again, a physician who wishes to obtain recognition as a specialist from one of the national accrediting boards will not even be considered unless he is an AMA member." (Committee on Research in Medical Economics: **Restrictions on Free Enterprise in Medicine, p. 9.**)

14. The move to draft Dr. Fred Shadid was stopped by local action supporting the cooperative—a resolution by the city Chamber of Commerce declaring him to be essential to the continued operation of the hospital, and a petition to the Government at Washington, signed by 13,000 persons, asking for his deferment. Another son, and the cooperative's dentist, had already been inducted into service.

15. Dr. Michael Shadid in **Cooperative Builder,** December 19, 1936, p. 18.

16. **Community Hospital Bulletin** (Elk City, Okla.) October 1950.

17. The Bureau was organized as a nonprofit enterprise in 1939, under the leadership of William David Parmer. It provides direct medical and surgical care through a panel of physicians who are compensated on a capitation or unit basis. It has some 10,000 members. Certain features of this plan are open to question, notably the contract between Mr. Parmer and the Bureau, whereby he was hired for 20 years, the contract being inheritable (and his widow succeeded him in the position of business manager at his death). For his services he was to receive 25 percent of all monthly dues and other income (this was estimated to have netted him some $20,000 per year). His compensation was reduced to 10 percent of the monthly dues in 1946, and he waived his share of the "other income."

18. Resolutions to that effect were passed by the Cooperative Health Federation's annual meetings of 1948 and 1949.

19. It is estimated that organizing a cooperative hospital and getting it open for business requires at least 1½ to 2 years. Actually, in certain cases two or three times that period have elapsed between organization of the cooperative and the opening day.

20. Dr. Shadid enumerates these as follows: The doctors (1) have complete control of the professional features of the plan, (2) are well compensated, (3) are freed from bookkeeping, economic worry, and collections, (4) have adequate paid vacations, (5) have better professional and social relations with the other doctors than usually obtains where all are competitors (6) have the advantage of receiving the patients at an early stage, instead of when the disease may be too advanced for cure, and (7) have the respect of their patients, because the latter know the doctor has no personal ax to grind. He might also have added the benefit to both doctor and patient that is obtained through discussion and consultation on current cases among the clinic staff members.

CHAPTER 29

1. Weld, L.D.H.: "Cooperatives in Minnesota." (In **Papers and Proceedings of Seventh Annual Meeting of Minnesota Academy of Social Sciences,** 1914, p. 70).

2. Late in 1954 the revised version of the film was issued, with opening and concluding remarks by a spokesman for the REA. The revision removes the previous emphasis on co-ops (they are mentioned only once), which now appear only as a last resort, when telephone service can be obtained from no other source.

3. That some of the original termite tactics are still in use was revealed during the course of the 1954 Senate

Anti-Monopoly hearings. A former official of a southern utility testified that the company eliminated cooperative competition by building duplicate lines and providing "super-duper" service and lowering rates below cost in the area intended to be served by the cooperative. This would continue until the cooperative was killed, and then service would fall and rates rise to normal. In one case REA officials were reported to be reviewing a cooperative's loan, to get "some kind of leverage" by which it could force the cooperative to sell out to the power company. (J. D. Stietenroth, former secretary-treasurer of the Mississippi Power & Light Co., reported in **Washington Post & Times Herald**, October 2, 1954.) This testimony must have had a very familiar ring to the ears of the old-time REA people.

4. Cooperatives and others pointed out that few cities or States—and no cooperatives—could undertake the development of multi-purpose projects. Only the power companies were large enough to build dams, power plants, and transmission lines; and the Department must therefore have had them in mind when it spoke of "local interests."

The change in policy did not, of course, change the law whereby preference is accorded to cooperatives and public power districts. However, as was pointed out, the law "is meaningless without vigorous administration sympathetic to the law."

5. Since expanding cooperatives could not anticipate their needs so far in advance, and the new contracts would contain no provision for recapture of power to satisfy their needs, the added current would therefore have to be bought from commercial companies at whatever rate they saw fit to charge. Secretary McKay said, truly, that the new policy gave the commercial companies "a new bill of rights."

Such strong opposition developed that the Department "clarified" its stand to assure that "preference" customers would receive power and that current not now needed by them would be sold to nonpreference buyers only on short-term contracts.

6. Actually, over 80 percent of the power facilities in the United States are owned by the commercial utilities.

7. Quoted in **Pacific Northwest Cooperator**, October 1954.

8. Senator Neuberger of Oregon commented: "Somehow it's called 'creeping socialism' for government to invest in a good pay-off dam, and its called 'progressive conservatism' for government to invest in a site the power companies don't figure will pay large profits."

CHAPTER 30

1. The Mutual Insurance Co. of the City of New York, oldest company in New York, was also formed during this period (1787), under a deed of settlement. This company passed out of the mutual group when it reorganized as a capital-stock company in 1809; its name was changed in 1846 to Knickerbocker Fire Insurance Co.

2. Mutual Benefit Life Insurance Co. of Newark, N. J.; New England Mutual Life Insurance Co. of Boston, Mass.; State Mutual Life Assurance Co. of Worcester, Mass.; and Connecticut Mutual Life Insurance Co. of Hartford.

3. Nebraska also has an organization, Farmers Union Industries Mutual Insurance Co., which writes fire insurance on buildings owned by all types of Farmers Union cooperatives in that State. Its coverage was extended to Kansas and South Dakota in 1953.

4. The companies are also entering other fields of business. In 1951 the National Casualty Co., licensed to operate in 48 states, was purchased. This was for investment only; although Murray Lincoln was elected president of the company in 1954, it was said that the latter would continue to operate independently.

Through various subsidiaries, the Farm Bureau Insurance Companies now own or control companies manufacturing fractional-horsepower motors and TV accessories and light-weight, fireproof building materials.

One subsidiary, Peoples Development Co., not only developed a model town, Lincoln Village, near Columbus, but bought five housing projects in Bridgeport, Conn., and gave the tenants in them the opportunity to buy their residences, and guided the formation of a housing project in each. A sixth organization, Bridgeport Mutual Management Corp., was organized by the five cooperatives to take over the management of the projects.

The Ohio insurance companies also own four radio stations—at Cleveland and Worthington, Ohio, Trenton, N. J., and Fairmont, W. Va.

5. **Pacific Northwest Cooperator** (Walla Walla, Wash., Pacific Supply Cooperative), April 1951.

6. Another interesting organization was affiliated with the consumers' cooperative movement in the early years, although it was not strictly a consumers' association. This was the group of five companies operating under the name Associated Cooperative Fire Insurance Co. of Sullivan County, with headquarters at Woodridge, N. Y. They operated on the Rochdale principles of one member, one vote, and no proxies. Their line of business was the insuring of boarding houses and hotels (mostly Jewish) in the Catskill Mountains.

Because of their out-of-the-way location and lack of local fire protection, insurance rates for these properties were very high; the companies were able to save the members from 25 to 50 percent on premiums.

7. Mutual Service Casualty Co. is licensed for Minnesota, Wisconsin, and the Dakotas; Mutual Service Life and Mutual Service Fire are licensed for Minnesota, Wisconsin, and Michigan.

8. But Midland Mutual Fire Insurance Co. later withdrew and, because of unrestricted use of proxies, gradually lost its cooperative character and passed out of the cooperative movement.

9. And the National Rural Electric Cooperative Association has an agency for fire and casualty insurance.

10. The original members are:

Farm Bureau Mutual Insurance Cos., Columbus, Ohio.
Mutual Service Insurance Cos., St. Paul, Minn.
CUNA Mutual Insurance Society, Madison, Wis.
The Farmers Union companies, Denver, Colo.
Group Health Mutual, St. Paul, Minn.

11. These are—

Consumers Insurance Agency (subsidiary of the regional wholesale, Consumers Cooperative Association, Kansas City, Mo.).
Self-Help Mutual Life Assurance Society, Chicago, Ill.
Group Health Insurance, Inc., New York City.
Cooperative Life of America, Salt Lake City, Utah.
Hospital Benefit Association, Phoenix, Ariz.
NRECA Retirement, Safety and Insurance Department, Washington, D.C.
Members Mutual Insurance, Dallas, Tex.
Cooperative Life Insurance Co., Regina, Sask.
Pool Insurance Co., Winnipeg, Man.
Cooperators Insurance Association, Toronto, Ont.

CHAPTER 31

1. The phrase "cooperative banks" may bring to the mind of the reader the so-called "cooperative banks" of Massachusetts (which, however, are savings and loan associations, and not cooperatives).

2. The cooperatives were not authorized to do a general banking business. They could deal only with their members, taking their deposits and making loans to them.

3. The rate is often set in the credit union law; a common requirement is that it shall not exceed 1 percent per month on the unpaid balance. Thus there are no extras, no "investigation" or other fees, and no hidden charges.

4. In New York these had been formed under the sponsorship of the Jewish Agricultural and Industrial Aid Society and were the first agricultural credit unions in this country. Between 1911 and 1915 the society sponsored 19 such associations (8 in New York, 5 each in New Jersey and Connecticut, and 1 in Massachusetts). This phase of the society's work was not a success, for the farmer members regarded the credit unions as "free loan societies." Beginning in 1918, they were gradually liquidated, and by 1924 all were gone.

5. Later its name was changed to La Caisse Populaire St. Marie. In 1922 it was still the only credit cooperative operating under special charter in this country. At last reports it was still active but had long ago been transformed into a commercial bank.

6. The first issue of **The Bridge** was that of June 1924.

7. Either they saw no need for special loan agencies for their employees or they were skeptical of the feasibility of worker-managed associations; and they hated the word, "union." Others opposed credit unions because they wanted their employees to invest their savings in company stock—thus tieing the workers' fortunes doubly to the company. Such plans slumped considerably in popularity during the depression, when the value of the stock depreciated or was wiped out altogether.

8. Some personnel officers or supervisors either had investments in small-loan banks or themselves made loans to employees at high rates. Such people, of course, could be counted upon to resist the organization of a credit union in their plants. One personnel officer prevented the formation of a credit union in his employer's factory as long as he lived.

9. Among them were A. S. Goss, who played such an outstanding role in the Grange cooperative movement in Washington State in the 1920's; Ralph Long, of Illinois; Leo Kaminsky of Indiana; Joe DeRamus and Earl Rentfro of the Rock Island Railroad; Charles Hyland, La Crosse fire fighter; Herbert Rhodes of North Carolina (now CUNA's Washington, D. C. representative); Claude R. Orchard of Nebraska (later to become the first administrator of the Federal Credit Union Act); Miss Agnes Gartland (for many years assistant executive secretary of the Credit Union National Extension Bureau); and many others.

10. By October 1, 1927, the number of postal credit unions had risen to

83. They had 16,257 members and over a million dollars in assets. The first one had been organized in the Brockton, Mass., postoffice on January 5, 1923, with 8 members and $18.50 in capital.

11. Building and loan associations defeated the bills in Missouri and California in 1925, and in Connecticut a State senator on the banking committee was able to knock out bills year after year. A Cleveland banker "strangled our bill with his bare hands" in committee in Ohio in 1929. The battle was even grimmer in Washington State. Beginning in 1925, when the credit union bill was passed by practically unanimous vote, Governor Roland Hartley (under the influence of the money lenders) vetoed or failed to sign one bill after another and it was not until his political defeat in the primaries in 1932 that a law could be passed in 1933. In 1931, in spite of powerful loan-shark resistance, a law was obtained in Arkansas. (Bergengren: **Crusade**, various pages.)

12. In one case, bank officials had even unloaded some of the bank's investments on the unwary credit union just before the bank crashed; these securities depreciated 60 percent in the next 3 months. In many other cases, depreciation of investments caused losses of varying seriousness.

13. Even then, however, Mr. Filene agreed to subsidize the work (through his Twentieth Century Fund) by $25,000 during the first year and $5,000 less each year through a 5-year period. Also, the salary of Mr. Bergengren was paid by the Extension Bureau that first year.

14. He was active in the local movement in Vermont and president of the State Credit Union League (until his death on November 11, 1955).

15. An application from Messrs. Filene and Bergengren to the Twentieth Century Fund (organized and endowed by Mr. Filene) was rejected! True, as Mr. Bergengren later wrote. "All that we were offering [as security] was an idea backed by unlimited faith."

16. Thus, in the early 1940's, "central" credit unions began to be formed, to serve the directors and committee members (who were barred from borrowing from their own organizations while in office) and to provide a repository for surplus credit union funds.

Such funds can be and have been used also to finance cooperative activities of various kinds. In Michigan the credit unions, through their State League, bought the Litchfield Savings Bank, and in 1951 also took over the control of a savings and loan association in Detroit. These organizations receive the deposits of and make loans to credit unions and others.

17. In striking contrast in courage was the experience of the Hawaiian Air Depot Federal Credit Union, at Hickam Field, Pearl Harbor—the only American credit union to come under enemy fire. Its office and records were wiped out by an enemy bomb and its treasurer was killed while trying to save the records. A new office was opened immediately after the raid, new passbooks were issued, and within 30 days the association was back in business again. (Bergengren: **Crusade**, pp. 351, 352.)

18. Much of my own satisfaction, in my long service in the U. S. Bureau of Labor Statistics, came from association with people like Mr. Orchard and the late R. H. Elsworth, long-time cooperative statistician in the Farm Credit Administration and head of its Division of History and Statistics until his retirement. Notwithstanding the heavy demands of their own work they were never too busy to cooperate with me and lend assistance and encouragement.

19. The **Wall Street Journal** (March 10, 1955) declared it was the bankers who first suggested the plan to President Eisenhower. "Credit union movement grows—to banks' annoyed alarm. Banks seek laws to compel these competitors to carry savings insurance—an expense that would narrow competitive cost advantages."

CHAPTER 32

1. The names of some of the student cooperatives reveal whimsy and the members' youthful exuberance—Seldom Inn, Panthers Lair, Spartan Hall, Three Squares, Valhalla, T.L.O.K. (The Lord Only Knows)—as well as some knowledge of cooperative history—Rochdale, Ann Tweedale, Robert Owen, etc. Some were named in honor of persons whom the members especially admired—as Norris House (Senator George W. Norris), Elsworth House (R. H. Elsworth, Federal cooperative statistician), Ulrey House (Prof. Ulrey, of Michigan State College, under whose encouragement the cooperative houses there were started), Campbell House (Wallace J. Campbell, director of the Washington office of the Cooperative League of the USA), etc.

2. A survey in Nebraska revealed an average saving of about $75 per semester for students in cooperative houses, as compared with current local charges.

Figures released by the National Committee on Student Cooperatives in 1938 showed that the average saving through the cooperative bookstores was 10 percent, through the eating clubs and dormitories 40 percent, through cleaning and pressing arrangements 60 percent, through buying clubs 15 percent, and through miscellaneous enterprises 35 percent.

3. In the first association the sponsor is the Bremerton lodge of the Fraternal Order of Eagles; in the second, four women, members of the Business and Professional Women's Club of Bremerton.

4. Of these, 5 were in Illinois, 4 each in Michigan and New York, 2 in Minnesota, and 1 each in the District of Columbia, Missouri, and Washington.

5. Miss Arnold's cooperative activities were preceded by service as an agent of the Federal Office of Indian Affairs, special courses in dietetics in California and Cornell Universities, operation (with Mabel Reed) of a cafeteria for students, and employment in the Bliss Torpedo Works during the First World War. In 1919 she and Miss Reed operated a cafeteria which later became the first of a series operated by Our Cooperative Cafeteria (now Consumers Cooperative Services). Miss Arnold was general manager of this organization from 1920 to 1937, besides serving as treasurer of the Cooperative League of the USA from 1924-37. In 1938 she went to Nova Scotia where she initiated and directed a successful housing project among the miners and fishermen. Upon her return to the United States after the project was completed, she helped to organize the Philadelphia Area Cooperative Federation which, beginning as an educational and coordinating body, evolved a plan for area-wide merchandising and store supervision that was in effect for several years. Later Miss Arnold served as acting manager of Eastern Cooperative Wholesale, during the period of its reorganization; she had been its president for several years.

Miss Arnold was succeeded as general manager of CCS by Mary Coover Long (widow of Cedric Long) and she, in turn, by Eulah Feemster.

6. Later Judge of Municipal Court. For many years Miss Kenyon has acted as attorney for Eastern Cooperatives, Inc., and other cooperatives in New York. She served for a time as United States delegate to the UN Commission on the Status of Women.

7. The history in this State included: (1) A ruling by the Attorney General in 1932 that a cooperative could operate legally if it employed a licensed embalmer; (2) A decision by the Iowa Supreme Court (1936) enjoining operation of the cooperative at Fremont but with a loophole by which the cooperative could escape; (3) A 1937 amendment to the embalming law that raised license fees—for cooperatives only; (4) "ouster" cases brought by the Attorney General in 1943, charging operation of a business not authorized by cooperative law and violation of embalming law, all of which were dismissed by the court; on appeal the State Supreme Court in 1946 ruled in favor of the cooperatives on all counts and overturned its own previous decision, by deciding that embalming is a business and not a profession.

8. Of these, 15 were in Minnesota, 10 in Iowa, 4 in South Dakota, 3 in Illinois, and 1 each in Arkansas, California, Michigan, Missouri, Oregon, and Wisconsin.

9. Not all of the cooperative plants were independent associations. Some were departments of cooperatives whose main business was marketing of farm products or running a cooperative store.

10. There have, however, been numerous instances of laundries started by laundry workers in the course of strikes, to provide employment and to assist in winning the dispute by competition with the "struck" plant. Usually, these have lasted only until the end of the strike. Others were opened because the strike was lost, to provide work. All of these operated as workers' productive associations, not as consumers' cooperatives. Theirs is another story, that may some day be told.

CHAPTER 33

1. Among the exceptional producer cooperatives in Alaska are a sawmill at White Mountain and a factory at Nome where native women make fur-lined parkas and other outer clothing. Other types of Indian cooperatives include a cranberry raising and marketing project, an oyster bed, and a salmon cannery.

Some of the Indian cooperatives were assisted under the Indian Reorganization Act of June 18, 1934, authorizing the formation of nonprofit organizations for economic welfare. A revolving fund of $10 million was appropriated for the purpose.

2. The geographical distribution of these was as follows: District of Columbia and Illinois, 9 each; New York, 8; Michigan and Ohio, 7 each; Indiana and Mississippi, 4 each; Alabama, Georgia, Maryland, New Jersey, North Carolina, Ohio, Pennsylvania, Tennessee, and Virginia, 2 each; and Arkansas, California, Connecticut, Florida, Kansas, Louisiana, Minnesota, Missouri, South Carolina, Texas, Washington, West Virginia, and Wisconsin, 1 each.

3. Associations believed to be still operating (and year of latest report to the Government) are the following:

Gee's Bend Cooperative Association, Alberta, Ala. (1950).

Peoples Cooperative Association, Tuskegee, Ala. (1952).

University-John Hope Homes Cooperative Store, Atlanta, Ga. (1951).

Mileston (Miss.) Cooperative Association, (1954).

Consumers Cooperative of Hackensack, N. J. (1949).

Cooperative Enterprises, Inc., New York, N. Y. (1954).

Tillery (N.C.) Community Cooperative Association (1947).

Weirton (W. Va.) Cooperative Association (1952).

4. Among its leaders were Jacob L. Reddix (then principal of a local high school; later president of Jackson, Miss., College), who was its president; and Leslie Joseph, a post-office employee, who became its manager.

5. I have read of many such cases. One that comes to hand was reported in the **Cooperative Builder** of December 24, 1953. In recounting the history of the Hibbing (Minn.) Consumers Cooperative Store, it noted that "Mr. Emil Panula, of the board of directors, once mortgaged his house to save the co-op from going under." In Marengo, Wis., also, a member mortgaged his farm to save the store.

6. At Waukegan, Ill., Fitchburg and Maynard, Mass., and Cloquet and Virginia, Minn.

7. Its general manager, Arvo N. Rivers, previously manager of the association at Rock, Mich., has also served on the boards of Eastern Cooperative Wholesale and the Cooperative League of the USA.

8. Another Finnish cooperative, United Cooperative Society of Norwood (1909) went out of business in 1951, after operating for 42 years.

9. Fitchburg, Gardner, Maynard, Norwood, Peabody, Quincy, and Worcester, Mass., and Milford and New Ipswich, N. H.

10. Eventually, the New Hampshire stores, and that in Gardner, Mass., became branches of Fitchburg. The Worcester store operated independently until 1929, when it became a branch of Maynard. The Quincy store also is still operating. The Peabody and Norwood associations went out of business, the latter, however, surviving until 1951.

11. I.e., the Bear Park Cooperative Mercantile Co., at Gary, which reorganized under the State cooperative law in 1919; the semicooperative Scandinavian Cooperative Mercantile Co. at Two Harbors, which is still operating under corporation law; and the Nelson & Albin Cooperative Mercantile Association, organized in a Norwegian community north of St. James. These three are now among the oldest consumers' associations in the United States.

The fourth organization, Lake Shore Cooperative Mercantile Co., at Butternut, although incorporated under corporation law (since there was not yet a State cooperative law), followed the Rochdale principles from the first. The store was sold in 1945 to a man who had been manager of a nearby cooperative.

12. The fourth association, Turlock (Calif.) Consumers Cooperative (1937), ceased operation during World War II.

13. Of these, 8 were in Massachusetts, 7 in Pennsylvania, 2 each in Illinois and Michigan, and 1 each in Connecticut and New Hampshire. The location of the other 2 was not given.

14. There were 2 in California and New York, 1 (of textile workers) in Connecticut, 11 in Illinois (mostly coal miners) 6 in Massachusetts, 4 (mostly coal miners) in Pennsylvania, and 1 each in Michigan, Minnesota, New Hampshire, and New Jersey.

15. Of this group, the Italian Colonial Cooperative at Leominster (1919) was in operation until about 1953; and the Workers Cooperative Union at Sagamore (1921) until 1948.

16. I.e., Sioux Center, Iowa (1924), Holland, Mich. (1919), and Edgerton (1937) and Long Prairie, Minn. (1931).

CHAPTER 34

1. Many labor stores, however, were too small for efficient operation and some were run on unsound principles. The Cooperative League noted with dismay the "critical situation" in the labor cooperative movement. The trade-unions, it said, were adopting methods in their stores that had failed wherever tried. (**Cooperation**, June 1920, p. 90.)

2. Mr. Walker dropped out of the cooperative movement after the failure of the American Plan, though he continued in the labor movement until about 1945. He died in 1955 at the age of 83.

3. Dr. Myers had been known as a friend of labor for many years. As industrial secretary of the Federal Council of Churches of Christ in America, he had made surveys of industrial conditions, studied labor relations, and was active in the mediation of labor disputes. He also served on the board of directors of the Cooperative League for several years in the late thirties. In 1940 he wrote a pamphlet entitled **Organized Labor and Consumers' Cooperation.** Revised editions were issued in 1943 and 1944 under the title, **Labor and Co-ops.** He also prepared a 4-page flier **Organized Labor, Organize as Consumers.** In 1948 he joined the staff of the National Child Labor Committee as assistant secretary, in charge of membership.

4. Elmer E. Milliman, president of the Brotherhood of Maintenance of Way Employes, was appointed chairman of the committee. The September 1944 issue of the **American Federationist**

carried, under the title, "Here is Tomorrow," an article by Mr. Milliman urging the advantages of cooperatives to organized labor. For some months preceding his death, he carried in his union's magazine a series of articles to acquaint the members with the various types of cooperatives, how they worked, and what they had done.

Upon his death, Arnold Zander, president of the American Federation of State, County and Municipal Employees, succeeded him on the committee and is still acting in that capacity.

5. The UAW-CIO published two pamphlets: **How to Organize a Cooperative in Your Community**, and **Are You Just Half a Man?**

Publications of the AFL include the following: **Workers Discover a Money-saving Idea, Business "of the people, by the people and for the people," Homes for Union Members**, and **When it Rains** (credit union pamphlet).

6. This period also brought forth two innovations: (1) Case lot sales in union halls, as a substitute for stores. This plan began in mid-1947 and spread like wildfire. It burned out as quickly. Some were intended only as temporary measures against current high prices. In others the expected great savings did not fulfill the hopes of the proponents and few lasted out the first year. (2) Warehouse-type retail units already described (see Chapter 25). The UAW-CIO was the chief exponent of this type of operation, but the 1948 AFL convention also endorsed it.

Both plans had been viewed with some concern by experienced businessmen among the cooperators. The latter were also afraid that the unionists' enthusiasm would run ahead of the making of real cooperators to support the cooperative enterprises and before sufficient capital and trained personnel were available.

7. The organizations most frequently mentioned by the cooperatives were, in descending order of frequency, the following:

International Union of Auto Workers (CIO).

United Steelworkers of America (CIO).

International Brotherhood of Carpenters and Joiners (AFL).

International Brotherhood of Electrical Workers (AFL).

International Association of Machinists (then independent).

International Union of Mine, Mill & Smelter Workers (CIO).

American Federation of State, County & Municipal Employees (AFL).

Textile Workers Union of America (CIO).

Amalgamated Clothing Workers of America (CIO).

The National Education Association and the American Federation of Teachers have both published considerable material on consumers' cooperatives for the benefit of their members.

8. In 1947 Philip Murray endorsed cooperatives and William Green issued a statement saying he regarded the consumers' cooperative movement as "thoroughly democratic," and pointing out that the Federation was working for its growth. Walter Reuther spoke up in favor of cooperatives on many occasions and it was largely due to his support that his union was so active in promoting cooperatives. In 1953 John L. Lewis, president of the United Mine Workers, gave his personal endorsement to cooperatives as one of the "checks and balances" in the national economy.

9. Its manager, Rudolf Schubert, was active in private and public welfare work in Germany. He spent several months in a concentration camp when he refused to join the Nazis. After his release he escaped to England in 1937, with the help of English Quakers. Coming to the United States in 1938, he managed a dairy farm for 2 years, then taught German in Connecticut Union College in 1940. He became manager of a cooperative in Watertown, N. Y., in 1941.

10. One of these is the issuance of a "co-op buck" for every dollar spent at the supermarket; these are usable at monthly auctions (which are also special events) of housewares and appliances. Its manager is A. J. Choat, who had had 12 years' previous cooperative experience.

11. Representatives on the new council's board were Laurie Lehtin and James L. Proebsting (Central States), Robert L. Smith and Leslie Woodcock (ECW), and Harland H. Allen and Percy S. Brown (Good Will Fund). Rochdale Institute, which had been one of the three sponsors of the Council for Cooperative Business Training, was not associated with the new council.

12. The council's original co-chairmen were Arnold Zander (AFL) and Victor Reuther (AUW-CIO). Mr. Reuther was later succeeded by Joseph W. Childs (rubber workers—CIO).

13. In 1936 Central Cooperative Wholesale concluded contracts with AFL unions, whereby the proposed scales became effective "when all private employers [in the area] accepted the same schedule." In 1938 the Cloquet Cooperative Society notified its employees that either hours would have to be increased or wages decreased, in order to bring conditions into line with those in other business in town. This resulted in a 1-week strike by its employees.

In New York a large cafeteria organization had been forced to pay wages considerably in excess of those its competitors were paying; this continued for some years. By the union's own admission, this cooperative had pioneered the 5-day week in the restaurant industry, led the way in vacations, in retirement pensions, in abolition of nightwork, equal pay for men and women, employment of Negroes, etc.

14. These two studies were corroborated by others. Thus, Fowler commented (**The Cooperative Challenge**, p. 253) that managers were generally overworked and underpaid. He cited the case of the general manager of a cooperative wholesale, who received an annual salary of about $5,000. His organization bought a privately owned refinery, and he found himself supervising department heads receiving up to $15,000 a year.

15. This applies not only to the distributive cooperatives but also to the insurance companies in Ohio, the North Central States, and Nebraska, to the credit unions, and to electric power cooperatives.

16. Retirement plans were adopted by Midland Cooperatives in 1944; by Farmers Union Central Exchange in 1945; by Consumers Cooperative Association in 1946; by Pacific Supply Cooperative in 1947; by Farmers Union State Exchange in 1950; and by Utah Cooperative Association in 1951. For details of plans see U.S. Bureau of Labor Statistics Bulletins Nos. 964 (pp. 13-15) and 1073 (pp. 12, 13).

CHAPTER 35

1. Of the other wholesales connected at any point with the consumers' cooperative movement, the Farmers Union State Exchange (Nebraska) and the Utah Cooperative Association will accept nonfarm members, the former up to the limit allowed for tax exemption, the latter up to 10 percent; Farm Bureau Cooperative Association (Ohio) and Consumers Cooperatives Associated (Texas) will admit farm cooperatives only; Indiana Farm Bureau Cooperative Association, Farmers Union Central Exchange (Minnesota) and Pacific Supply Cooperative (Washington), while admitting only farm cooperatives as members, do business with nonfarm cooperatives (and pay them refunds on patronage). age).

2. U. S. Senate. Committee on Agriculture and Forestry. Subcommittee (76th Cong., 1st sess.): **Hearings on S. 2605**, pp. 72-75.

3. Daniels, John: **Cooperation, An American Way**, p. 270.

4. It is for this reason that I believe the oft-suggested merger of United and National will never come to pass unless National comes under the complete control of the producer-minded members. United was a charter member of National but withdrew in 1939. Its reasons for so doing were never announced publicly.

5. Merritt H. Crouch (then its general manager), quoted in **Midland Cooperator**, July 23, 1947. Mr. Crouch went on to say: "Some of our own so-called agricultural leaders are trying to tie some of our agricultural cooperatives to these groups which are primarily dominated by the labor group." (The labor reference may have been to the invitation by the Cooperative League to Walter Reuther, to speak at its 1946 congress.)

6. Farm Bureau Cooperative Associations of Indiana and Pennsylvania, Farmers Union Exchanges of Minnesota and Nebraska, Consumers Cooperatives Associated (Texas), and Consumers Cooperative Association (Missouri).

7. An exception is Consumers Cooperative Association which withdrew from the League for personal reasons but still makes a financial contribution to it.

8. **Journal of Farm Economics**, February 1935.

9. John Daniels said: "Their feet are on the ground—but too heavily. Their near sight is better than their far sight. They could do with more leaven and lift." (In **New Leader**, quoted in **Cooperative Builder**, March 17, 1949.)

10. Even as late as 1949, Associated Cooperatives (California) reported to its members that one of the reasons for abandoning its farm-supply department was that the farmers were "unwilling to be closely associated with a whole in which the dominant philosophy was that of an outspoken consumers' cooperative." (Its **Annual Report**, 1949, p. 5.)

11. An exception is the National Farmers Union, whose annual meeting in 1955 adopted a resolution declaring that "As farmers we recognize that our welfare and that of working people everywhere is closely bound together, and we welcome the support of organized labor in our mutual effort to attain parity for all." This farm organization also supported organized labor's unsuccessful effort to raise the minimum hourly wage to $1.25 in the Federal bill in 1955.

12. In 1946, Mr. Babcock quoted with approval the remark of a "veteran cooperator" who, he said, was "noted for liberality," that the Cooperative League was "controlled by ultra-liberal and leftist factions largely predominant in the consumer cooperative group and radical labor circles." (Quoted in **Midland Cooperator**, December 27, 1946.)

CHAPTER 36

1. Formerly known as the Federal Council of Churches of Christ in America.

2. Dr J. Henry Carpenter, executive secretary of the Brooklyn Church and Mission Federation, was appointed chairman and Rev. James Myers, secretary of the Council's Industrial Division, secretary.

Dr. Myers was also for many years chairman of the Cooperative League's committee on cooperatives and labor.

Pamphlets issued by the League during this period include the following:**Cooperation and Religion: The Relationship Between Religion and the Cooperative Movement Defined and Expounded**, by Dr. M. M. Coady (1939). **Bear Ye One Another's Burdens** (1943), **Bethlehem and Rochdale**, by Benson Y. Landis (1944), **The Social Significance of the Cooperative Movement**, by Dr. M. M. Coady (1945), and **Christianity and Cooperation**, by E. Stanley Jones (1945?).

3. Among them may be cited **Committee on the Church and Cooperatives** (1938), **The Church and Credit Unions**, by Benson Y. Landis (1940 and 1947), **Manual on the Church and Cooperatives**, compiled by Benson Y. Landis (1940 and 1945), **Churches in Social Action: Why and How**, by James Myers, (1942), and **In Business for Service—Religious Implications of Consumers' Cooperation**, by James Myers (1946).

4. Popes Pius XI and XII, Bishops Muldoon, Schrembs, Hayes, Russell, Ryan, and Muench, and Msgrs. Ligutti and Coady. For quotations of some of their statements, see **Catholic Churchmen and Cooperatives** (co-sponsored by Catholic Cooperative Committee, The Queen's Work, and National Catholic Rural Life Conference).

5. Quoted by Landis in **Bethlehem and Rochdale**, p. 31.

6. Among them are **Consumers Cooperatives**, by Rev. Edgar Schmeideler (1937) and **Credit Unions**, by Frank O'Hara (1937). (Its Social Action Series Nos. 5 and 7.)

7. **Catholic Churchmen and Cooperatives.**

8. Among the distributive cooperatives in the organization of which churchmen are known to have taken an active part were Central Consumers Cooperative of Cambridge, Mass.; East Lynn (Mass.) Cooperative Society; Jamaica Plain Cooperative Society, Boston, Mass.; Lane County Cooperative Association, Eugene, Oreg.; Thurston County Consumers Cooperative, Olympia, Wash.; Pacific Cooperative Services, Oakland, Calif.; Humboldt Park (Ill.) Consumers Cooperative; North Shore Cooperative, Evanston, Ill.; Knickerbocker Village Cooperative, New York City; Lackawanna (N.Y.) Consumers Cooperative; Adamant (Vt.) Cooperative. All except the last-named association are now out of business.

9. As one minister whose advocacy of cooperation cost him his church put it: "I am not optimistic about the possibility of ministers taking a truly active part in promoting the consumer cooperative movement. They are under too heavy an obligation to the **status quo** to function in this connection."

10. Quoted in **Information Service**, (New York, Federal Council of Churches of Christ in America), March 23, 1940, p. 8.

11. At the end of 1953, there were 340 Federal credit unions with religion as the basis for membership. No data are available as to the number chartered under State laws.

12. Ward, Leo: **Ourselves Inc.—The Story of Consumer Free Enterprise**, p. 7.

CHAPTER 37

1. Even in 1954, the Farmers Union State Exchange reported a price war in Nebraska that lasted for about half the year.

2. I am not informed regarding other Government agencies, but at least one of them, the U. S. Bureau of Labor Statistics (as the one interested in consumers' cooperatives), was bombarded with letters intimating that the Bureau (or the Government generally) was promoting or favoring cooperatives, and demanding that this be stopped and that "the cooperative menace be curbed." I remember one or two correspondents who (ignorant of the provisions of the law under which the Bureau functioned) even thought that the welfare of profit business should be the aim of the Bureau as well as of the Department of Commerce.

3. Correctly deducing that education is fundamental to cooperative expansion, cooperative adversaries tried unsuccessfully in 1943 to repeal the Wisconsin law requiring the teaching of cooperation in schools receiving State aid and to remove the authority of the State Department of Agriculture and Markets to encourage cooperatives. In 1954, North Dakota opponents of cooperatives made an unsuccessful effort to prohibit the use of any money by cooperatives (or labor unions) for educational purposes.

Bills introduced in Minnesota in 1941 would (1) have prohibited cooperatives from selling any article not regularly carried in stock and (2) limited to 3,000 gallons any load of gasoline or other inflammable fluids carried by transport trucks (only cooperative trucks actually carried larger loads). Neither passed. Also in 1941, a Massachusetts bill to impose a gross-receipts tax of 1 percent—on cooperatives only—failed to pass.

In the same year an amendment to the appropriation bill for the Farm Security Administration was introduced in Congress, prohibiting the lending of money to any type of cooperative that might be in competition with private business. It also was unsuccessful.

4. The year 1947 was remarkable for the unusual number of attempts to harm or hamper cooperatives through legislation. There were tax bills or restrictive measures against consumers' cooperatives in 7 States; three bills aimed at the Farmers Union insurance associations in North Dakota; and legislation intended to harm REA cooperatives in 22 States. Fortunately for the cooperatives, most of these efforts failed.

5. Among those that have come to my attention were the proposed imposition of a gross-receipts tax on cooperatives only (in Montana in 1951); requiring the payment of income tax on all patronage refunds if any business at all was done with nonmembers (in North Carolina in 1953); of a tax on patronage refunds (in Maryland in 1945 and 1954, and in Colorado and Kansas in 1951), and on those deferred (in Kansas in 1945) or paid in patrons' equity certificates (in Minnesota in 1949); and on all merchandise shipped into a warehouse and later removed to retail outlets (in North Carolina in 1953). None of these moves succeeded. The North Carolina bill failed because it would also have affected grocery chains, one of which declared that it would cancel its plans for building a new warehouse in the State if passed.

6. According to the U. S. Department of Agriculture, the combined assets of farmers' cooperatives are less than $2.9 billion. In comparison, three giant profit corporations each have assets exceeding this figure—Standard Oil of New Jersey (5.4 billion), General Motors ($4.4 billion), and United States Steel ($3.2 billion).

7. Barnard, Charles: **Cooperation as a Business**, p. 216.

8. That not all sectors of the business world go along with this is indicated by a recent article in the **Wall Street Journal** which commented in part as follows:

"So [since postwar competition is very tough] the auto dealers want a law passed to stop cut-rate sales of new cars; ultra high frequency TV operators want the expansion of very high frequency stations stopped; airlines want their subsidies untrimmed; druggists, jewelers, and appliance dealers want more 'fair trade' laws.

"Not that any of these good people are against 'competition' as such. Competition, as they will all testify, is the backbone of the free enterprise system, and the life line of the nation's expanding economy. But when competition gets tough, somehow it seems also to get unfair."

CHAPTER 38

1. Arizona, Delaware, Georgia, Indiana, Louisiana, Maryland, Mississippi, New Hampshire, Texas, Utah, West Virginia, and Wyoming.

2. On the other hand, the Ohio law consists merely of two short sections, permitting the formation of "trading associations dealing in articles of merchandise" and authorizing the distribution of earnings in proportion to purchases. Tennessee's law has three sections permitting associations to buy or sell agricultural products and merchandise and specifying the number of persons necessary for incorporation. Vermont's general act merely prohibits the use of "cooperative" in an association's name unless it conforms to the cooperative principles set forth in the section.

3. Some of the State laws have undergone an almost continuous process of amendment. Others that badly need revision have had little or no attention. Thus, the two-section Ohio act has remained unchanged since enactment in 1867. The same is practically true of the Pennsylvania of 1887, (although an attempt was made in 1937 to remove the provision that makes each member of a consumers' cooperative liable to suit for debts of a cooperative). The law's only changes were extra sections added in 1923 to allow cooperatives to take advantage of the Farm Credit Act. Naturally, the most liberalizing revision has occurred in the States in which consumers' cooperatives are strongest.

4. President Taft, in a special message to Congress, March 13, 1912, called attention to consumers' cooperation as a means of lowering the cost of living.

In June 1923, in a speech at Idaho Falls, Idaho, President Harding proposed "a plan of cooperation among consumers financed, in part at least, through a carefully organized and supervised adaptation of the principles of the building and loan society." As Mr. Harding died 2 months later, nothing came of this nebulous proposal.

His successor, Calvin Coolidge, in February 1924 praised cooperative marketing and noted the need of urban consumers' cooperatives and a closer working arrangement between the two as the "ideal toward which economic efforts should be directed."

The attitude of President Roosevelt was implicit in the many cooperative aspects of his Administration.

General Eisenhower was reported in the cooperative press to have told James G. Patton (president of the National Farmers Union), while campaigning in 1952, that cooperatives were fine for marketing farm products, "but when they 'go so far' as to own their own oil wells they become 'dangerous'." (Quoted in **Cooperative Builder**, October 2, 1952.)

5. But since 1926, advice and service, research on farm cooperatives and their problems, collection of statistics and educational materials have been provided for farm cooperatives. These functions are now performed by the Farmer Cooperative Service (formerly the Cooperative Research and Service Division of the Farm Credit Administration).

6. Thus, the collection of data on State-chartered credit unions was shifted to the Bureau of Federal Credit Unions and on medical-care cooperatives to the Social Security Administration. The annual statistical studies have been discontinued pending, it is said, the making of a Federal census of wholesale and retail trade to provide a benchmark for future estimates.

7. The District law, intended as (and in most respects) a model law, is faulty in at least one respect. It provides for the redemption of outstanding shares at par value only. This presupposes that all cooperatives will operate profitably, so that their shares will be worth par value. But if, because of operating losses, the book value has fallen below par, the cooperative is then on the horns of a dilemma. On the one hand, to pay the withdrawing member par value is to discriminate against the loyal members who remain. On the other, the association cannot ethically continue to recruit new members and expect them to pay par for shares which are actually worth less than their face value. The only alternatives open to the cooperative are (1) gainful operation long enough to restore the par value or, failing this, (2) reorganization, wiping out the amount of share depreciation. In the meantime it is stalemated. The law needs to be amended, adding a phrase allowing redemption at par, "or book value, whichever is less."

8. In the Midwest the hearings stirred up such a hornet's nest among the farmer cooperators that the Republican Party leaders began to be concerned for the elections, and the rest of the hearings were cancelled. The West Coast hearings turned out to be a fizzle and the investigation was called off after a short time. (Amusingly, one of the most vociferous anti-cooperative witnesses was a honey distributor who, it was revealed, did not himself pay any Federal income tax, as his firm was a partnership.)

9. Main representative of NTEA views in the House has been Congressman Noah Mason (R.—Ill.), who has been the sponsor of several anti-cooperative bills (all unsuccessful): In 1950 a bill to tax unallocated reserves and earnings from "sideline" businesses of farm cooperatives, and impose a 10-percent withholding tax on interest paid on cooperative shares; in 1951, a bill to subject all patronage refunds to tax unless paid in cash or merchandise within 75 days after the end of an association's business year or paid half in cash and not over half in 2-year obligations bearing not less than 3 percent interest; in 1953, a bill calling for a special tax on cooperative patronage refunds; in 1954, a proposal to impose a tax on the earnings of saving and loan associations and mutual savings banks, at the regular corporation rate of 52 percent, as well as on all patronage refunds not paid in cash.

Also in 1954, Senator Williams (R.—Del.) proposed a tax on certain forms of patronage-refund certificates, which was defeated on a voice vote.

Similar bills were introduced in the the first session of the 84th Congress by Representatives Mason and Davis (D.—Tenn.), but Congress adjourned without taking action.

10. John H. Bolin, manager of the Auditing Service for Cooperatives (Omaha, Nebr.) believes that some of the misunderstanding would disappear if cooperative patronage refunds were described as the same as "trade discounts" used by profit business, on which no income tax is paid.

11. Arthur J. Smaby (general manager of Midland Cooperatives, Inc.), at annual meeting December 6, 1954.

CHAPTER 39

1. But only one of them (N. O. Nelson) actually represented a cooperative.

2. Since its organization in 1896, the Alliance has been the representative and spokesman of cooperatives throughout the world. Its membership has fluctuated with world conditions, reaching a peak (117 national federations in 40 countries) in 1930, then gradually decreasing as Fascism and Nazism put out the lights of freedom in one country after another. Membership rose by some 8 million from 1949 to 1950, to a total of 105 million (not including Communist-dominated countries most of which failed to report). By the end of 1954, the Alliance again included 117 million cooperators in 35 countries.

3. Leclaire Cooperative Association (Edwardsville, Ill.), Cooperative Union of America (Cambridge, Mass.), and American Cooperative Union. The only "voting" member listed in 1897 was the cooperative at the Ruskin Cooperative Colony in Georgia. By the turn of the

century, the Pacific Coast Cooperative Union and the Rochdale Wholesale Co., San Francisco, had joined the Alliance. Later the membership was held by the Pacific Cooperative League.

4. These were the Leclaire Cooperative Association, Edwardsville, Ill.; Co-Workers' Fraternity Co., Boston (Bradford Peck's organization); Cooperative Union of Kansas (educational federation); Pacific Coast Cooperative Union (educational federation); Rochdale Wholesale Co., San Francisco; and a workers' productive association, Union Fishermen's Cooperative Packing Co., Astoria, Oreg. In 1909 the Right Relationship League, Minneapolis, affiliated and 3 years later Hyman Cohn's Cooperative League. The First National Cooperative Society, Chicago, also claimed to have been accepted into membership in 1906, but available records do not substantiate this.

5. In 1945, Howard Cowden and Murray Lincoln became members of the Committee and the latter was elected first vice president of the ICA in 1946. Mr. Lincoln was also elected to the Executive Committee, being succeeded in 1951 by Mr. Cowden.

The number of United States representatives on the Central Committee was increased to five in 1954 and to nine in 1955. They are Mrs. Harold Robison, Murray Lincoln, Felix Rondeau, A. J. Smaby, Jerry Voorhis, Samuel Ashelman, Wallace Campbell, George Jacobson, and J. W. Koski. Also, Howard Cowden will represent Consumers Cooperative Association, now an ICA member in its own right.

6. Present (1954) trustees of the Fund are Murray Lincoln (president), Frank W. Hussey, W. Gordon Loveless, Robert L. Smith, and Jerry Voorhis.

CHAPTER 40

1. Ryan, **Right Rev.** John A.: **Distributive Justice**, pp. 167, 168.

CHAPTER 41

1. But now the tendency is to stock, also, other "variety" items that provide greater earnings. The Greenbelt cooperative has gone so far in this direction that it calls its new Takoma Park store a "general store." Such stores can still make substantial savings. Thus, those at Herman and Wisner, Nebr., had earnings in 1953 amounting to 6.34 and 6.5 percent on sales.

2. In Minnesota the University reported that farmers' buying power in that State early in 1955 was at a 16-year low.

3. Quoted in Cooperative Consumer (Kansas City), April 14, 1954.

Appendix A. — CENTRAL ORGANIZATIONS

Below are shown (1) the regional cooperative wholesales connected with the consumers' cooperative movement through the Cooperative League, National Cooperatives, or both; with year of organization and trading territory; (2) members of National Cooperatives, and year of admission; (3) the service federations, with year of organization and services provided; and (4) the productive federations, with year of organization and commodities produced.

REGIONAL WHOLESALES

Year organized	Name of Wholesale	Trading Territory
1914	Farmers Union State Exchange (as dept. in Farmers Union), Omaha, Nebr.	Nebraska.
1917	Cooperative Central Exchange (now Central Cooperative Wholesale), Superior, Wis.	(roughly) northern halves of Minnesota, Michigan, and Wisconsin; grocery cooperatives in the Dakotas.
1920	Farm Bureau Services. Lansing, Mich.	Michigan.
1921	Indiana Farm Bureau Cooperative Association. Indianapolis, Ind.	Indiana.
1926	Minnesota Cooperative Oil Co. (now Midland Cooperatives), Minneapolis, Minn.	(roughly) southern halves of Minnesota, Michigan, and Wisconsin; northern Iowa.
1927	Farmers Union Central Exchange St. Paul, Minn.	The Dakotas, Minnesota, Montana, and Wisconsin.
1928	Union Oil Co., Cooperative. (now Consumers Cooperative Association), Kansas City, Mo.	Colorado, southern Iowa, Kansas, Missouri, Nebraska, the Dakotas, Oklahoma, and Wyoming.
1929	Eastern Cooperative Wholesale (now Eastern Cooperatives, Inc.). Three warehouses—	
	New England Cooperatives.	New England States.
	Mid-Eastern Cooperatives.	New York, Connecticut, northeastern Pennsylvania.
	Potomac Cooperators, Inc.	District of Columbia, Maryland, Virginia, southeastern Pa.
1931	Consumers Cooperatives Associated. Amarillo, Tex.	Arkansas, Colorado, Louisiana, Mississippi, New Mexico, Oklahoma, and Texas.
1933	Pacific Supply Cooperative. Walla Walla, Wash.	Idaho, western Montana, Oregon, and Washington.
	Farm Bureau Cooperative Association. Columbus, Ohio.	Ohio.
1934	Farmers Cooperative Exchange. Raleigh, N. C.	North Carolina.
	Pennsylvania Farm Bureau Cooperative Association. Harrisburg, Pa.	Pennsylvania.
1935	Utah Cooperative Association. Salt Lake City, Utah.	Utah.
1936	The Cooperative Wholesale. (now Central States Cooperatives), Waukegan, Ill.	Illinois, Indiana, Ohio, and lower Michigan.
1939	California Cooperative Wholesale. (now Associated Cooperatives), Oakland, Calif.	California, Nevada, and Pacific islands.

National Cooperatives, Inc.

The members of National Cooperatives, as of the end of 1954, and years of affiliation, were as follows:

UNITED STATES

Regional Wholesales:

Associated Cooperatives (Calif.) 1941.

*Central Cooperative Wholesale, 1933.

Central States Cooperatives, 1937.

*Consumers Cooperative Association, 1933.

Consumers Cooperatives Associated (Texas), 1934.

Eastern Cooperatives, Inc., 1936.

Farm Bureau Cooperative Association, (Ohio), 1939.

Farm Bureau Services (Michigan), 1939.

Farmers Cooperative Exchange, 1940.

*Farmers Union Central Exchange, 1933.

Farmers Union State Exchange, 1945.

Indiana Farm Bureau Cooperative Association, 1939.

*Midland Cooperatives, 1933.

Pacific Supply Cooperative, 1934.

Pennsylvania Farm Coop. Assn., 1939.

Tennessee Farmers Cooperative, 1946.

*United Cooperatives, 1933. [1]

Utah Cooperative Association, 1945.

Other:

Wisconsin Electric Cooperative, 1950.

CANADA

Regional Wholesales:

Alberta Cooperative Wholesale Association, 1945.

British Columbia Cooperative Wholesale, 1946.

Cooperative Federee de Quebec, 1947.

Manitoba Cooperative Wholesale, 1945.[2]

Maritime Cooperative Services, 1947.

Saskatchewan Federated Cooperative, 1940.[2]

United Cooperatives of Ontario, 1937.

*—Charter member.
1.—This association withdrew in 1939.
2. These wholesales merged in 1955, forming a new organization, Federated Cooperatives, Ltd.

Service Federations

1917: Equity **Audit** Co., Aberdeen, S. Dak.

1929: Mesabi Range Cooperative **Park** Association, Hibbing, Minn.

1935: Cooperative **Auditing** Service, Minneapolis, Minn.

1936: Northland Cooperative **Mortuary**, Cloquet, Minn.

1937: Midland **Credit** Corporation, Minneapolis, Minn.

1938: Farmers Union Cooperative **Credit** Association, St. Paul, Minn.
Business Service Association, Des Moines, Iowa (Auditing, tax service).

1939: Cooperative Press, Minneapolis, Minn. (Collective purchase of printing and of office supplies).

1940: Farmers Union Agency, St. Paul, Minn. (Agency for fire and casualty insurance and employee bonds).
Central **Finance**, Inc., Superior, Wis.

1942: Valley Cooperative Services, Appleton, Wis. (Funeral service).

1943: National Cooperative **Finance** Association, Chicago, Ill. (not yet in operation).

1944: Federated Cooperatives of Maryland, Frederick, Md. (Management service, financing, collections).

1948: Cooperative **Finance** Corporation, Oakland, Calif.

Productive Federations

1933	Cooperative Mills, Auburn, Ind. **Members:** (originally) Eastern Cooperative Wholesale, Central Cooperative Wholesale, Central States Cooperatives, and Indiana Farm Bureau Cooperative Association. Became department of National Cooperatives Jan. 1, 1947. Sold in June 1948.	Flour.
1934	Cooperative Publishing Association, Superior, Wis. **Members:** Central Cooperative Wholesale and 150 local associations.	Printing, book and job.
	Grange Printing Association, Seattle, Wash. **Members:** Grange Cooperative Wholesale and four other Grange organizations.	Printing.
1936	Cooperative Fertilizer Service, Baltimore, Md. **Members:** Pennsylvania Farm Bureau Cooperative Association and Southern States Cooperative.	Fertilizer.
1937	Cooperative Printing Assn., Minneapolis, Minn. **Members:** About 125 local associations.	Printing.
1938	Fertilizer Mfg. Cooperative, Baltimore, Md. **Members:** Farm Bureau Cooperative Association (Ohio) and Coop. GLF Exchange, Ithaca, N. Y.	Fertilizer.
1940	National Farm Machinery Coop., Bellevue, Ohio. **Members:** Farm Bureau Cooperative wholesales of Indiana, Michigan, Ohio, and Pennsylvania, Cooperative Service Co. (Iowa), Midland Cooperatives, Farmers Union Central Exchange, Consumers Cooperative Association, Farmers Union State Exchange, Pacific Supply Cooperative, Central Cooperative Wholesale, United Farmers of Ontario, and Saskatchewan Federated Coops. This association went out of business in 1953.	Farm equipment.
1942	Cooperative Mills, Cincinnati, Ohio. **Members:** Farm Bureau Cooperative Associations of Ohio and Pennsylvania, Southern States Cooperative, and Georgia Cotton Growers.	Feed.
1943	National Coop. Refinery Assn., McPherson, Kans. **Members:** Midland Cooperatives, Farmers Union Central Exchange, Consumers Cooperative Association, Farmers Union State Exchange, Central Cooperative Wholesale, and Iowa Farm Service Co.	Crude oil and refined fuels.
1944	Cooperative Plant Foods, Schererville, Ind. **Members:** Indiana Farm Bureau Cooperative Association, Midland Cooperatives, Illinois Farm Supply Co., and Wisconsin Cooperative Farm Supply Co.	Fertilizer.
	North Iowa Cooperative Processing Association, Manley, Iowa. **Members:** 43 local associations.	Feed and soybean oil.
	International Lumbering Assn., Vancouver, B. C. **Members:** Farm Bureau wholesales of Indiana and Ohio, Midland Cooperatives, Farmers Union Central Exchange, Consumers Cooperative Association, Pacific Supply Cooperative, Central Cooperative Wholesale, Alberta Cooperative Wholesale, Manitoba Cooperative Wholesale, Saskatchewan Federated Cooperatives and United Farmers of Ontario. This association went out of business in 1949.	Cedar shingles.
1945	Northwest Cooperative Mills, St. Paul, Minn. **Members:** Midland Cooperatives, Farmers Union Central Exchange, Central Cooperative Whole-	Feed, fertilizer, and soybean oil and meal.

Year	Organization	Products
1945	sale, and Farmers Union Grain Terminal Association.	
	Farm Bureau Chemical Corp., Glendale, Ohio. Members: Indiana and Ohio Farm Bureau cooperative wholesales.	Fertilizer.
	Producers Coop. Oil Mill, Oklahoma City, Okla. Members: Consumers Cooperative Association, Oklahoma Cotton Growers, Oklahoma Farmers Union, and 60 local cotton-gin associations.	Feed, cottonseed oil, and cotton linters.
1946	Millers Creek Coal Coop., Paintsville, Ky. Members: Farm Bureau wholesales of Indiana and Ohio, and Midland Cooperatives. Indiana became sole owner in 1950; the business was sold by it in 1951.	Coal.
1948	Premier Petroleum Co., Longview, Tex. Members (owners of "substantial" interest): Midland Cooperatives, Farmers Union Central Exchange, and Illinois Farm Supply Co.	Crude oil and refined fuels.
	Petrol Refining, Inc. Members: Pennsylvania Farm Bureau Cooperative Association; Southern States Cooperative; and Coop. GLF Exchange.	Crude oil and refined fuels.

Appendix B. — LEAGUE DIRECTORS, 1916 Through 1955

In the following list are shown periods of service of the directors of the Cooperative League or, rather (in most instances), the terms for which elected. Death or resignation sometimes occurred before completion of term (as in the case of Cedric Long and Eskel Ronn); the records now available do not show whether a complete term was served, and those for the earliest years are incomplete.

League directors are elected at the biennial Cooperative Congresses, always held in the autumn; they take office in the following January. In each case the years shown are inclusive; thus, 1927-34 means elected in the fall of 1926 and took office in January 1927 to serve through 1934.

In the compilation of this list I am greatly indebted to Miss Martha Hanes of the Cooperative League staff.

Cooperative League Directors

Dr. James P. Warbasse, 1916-41; President emeritus, 1942—present.
Scott Perky, 1916, 1917.
Peter Hamilton, 1916-20.
Rufus Trimble, 1916-20.
Emerson P. Harris, 1916-20, 1923, 1924.
Albert Sonnichsen. 1916-27.
Mabel Cheel, 1917-20.
M. Fainberg, 1918-20.
Joseph Cannon, 1918-20.
Elias Lieberman, 1918-20.
James A. Duncan, 1921.
Robert McKechan, 1921.
Senator Morris L. Sheppard, 1921.
Aaron Stolinsky, 1921.
Rev. Raymond A. McGowan, 1921, 1923.
John F. McNamee, 1921, 1923.
Joseph Schlossberg, 1921, 1923.
W. C. Lansdon, 1921, 1923, 1924.
A. P. Bower, 1921, 1923-25.
John Nummivuori, 1921, 1923-25.
L. S. Herron, 1918-33.
A. W. Warinner, 1921, 1927-35, 1937, 1938.
Waldemar Niemela, 1921, 1923-30, 1933-39, 1940-44.
R. H. Salter, 1923.
Warren S. Stone, 1923.
Thomas J. Donnelly, 1923, 1924.
Daniel W. Hoan, 1923, 1924.
John H. Walker, 1923-28.
V. S. Alanne, 1923-39.
Edward Solem, 1925.
Cedric Long, 1925-31.
Eskel Ronn, 1925-31.
Harold Nordby, 1925-32.
Albert S. Goss, 1925-36.
Matti Tenhunen, 1927-30.
Adolph Wirkkula, 1925-30.
O. Saari, 1927, 1928.
Colston Warne, 1925, 1927, 1928.
Otto Endres, 1927-30.
Jacob Liukku, 1927, 1928, 1931-35.
Mary Arnold, 1927-35, 1937, 1938, 1945-50.
Dr. G. L. Kennedy, 1929, 1930.
F. W. Wenschoff, 1929, 1930.
H. V. Nurmi, 1929-35.
Joseph Blaha, 1929-37.
George Halonen, 1930-35, 1937, 1938.
E. E. Branch, 1931, 1932.
K. E. Grandahl, 1931-34.
Joseph Martinek, 1931-34.
J. J. Nylander, 1931-34.
Meyer Rubinson, 1931-35.
Gideon Edberg, 1933-35, 1937, 1938.
A. E. Kazan, 1933-35, 1937, 1938.
John Hofmann, 1935-39.
Ralph Ingerson, 1935-37.
Quentin Reynolds, 1935-37.
George W. Jacobson, 1935-37, 1955—present.
Ferdinand Foernsler, 1916-20.
William Kraus, 1916-20.
Isaac Roberts, 1916-20.
Hyman Cohn, 1916-20.
Leslie E. Woodcock, 1935-39, 1941-48.
I. H. Hull, 1935-37, 1939-50.
Howard A. Cowden, 1935-37, 1939-52.
Murray Lincoln, 1935-37, 1939—present.
Edward Carlson, 1937, 1938.
George Barrett, 1937-39.
James Myers, 1939-41.
Carlos C. Palmer, 1939-42.
E. G. Cort, 1939-42.
R. N. Benjamin, 1939-50.
William Liimatainen, 1939-52.
Perry L. Green, 1939—present.
Mrs. Ella Fowler Douds, 1941, 1942.
James L. Proebsting, 1941-44.
Andrew P. Jensen, 1941-48.
Dwight Townsend, 1941-52.
A. J. Hayes, 1943-46.
Charles Baker, 1943—present.
Arthur J. Smaby, 1943—present.
Mrs. S. R. Logan, 1945, 1946.
J. Orrin Shipe, 1947, 1948.
E. A. Whitney, 1947-52.
Richard Leekley, 1949, 1950.
Elmer Christoph, 1949-52.
Leonard Cowden, 1949-52.
Chris Ellingsen, 1949-52.
W. Gordon Loveless, 1949-52.
Dr. Joseph A. Geddes, 1949—present.
Robert Neptune, 1949—present.
Felix F. Rondeau, 1949—present.
Jerry Shea, 1949—present.
D. M. Hall, 1951, 1952.
Clark McWhorter, 1951, 1952.
Robert C. Scott, 1951-54.
Charles Folda, 1951—present.
Paul D. Grady, 1951—present.
Mrs. Harold Robison, 1951—present.
Larry Offenbecker, 1953, 1954.
Clyde Seybold, 1953, 1954.
Robert L. Smith, 1953, 1954.
Walter Allen, 1953—present.
Howard Custer, 1953—present.
George Dunlap, 1953—present.
J. W. Koski, 1953—present.
Jack Kyle, 1953—present.
Frank Lair, 1953—present.
Brynolf Peterson, 1953—present.
Rafael Pol, 1953—present.
Walker Sandbach, 1953—present.
Holten Svendsen, 1953—present.
W. V. Thomas, 1953—present.
Samuel Ashelman, 1955—present.
William Bergeron, 1955—present.
Clyde Ellis, 1955—present.
Florence E. Parker, 1955.
A. G. Rose, 1955—present.

BIBLIOGRAPHICAL NOTE

The list of sources used in the compilation of this history has been omitted for reasons of space. It is not by any means an exhaustive bibliography of literature on consumers' cooperation (since it includes only publications *used*). However, if there appears to be any considerable demand for it, it will be duplicated by The Cooperative League of the U.S.A. and supplied to inquirers for fifty cents per copy.

INDEX

D

E

G

I

J

K

L

N

Q

R

S

V

W